D0594548

Reprints of Economic Classics

THE GROWTH OF THE MANOR

SOME PRESS OPINIONS

THE GROWTH OF
THE MANOR

SIR PAUL VINOGRADOFF
M.A., LL.D., D.C.L.

REPRINTS OF ECONOMIC CLASSICS

AUGUSTUS M. KELLEY · PUBLISHERS
NEW YORK 1968

First Edition 1904

Second Edition 1911

(London: George Allen & Unwin Ltd., *Ruskin House,*
40 Museum Street, W. C. 1)

Reprinted 1968 by

AUGUSTUS M. KELLEY · PUBLISHERS

NEW YORK NEW YORK 10010·

By Arrangement With GEORGE ALLEN & UNWIN LTD.

LIBRARY OF CONGRESS CATALOGUE CARD NUMBER

52-27922

PRINTED IN THE UNITED STATES OF AMERICA
by SENTRY PRESS, NEW YORK, N. Y. 10019

PREFACE

SOME twelve years ago I attempted to treat the difficult
subject of villainage in a volume which was intended to
pave the way towards a discussion of the origins of the
Manorial System. Various professional duties have prevented me hitherto from following up the thread of my
investigations, and, now that I am free to return to these
studies, I find that their ground has been to a great extent
shifted by the remarkable work achieved in the mean time
by English scholars. Professor Maitland, Mr. Seebohm,
Mr. Round and others have approached the problem from
new points of view, have brought to bear on it a vast amount
of new evidence, and have sifted the materials at our disposal with admirable skill. If I still beg leave to be heard
on the subject, I may plead in excuse the nature of the
problem and the stage at which the inquiry has arrived
at the present moment. In a study of such magnitude
and complexity there are, and will be for a long while yet,
insufficiently explored fields awaiting labourers. I may
point out, for example, the analysis of Domesday, and the
study of the " Danelaw," as parts of the inquiry which
will, according to the best authorities, yield fair results to
conscientious explorers. Indeed, it is my hope to be able
to publish in no very distant future a second volume of
the " Essays in English Mediæval History," of which
" Villainage in England " was the first instalment.[1]

But there is also another aspect from which new attempts
to approach the questions at issue seem warranted. If I
am not mistaken, the very success of modern special investigations has rather disarranged our conceptions of
English social development, and the want of co-ordination

[1] "Villainage in England. Essays in English Mediæval History."
Oxford University Press.

v

of results makes itself felt more and more. We were clearer in our mind before recent researches had laid bare the many hidden pitfalls which underlay our hasty generalisations. We shall be able to bring order into our ideas once more when the balance of our newest acquisitions has been carefully drawn, and latest discoveries assigned their proper place in the general course of inquiry.

Not in disparagement of eminent scholars, on whose work I shall have to rely all along, but in order to give a more concrete application to my general contention, I should like to suggest at the very outset that the principal achievements of later years may become the starting points of further reflection and inquiry. No one has done more than Professor Maitland to unravel the mysteries of legal antiquities in the light of mediæval Common Law and modern common sense ; no one has subjected to a more searching analysis the organising influence of kinship, the conceptions of mediæval communalism, the speculations as to hide, early manor, etc. But in some cases people with a hopeful turn of mind may venture on reconstruction where his subtle scepticism has dissolved ; and perhaps in the end we may get a better insight into historical peculiarities of thought and social arrangement.

Mr. Round has been specially conspicuous as a past master in the arts of social calculus which are so necessary to exponents of Domesday and other fiscal documents. But as, after all, no society can depend entirely on symmetrical computations, and no government has ever succeeded in mastering organic growth, the clues given by the artificial terminology and the neat numbers of the surveys will have to be adjusted to the requirements of actual husbandry and landholding.

Mr. Seebohm's researches have been always distinguished by their grasp of reality and their synthetic aims ; but he has been attracted in turn by one element of mediæval life after the other ; first, by the servile community and then by the tribe, by the freedmen after the slaves, by Roman culture and Celtic influence. No wonder that the very energy with which he urges his points prevents him from attending sufficiently to the equilibrium of the whole.

Altogether, the clash of opinions and arguments seems to call for harmonising combinations, for a summing up of results, for estimates of the manner in which recent researches counteract and limit, or supplement and support each other, for attempts to trace the general course of social evolution. Such attempts are especially needed, not so much by scholars engaged in current controversies, who have their hands full with their particular investigations, as by students of general history and the public at large, who have a right to know what the labour of searchers has achieved in the way of results.

Such are the considerations that have prompted the present work. I have tried to present an outline of the growth of the Manor, as a social institution passing through all the stages of English history. Dwelling only on the main facts and the decisive moments, I do not pretend to start an entirely new theory on the subject, but I have had to choose my way between conflicting theories and arguments and to set forth as clearly as possible the leading ideas to which, according to the best of my knowledge, details have to conform. I shall address myself primarily to students of general history and try to make my sketch intelligible to them, but it would be misleading not to state shortly the reasons for taking up this or the other position, and I hope the notes at the close of each chapter may be deemed sufficient for this purpose.

It is hardly necessary to dwell on the importance and interest of the subject, and I will merely venture to state the chief reasons for the personal fascination it has exercised over me.

When observing the classical world, we are apt to fix our attention on the city, " civitas," " πόλις," as the most complete expression of ancient society. If we look out for something as marked and as peculiar in mediæval life, it is impossible to choose anything but the Manor as the subject of discourse. As in the case of the Classical City, economic, social and political institutions and ideas are con-

centrated in its mould. It has not been devised or arranged
by any one in particular, but slowly evolved by the needs of
generations. If the direct intercourse of the city, the active
participation of citizens in its corporate life, gives its peculiar
stamp to ancient life, the rural work of the Manor, the customary constitution of its lordship, the curious intermixture of
local interests and rights in the position of its tenants form
the social nucleus of mediæval life. Then again, the Manor
in its special framework appears as a thoroughly English
institution, and at the same time it affords the best example
of the feudal organisation which extended its sway over the
whole of Western Europe. It may be said, in a sense, that
by the strong constitution and the customary self-government of its Manorial system England has got quite as much
the start of her continental neighbours in point of social
development, as she obtained political precedence over them
by the early consolidation of her parliamentary institutions.
And at the same time there is so much affinity between the
English "Manor," the French "Seigneurie," and the
German "Grundherrschaft," that a careful study of every
one of them is sure to throw light on the development of
the others, and so one of the best modes of checking theories
as to the growth of any of the three consists in applying
these theories, with due allowance for the difference of
circumstances, to the kindred cases.

All periods of English history have had their bearing on
the life of the Manor. Some germs of manorial institutions
may be found in the Celtic age ; the Roman occupation
of the island had undoubtedly a powerful influence on
its economic arrangements ; the Old English period is
marked by the full development of the rural township ;
the feudal epoch finds the Manor at its height ; the dissolution of the Manor forms one of the processes by which
modern commercial intercourse was brought about, and
survivals of the Manorial system and of its component
elements may still be observed all over England. More
is known, of course, about later than about ancient times,
and this will make it necessary on many occasions to turn
to well ascertained later facts in order to form a judgment

about ancient conditions. But it is not necessary to invert the sequence of epochs in the sketch of historical development, and by following the chronological order we may guard against carrying into the distant past conceptions of comparatively modern growth. It is not so much the fact of studying later stages before the earlier that constitutes the method of investigation from the known to the unknown, as the careful distinction between evidence and inference, and the systematic use of both.

I am deeply indebted to several friends who have kindly read through the proofs of this book and given me the benefit of their advice. To Prof. Rhys and Prof. Anwyl I owe many valuable suggestions on Celtic questions, while Mr. Haverfield and Prof. Pelham have warned me against dangers in my survey of the Roman period, and the Rev. C. Plummer has given me invaluable assistance in regard to the Old English portion of the work. From Mr. F. Seebohm I have received weighty advice on the general conceptions of the book as well as on many details, and Mr. T. Darlington has done everything in his power to supply my deficiencies in point of language and style. My friend and pupil, Mr. A. Savine, has kindly compiled the index to this volume. Altogether, if this book has not turned out more satisfactory, it is certainly not the fault of my friends and advisers. I may add that the essays now published as a book have formed the basis of lectures delivered in Oxford in the Summer term of 1904.

Prefatory Note to Second Edition

IN submitting the second edition of *The Growth of the Manor* to the judgment of the public, I have tried, besides correcting misprints and mistakes, to bring the book up to date by noticing briefly the chief contributions to the subject made in the course of the last five years.   I did not find it necessary to modify my conclusions or the general line of my argument, but several points of detail had to be reconsidered and stated afresh.   I hope these alterations may prove to be improvements.

P. VINOGRADOFF.

OXFORD,
   January, 1911.

CONTENTS

PREFACE   *page* **v**

BOOK I. THE PRE-ENGLISH PERIOD

CHAP.
  I. *Celtic Tribal Arrangements*   **3**
  II. *Roman Influence*   **37**

BOOK II. THE OLD ENGLISH PERIOD

  I. *The English Conquest*   **117**
  II. *The Grouping of the Folk*   **135**
  III. *The Shares in the Township*   **150**
  IV. *The Open-Field System*   **165**
  V. *The History of the Holding*   **200**
  VI. *Manorial Origins*   **212**

BOOK III. THE FEUDAL PERIOD

  I. *The Principles of the Domesday Survey*   **291**
  II. *Ownership and Husbandry*   **307**
  III. *Social Classes*   **332**

Notes to Book I   **88**
Notes to Book II   **236**
Notes to Book III   **366**
Index   **381**

First Book
PRE-ENGLISH PERIOD

CHAPTER I.

CELTIC TRIBAL ARRANGEMENTS.

I. KINSHIP.

THE most ancient society on British soil about which we can form a more or less definite notion is Celtic

Materials for the History of Celtic Institutions
society. We know indeed that the Celtic race was preceded in the British islands by earlier inhabitants, but as to the culture of the latter we can guess only very little.[1]
Even as to the Celtic epoch a good deal depends on inferences and probabilities, but for these there is a solid and extensive foundation. We are not restricted to half-legendary narratives ; there is a vast store of materials in ascertained facts of later times. We can use legal enactments of the Welsh, the Irish, and, in a lesser degree of the Scotch people, which have come down from the tenth, eleventh, and twelfth centuries. There are Welsh surveys which, though not earlier than the fourteenth century, present customs and arrangements bridging over the Conquest and dating from the period of the independence of Wales under its native princes. We hear a good deal of the peculiar institutions of Ireland and Scotland in the seventeenth and eighteenth centuries when these institutions were partly arrested in their progress, and partly destroyed by the impact of the English. Even now there may be noticed customs in the life of Irish, Welsh, and Highland societies which are best explained by the peculiarities of their remote history. And even in French Brittany, and in the records of the Celtic tribes on the continent there may be found some illustrations of habits which prevailed among the Celtic population of Great

3

Britain. We have the right to use these materials, scattered through many lands and many centuries, because, notwithstanding all the variety of details, they present a remarkable unity of fundamental arrangement and a not less remarkable contrast with the institutions of neighbouring races. This unity and this contrast are so striking by reason of a common and ancient origin of institutions, and to that common and ancient origin we may attempt to trace them back in a spirit akin to that which prompts the students of comparative philology when they try to trace the observable affinities of dialects to common stems and original forms. Needless to say that this kind of work requires great precautions, the neglect of which actually explains a good many current errors and misapprehensions. Everybody understands that it would not do to carry back into pre-Roman Britain all the features described in the Welsh surveys of Edward I., every trait noticed in the life of a Scottish clan following the Pretender, or of an Irish sept as described by the lawyers of James I., but much disagreement may arise as to the extent to which one may be allowed to borrow traits from these later pictures in order to reconstitute the earlier one. A good deal will always depend on the individual sense of the apt and the probable, but some general guiding considerations had better be stated at the outset in the hope that they may prove useful in the course of the inquiry. Some of them are negative, others positive, and, as usual, it is more easy to perceive the negative points.

We must, evidently, take special precautions against carrying into old Celtic domain facts connected with demonstrably later conditions ; it will not do, for example,

Precautions to be used in the study of the Materials

to assume that agricultural arrangements of a time when agriculture had become the mainstay of economy, are to be considered as representative of agrarian origins, or that the powers of territorial lords granted by the English Crown point to the methods in which lordships were organised, when the tribes were independent. Another warning may, perhaps, be formulated in the following manner ; even features connected with very peculiar Celtic institutions must not be thought to have been as completely developed at the time when Celtic civilisation was a unity by itself ; it must be borne in mind, that if these features are borrowed from later history, they are sure to bear, to some extent, the stamp of later history ; in other words, that they are, as it were, hardened and sharpened even in those parts which remain true to the original cast—hardened and sharpened, because the life of the people has been proceeding for long periods in the same peculiar groove. The elaborate arrangement of a Highland clan, for instance, is certainly very characteristic of the principle of patriarchal organisation, and must be used to illustrate and to demonstrate the strength of this principle. But it would be wrong to assume that in the Celtic Britain of Cunobeline, or even in the Ireland of the tenth century, the clan had reached the stage described by eighteenth century observers of clan customs. I am inclined to submit one more negative proposition : we must guard carefully against the tempting idea that a state of a society, even of an ancient one, may be treated as a system. It appeals, undoubtedly, to our sense of order and wish for clearness to reconstruct in our mind the fabric of a by-gone society as if it were a bee-hive, the cells of which are formed and repeated in one and the same way, according to unfailing processes, so that one clue will lead us through the whole labyrinth. It would be impossible to enumerate the instances when such convenient simplifications have suggested false solutions of difficulties, or when the dislike to admit the concurrent influence of more than one main principle has blocked the way towards right solutions. I will venture to point out, as an instance, that if we were to construct an ancient society purely on the ground of relationship through mothers, the system would exclude the possibility of a rise of the opposite, or patriarchal system, quite as much as a construction on the basis of the latter would not explain the various facts which indicate the social influence of the conception of maternity. In fact a system is a system only as long as it excludes other systems, and in real life such exclusion is impossible because life is movement. We have no other means of explaining life than by shewing its inherent contradictions and transitions.

The warnings contained in these negative considerations may suggest some hints as to the direction in which positive **Hints as to** results are to be sought. As we have to take **Methods** our facts mostly from later periods, and from periods, too, which lie on different historical planes, our endeavours ought to be directed as much as possible towards getting hold of the peculiar conditions which have influenced the earlier stages of development in comparison with the later. We must, for example, make out by what means people got their living at the time when the Celtic tribes formed their distinctive arrangements of society, and in what respects their economic pursuits are to be distinguished from other and later modes of husbandry. Then again, we must be careful to note with what kind of political conceptions we have to reckon at that stage, and in what respects these political conceptions differed from those of a feudal and of a modern state.

A second indication is afforded by the necessity of making a considerable allowance, even in the recognised peculiarities of Celtic development, for the gradually increasing onesided-ness and artificially elaborate character of arrangements which have been going on for a long time in a special groove. Our endeavours ought to be directed not so much towards reproducing the actual structure of these earlier stages—an attempt hardly likely to be successful—as towards formulating the types and tendencies of development of Celtic society. The Highland clan may not serve as an example of what the old Celtic sub-section of a tribe may have been, but it certainly shews that we have to look to the gathering of agnatic relations as to the fundamental bond of that old Celtic society from which the varieties of Welsh, Irish, and Highland tribal organisation have sprung.

And lastly, if we are unwilling to admit that every trait of social life ought to be explained in reference to one ruling standard, we must have our eyes open to the possibility, that, alongside of customs and institutions derived from one stem, there may have existed customs and institutions claiming other origins, either as competing forces, or as survivals, or as germs. Our study will, in fact, concern itself, not only with the task of bringing the facts under the organising rule of prevailing principles, but also of showing in what combinations such principles stand to each other, and in what direction such combinations were undergoing change.

Need I remark that I am putting forward these general considerations with a view, not of giving an exhaustive statement as to methods, but rather of exemplifying the difficulties one has to contend with in actual work ? My readers may, perhaps, think that in a short and popular account of the phenomena of social history, it is not necessary to enter into such questions, inasmuch as the actual work of investigation will, to a great extent, remain concealed from the eyes. But, in my view, this is rather an additional reason for making clear to the reader the character of the statements he will have to deal with. I may add, before starting on our review of the subject, that though I have made some use of Irish and Scotch evidence in as far as the best modern books enabled me to do so, it is especially to Welsh conditions that I have tried to draw the attention of the reader, and this for two reasons—because the Welsh material has been shown lately to be especially suggestive and complete, and because the Welsh facts are more characteristic of Celtic society on English soil than the Scotch or the Irish. Besides, Celtic evidence helps to explain Germanic facts of tribal custom.

There can be no doubt as to the ruling principle according to which Celtic society was arranged : it was the union of **Agnatic Principle** persons descended, or supposed to be descended, from the same ancestor through males, the union of *agnatic* relations. This was expressed in Scotland by the well-known " clann," which means children or descendants, but is made to apply in a special way to the descendants by males.[2] Walter Scott's novels have made everybody familiar

with the general character of this grouping of society.
What effect the stretching of agnatic organisation outside
the bounds of the natural family produced may be illustrated, for instance, by a fact which occurred well within
observation of responsible witnesses in 1606.   A whole
kindred of Grames was moved by the English government
from Cumberland, where it was troublesome, to Ros-
common.³   It consisted of thirty-three families, and included one hundred and twenty-four members, all bearing
the name of Grame from the chief, the "gude man of
Netherby," down to the servants.   What seems to be
especially worthy of notice is the social completeness
of the arrangement : chieftain and followers, warriors and
workers, masters and servants, are all included in the same
organic group, all related to each other and separated from
strangers by blood.

The same arrangement meets us when we look at the
condition of Wales and Ireland, and indeed we gather
from these regions significant details, ascertained by
documents of more ancient date than those which have
been preserved for the Highlands of Scotland.   Fourteenth century extents of Welsh manors disclose a state
of things very different from English manorial practice.
The Record of Carnarvon, drawn up in 1354, and the
extents of North Welsh manors of 1335, mention constantly the holding of land by communities of joint tenants called weles (gwelys),⁴ a word meaning "beds"
(lecta).   The extent of the honour of Denbigh, of 1335,
gives a very full enumeration of the persons forming such
beds, shewing them to be sets of agnates descended from the
same ancestor,⁵ and the Welsh laws trace the influence of
agnatic relationship in some cases up to the ninth generation,
that is to sixth cousins.⁶   In Ireland, the Brehon laws,
besides bearing testimony to a development of septs and
tuaths akin to the Highland clans and tribes, disclose an
inner kernel of the arrangement in their regulations as to
nearest relations.   These form the Finè which stretches
according to certain rules and gradations over the sixteen
nearest agnates of a person, and connects them into a

specially close union in regard to defence and inheritance, but at the same time provides for a further connection between this narrow community and the larger tribe by the passage of supernumerary members out of the inner circle into the outer, and *vice versa*.[7]

As I say, there can be no manner of doubt as to the prevalence of the agnatic clan arrangement among the Celts of historical times. This fact does not exclude a certain influence of different and earlier systems. On the contrary, there are distinct traces of an older mode of reckoning relationship among the Celts : the rule of so-called Pictish succession which prevailed, according to the testimony of Bede (i. c. i.) in regard to the devolution of the Crown among the Picts of Scotland, gave precedence to the claims of maternal kin, and there are many traits in the Irish legends and in ancient Gaelic inscriptions which point the same way.[8] Cæsar tells of another custom which, though not implying a construction of a relationship of cognates or persons allied by maternity, still points to a state of tribal organisation which does not admit of the establishment of agnatic pedigrees. He mentions the fact that among the Celtic people in Britain, polyandry was common, several brothers having the same wife (*De Bello Gallico*, v. 12). But all such traits belong either to earlier stages of social development, to which it is not only difficult but needless for our purpose to seek access, or else they represent stray survivals of these older stages, and do not alter the main fact that in all the branches of the Celtic people on British soil we come across the formation of agnatic clans resembling the *gentes* and γένη of the classical world and the patriarchal tribes of the Hebrews. This arrangement had, in historical times, become the dominant fact of social organisation. It would be wrong to assume that the predominance of agnatic organisation necessarily implied a denial of all other modes of relationship, and that it always led to a complete subjection of the married women to the sway of their husbands. The recognition both of relationship through females and of independent rights of women could exist in agnatic groups as subsidiary facts. We

(marginal note:) **Recognition of Relationship through Women**

find, indeed, that every tribesman was conscious not only of the ties which bound him to his father's kin, but also of those which connected him with the relatives of his mother. The prevailing agnatic union did not exclude the existence of feelings and interests derived from relationship through females. To begin with, separate property was allowed to the wife, and therefore a separate inheritance proceeded from her to her children and eventually to members of her personal kin.[9] She was by no means at the mercy of her husband, and not entirely separated from her father's house and from his relations even after marriage. On very important occasions, when a man had to look for defence and revenge to his relations, or to rely on their support when called upon to satisfy claims, he did not lean exclusively on his agnatic relations, but also sought support from his mother's kinsmen.[10] But though, in the case of a settlement of claims in regard to the murdered man's " galanas," the portions assigned to single individuals depended mostly on the degrees of relationship in which they stood to the victim, the blood feud groups which enforced the payment of the fines, and bore the feud in case fines were not paid, were permanently organised clans or kindreds, and not associations formed on different lines in every single case. These are facts well established in Irish and in Welsh law, and sufficiently indicated in Highland custom, and as facts stand against facts on both sides it is impossible to get rid of one or of the other set. It would not help to argue that the predominance of agnatic relationship must have entailed the rightlessness of women, and the exclusion of all relationship through women, or *vice versa*, that the recognition of rights proceeding through women is to be considered a bar to any working arrangement of agnatic kinship.[11]

After all, the compromises which have to be effected between the two sets of rights and obligations are not so artificial or

Compromises in the organisation of Kindred intricate as to make it impossible to unravel their meaning. In one way, the close connection of a woman with her own kin even after marriage may be even considered as a direct outcome of the principle of agnatic union. The taking of a wife in those old times was by no means always a taking by force, a rape and a conquest. Without going far into ethnological inquiries, we may simply point to the fact that marriage by a contract between two kins of more or less evenly balanced strength was quite as much a possibility as a marriage by violence, and that, even apart from the influence of Christianity, the fact of getting a wife whose life and rights were protected by powerful kinsmen led to a union of a higher order than the violent acquisition of a woman who might be treated as a slave.[12] The existence side by side in a settled social order of powerful agnatic associations was the best guarantee against an arbitrary treatment of married women and of their recognised offspring ; no wonder that certain acknowledged legal ties proceeded from it, that the wife could sometimes seek refuge from ill-treatment at the hands of the husband in her father's house, or under the protection of her brother, that her murder was avenged primarily by her own kinsfolk, who had to receive fines for her death, that she had some private property which could not be encroached upon by the husband and his people. Altogether we may say that the strong stress laid on the woman's agnatic ties even after marriage does not weaken the impression that agnatic kinship was of first rate importance in social life.[13]

This involves a series of consequences for the offspring of contractual marriages. Though, at the first period of their life, they were exposed to rejection, and even extermination by the father, once accepted, they grew up to stand in distinct relation not only to their father's but also to their mother's kin, and in the most important matter of social protection could appeal to both sides. But here again we need not develop the divergence of protecting ties to the extent of assuming that no agnatic organisation mattered because there mattered two or possibly more. It was a case of bringing to bear as much protecting influence as possible from all available sides, and the Celtic law expresses it very pertinently by the rule that apart from specified payments to helpers of divers kinds —

adoptive children, foster-brothers and the like, two-thirds of the fine for murder were to be paid to the father's agnatic relations and one-third to the mother's.[14]   Let it be noted that this rule does not lead to a computation of the eventual shares of relatives in their personal positions in regard to the murdered man ; it is an arrangement for adjusting the claims of two organised and allied bodies.   The organised existence and the predominant importance in practice of the agnatic group were guaranteed by the rule that women did not inherit land and that the territorial basis for applying all the advantages accruing from the possession of immoveables was originally bound up with agnatic relationship.[15]   Two powerful factors make in this way for agnatism : the natural preponderance of strength accruing to the armed sex in primitive communities, and the settlement in separate households which led to permanent marriages and to the establishment of patriarchal administration within the limits of the household, and on the basis of the land assigned to it.

The cross influences which arose from such a recognition of different sources of affinity are, of course, not to be considered in the light of a standing, well balanced compromise in which the acting forces were so united as to ensure a permanent combination.   It is clear that, in real life, there was not only room for many collisions, but that there existed permanent germs of discord and disruption.   Apart from the fact that there were divergent interests to be adjusted, changes in the general conditions of life might indirectly loosen and explode the combination.   When, for instance, the development of private property reached a stage in which women were allowed to inherit land— such a change was bound to react in a very disturbing manner on the territorial distinctness of agnatic groups, and thereby on their very existence.   Then, again, the rise of individuality, and the weakening of the political attributions of the clans, might lead to the gradual substitution of the idea of an all-round relationship to the conception of membership in a distinct agnatic association supplemented by ties in other similar groups. But these possibilities and eventualities ought not to be treated as if they were an immediate consequence to be drawn from accepted premises, which rendered all compromise and combination impossible at the very outset. As a matter of fact, a working combination of the conflicting tendencies existed for many centuries under the prevailing influence of agnatic kinship, and it is with this combination that we have mostly to do in the domain of early Celtic law.

Nothing could be clearer than the Welsh evidence
The Gwely as to the gradual development of higher agnatic units from the family household, and as to the passage from the primary family to the joint family and from thence to the kindred. Mr. Seebohm has elucidated this matter with great abundance of detail.[16] His Denbigh documents shew us how the household of Lauwarghe ap Kendalyk or of Vaughan ap Asser spreads into a *gavell* in which the three sons of Lauwarghe or the four sons of Rand hold together as a joint family united in its work, rights and duties, and the grandsons have to wait till all the sons are dead before coming forward with their claims as to full and equal rights. Further, in the third generation we see gavells of grandsons springing up within the *bed* (wele or gwely) of Lauwarghe or Vaughan, and on the one hand combining for purposes of husbandry, on the other hand vouching for an eventual redivision of rights, on the passage of the land to the next generation. And when the third generation has died off, the descendants of Lauwarghe become a *progenies* in which the beds and gavells represented by second cousins still keep together as a political and economic union. Recorded Welsh law breaks off the nominative reckoning at this stage, that is at the fourth generation, but the obligation of joining in the payment and receipt of galanas is carried expressly to the seventh generation, and expected even of those—who do not stand further than the ninth generation—sixth cousins.

In Irish law, as we have seen, the express reckoning is

followed to the fifth generation, but there also it is probable that the limitations were not more than expedients for simplifying the legal application of the principle of agnatic solidarity. As a matter of custom and tradition, all the hundreds and thousands of O'Kellys were considered as more or less distant relations, and could be stirred to common action by the wrongs or the prowess of one of them. In such cases, undoubtedly, a point of first rate importance was material proximity, community of local interests and a distinct territory to help and uphold the sense of relationship. In the Wales of the fourteenth century we already notice the disruption of these local foundations, and, in connection with this, a weakening of the tribal ties. Beneath the mail-links of English feudalism, it is not possible to reconstitute the old divisions into local tribes and septs. It is only in the lower units that the agnatic grouping makes itself felt, and even there the beds and kindreds stretch from one place to another. But in the Highlands, and in Ireland, the country was, until late times, actually divided between the kindreds, septs and clans, so that the territorial basis of the agnatic arrangements becomes very conspicuous. In the country of the Campbells, it is natural that the pedigree of the Campbells should be looked to as the chief direction in the apportionment of rights, dignity, and power, and even in Wales, on a lower scale, it was primarily to the members of the households included in the gwely and not to cognates however near, but belonging to other local unions, that any descendants of a *progenies* had to look for support and co-operation.

If we now ask, in what way that support and co-operation was provided, it seems that it is hardly necessary to dwell at great length on the point of co-operation for mutual defence, because this point is very obvious, and only indirectly connected with the vicissitudes of the economic arrangements which form the direct object of our study. It may be sufficient to say that the system of mutual defence, as embodied in the rules of revenge and composition, of legal support and participation in claiming and paying fines, was certainly an institution as to the vital importance of which

it is hardly possible to form an exaggerated opinion. In
those days of violence, the mutual insurance of powerful
combinations of kindred was not only the means of checking, to a certain extent, lawlessness and greed, but, as we
can judge at a glance from any barbaric code, it provided
a machinery which was constantly in motion, and which
impressed the mind of the people more than any other
institution. But there is another side of co-operation
which we have to examine more carefully, as it had a direct
bearing on the development of landed property and on
agrarian questions in later days. I mean the land settlement, as it appears in Celtic parts.

II. LANDHOLDING

It has been pointed out that in the very mode of con-
structing houses, as it is described in the Welsh Codes, we
Homesteads   may perceive a trace of the powerful tendency
and Hamlets   of Celtic families to keep together as long as
possible. The house of the tribal king, and, in a smaller
degree, that of the better tribesman, the "uchelwr," is not
meant to be the dwelling-place of a small family household
surrounded by a certain number of dependents. It is adapted
for the joint occupation of a number of tribesmen living
together. The great hall, opening between trees, the boughs
of which met to form the roof of the house, was the common
room and the dining hall of the whole household, and in
the aisles on the right and left of it lay the beds or compartments of the families which constituted it.[17] This mode
of building answers well to the indications of the laws and
extents as to the joint management of affairs by members of gwelys. The more usual course was however to
provide a young man when he married with a tyddyn, a
separate dwelling of modest size and light construction.[18]
These tyddyns sometimes lay in proximity to each other,
and were grouped into small hamlets or villages [19] (trevs),
in which the inhabitants clustered according to their dis-

tribution in kindreds and "beds." In other instances
the tyddyns were set up in the centre of allotments made
to the different families, and moved in the case of important
redivisions. This would account for the scattering of farms
over the territory of Ireland. In the more mountainous
districts of Wales, and of the Highlands, this scattering
was rendered necessary by the very conformation of the
soil. There is, however, no reason for laying too much
stress on this feature, and especially for turning it into a
kind of distinctive Celtic arrangement.[20] The peculiarities
of Celtic agrarian occupation could be met in all three
cases. In all, the strong influence of the agnatic
group on the arrangement of the rights of its component
households is making itself felt—by settlement in tribal
houses, by the clustering of dwelling-houses into villages
and hamlets, and by the scattering of them for the purpose of their pastoral occupations.

All our sources of information as to Celtic antiquities
show us the people living chiefly on the produce of their

Pastoral Pursuits
herds. Every household, even that of the low-
standing Welsh taeog, is supposed to possess
cows. Sheep, pigs, and goats are also constantly mentioned, and the careful distinctions drawn between animals
of different age and quality show a minute acquaintance
with their species and habits. The tariffs of compositions
are all fixed in cows. The occupations and products of
dairy-farming, the use of milk, the making of cheese,
the salting of bacon, etc., are a subject of constant attention
and description.[21] By the side of this chief calling appear
pursuits connected with the forest and the stream—hunting,
fishing, tending of bees. It would be impossible to say
when the cultivation of the soil arose, and to what extent
it was carried on. No statement can be made in this respect
beyond the very general one, that the cultivation of arable
is already mentioned in the case of the British Celts of
Cæsar's time,[22] but that it played everywhere a more or
less subsidiary part in contrast with the prevailing
grazing husbandry. This statement is not unimportant because it prepares us to find that individual

property in land was not much developed in Celtic parts. It is not necessary, and it is even mischievous, for communities of graziers to divide strictly the area on which their herds pasture. As no artificial cultivation has to be carried on, and no particular implements or capital have to be provided to make use of the grass freely growing in the open, the most appropriate distribution of land in such communities is the parcelling into large tracts for the convenience of the great divisions of the people—the tribes, clans, septs or kindreds—and the intercommoning of the herds of each division within its boundaries, according to certain rules. In view of such a state of affairs, we may expect to find, and we do find, rough but marked boundaries between the territories of clans and kindreds, and a great deal of shifting and redistribution between the families and households which go to form the kindreds or septs. Perhaps the most striking example of that arrangement is to be found in Ireland, where the land is divided from immemorial time, very symmetrically, into districts (bailies) and quarters (cartrons), by ditches and fences, the object of which is primarily to guard against the trespassing of foreign cattle, while the area within the cartron admits of frequent changes of settlements.[23] In Scotland, the larger part of a village territory was occupied by grazing tracts outside the herd fence marking off the area of agricultural cultivation in outfield and infield.[24] Ancient Welsh documents dwell frequently on a feature which seems to have been common to all Celtic districts in mountainous country, namely, on the summer migrations of the herds and herdsmen, and the erection of summer dwellings on the slopes of the mountains, in regions where the soil was not subdivided for private occupation by individuals, but kept the common property of the tribes, while made use of according to the pasturing requirements of the several households.[25]

If the notion that the soil was only the common basis of rights of usage within the septs is especially conspicuous

Agriculture in regard to the chief economic pursuit— the grazing of cattle, the methods of agriculture, and the treatment of the arable point with certain

modifications the same way.[26] The communalistic origin
of property in land has been lately much contested. But
in so far as agriculture is historically developed out of
pastoral husbandry, there seems to be hardly anything
more certain in the domain of archaic law than the theory
that the soil was originally owned by groups and not by
individuals, and that its individual appropriation is the
result of a slow process of development. In the case of the
land reserved for crops, the distribution of labour and of
claims takes necessarily the shape of a delimitation of
the soil, and that delimitation may be lasting if the
labour and capital applied bring about a thorough-going
change, extending, with its indirect results long over the
removal of the harvest : such is evidently the case when
complicated systems of rotation of crops come in, when the
soil is systematically manured, when improvements of any
kind get sunk into the soil. Or else, tillage being superficial, application of capital slight, and natural conditions
more or less equal, the apportionment of the soil lends
itself to frequent readjustment in the interest of the community which had to provide for an appropriate outfit of
its members out of the common land fund. Even in later
days the processes of agriculture in Celtic parts were characterised by their very extensive character, and the slight
application of labour and capital. Such manuring as there
was came chiefly from letting the cattle and sheep remain
on the stubble. The only considerable outlay in the way
of providing implements was entailed by the starting of
ploughteams—big, clumsy, and costly concerns, to which
four or even eight oxen had to be yoked. The treatment
of arable was in keeping with these premises : the so-called
run-rig system seems to have been widely employed.
It is attested by customs which have been preserved
even to our times, and indicated by many passages of
ancient records. The point in this system was that the
soil was not allotted once for all to particular owners,
but remained in the ownership of the tribal community,
while its use for agricultural purposes was apportioned
according to certain rules to the component households,

strips for cultivation being assigned by lot.[27]   The Welsh laws disclose an even more communalistic practice, namely, the distribution of strips in the open field between the several members of an association formed for keeping a plough, each receiving the use of a strip, according to his share in the undertaking, one for providing the ploughshare, another for acting as a ploughman, a third for driving the oxen, a fourth, fifth, sixth, seventh, and so on, for contributing the oxen.[28]   In later times these unions for coaration are treated as free contractual associations and there are rules in the laws to meet such cases, but there can be no doubt that originally they were the outcome of the very close ties of settlement and co-operation between members of the large households of which we have already given some account.   People living in the same tribal house, gathered in some tribal trev, or even holding together as members of the same tribal grazing community, were evidently the most likely to join in those processes of cultivation which, in opposition to our present ideas on the subject, entailed a good deal of co-operation, and very little individual labour, and it would be difficult to understand the assignation of erws on any other principle.

The communalistic management of property in land is very definitely described in the Welsh documents.[29]   The **Trevgyvriv** extents present to us two varieties of village organisation, the *trevgevery* (trevgyvriv) or holding by joint account, and the *treweloghe* (trev and tir-gweliaug) or holding by gwelys.[30]   The Codes accordingly describe two modes of acquiring land, by allotment of strips and by dadenhudd or succeeding to one's father in a gwely. There is this marked difference between the two modes of getting and holding land, that in the first case each full-aged inhabitant of the village is entitled to an equal share in the land occupied by the village, irrespectively of his genealogical position,[31] so that if there are twenty men in the village each will have one-twentieth share in the land allotted to him in a certain number of strips, certain rights and duties as to coaration, pasturing, hunting, fishing, etc. If two of the twenty die, the share of every survivor will

be increased and become one-eighteenth of the whole ;   if,
on   the   contrary,   two   members   are added   to   the   group,
say   by   the   coming   of   age   of   two   youths,   there   will
be twenty-two shares in the whole.   If there remain but
one of the shareholders in the trev, his will be all the land,
and he will have to perform all the duties incumbent on it.
In this system there is no difference in regard to rights
between father and son, uncle and nephew, if they are full-
bodied men : they rank equally as sharers.   The amount
of land actually held may be, of course, different in different
cases,   but   it   was   considered   that   a   plain   freeman,
in order to get a sufficient living, ought to be entitled to
not less than four or five erws (strips), while joining according to strength in coaration and other common usages.   For
a man of higher standing eight erws was assumed to be
the required minimum, and we have to infer that if tnere
was no room for locating all the necessary erws, the village had to seek additional means of meeting the requirements of population by reclaiming land, starting a colony,
and the like.   In the extents, holding by trevgyvriv is
restricted to the so-called native trevs, the villages in
which the dependent peasantry was settled.   But legal
maxims speak of allotment of strips to free and privileged
tribesmen, and the descriptions of Irish gavelkind imply
constant allotments and redivisions amongst freemen.[32]

Treweloghe   The other arrangement, the coming to land
               by dadenhudd, (literally '' the uncovering
of   the   hearth '')   though   less   equalising   and   more
adapted to genealogical reckonings, was, nevertheless,
based on the same communalistic assumption that there
ought to be land for every tribesman.[33]   The characteristic feature of dadenhudd lay in the idea that every
head of a household ought to be put on an equal
footing with the men of his generation within the gwely.
Theoretically the founder of the *gwely* was considered as
if he had effected the first settlement on the land, and
taken possession of the whole of that land.   At his death
each of his sons got an equal share with his brothers :
if, for example, there were four sons, four shares were

formed in the gwely ; if after a time one of the sharers, say A, died, leaving two sons, these last entered provisionally as half sharers [34] for the part which their father had held, so that instead of four shares there were henceforth three full shares and two half shares ($\frac{a}{2}$, $\frac{a}{2}$, b, c, d). Suppose B died leaving three sons, and C, leaving four, as long as D was alive the division would be into one full share, two half shares, three thirds and four fourths ($\frac{a}{2}$, $\frac{a}{2}$, $\frac{b}{3}$, $\frac{b}{3}$, $\frac{b}{3}$, $\frac{c}{4}$, $\frac{c}{4}$, $\frac{c}{4}$, $\frac{c}{4}$, d). But on D dying and leaving, say, one son, the whole apportionment would be readjusted, each of the cousins forming the third generation taking one-tenth share in the whole gwely. By the same process the shares of the great grandsons of the founder would be formed inside their father's lots as long as there was a single member of the third generation alive, but on the death of the last grandson, the second cousins would redivide the whole into, say, twenty equal shares. If, however, one of the grandsons had died before that redistribution of the fourth generation his sons could seemingly not inherit full shares with their uncles, and were precluded for ever from taking part in the redistribution on a footing of equality with their contemporaries, the third cousins of the fifth generation. The appeal to the gwely of the original founder was barred after the fourth generation, the process of equalisation going on nevertheless, but starting theoretically not from the first founder but from every one of his sons ; though in practice many of the gwelys must have held out longer. Of course, in order to carry out such a system people had to reclaim new land and to send out the surplus of the population when the conditions of settlement got tight. As a matter of fact, redivisions in " gavelkind," as the English writers termed the arrangement, tended towards a pulverisation, if not of the holdings, at any rate of the shares, and the inevitable result is noted by later observers.[35] Originally, as is fully established by the surveys, attributions of real allotments were not practised, and would have been absurd even in the case of treweloghe, not to speak of trevgyvriv : what was meant was the admission of more or " fewer " persons into a community, and the appreciation of their respective ideal shares in the concern : only the settlement in the tyddyn had to be necessarily real.[36] But in course of time the eventuality of real partition had to be considered more and more often ; indeed, the Codes express the sound opinion that nobody is bound to hold in joint tenancy if he refuses to do so, and provide for cases when objects came into partition which did not admit of real division.[37]

Let us notice the very important fact, that the unity of the gwely, which is so strongly exemplified by the process **Familial** described, is emphatically the union of a com-**Communities** munity of joint tenants. The Codes do not mention any one who acts as a chief of the gwely, not to speak of any one who has a right of property in it in opposition to rights of maintenance claimed by the rest.[38] In all the free gwelys and in those native villages where the bondmen held according to treweloghe, the shareholders, the fathers of households, are on an equal footing, and if some enactments seem to suggest a claim of the elder brother to the whole, as taking precedence of the claims of younger brothers, a comparison with the numerous paragraphs testifying to an equal distribution of rights between brothers shows that the elder brother plays a peculiar part, not as an only or privileged inheritor, but as the representative of the gwely as a whole. This representation had of course considerable consequences in practice, inasmuch as on many occasions the members of the gwely had to act as a whole, and to support each other by oaths and goods, as the law terms it.[39] But there is no question of exclusive ownership or even chieftainship in this case. The *penteulu* mentioned in some enactments does not belong to this connection at all : he is either the chief of the Royal household, a kind of major domus, or a simple householder (father of a family).[40] Of the chief of the kindred and of the landlord we shall have to speak later on, but they are certainly not chiefs of gwelys and indeed I do not find any chief of wele in the Welsh codes. Normally it was a community of second cousins, numbering some 12 to 15 households, and probably some 50 to 60 members, but it did not necessarily coincide with a kindred, and when it coincided the part it played as a kindred was distinct from the legal arrangement of property and inheritance described by the codes. I lay stress on this point not because I want to minimise the effect of these peculiar arrangements, but because it is necessary to make clear that the Welsh tribal arrangements are not to be construed on the basis of a sole ownership in land of the "patriarch." They are based on gavelkind in both their main developments, and both systems are directed towards an equalisation of shares as to land, though in one case this is achieved in a more complete fashion, while in the other the attribution of shares is adapted to the relative position of men according to pedigree. We have to add that the often recurring claim to land by kin and descent is a distinct form of pleading. A man had to claim kin and descent, if he could not rely on dadenhudd (" uncover the hearth "), that is establish a definite position through father, grandfather and so forth in a particular gwely and within the fourth generation. By claiming kin and descent he contended either that the persons who were holding him out of the possession of land were either strangers to the land, usurpers who had no kin and descent to fall back upon, or else that there was no one in the kindred nearer him, though he himself did not belong to the close community of the four generations. If they were settled according to dadenhudd kin and descent gave no claim against them.[40a] This seems very clear in the documents, and there is nowhere an indication of a double title to land—one by dadenhudd in the ordinary course of inheritance, and the other by kin and descent as flowing from a claim to maintenance. In fact I cannot discover any special right of maintenance of the free tribesmen in distinction from their right as actual or potential shareholders in the land which came to them by reason of their taking part in one of the tribal communities or of the settlement of their forefathers in a particular trev.

Does this lead us to the conclusion that Celtic tribal society was entirely actuated by democratic ideas, and that special

care was taken in it to place all men on an equal footing ?
Aristocracy and Nothing of the sort. The fact that land was
Democracy considered primarily to be the common property of clans, septs or gwelys, does not preclude in the least
that other commodities were distributed without any regard
to the allotment of shares, and that very marked ranks and
privileges were built upon this foundation as well as upon
special forms of landownership. It remains to be seen
how far the communalistic ideas acting on one side counter-
balanced or did not counterbalance the individualistic and
aristocratic leanings in other respects. Hitherto we have
only treated of the relation of tribesmen to land in agnatic
communities. The communalism we noted was produced
by a conception of the value and the use of land very different
from our own, or from the feudal one for that matter. It
was connected with the necessity of considering the
welfare and the feelings of tribal warriors which were
the most important element of that society, important not
only for themselves, but also as impersonating the strength
of the tribe and its political capabilities.[41] The armed free
tribesman was undoubtedly endowed with a rough average
of rights, though the recognition of his social status had
nothing to do with modern democratic theories.

Let us now turn to the aristocratic elements of the problem. In order to realise their strength one has to
Slaves and take into account the dependent classes.
Taeogs Tribal society did not merely consist of free
tribesmen. Besides those, there were slaves (*caeths*) villains—*taeogs*, *aillts*, etc., and there were strangers, *alltuds*.
Attending to the first of these classes, we may notice that
the element of personal bondage, the notion that a *caeth*
is a thing, is sometimes expressly put forward : the
king may not have any fine for the killing of the bondmen belonging to another person ; that is a fact which
entirely concerns the owner, for a person has the property of his bondman " as of his animal." [42] There is such
a gulf between a freeman and a bondman (*caeth*) that if the
first strikes the latter, he has to pay twelve pence ; but
should the latter strike a freeman, he loses his arm.[43] In

Ireland the *cumal*, the female slave, appears as a standard article of trade and a unit in reckoning. As for the *taeogs*, they appear as *nativi*, as serfs, settled on the land, bound to perform certain duties and pay certain rents ; but holding personal property and following fixed customs in their daily life, and their relations to each other or to their lords. There are taeogs of the king and taeogs belonging to private persons. The bulk of the *nativi* evidently came from the remnants of the aboriginal population which held the country before its invasion by Celtic tribes. We find the recognition of this fact in Irish accounts.[44] Even if no such recognition were forthcoming we should have to surmise something of the kind, as there is ample anthropological evidence of strong pre-Celtic elements in the composition of the Welsh, Irish, and Highland Scotch people ; and we should have to assign to these pre-Celtic elements, in accordance with the usual course of events in history, the lowest place in social organisation.

Economic Subjection It seems natural to suppose, with the authors of the book on the Welsh people, that the Celtic conquerors formed the upper layer of society, and not even a very voluminous one, and made use of their political superiority to throw on the aborigines the burden of tedious farm work, and make drudges of them.[45] Such an account would altogether seem to be more in keeping with the latest fashion of understanding ancient society[46] than any idea which might be construed as carrying back modern notions of democratic freedom into these ancient times. It seems almost preposterous on my part to contest the adequacy of such a reading in regard to Celtic history, but I venture to submit that there are other combinations to be reckoned with than the two of free democracy and of an association of idle conquerors living on the work of natives, and that the Celtic arrangements do not fall either under one or under the other of these heads. The clearest view of these matters is presented in the Welsh documents. Looking at the extents, we find that the population is not unevenly divided into freemen and natives, and that each class is grouped in

separate trevs.[47]   Exceptional instances, when in the same
trev one part of the inhabitants are free and the rest villains,
confirm the rule as to the division of both classes, because
the free and the serfs are placed on the same level, the first
holding some of the gavells of the trev, and the second the
others.[48]   Both the free and the unfree tenants are bound
to perform certain duties and pay rents ; and though these
duties are not identical, it is material that both kinds are
directed to the use of the chief's household, and *the taeogs
are not, as a rule, subordinated in their work and payments
to the free.*[49]   In this manner we see that the very numerous
free population stands by the side of the unfree population,
and is not supported by it. The registration of the personnel
in the Denbigh extents especially is so careful, and the numbers of the freeholders in treweloghe so large, that it would
be out of the question to suppose a kind of two-storeyed
occupation in free trevs in contrast to a single-storeyed one
in unfree trevs.[50]   The 15 or 16 freemen concentrated in
a gavell, the 50–60 forming a gwely are evidently taken
to be the holders of the gavell and of the gwely, and
if they are taken to be so in the half-feudal fourteenth
century extent, it is difficult to make out that their
ancestors were anything different in the time of independent tribal Wales.   If we turn to the Codes, we find a
curious description of the division of a *cymwd* into 50
trevs, of which two are reserved for cultivation as royal
board land, eight are set apart as office land for the use of
domanial officers, sixteen are entered as trevs held by taeogs,
and the rest, twenty-four, belong to free tribesmen.[51]   It
may be argued that the arrangement could not have been
carried out with this arithmetical precision and symmetry ;
but undoubtedly the passage gives us an insight into the
usual, the normal distribution of villages and groups of
tenants in ordinary cymwds, and such a distribution
certainly does not resemble in the least the arrangement
of the feudal districts of England : there is no attempt to
build up a system in which the natives would be made to do
work and to act as drudges for the free.   Both are harnessed
to the same yoke, although the natives had to draw a

heavier burden, as we shall see by-and-bye. Looking back from these ascertained facts to a period when the tribal organisation was in full work, and not yet complicated by English feudal influences, we may suppose, with some certainty, that the way the conquered aboriginal population was treated in Wales was not the reduction of it into slavery or a serfdom intended to provide the conquerors with the working men necessary for the cultivation of their holdings, but its subjection into a tributary state in regard to the clans and their chiefs. The natives were grouped in some parts of the country, while room was made for the tribesmen in other parts ; some slaves these latter undoubtedly had, but these were not many, and did not enable their proprietors to live, as a rule, on the produce of servile work and to dispense with work of their own. It may be found, on reflection, that such a situation was not unlikely to arise in a country with predominant grazing and hunting pursuits, very scanty cultivation, most imperfect ways of communication, poor markets, and weak State control. It appears that the arrangement of society on the basis of slavery or of serfdom is not so easily carried out as many suppose, and that it is, perhaps, a more complex result of historical development than even primitive democracy. In order to employ slaves extensively one ought to be able not only to get them, but also to feed, to keep, and to supervise them ; in order to use profitably the labour of serfs, one ought to be able to organise it and to apply its produce regularly to home-consumption and to sale. If these conditions of regularity could not be attained, the employment of slaves and of serfs might turn out to be a burden, and it was more natural for the conquerors to impose tribute on the subject households and to leave the more intensive employment of servile labour to the few people in a position to make profitable use of it— to the kings, chieftains and other highly privileged persons. With the rest of the inhabitants of Scotch and Welsh mountain valleys and of Irish bogs, slaves might be an exceptional commodity, female slaves might even be specially sought for different purposes ; but there could be no slave-

holding husbandry arrangements. The pasturing of herds,
the work of the dairy farms, the collection and preparation
of honey, even the ploughing and harrowing operations,
were mainly performed by members of the free households
themselves, with such occasional help as they might find
from dependants of different kinds—domestic servants,
strangers, clients. It must be added that the possession
of taeogs not being common and usual, it must have given
special prominence to those who were able to dispose of
them, and, as it was coupled with privilege, must have
served to enhance that privilege. The owners of slaves
and serfs naturally get ascendancy among the free.

If we now turn to the repartition of duties to the tribe
between the freemen and the taeogs, we find that the

Services and Rents   first had to act primarily as military men, to
serve in the hosting, to follow *feacht* and
sluaged,[52] as they said in Ireland, and to attend the courts
as assessors.[53] The military obligations of the free were
graduated according to their personal status, no one being
required to serve on horseback (as a marchog) if he was
not the chief of a family, if he had not ascended to the
state of his father. The taeogs also came to the host,
but only as hatchet men, to help to erect camps. For the
erection and the keeping up of castles both classes were
called up. The taeogs were assessed differently when
they were settled in Maer trevs, that is in villages under the
management of stewards, and when they lived in tributary
villages in trevgivriv, or in treweloghe. In the first
instance they had to perform all the necessary agricultural,
pastoral, and carrying work for the demesne; but these cases
are exceptional, and testify more to the gradual rise of
demesne cultivation on the land of the chieftains than to the
general condition of the country.[54] As a rule, the villages of the
nativi were left to manage their own affairs, but were bound
to pay certain rents in food-stuffs, and to provide the king's
servants and strangers under his protection with lodging
and maintenance (dovraeth).[55] As to the king himself,
when he went on progress he had to be feasted by his free
subjects, and the villains or taeogs were called up chiefly to

" raise " houses for him, with the exception, however, of two great annual progresses, which fell as a burden on the taeogs as well as on the free.[56]   The feasting and the provision of food was the most characteristic and profitable part of this system of assessment.   It did not require any very close supervision or frequent intrusion into the life of the dependent people, and it dispensed with an intricate arrangement of domanial husbandry.   This barbarous system of exploitation was not burdensome, because it lacked the organisation and continuity of purpose to make it burdensome, but the strain it put on the tenant in extraordinary cases shows that it was not rendered easy out of consideration for the tenants.   One curious method of drawing income from taeogs was to let the maer fasten on them in turn, going from one to the other every year in order to avoid the complete ruin of the bondmen concerned.[57]   Another mode of exploitation was to quarter on the taeogs youths who were to be fostered according to their requirements and condition, and even received a claim to a son's portion of the inheritance of the taeog, but might be useful to him later on by giving him protection or material help.[58] It must be added that as the food rents and feasting were to a great extent exacted from the free people as well as from the taeogs, both had to contribute to the tunc pound, the money tax which was laid on the land in commutation for the food rents.[59]

A second element of dependence with which one has to reckon in ancient Celtic society arises from the position of **Strangers in Blood** strangers in blood, of *alltuds*.   They might have come from over the border, or they might be kin-shattered men who, for some reason—a quarrel, a murder, economic difficulties—had had to forsake their home and kindred.   Their personal freedom was recognised, and if they took care to move from one place to the other, and to seek protection with different people, they remained quite distinct from the *aillts* or taeogs.   But their position was very difficult in a society in which security was guaranteed primarily by the help of relations and friends. As they had no relations, they had to seek friends at any

price, and this price could be no other than the surrendering
of a part of their independence and earnings. Gradually a
kindred might grow up around a family of alltuds, and if
this family had succeeded in keeping its personal freedom
through three generations, in the fourth it might take rank
with the free-born Welshmen of the Wyrion gwelys.[60] But if,
as was even more likely, the fourth generation found the
alltud family sitting on the same land, and under the same
protection which its great-grandfather had obtained, it
lapsed into perpetual dependence, and it is not unlikely
that some of the settlements of *nativi* had had no other
origin.[61]

Thirdly, personal dependence might be the consequence
of economic processes going on in the midst of the free

Patrons and Clients communities themselves. The economic
balance of households chiefly dependent on
pastoral or semi-pastoral pursuits is even more easily disturbed than the economy of agriculturists, and notwithstanding the precautions which were taken to give all the
free tribesmen a fair start in life, it often happened that
some got ruined in consequence of murrain, bad seasons,
war, fire, and the like. Even apart from that, there must
have been constant inducements to one or the other among
the people to speculate on larger profits by getting an
additional outfit of stock. Loans of cattle are most commonly mentioned, but loans of agricultural implements and
seed occurred also, and the consequences of these operations
were peculiar. The Irish laws give the fullest description
of the degree of personal dependence which was incurred
by free householders who had been reduced to take loans
from chiefs or from more prosperous neighbours. It is
not to be wondered at that interest was high, and the
conditions for repayment hard, as, evidently, there was
no accumulation of capital to speak of, and the
security of such transactions could not be great. And so
the debtor sank easily, and often passed from the position of
a free dependent (*saer ceile*) to that of a bond one (*daer
ceile*).[62] In any case these operations in cattle and agricultural outfit produced something very different from

CELTIC TRIBAL ARRANGEMENTS

personal indebtedness : they led to dependence, to a position of clients in regard to great men which, without actually destroying the free status of the debtors, still reduced their social value, and, on the other hand, helped to create aristocratic positions and pretensions. It is obvious that Cæsar had something of the kind in view when he spoke of the factions in the tribes of Gaul, and of the dependence of *Clientes* and *Obœrati* on a few leaders.

In this way we observe in the development of Celtic society two distinct currents, one produced by the hierarchical organisation of tribal society, the other by various causes favouring inequality among the people and the personal influence of powerful men. We are led to the same general conclusion by observing the different manners in which leadership appears in Celtic documents. There are two terms expressing authority with which one has to deal in Welsh evidence—*pencenedl*, the chief of kindred ; and *argluyd*, the lord.[63]

If we turn to the opposition between the chieftain and the lord, we shall have, evidently, to take into account that **Chieftain and** the first of these authorities is the more archaic **Lord** one, as it comes from the agnatic arrangement of society, which answered to the original half-pastoral state of the folk, whereas the second connects itself with those personal influences making towards economic inequality and privilege, which tended to modify the tribal arrangement. Looking at the Welsh laws, one finds the chieftain often mentioned, but not many functions are distinctly attributed to him : he appears mainly in the act of admitting or refusing admission to those who claim to be members of the kindred, and who have not had a father to admit them, a ceremony which was certainly very material to the constitution of that body and to the establishment of claims on the basis of pedigree. It may be noted that it is supposed that in each case the chieftain does not act alone, but in agreement with his kinsmen, and even his kinswomen— this last probably because cases occurred when the father was dead or a stranger, and the mother had to testify to the link of blood-relationship. In disputed cases which ended in a refusal, the chieftain appears with six kinsmen to help him ; and the eventuality of a kindred without chief is distinctly recognised. In this last case the kindred is represented by twenty-one best men in Gwynedd ; while in Powis fifty men are required to take part in the decree.[64] Apart from this we find the chieftain concerned with paying rents and performing duties in regard to the king. But in Ireland and in the Highlands the chieftain of the sept or of the clan appears as the principal authority over tribesmen. They are ranged under him in all concerns of life ; they look up to him as the military commander, the judge and the regulator of claims as to land. As late as in 1724 an acute and trustworthy observer of Highland customs described the life of the Highlanders as bound up with the organisation of branches of kindred of some fifty or sixty men standing under the arbitrary authority of chieftains, who acted not as landlords, but as patriarchs.[65] Still, it would be hardly right to represent the Highland chieftain as an absolute ruler and the rights of the clan as vested in his person. Such positions are not governed, of course, by strict constitutional limitations ; but custom and the natural authority of the elders and heads of families exerted certainly a good deal of influence, and kept a chieftain within bounds. We hear occasionally of meetings of tribesmen to arrange their affairs (Nabacs, Mods) in Scotland,[66] and from Ireland we get curious information as to customary limitations to the authority of the chieftain and as to its occasional expansion. The chief of the Mac Guires, for instance, is said to be restricted to a comparatively modest position in time of peace ; he owns only four bailies of land out of the fifty-one-and-a-half, which belong to the tribe, and cultivates only one bailie as demesne in connection with his castle at Inniskillen ; besides this he gets a tribute of 240 beeves from seven bailies. In time of war, however, his rule becomes arbitrary ; he makes himself self-owner of all, and burdens the country with whatever dues he likes in order to carry on military operations.[67] The passage from the authority of a chief to that of a feudal lord is very simple in

Scotland : it was unmistakably the result of influence from without, of pressure brought to bear by the governments to which Scotland was subjected. As to the Highlands the transformation was achieved by the break-up of the clans after the rising of 1745, and the compulsion of the inhabitants of the Islands and Highlands to " show their holdings," [68] that is, to exchange their tribal occupation for modern land-tenancy. In the Lowlands the same process had been going on under feudal influences, even from the formation of the thanages under the first dynasty of Scottish kings to the seventeenth century. But apart from that process of political feudalisation may be noticed the conclusion of contracts of *manred*, by which men became tenants under well-to-do landowners, paid rents and gave *calp*, i.e. one of their best beasts, on a change of tenantship.[69] In Ireland the way towards analogous results was paved by the specialisation of Church land and Royal offices on the one hand, and the process of commendation through cattle-ownership and land-tenancy on the other. The Airès rose from the tribe as owners and lenders of cattle, and then of reclaimed and privately appropriated land. Very interesting and circumstantial evidence may be gathered from Welsh documents. The *argluyd*, the lord, is not only often mentioned by the side of the *penkenedl* in the Welsh codes, but he is sometimes treated as his superior. The chieftain has to pay rent to him, and if he grants some office within the kindred, a fine of one pound is to be given to the lord.[70] The lord appears on other occasions as the president of a court composed of freeland-owners, of *gwrdas*.[71] He conducts the proceedings, and execution is done in his name, although the decision comes from the judges and the free assessors of the court. As the courts of which these paragraphs treat are the courts of the cantrev and of the cymwd—the hundred and the half-hundred—the lord must be considered as a magnate who has received from the king the office of chief of a cymwd or a cantrev, a kind of thane, like those of whom we hear in Scotland in the eleventh and thirteenth centuries, a hereditary official holding by feudal tenure from the king, but deriving his popular authority, to a great extent, from his being the successor of the traditional tribal princes of old.   Although the connection of Welsh lords with tribal chieftainship remains a matter of inference, it seems the most natural explanation of their position at the head of the great divisions of the country, and of the subjection of the chiefs of kindred to them.

At the same time there is an element of personal patronage in the influence exercised by the argluyds.   A free Welsh-

Comitatus
man usually joins an argluyd at the age of 14, and he gets an outfit from him,[72] the gift of some *da*, some cattle or other chattels, after the taking of which he becomes personally pledged to fidelity to his chief.   We hear even that land is usually conferred by the chief on a follower who has reached the age of 21,[73] though this looks like a later development of the original maxim about the gift of the *da*.   As the relation is a personal one, the election of an argluyd seems to have been optional, and the patron in such a case would not be necessarily the head of the cymwd where the youth was born, or of any other ; any great man with ample means may have done ; and in regard to means, the ownership of a good deal of land in private or official property must have been one of the conditions enabling a man to gather followers.   At any rate, we get a glimpse of relations which stand in marked contrast to the ordinary grouping of the population into kindreds and gwelys.   We have again an example of competition between institutions which, if developed in a one-sided manner, would have excluded each other. On the one hand stands the grouping according to pedigree and the association of free tribesmen in the gwely, the kindred, the sept, and clan ; on the other,—the formation of voluntary ties of patronage and command around men of exceptional authority and wealth.   Lastly, we have to take into account the imposition of political authority from above, by the influence of kingship, and the consequent arrangement of local subdivisions for the purpose of administering justice, collecting revenue, and organising the host.

In consequence of the action of these various causes, we find tribal society differentiated into classes. The Irish laws present an exceptionally complicated series of grada-

Classes
tions, according to property and patronage.[74] The Welsh system is much simpler. The free tribesmen are either *uchelwrs* (*breyrs*) or innate *boneddigs*,[75] and the distinction between those ranks is expressed among other things in their *galanas* or wergeld : where an uchelwr is paid for by 126 cows, a boneddig is only worth sixty-three cows. Sometimes the father of a family is estimated at a somewhat higher price than the unmarried boneddig, namely, at eighty-four cows.[76] The dignity of an uchelwr became hereditary and depended on high birth, patronage, wealth, or an office. There is nothing to show, however, that the position of an uchelwr was widely different from that of common tribesmen, or implied necessarily a lordship over them. In any case the aristocracy proceeds from an internal process of development within the mass of free tribesmen. The typical freeman is still the boneddig, and in the extents we lose sight of the division ; both classes are merged into the one of free tenants.

If we now consider Celtic society from the point of view of its relation to the coming manorial system, we shall

Summing up
notice, without difficulty, that it contained some of the elements which went towards the formation of the manor, but that these elements were in an incomplete and disconnected state, and overshadowed by the influence of other principles. Landownership began to be recognised as a force, but there was as yet no regular organisation of the estate in which dependent labour would be gathered round an economic centre ; many serfs lived by the side of free proprietors and free tenants ; but they formed separate communities, and were not arranged to bear the burden of work for the benefit of the free people. Both serfs and free were subjected to food tribute, and providing maintenance for the chiefs and kings ; but other-wise their position was that of independent householders. There were many aristocratic ranks and degrees in the

folk, but the passage from one to the other was easy, and the differences of pedigree, wealth and influence which led to their formation were constantly shifting, so that there could be no question of a settled system of hierarchical privilege and patronage. The segregation of political power, as distinct from tribal authority, had begun, and had produced some attempts to arrange society into rough, symmetrical compartments ; but for the chief purposes of defence and of economic organisation the tribal grouping still remained the principal scheme of society. The ideas underlying tribal order, affinity in blood and association through origin from one and the same household, contributed powerfully towards keeping up a spirit of co-operation and safeguarding the interests of every born tribesman as member of a kindred. I should like to say, in conclusion, that the value of these Celtic facts does not only consist in their possible connexion with traits of the manorial system. They are important also, because they help us to understand the conditions of tribal society in its simpler forms. The observations made in regard to them will have to be taken into account when we come to treat of the more complex and contradictory arrangements of Old English Society.

CHAPTER II.

ROMAN INFLUENCE

I. Romans and Celts in Britain

In the case of Britain, as well as in that of Gaul and Germany, the process of spontaneous social evolution was interrupted and modified by the intrusion of a powerful foreign element—Roman civilisation. **Romanisation** How far did it extend, and what features of the life of Rome were transplanted to British soil ? It is easier to answer the second of these questions than the first, but it is necessary to form an opinion as to both.

It seems pretty clear that the conquest of Britain by the Romans did not produce the same thorough Romanisation of the people as was achieved by the conquest of Gaul or Spain. England has not grown to be a Romance country with a people speaking a language directly proceeding from Latin, and whatever our subsequent opinion as to the effect of the German settlement may be, we must in the first instance look for an explanation of the fact in the comparatively slight impression produced by Roman dominion on the Celtic population of the British Isles. There are many signs to show that the absorption of Celtic nationality by Roman culture was by no means complete, and had not even been carried very far, when the Saxons broke in, and Roman rule collapsed. Even the general aspect of Roman remains in Britain is different from that which they present in other provinces of the West. As one of the authorities on the subject has expressed it—most of the objects and inscriptions found in Britain bear a military stamp on them : they refer either to the military occupation of the island, or to the material and religious life of the people connected with this military occupation.[1] The traces of the road system point, of course, to work which facilitated intercourse and commercial development, but they are primarily explained by strategic and administrative requirements. Although some thirty-three town settlements of various forms and degrees are noticed in Roman times, the vestiges of municipal life which form such a conspicuous element in other provinces are insignificant—in fact not a single municipal inscription of any importance has come down to us from Britain. There are many remnants of Roman houses and villas, and they point incontestably to the existence of a numerous well-to-do class used to the ways and comforts of Roman life, and thus the account given by Tacitus of the captivating influence of Roman blandishments on the natives, gets substantiated by remains of objects which have been in actual use. But such remains do not necessarily indicate an influence stretching wide and deep through the country : in fact, they are grouped across it, as it were, in patches.

The South Coast on one side and the Wall of Hadrian on the other present, of course, the most remarkable traces of connected occupation, and behind those **Villas** outer lines some districts appear to have been rather thickly studded by Roman settlements. Gloucestershire and Lincolnshire may be pointed out as instances, and it is not unlikely that their considerable Romanisation may be accounted for by their forming, as it were, feeding centres which supported the military concentrations in the West and in the North. But by the side of such districts appears the Midland region, in which Roman remains are very slightly represented, and in the very centre of thickly populated and strongly Romanised Kent and Sussex there stretched a vast forest tract, the Weald, which remained a wilderness right into the middle ages.[2]

Without venturing into details as to explorations of villas I may just point out that they testify to curious contrasts between an exotic culture of a very high order and a vernacular culture of a very primitive kind. Let us take the

remains of the villa in Brading, Isle of Wight, as an instance.
The mosaic pavements are remarkable : they remind one of
Pompeii. But the Orpheus in the hall looks at us with
Southern eyes, and the very choice of the subject for this
picture, though not uncommon, has an emblematic significance which hardly testifies to a thorough blending of Roman
and native elements. Orpheus has indeed succeeded in
charming the animals around him by the civilised strains
of his lyre, but the monkey, the peacock and the coot,
though tamed, are animals after all. And as for the elaborate provisions for heating the rooms by hypocausts, they are
too much in advance even of modern civilisation to be attributed to anything but a delicate exotic varnish.

At the other end of the ladder stand the remnants of
village dwellings of Roman Britain, as illustrated by the
finds of General Pitt-Rivers in Cranbourne Chase on the
border of Wiltshire and Dorsetshire. The remnants of Roman
pottery, ornaments and coins speak of Roman influence,
though the excavated villages are of the same type as that
of Standlake in Oxfordshire, where only stone implements
were found. Again we come across rude heating apparatus
constructed of stones, but some of those seem to have been
used for boiling meat by the rude expedient of throwing
red-hot stones into the cauldron. And the village itself was
built in a most primitive fashion, the dwellings being connected with pits used as storage-rooms, refuse sinks and
burial places, in a very strange promiscuity of needs of the
living and of the dead. The corpses are often found crouch-
ing in positions which were never adopted in Roman burials,
and correspond to the habits of inhumation of primitive
tribes. Altogether Roman civilisation does not seem to
have altered much in the modes of life of the lower classes,
as illustrated by these pit villages.[3]

There is also other evidence of the fact that Celtic
elements were still quite alive, and capable of emerging
from their subordinate position at any given
Celtic Revival opportunity. There can be no dispute as
to the permanence of Celtic language and culture in the
North and in the West of the island. Not to speak of the

country beyond Hadrian's wall, which was given up to the Caledonian tribes after Septimius Severus, the shires which formed the southern part of Strathclyde (Cumberland, Westmorland, Lancashire), the whole of Wales, Devon, and Cornwall are vindicated for Celtic nationality by their well known later history, and notwithstanding the garrisons in Chester and Caerleon, and the Roman roads cutting through the mountains and reaching the coast, the removal of Roman official rule disclosed in those parts a population still living according to old Celtic habits, and still possessed of peculiar economic and political institutions.[4] It would not do to ascribe the tribal customs of Wales and the clear traces of Celtic life to the mere influence of a late revival, as the very width of the Celtic zone and the traditional peculiarity of Celtic customs point to their continuous and firmly rooted existence. The Celtic trevs and kindreds are not likely to have been constructed anew by emigrants from a few outlying districts on soil where they had been previously eradicated. This is a fact of primary importance, because it shows that the Romans did not attempt to uproot these customs and institutions in the western part of Britain, but had to be satisfied with very superficial allegiance. And even in the rest of the country the great mass of the population must have remained true to Celtic speech and therefore to Celtic traditions, notwithstanding the influx of Latin and Romanising influences. Only on this assumption can we account for some well-established facts. There is firstly, the marked reappearance of the Celtic element in the protracted struggle with the Northern and Eastern invaders during the fifth and sixth centuries : let me just remind my readers that the Saxons and Angles are described as fighting and conquering British Celts : the admixture of Roman provincialism at this time is not entirely absent, but disappears with significant rapidity. The second and even more characteristic fact is that during these same fifth and sixth centuries, in the general turmoil of migration and invasion, the population of Great Britain plays not only a passive but also an active part, and not only defends itself against Saxons, Angles and Picts, but also comes forward in a powerful offensive movement against the French shore, occupying Brittany and a good deal of the adjoining country along the Loire. The point is that this wave of immigrants rushing from Great Britain to the Armorican shore is strongly Celtic, and to that extent alien to Roman sentiment and institutions that it actually destroys them in the Gallo-roman districts it appropriates. Latin is stamped out and replaced by the dialects of the Dumnonii, Cornubii, and other Britons which came over in those troubled times [5] ; and the influx of these Celtic elements is so powerful that it has held its own against the general course of French history even to the present day, maintaining the well-known peculiarities of Breton speech and custom in the so-called *Bretagne bretonnante*.[6] The people who brought about this result certainly did not speak Latin or submit to Romanisation in the country from which they came, if they acted in this manner in their new home. It is impossible for us nowadays to realise with anything like precision the shades and variations which led from the considerable Romanisation of parts like Kent or Hertfordshire to the militant Celticism of the West. But one thing seems clear : there is not the slightest probability that the marked assertion of Celtic speech and nationality both at home and abroad in the course of the fifth and sixth centuries proceeded entirely and exclusively from those parts of Wales or Devon and Cornwall which had been left more or less untouched by Roman occupation, although the political and intellectual leaders in the struggle against the Saxons and in the movement of emigration which brittanised Armorica seem to have come chiefly from these parts.[7] At a time when Celtic traditions came to the fore and the most thoroughly Celtic regions became the strongholds and centres of action against an invasion from the East, Wales and " West-Wales " obtained naturally a leading position, and supplied chiefs and organisation to the movement of Celtic revival at home and abroad. But the strength of that revival lays claim to a broader basis, and implies a more superficial hold of the Romans on the whole province than has been supposed by those who have argued from the traces of Roman architecture and coinage to a more or less complete transformation of the vernacular elements.

It may be supposed that the emigrants to Armorica, though led on most occasions by Welshmen and Dumnonians, consisted to a great extent, if not mainly, of people who had been driven from their homes in central and eastern Britain by the Saxon and Pictish invaders and, after collecting in a shattered condition in the West, became organised there, and carried Bryttonic speech and manners over the Channel into Brittany. By the side of the Cambrians and Dumnonians the Cornovii appear as a tribe which took a great part in organising the advance, and this brings us already on soil occupied now by purely English counties, as the territory of these Cornovii seems to have covered the region stretching from Chester and Hereford in the west to Warwick in the east.[8] Some bands may even have had leaders from the district adjoining the Roman wall.[9]

From our special point of view it seems pretty clear that, as the great wave of Celtic immigration which turned the Armorican peninsula from its Romanised state to definitely Bryttonic condition came from Great Britain, it testifies to the prevalence of Celtic speech and customs in the Great Britain of the fifth and sixth centuries.[10] In short, only by admitting a strong under-current of Celtic life may we account for the powerful Celtic revival of the fifth and sixth centuries. One has to keep this well in mind from the very beginning while drawing up an estimate of Roman influence on Britain. That Roman influence must have been considerable in any case is not a point which need be disputed. But in order to speak of it rightly we must remember that the Romanisation of outlying provinces is at the same time the barbarisation of Rome. In consequence of the swallowing up of so many nations in a primitive state of culture the Empire had necessarily to lower in every respect its standard of culture, and it is not only

Survey of Roman Occupation

on account of defeats, of an intolerable strain on the resources of society, and of the enervating influence of political
despotism that the achievements of Imperial civilisation in
politics, science, arts, economics, in the very use of language,
appear in such a miserable form in the third, fourth and fifth
centuries as compared with its work in the first and third :
we have to deal in this lower period with a barbarous
Rome, with a degenerating coinage, as it were, in which the alloy
of baser metals is more and more driving out the gold it pre-
tends to be in name.[11]   I shall try in the following pages to
make this clear ; but one warning as to the treatment of
this subject must be given beforehand.   We have not the
means to draw a complete picture of Roman social
institutions as they existed in the special case of Great
Britain.   Archæological study enables us to form an
opinion as to the character of material civilisation and
as to its spread over the country.   But it does not tell
us what institutions, political and social, were brought
by the Romans and what compromises were effected
between these imported forms and vernacular traditions.
Even if we knew all about the topography of Roman
villas and all the details of their construction and decora-
tion, we should still be in the dark in regard to the legal
and economic organisations to which they belonged.[11a]
In fact any attempt to describe these with anything like
precision must consist mainly in inferences from facts
ascertained in regard to other provinces and to the Empire
in general.   Such a method has certainly to leave a
margin for doubts as to how far such observations fit
the particular case.   Still, no one will dispute that a careful survey of the conditions which prevailed in the more
backward parts of the Empire, and especially of the
processes of Romanisation of Gaulish tribes affords the
nearest approach to direct information about Roman Britain.

Even from the cursory descriptions of historians and
literary men, we may gather that the country had made
Material great progress in point of material culture
Progress from the time of Cæsar to the time of Constantine.   Instead of being the dwelling-place of pastoral

and hunting tribes, with a small fringe of agricultural occupation on the south-eastern border, it is extolled as an area of prosperous farming, and it certainly played a part in keeping the troops on the German frontier supplied with corn.[12] The Bryttonic language, which has to be taken as the strongest proof of independent Celtic vitality, presents a vast number of words which testify to the influence of Rome in domestic economy and cultivation. Such words as solium (Welsh sail, Eng. threshold), paries parwed, wall), cultellus (cullel, knife), caseus (caws, cheese), culter (cwlltr, ploughshare), catena (cadwyn, chain), soccus (swcch), stipula (sofl, stubble), furca (fforch, fork), scala (yscol, ladder), fustis (ffust, flail), funis (ffun, rope), stabellum (ystafell, stable), cella (cell), major (maer, steward), grex (gre, stud), admissus (emys, stallion), catta (cath, cat), porcellus (suckling pig, porchell), soldus (swllt, shilling), pagus (pau, a district), and many others of the same kind, not to speak of military and scientific terms, show conclusively that Roman expressions permeated to no inconsiderable extent the Celtic every-day speech even of the most backward portions of the population.[13] It has to be added at once, however, that by themselves these facts do not prove a complete transformation of the manners or institutions of the people : the like and perhaps more may be shown in regard to the German tribes,[14] which certainly did not lose their individuality, notwithstanding such borrowings. In regard to the use of the most important agricultural implement, the plough, an implement which has played the part not only of a technical, but one may say of a social agent in history, it was of the same kind in Britain and in Germany—the big plough with large iron ploughshare mostly drawn by four oxen and more.[15] This was certainly not the Italian two-oxen plough, but a contrivance particularly adapted to the soil and the methods of work north of the Alps : in northern parts, cultivation had to reckon with heavy soil, a plentiful supply of cattle, and a lack of untiring individual energy in the labouring men. Whether the big plough was Celtic or even pre-Celtic in

its origin we cannot tell; it was certainly not specifically Teutonic, and it is very probable that intelligent Roman agriculturists did a good deal to propagate its use in the barbarous
parts of Britain, Germany and northern Gaul.[16] Neither
can it be doubted that the handicrafts of masons, wall-
painters, mosaic-workers, and other artisans as represented
by the manifold remnants of town houses and villas, mostly
owed their rise and development to the immigration and the
teaching of Romanised workmen from Gaul, Italy, and,
perhaps, other parts of the Empire.

Taking our stand on these characteristic traits of material
conditions, we may assume safely that the Britain of the
Roman Policy Romans was by no means a homogeneous
in regard to con- and thoroughly centralised body. On the
quered Nations contrary, we may be prepared to find on its
soil all the varieties of social arrangements of the time, from
the most rudimentary tribal customs to the most complete
specimens of urban and rural Romanism. Everything we
know of the general policy of Rome on conquered soil
points in the same direction. The Romans, as we are
taught by our authorities, never attempted to introduce
their own ideas and institutions by means of a direct and
sudden centralisation. On the contrary, after providing
for undisputed sway and financial exploitation, they were
content with throwing the seeds of town life and rural life
into the new soil, leaving those seeds to bear fruit under
the propitious influence of the advantages connected
with high civilisation and the prestige of the conquerors of
the world. Romanisation became in this manner more an organic process than a mechanical contrivance for administrative purposes. In private law the customs of the vanquished
were tolerated as long as they did not stand in the way of
some recognised doctrine of the predominant law and did
not claim more than a local acceptance.[17] And as to
social order, the typical Roman arrangement of the city,
with its resident burgesses administering the country
around them, was not and could not be transplanted into
barbarous countries by a stroke of the pen ; it had to grow

as gradually as circumstances permitted, and to put up with much obstruction and conflicting tendencies in proportion to the strength and vitality of native arrangements. It is the more characteristic of the strength of this local opposition that the goal towards which Imperial policy tended presented undoubtedly a position of conspicuous privilege— the rights of Roman citizenship were bestowed on those who were ripe for municipal organisation. But still even at the time of Caracalla, who proclaimed the principle that every municipal citizen in the Empire was to be considered a citizen of Rome, numbers of Roman subjects remained outside the pale of the measure because they had not reached the stage of municipal organisation, but stuck to tribal and cantonal arrangements in their modes of life.[18]   We know for instance, that the Romans never succeeded in breaking up the native clans of the Berber and Moorish tribes in Mauritania and Numidia : five hundred and sixteen clans are mentioned, ruled by their chiefs.[19]   Even in the time of Augustine there were people in Africa who continued to speak dialects of Phœnician.   In Spain, Macedonia, and Pannonia are also to be found survivals of tribal organisations.[20]   But the most interesting case for our purpose is that of the continental Celts, as their original institutions had been the same as those of the island Celts and the processes of Romanisation applied to them were evidently of the same kind as those which were brought to bear on the Britons.   It must be added that, as the influx of southern population, material culture and ideas was much more prolonged and stronger on the Continent than on the island, it is not so much in the latter as in the earlier stages of the development of Gaul that we have to look for illuminating analogies to the history of Britain.

Now it is an acknowledged fact that the social constitution of the Celts, their territorial divisions, the grouping of their population, the character of their organising centres, were for a long time vastly different from the Roman local arrangements of the same period.   Instead of the preponderating part played by city life with its bodily concentration of landowners in

Peculiarities of the Celtic Districts

the towns, its subordination of rural districts to the town authorities, its complete dependence of rural population upon the will and the interest of urban masters, we find people scattered in hamlets over the whole territory of the district, coming to town only to transact exceptional affairs, to seek defence and justice, to buy and sell, to transact some business with the few merchants and craftsmen of the town, or to meet other inhabitants of the district for the settlement of some common affair, etc. ; in connection with this, we see institutions for organising the district as a whole, and its component parts as villages or clusters of hamlets.[21]   And the Celtic land system was not only opposed to the Roman city, but held its own stubbornly after the conquest.   It may be easily understood how difficult it was to bring the people not merely to recognise the political sway and the superiority of culture of the conquerors, but to alter their habits as to places of residence, interests, and occupations, and their habitual relations between neighbours. As a matter of fact, the Romans never attempted to turn everything upside down at once, and actually recognised the land districts of the Celts and the peculiarities of their grouping on the land, merely introducing the city as the head and centre of the land district.[22]   They trusted that the cities would gradually attract the better people, and in this way would come to dominate over the lesser people left in the villages. and they were not mistaken on the whole, but two significant facts have to be noted, nevertheless, in connection with this process of Romanising municipalisation.   During the first periods of Roman sway, it went on most energetically although it had to meet vernacular formations of very definite shape and tenacious strength, but it not only slackened in the latter period, especially in the third and fourth centuries, but even gave way to a movement of recoil created by the growing importance of rural life and its striving towards independent organisation.   When the time of the undisturbed Roman peace was over, the powerful intercourse of trade, with its concomitants in the application of capital, the considerable division of labour, and the varied forms of husbandry based on money exchanges, was

rendered insecure, and the rural elements came forward in
every respect as more adapted to primitive forms of natural
husbandry.[23]   On the other hand, there can be no doubt
that even when the city system was introduced, it had to be
compromised with many survivals of former institutions, and
that the further we proceed from south to north, the more
marked and considerable these survivals become. Originally
the rise of the central city was both artificial and superficial ; the older units of population continued to exist, and
it could be said, for instance, that a district included two
chief towns and nineteen other townships of a lower kind,
or that it was treated as an adjunct of an important munici-
pality although it possessed twenty-four towns of its own.[24]
When natural features of the country helped to keep up
those peculiarities, as in the Alps, the national type became particularly accentuated.[25]

Sometimes we get a glimpse of the agnatic organisations,
of the clans which were historically at the root of this grouping into districts : clans, (*gentilitates*) are, for instance, mentioned on Spanish soil.[26]   But, as a rule, the characteristic
territorial divisions of the Celts are termed *pagi* as the land
districts into which the *civitates* were divided.   By *pagus* was
meant both a territory forming a certain whole for geogra-
phical or historical reasons, and the association of the
land-people settled in it.[27]   The members of the *pagus*,
the *pagani*, the δῆμος in Greek provinces, form the counterpart to the *plebeii* in the towns ; their association was
not only recognised for the sacral purpose of upholding the
ancient rites of local deities: it was also a social one[27a] :
they owned property, erected and kept in repair buildings,
elected common magistrates (*magistri pagi, œdiles*), and had
to manage such interests as must arise between country
neighbours—questions about the maintenance of vicinal
roads, rights of way, common rights in regard to undivided
and waste lands, the settlement and preservation of
boundaries.[28]   There can be no doubt that this organisation of the land-folk, which showed such a vitality in
Gaul and even Italy, must have played a large part in the

history of Britain. To judge from Wales and West Wales, its features must have held on long in backward regions, whereas in more advanced parts of the country the organisation of the *pagi* had to adapt itself to lines more resembling those of Roman municipalities with meetings of members and elective magistrates.

The provinces of the Empire, which through the peculiarities of their rural organisation had succeeded in **Vici-Villages** preserving their native districts in opposition to the prevailing municipal system, naturally show a further grouping of population in lower and more intimate stages of life. I mean the grouping into villages (*vici*). Even apart from the actual distribution of dwellings in large accumulations, small clusters or single farms—there was a call for a village organisation of some kind in all cases when the owners of the land were spread about the country and not concentrated in the cities. The *pagus*, in fact, could not do without the *vicus* to support it for the settlement of all immediate neighbourly concerns. If the peasantry and the owners were actually congregated in rural centres, such an organisation must necessarily have assumed the form of village meetings and of village elder-ship of some kind. But even if the dwellers in the open country did not live close by each other, they had still many interests in common and were drawn together for civil purposes into a kind of civil parish, as they certainly were around common temples or churches in rural colleges or parishes. The process of social organisation we are mapping out is not a product of guesswork or imagina-tion : from all sides of the Empire comes evidence as to the existence and activity of organised villages (*vici*). They are the more significant as from the legal point of view the " *vicus*," as a rural community, with an independent organi-sation, forming the medium between the individual and the city, did not exist for the Romans. A village was considered by the Romans on their own soil merely as a matter-of-fact agglomeration of buildings which had to look for organisa-tion to the city on whose territory it was situated. To say that anybody was born in a village was the same as to say that he was born a citizen of the city to which the village formed an adjunct.[29]   But in conquering the world, the Romans came across people who had other conceptions and other institutions, and they accepted these heterogeneous elements more or less in the same spirit as they accepted foreign deities, joining them on, in a sort of compromise, to their own municipal institutions.   Festus speaks distinctly of villages which form commonwealths and unities of jurisdiction, and of others which, though not so city-like, have still to be considered as economic bodies, and, e.g., hold their own fairs and enjoy a special administrative organisation.[30]   Indeed, we come across village magistrates, and find that the villages hold property, bear expenses, and, consequently levy rates.[31]   From the point of view of strict Roman law, these independent organisations had to claim their powers as corporations, colleges of private law invested with sacral attributions and religious sanction.[32]   But it would hardly be safe to trust too much or too long to such a construction.   Certainly the point of view of the analogy with the commonwealth of a city and of the participation in its powers, taken up by Festus, does not favour such a narrow interpretation.   As is often the case in the domain of local institutions, it is impossible to carry out to their ultimate consequences rigid attempts to restrict the local units to mere subordination to higher powers, and to bereave them of all political significance.   In those provinces where the *vicus* was a historical pre-Roman growth, and sprang naturally from the rural basis of social life, it had to be accepted as a small self-governing unit and fitted into the system of local institutions either in connection with the *pagus*, or as an adjunct to the city, or under cover of the extra-municipal organisation of a lordship, a private *saltus*.   These observations are not affected by the fact that, as in the case of other self-governing units, the Emperors sometimes subjected the villages to the tutelage of nominated managers : that occurred in the same way in municipalities, but even these cases did not result in the complete destruction of all self-government in the village.[33] In a word, though we hear very little of the daily life and the humble affairs of these villages of the Roman Empire, we know enough of their organisation to warrant the assumption that they were associations of small land-owners or tenants closely connected with each other in agricultural matters, managing their concerns mostly by means of elective officers and meetings of the more impor-tant villagers, and capable on many occasions of seeking redress of grievances and affording protection to those of their numbers who suffered wrong. The position of these villagers was different according to the eventualities of their living on their own, or on the Emperor's, or on great people's land, but in any case it was neither defenceless nor broken up into isolated interests. We happen to know more defi-nitely of conflicts between rural corporations on imperial domains and stewards of these domains because the high intervention of Majesty gave especial publicity to these conflicts, but there are many glimpses of similar assertions of rights and measures of redress and protection in regard to communities of free peasants, and there can be no doubt that the law of the Empire gave to these last and to the tenants of private landlords even a better legal standing in the tribunals than to the occupiers of the imperial domains.[34] However, it is too early yet to speak of these relations from the point of view of civil law and of economics : what concerns us now is to show that there existed all over the Empire rural communities with a modest but definite measure of self-government ; and that these bodies did not give way either before the spread of municipal civilisation or before the developement of private ownership with its individualising tendencies. It is not meant thereby that this state of things was the only one possible, or that, in the case of dependent villages growing up on private soil, no other organisation was possible. On the contrary, it is evident that there were strong forces acting on the side of individual-ism, and that, in many cases, great landowners and their agents had it their own way.[35] But such was not the course of events everywhere, and though no statistics can be given, the numerous testimonies to the activity of rural self-

government must be noted and considered carefully, especially in instances when the pre-Roman antecedents certainly
worked that way.   It would be preposterous to picture the
settlements of barbarian *læti* on the frontiers and even of
barbarian *coloni* in the interior of the Empire on lines of
complete subjection to the will of landlords and stewards.
Indeed, some form of rural community would have to be
postulated for these frequent and symptomatic cases.[36]
But, apart from them, have we not the right to ask whether
the Celtic tribes when they came under Roman sway broke
up unresistingly into numbers of isolated individuals
connected with each other merely by municipal ties or by
relations of private contract, or whether there are indications to show that some of them, at any rate, preserved
ánd developed village organisations ?   When the Helvetes
came under the observation of Cæsar, they were divided
into four hundred *vici*, which have, no doubt, to be taken
as the territorial equivalents of as many kindreds.   All
that we learn of their subsequent life in Switzerland under
Roman sway speaks for the continuance of such local
divisions, though settlements of the Roman type—towns
and villas—break in and spread to a certain extent among
them.   The same may be shown in regard to other Alpine
tribes.   In Gaul the Romans were more successful in most
cases but in Britain the distance from the Roman centre
and the comparative shortness of its occupation may have
nad much the same effect as in Switzerland.   In any case, the
Welsh trevs, and the *plou's* of Armorica, testify to the
vitality of village organisations which have bridged over
the period of the Roman conquest from the times of purely
tribal arrangements ;[35] and the vestiges of municipal organisation in Britain are too sparse to admit of a complete
administrative arrangement of the country under the rule
of cities.

II. PRIVATE PROPERTY IN LAND AND TAXATION

One very important result of the Roman occupation
was undoubtedly its powerful influence in furthering private

property and private appropriation of land. The Roman

law, as represented by the jurisprudence of the imperial jurists, was conspicuously a law based on individualistic conceptions. The new field opened to the transactions of Roman capitalists was opened at the same time to the spirit of private enterprise, private speculation, private right.[38] The fact that Roman jurisprudence had a fully developed apparatus for the management of corporate interests and for the creation of corporate associations did not seem, at first sight, at any rate, to alter this fundamental position, because the societies of Roman law sprang from free private agreement or from direct institution by the State and entered into the general arrangement of private property as modifications of private persons—as fictitious persons. All these notions and rules were carried into the provinces, not merely by the appearance of Roman people and imperial tribunals, but also by the systematic operations necessary to establish and to regulate the financial burdens of the State. The general census of the Empire was planned and begun by Augustus, carried out by the time of Trajan, modified and supplemented by very important measures in the reign of Diocletian, and the operations of the census necessitated delimitation of the territory of the State, the overhauling of all its landed property with a corresponding determination of claims to meet the assessment, a valuation of the advantages connected with the land and of the forces employed on it. Of course, all these processes must have worked powerfully to put an end to the uncertainties and variations resulting from other and less civilised arrangements, and to assimilate, as far as possible, the peculiarities of provincial land-tenure to the standards of Roman possession even in those cases when the provincial customs had not given way at once before the superior merits of Roman notions and methods. A general tendency in this direction cannot be disputed, and has to be recognised as a powerful factor of social transformation.[35] But too much attention has perhaps been paid to this striving towards centralisation and uniformity, and not enough to the recoil in the direction of provincial peculiarities, a recoil which was the more marked the less a particular province was drawn into the general current of imperial life, and the further and less inviting it appeared from the point of view of political rulers, commercial speculators, and enterprising pioneers of civilisation.

Let us notice some characteristic limitations to that levelling process of economic and juridical development. Several operations have to be taken into account : the surveying of the territory, the determination of title and tenure, the valuation of property, the procedure of assessment, the collection of taxes. In each respect we find that there was left quite a considerable margin for adaptation to provincial circumstances, and very wide loopholes for the introduction of social peculiarities.

Surveying

The Roman treatises on surveying and on agrarian disputes give us a very accurate insight into the main points and even into the details of the first operation connected with the census — the delimitation of the territory. And they start with the sharp contrast between several modes of delimitation, the highly peculiar centuriation in rectangles being confined to strictly Roman soil, including the Roman colonies, but excluding all other varieties of municipal or rural organisation.[40] Even the modification implied by the division into strips (*per scamna et strigas*) was to be found only on soil which was very similar to that of the assignated territories, namely, on soil held directly from the State by private possessions paying rent.[41] But then come two other categories of limitation or rather two varieties of the same category, namely, the *agri arcifinii* and the *agri per extremitatem mensura comprehensi*. The first are not measured at all, but described in their frontiers according to the national features of the country—rivers, ditches, hills, villages, trees of striking appearance. The second method implies a certain measurement which, however, does not go into details, but only aims at giving the rough and general extent of the country surveyed.[42] We learn further that these modes of delimitation were employed when land was held by provincial possessors under the eminent ownership of the Empire and when it was surrendered to cities as a whole under the condition of their paying a certain tribute. Thus on provincial soil we come across two classes of land in the limitation of which all direct transfer of strictly Roman methods of surveying is renounced, and this accounts for two striking facts—namely, for the all but complete absence of traces of centuriation outside Italy, and for the constant recurrence of vernacular measures on provincial soil : let us just recall to mind the Greek plethra, the Gallic aripennis and the innumerable varieties of local acres.[43] We may thus safely assume that the work of the surveyors started by Augustus and Agrippa did not aim at or amount to a measuring up of the whole Empire acording to Roman measures and Roman methods of agrarian limitation. Indeed, it would have been absurd to attempt under cover of an operation of inquiry as to size a remodelling of the agrarian divisions. It was already a big task to ascertain, even by the help of local measures and with constant reference to local usage, the actual size and shape of the existing territorial divisions, even when in some cases the process did not go into details and left those to the settlement of the people locally interested.

The adoption of local measures and the necessary recognition of actual peculiarities in the division and use of the land leads us to the inference that in questions of **Title to Land** title also the Romans were not likely to upset all previous arrangements, but contented themselves with pressing them into a shape more or less approximating to the familiar rubrics of their law. It is certainly not to be supposed that they understood or cared to adapt themselves to the uncertain aspects of clan ownership with its complex conception of the communal property, the hereditary claims of Celtic gavelkind, the rights of free tribesmen to contingent shares and the right of chieftains and elders to regulate those shares. And, although they did not want to upset by force such customary arrangements as did not directly clash with their laws, they wanted to know who had to be responsible for the taxes of the land, and consequently who had to be considered its owner or tenant. There were several exits out of the difficulty in this respect : the assignation of portions of the soil to recognised local bodies—cities, pagi or villages— which would be held responsible for the tribute, but would be left to manage the questions and claims of customary title in their own way, and the provincial practices of delimitation held, as we have seen, that exit open for the provincial authorities. The other possibility was to recognise one particular kind of title to the land as accepted by Roman law, and to subordinate all other claims to this privileged title. The territory of a clan might, from this point of view, become the property of its chieftain, and all the clansmen would be looked upon as his tenants—more or less as was done in Scotland when the ancient tribal arrangements were broken up in favour of the common law of Scotland. Or else all the house-holders might be recognised as independent private owners, a contingency which is supported by the example of Gaul, where the great bulk of *fundi* appear originally as small and middle-sized plots, and coalesce into *latifundia* and *massae* only by being joined to each other.[44] Or again the property of a corporation, of a pagus, a town, or a village might be taken as the foundation of possessory claims. This eventuality has been less considered than the first two, but there is nothing to be said against it from the point of view of Roman law, and if we revert to the copious evidence as to the existence of rural groups with corporative constitution and rights we shall not be inclined to treat this settlement of the problem as an impossible or an unlikely one. There can be hardly any doubt, if one considers the conditions of the case, that all these expedients were actually adopted—with the result that the native organisations were indeed much shaken, disturbed and dispersed, but that they did not disappear completely : they were rather welded into a number of compromises and hybrid shapes in which the traditions of the soil lingered obstinately though disguised and hidden by Roman legal forms. We need not therefore feel astonished at the fact that a study of the details of rural arrangements discloses a good many points to which it would be hard to apply the ready conceptions of individual ownership and private interest.

As regards the processes of valuation and assessment, we are confronted by two facts which seem to militate strongly

Assessment against the theory which has been propounded just now in regard to the adjustment of title. We are told that the taxable quality of landed property was defined in a very circumstantial manner in the register of the census, the name of the plot as well as that of the neighbouring plots, the quantity of arable meadow, wood, vineyard and pasture, the number of heads of cattle and the *coloni* connected with it.[45] Specimens of descriptions drawn up in accordance with this scheme have been actually preserved. Then, again, we hear that the gist of Diocletian's reform consisted in dividing the whole taxable area into a certain number of fiscal units called *juga, capita, millenae, centuriae,* in the different provinces and supposed to represent approximately equal shares of landed property with all its belongings in soil, animals, and cultivators, the labourers and craftsmen not attached to particular holdings being grouped into corresponding units representing incomes similar to those embodied in the juga. One may well ask whether such attempts at exact assessment of values and incomes do not prove that the whole territory of the Empire was partitioned in *fundi,* in estates of the same kind, among which the *capita,* the heads of the land-tax, had to be distributed in accordance with relative fiscal strength, and in this case what would become of the districts not attributed to particular " fundi " and not taxed in detail by the central government ?   In other words, would it be possible to carry on both assumptions at the same time, the apportionment of territory and taxation to large groups with liberty for them to manage the land tenure and distribute taxation according to their notions and habits, and the detailed appreciation of property and population according to fixed standards of value ?

These questions turn out not to be so perplexing as they look at first glance, when we come to a closer examination of the evidence. The passages of Ulpianus and Hyginus giving the general form of the *census* read as very absolute prescriptions meant to be executed in a uniform manner everywhere, but a little consideration will show that they could not be executed in this uncompromising manner all over the Empire. They give the ordinary *formula* of censual description used in most cases in Italy, Gaul, Greece, Asia Minor, Africa, and the like ; but surely the cases of mountainous districts, of moors, of unreclaimed waste, of extensive common pastures, of half-nomad populations, of settled barbarians, of frontier settlers, required material modifications ; they did not admit in the same way either of exhaustive enumerations and measurements, or of the clear division of rights of ownership, or of a definite location of settlement, or of certainty in regard to neighbours. The *formula* had to be very much altered, partly simplified, partly complicated, to meet such cases, if it was meant to give anything like a trustworthy description of the state of things. It has to be noted, secondly, that the census alluded to by Ulpian and Hygin was a record of population and property meant to serve as a basis for the imposition of the *tributum*, a land-tax in money which was laid on the provinces in certain fixed sums and then distributed among the cities and other districts which had to assess their citizens according to their means, the burden of each being heavier or lighter in proportion, not only to his relative fiscal strength, but also to the general sum decreed as tribute. The repartition, in fact, went from top to bottom, as it were, and the censual description of the means of each proprietor was necessary to enable the government to form an estimate of the sum which could be imposed, and for the magistrates and bodies entrusted with the repartition in order to distribute the burden with equity and not to overstrain some individuals while favouring others. This being so, and the intermediate bodies, especially the cities, being collectively responsible for the payment of the tribute, the attempt at levying a " cadastre " of the Empire did not preclude all sorts of allowances in view of peculiar conditions in the provinces.

The departure taken at the time of Diocletian seems at first sight to initiate an entirely different system, insomuch as fiscal units are formed, and the composition of each fiscal unit settled in a definite manner in regard to land of different kinds. In such a case the individual equation drawn between so much capita and this or that particular estate, containing so many jugera of best, or middling, or indifferent arable, so many stocks of vine or olive trees, with so many head of cattle and so many labourers attached to them,[46] seems to present a constant basis which will have to support more or less tribute, in a definite ratio to the neighbouring properties equated with proportionate numbers of units. This scheme seems to render the action of the intermediate bodies superfluous, and pictures the Government as drawing directly on the resources of the individuals. But, as a matter of fact, the taxation of the fourth century was not more and probably less individualistic than that of the second. Even if we leave out of account the fact that Diocletian's system was devised for the levying of tribute in kind (annona), while the money contribution followed in the old way,[47] many traits show to what extent there was room for local variations and for the introduction of elements connected with social arrangements which are very different from the hard and fast distribution of individual property. The Syrian lawbook, from which we glean the definite scrap about the assessment of arable, vineyard and olive plantations, leaves out of the general reckoning mountain land and pastures, and prescribes rules for their assessment which have nothing to do with the apportionment by *capita*. Then, the labouring population is not mentioned, nor the farmers, the coloni, and we are left to surmise that they were either reckoned and taxed outside the scheme of the capita, or else formed " heads " of population by themselves. A similar observation may be made in regard to the cattle.[48] But, apart from these discrepancies and queries, we find that the meaning of the

fiscal units varied materially in the different provinces:
in one case, only the land was taken into account, in another
the land and the people on it, in a third mainly the people.
The very names of the units are different in connection with
these alterations of meaning; sometimes it is *jugum*,
sometimes *caput*, then again *centuria*, meaning a couple of
hundred jugera, sometimes *millena*.[49]   Then, again, though
the establishment of heads of taxation seems to be a step
further in its individualisation, collective liability is rather
increased than lessened in the Empire of Diocletian and
Constantine ; people are made not only to pay for their
insolvent fellow-citizens, but even to take upon themselves
the responsibility for the taxes of the land which had been
vacated by their neighbours (ἐπιβολή).[50]   The attempt to
reduce the varieties of taxed property to a certain number
of units of assessment turns out in this way to have been
consistent with an astonishing amount of provincial and
local varieties.   And last, but not least, it is evident from
the practice of general remissions of so many *juga* or *capita* to
entire provinces that the system of apportioning the *juga*
was not merely the outcome of a careful enumeration of
assessable objects.   It is clear that this last chiefly remained
as in the second century, a means of ascertaining the fiscal
capabilities of districts and of apportioning the fiscal liabilities of the population, but it did not work automatically
in this sense, that so many acres of, say, middling land were
always reckoned to constitute so many *juga*.   The letting
off of so many juga shows that already, in these later
Roman times, there existed in matters of taxation the curious
combination of appraising property on the strength of its
individual features and of treating the units of taxation as
something laid on from above to be distributed according to
circumstances known to the local authorities and bodies.
The idea of privileged capitation is the only one which can
reconcile these contrasts   The property in a district may
have been assessed at 32,000 capita, but the annona from
it may have been indicted as from 25,000, and, in this case
the local authorities could single out for total or partial
exemption some properties worthy of exemption on account

of a weakening of their resources, or of an increase of private liabilities or of services rendered to the State or district and the like. And, if a great mishap visited the country in the shape of a famine or of an incursion of barbarians, etc., and, say, 5,700 juga were taken off by the grace of the Emperor, it was possible not only to strike off the roll those who had been actually destroyed as economic units, but to reckon as half or three-quarters those who, from a formal point of view, might have been taken as entire units.[51] The extreme roughness of classification, and the absence from it of very material factors in the shape of an appraisement of capital, of industrial and commercial adjuncts, of profitable easements, etc., made such rough corrections necessary, and at the same time disturbed the simplicity and uniformity of the formulas devised for the purpose of taxation.

The net result of these considerations seems to be that we must not lay too much stress on the systems of tabulated estimates which were practised by the bureaucracy of the Empire. They do not imply, as they seem to do, a very close attention to the particulars of each case, and a very exact rendering of social conditions. On the contrary, they introduce a method of fictitious reckoning of values which, though expressed in concrete agrarian terms, presents, in truth, something between a repartition of totals into particular grooves of liability and the natural outcome of assessment according to ascertained means.

The Fundus The unit of land from which the normal " cadastre " starts is the *fundus*. It is described as containing so many jugera of every kind of soil, so many useful trees or stocks, and as provided with so many head of cattle and so many labourers or farmers to cultivate it; in fact, it forms a complete and self-sufficient agrarian organism. On the other hand, it is private property, or, at least, in most cases, in private possession of an individual or of a corporation, it is inscribed under the name of an owner, though it is not the changing present owner that is meant, but either the original organiser of the *fundus* or else the one under whose name it was registered the first time in the roll of the fiscal survey or "cadastre." [52] Such a mode of description is very characteristic; it means that, as a rule, the Roman financial administration considered the cultivated land to be divided into private estates, great, middling, and small, and fastened its arrangements for taxation to these estates. This is, undoubtedly, a very important point, both as a symptom of the prevailing mode of holding land and as a factor which must have worked powerfully to modify in that particular direction, arrangements which, by themselves, did not well fit into it. The practical importance of the scheme has been well illustrated, not merely by the couple of instances in which fragments of actual census descriptions have come down to us, but also by the interesting fact brought to light by French scholars, that a great number of the names of present French villages are derived from names of *fundi* either in their Roman form, as Savigny— fundus Sabinianus—or in a form slightly celticised by the adjunct of a Gaulish suffix as Polignac—Pauliniacus—or in some cases, as it were, translated into Frankish by the substitution of the name of a German owner or a mediæval saint, as Thionville—Theodonis villa.

The private estate, entirely dependent on the disposition of the master, and with a population of labourers subordinated to this master, seems to be firmly established by these facts as the foundation of land-tenure and land-law in the provinces of the Empire. But the matter requires a little more attention, and is not so simple after all. It is not difficult to see that the arrangement is, to a great extent, an artificial and a fictitious one. The *fundus* appears as an indestructible unity on the rolls of the cadastre, although, as a matter of fact, it is the very reverse of indestructible just because it is private property. The very name-giving has to be taken as a fiscal expedient and not a natural process : one could understand the immutability of the name, if it arose from the natural agency of tradition—a name once given to a place or to an estate is not likely to be changed often, easily, or at will. But, as a matter of fact, the name of the *fundus* must in many, if not in the majority of instances, have arisen at the moment of the inscrip-

tion on the rolls, detaching itself in this case from the time-
honoured name under which the place had been known
before, in the mouth of the people, or even driving away
that ancient local name. Mappalia Siga would thus become *Villa Magna Variana*. Even apart from the consideration that a number of these personal names must have
been produced by the inscription to the census and by nothing else, it is impossible to believe that even all the places
furnished with names of *fundi* in *anus* and *acus* never had
had any other designations drawn from local features and
provided with a more distinct Celtic stamp. And so it
looks as if the place nomenclature of the Empire had, indeed, been very strongly affected by the procedure of the
census, but as if this result had been achieved in a wholesale and artificial manner, and, in fact, right across the
natural lines of development.

Another artificial trait is disclosed by the tenacity of the
inscription under one and the same heading and as one fiscal
unit of estates which in the course of time had been subjected to a complete transformation as agrarian unity.
A *fundus Julianus* gets first described and enrolled as
the property managed by Julius in the time of Claudius,
when the first census roll was drawn up. It will stand as
fundus Julianus on the rolls of Marcus Aurelius, although,
as a matter of fact, it may consist now of six distinct properties, held partly by descendants of the original Julius,
and partly by people who had married his granddaughters,
or even by strangers who had bought some of the shares.
And so we come to the combinations of the Ravenna
charters when one person is described as holding $\frac{7}{12}$ of a
fundus, another $\frac{2}{12}$ of the same *fundus*,[53] etc. It is proved
by the description of boundaries that in such cases no real
unity is left in the management and organisation of the land,
although the fiscal unity is still asserted.[54] The converse
case is recorded as well, and is quite as striking. The *fundi*,
as originally inscribed, may be large, middle-sized, or quite
small. But in the interval between two censuses, some may
have been concentrated in the hands of one owner and entirely transformed in their economic aspect and plan of

management, may have become large grazing farms, for instance, instead of small agricultural holdings ; still they will be entered, not as a new whole, but as a combination of old ones, as a *massa* (fundorum), in regard to which the old names will still be kept for no other reason than that of the formal continuity of official tradition.

This being so, we may well ask whether the deeply individualising character of the census inscription vouches for the disappearance of ingrown peculiarities of husbandry and local arrangements in the provinces. One point has been very much discussed of late. Are the villages of Gaul to be taken as created by the management of private owners of *fundi*, as so many of their names seem to imply, or did they exist in a number of cases as units by themselves for administrative and possibly economic purposes which did not coincide with the *fundi*, and were left aside by the fiscal administration, inasmuch as they did not fall within the lines of the official formula of description ? [55] In view of all that has been said of the tenacious peculiarities of Celtic rural organisation, it seems hardly proper to decide in the first sense. Indeed, it has been shown that, in a number of cases, the argument from the names does not apply, as there is a sufficient number of instances when the *fundus* nomenclature did not impose itself. And, what is more important, even in many cases when it did impose itself, it would be rash to argue that the village did not exist as a real unit by the side of the *fundus*, or above it. If there ran, as it were, two threads of nomenclature through the country, they must have overlapped constantly, and the fact that the official designation so often got the better of the one drawn from the features of local grouping does not do away with this latter. Floriac as a village may have been much more than the *fundus Floriacus*, though it drew its name from that *fundus* in connection with one or the other circumstance in the census of the locality.

We may even safely go further, I think, and point out that the individualistic stamp given to the census entries by the notion of the *fundus* must not blind us to the existence in the actual world of many non-individualistic features.

We know, in fact, that the division of the ground into plots and estates in private property was supplemented everywhere, even in Italy, by numerous patches and tracts of land of which the use was common to several adjoining proprietors. The *subseciva* (or *subcesiva*) were often used in this manner where there was centuriation or limitation " *per strigas et scamna.*" Besides, *agri compascui* are mentioned frequently, and certainly formed an important item in husbandry, especially in the husbandry of districts in which pastoral pursuits played a great part.[56] And here we come to a point which ought to be taken into consideration over and over again. It must be borne in mind that, quite apart from minor economic varieties, there ran one very marked line of cleavage between the systems of husbandry of the Empire, at least of its western half. There was the intensive cultivation of the south, as most strikingly exemplified by the horticulture around Rome, the culture of the vine and of the olive, but not less characteristic in its methods of raising crops by the unsparing energy of tillage, the strong manuring of the fields, the small holdings, short furrows (the *actus* of the *jugerum*) and small handy ploughs of two oxen, and the very subordinate part played by cattle-farming in connection with it. Cato's precept for the farmer was *agrum bene colere, arare*, etc. This is the picture presented by the rural life of the centuriated fields of Italy, but also, with some differences in degree, of the agricultural parts of Spain, Africa and southern Gaul, and to this management the census description, with its prominence of the *fundus* and its reference to the individual management of the estate, seems perfectly adapted. If there existed exceptional traits and complications, as of course there were, they could be worked out without much difficulty by modifying the main formula. But things were very different in the north, where the climate was rough, the forests, moors, and other waste lands considerable, the labourers not numerous and not accustomed to hard work. Cultivation on an extensive scale, making as much use as possible of natural processes, and not relying particularly on the energy of man, was inevitable in these northern latitudes. And we find, accordingly, everywhere in those parts, as soon as we get to know anything about their economic aspect, systems of cultivation in which grazing plays a large, and sometimes the largest, part, while tillage appears as a sort of adjunct and long remains superficial, varying from occasional occupation of the waste in the Celtic tribal districts and in the earlier days of German migration, through reckless occupation of tracts fertilised by burning down of woods and grass, to open field culture with a two-course and three-course rotation of crops.[57] Even the big plough of the northern parts, with its long furrows, seems to be a rural implement—which goes well with systems in which oxen could be used unsparingly, while human labour was deficient in quality and in quantity. The great cleavage seems thus to lie between southern arrangements with individualistic bent and northern arrangements with a communalistic bent. I say communalistic and not collectivistic, because it is not the necessity of co-operation which strikes one so much in the northern treatment of the land as the difficulty of an individualistic apportionment of rights. The question of how far the people who held the land would be bound or would find it profitable to work together and to appropriate the produce jointly, is different from the question how far it was expedient for them to partition the land on which their herds were moving and their crops were raised, and in this latter respect it is hardly necessary to point out that extensive open-field cultivation and pastoral requirements made for forms of occupation in common and sets of usages adapted to communalistic rather than to individualistic arrangements. The question now is : are we to suppose that the Romans, when they came to those northern parts and obtained supremacy over the different barbarian tribes which lived in them, made it their aim to override all these natural leanings, and to cast northern husbandry into the individualistic mould of their *fundi* as known in Italy and southern Gaul ? It would hardly be reasonable to assume this on *a priori* grounds, and it would be impossible to do so in face of the fact that extensive cultivation, half pastoral habits, and communalistic arrangements of possession actually prevailed in the northern provinces after the occupation by Romans as well as before it, and this quite apart from the nationality of the barbarians who were conquered in the different instances. We find these extensive communalistic and open-field practices in Wales as well as in Flanders, in Norfolk as well as in Brittany, in the Agri Decumates as well as in the territory of Chartres.[58] There seems to be hardly any other explanation of the fact than the assumption that the barbarian populations of these districts were very like each other in their habits, whether Celt or Teuton, Goidhel or Briton, and that the influence of Rome went to further the economic development of these parts without altering the fundamental cast of extensive husbandry and communalistic arrangements in the occupation and distribution of the land.

It would be impossible to state definitely in what ways allowance was made for these features in the cadastre and the taxation of northern provinces. Whether the formula itself was modified or the usual items stretched to cover the peculiarities arising from the differences spoken of, in one way or another the survey had to conform to altered realities, and possibly some inscription may be discovered by-and-by which will acquaint us with some particulars. The parting of the ways between extensive and intensive husbandry on large estates is clearly illustrated even by extant evidence in the contrast between the *fundus* and *latifundium* on one hand, and the *saltus* on the other.

III. The Estates

Great and small Estates It would be wrong to picture to ourselves the Roman Empire as composed exclusively or even chiefly of large estates. Recent researches have shown that small proprietors were to be found everywhere, and formed in the latter times of the Empire, the numerous and socially important classes of possessors and of *vicani*.[59] The well-known jeremiads about the ruin of Italy and of the provinces by the growth of estates are based

on some exaggeration.[60] Certainly there were powerful
causes making for the concentration of property. In
the prosperous period of the Empire small owners lost
ground because they were bought out by speculators
against whose power of money and methods of trade
and agriculture they could not compete. The policy
of strengthening the stock of small proprietors by
distributing, again and again, land to soldiers who had con-
cluded their term of service did not succeed. The veterans
were badly equipped as landowners, inadequately provided
and especially deficient in interest, in the knowledge and
the habits necessary to make a good use of their allotments. Their plots became an easy prey of those who
speculated in land.[61] But it was much more difficult to
uproot the stock of those small owners and peasant cultivators who had sat on the soil for generations ; in all the
provinces, we find a good many of them ; they formed
probably the great majority of the landed class of the
Empire, as the normal conduct of municipal business and
the levying of taxes was connected with their existence and
activity.[62] There is every reason to suppose that in provinces newly reclaimed from barbarism, like Britain, their
number must have been especially large. The Romans
never considered it good policy to dispossess the lower
orders ; on the contrary, some measures were taken to
strengthen small proprietorship, and the social causes which
made for concentration of property, the application of capital
and the organisation of traffic on a large scale, and the
political influence of privileged people, had not had time to
act for a lengthened period. Indeed, we are not left without some direct evidence as to the traditional position of
the free peasantry and the efforts of the government to
keep it up.[63]

Although there is thus no reason to suppose that the
Roman power divided Britain, as by the stroke of a magic
wand, into a number of great estates, or that even at its
close these estates had attained to a crushing superiority—
either in regard to their number or to the development
of their internal structure, archæological finds show, in

many places in Britain, as well as in other provinces,
remains of large, carefully-built and decorated country house
villas, which evidently were erected as seats of great people,
and must have acted as centres of culture and husbandry
in the several districts in which they were situated. It
has been pointedly said about Africa that there were some
private persons there whose estates were as large as the
territories of entire cities, and that their villas were surrounded on every side by villages of their dependants as
by bulwarks.[64] Britain was very far from offering the
same inducements to great landlords as Africa, with its
wealth of sub-tropical products of vegetation. But in
Britain, too, the villas at Bignor, Woodchester, Andover,
etc., present striking examples of arrangements for a life
on a great scale ; and there can be no doubt, on the strength
of their evidence, that there lived a good many Roman
or Romanised magnates in those parts of the island which
were within easy approach of Roman stations and cities ;
and that we have to reckon with this element of rural
aristocracy in forming an estimate of the social situation
of Britain under the Empire.[65]

Saltus   The great estate appears in our sources in
two different aspects—as a *latifundium* or
massa, and as a *saltus*. In the first instance we have to
do with an agglomeration of *fundi*, which goes back historically to separate smaller properties thrown together
in course of time ; they may continue to be separate
economic organisations, or they may have coalesced into
one larger organisation. The latter must have been frequently the case for purely economic reasons, such as
the influence of capitalism and the advantages of production on a large scale. But it would be wrong to assume
that whenever we hear of a *latifundium*, or can trace
vestiges of a large property, we must at once think of an
estate managed systematically from a centre, with an
organised population of labourers around it. Some of
the latifundia were real estates, others merely *massæ* of
casually collected smaller properties, the component parts
of which may have presented many varieties of legal and

economic structure.[66] The *saltus* is taken in opposition
to the *fundus*, as a territory of difficult access and of backward culture, mostly consisting of mountain slopes, forest
and pasture land.[67]   It is often kept outside the jurisdiction
and taxation of the cities, and may be measured by less
careful methods than those applied on municipal territory.
The *saltus* we know of belonged chiefly to the Emperor,
but great landowners of senatorial rank were also possessed
of them.[68]   It is evident that the primitive condition of
Britain, the processes of colonisation on its soil, the
gradual social transformation of its aborigines as well as
the peculiar conditions of the extensive husbandry suitable to this province, must have made it especially adapted
to the formation of *saltus*, whereas the *fundus* had hardly a
sufficient basis in its conditions of life. It may be even
supposed, on the strength of some indications from other
provinces, that the mapping out of large districts as
Imperial saltus may have presented a convenient form
for bringing under legal classification and administrative
subordination many parts of the country which were rather
backward in their life.   This method must have presented
especial facilities for introducing Roman elements without
roughly disturbing inveterate habits : by its help Roman
politicians were able to avoid the ridiculous and dangerous
pedantry of treating the population of backwoods and
pastoral tracts as if it was composed of citizens of civilised
cities, accustomed to all the incidents of Roman governmental methods.   Of course, if we consider the *saltus* from
this point of view, we must be prepared to find it anything
but a model estate with an energetically centralised
administration, and submissive and rightless labourers
acting the part of economic machinery.

Patronage   Before we proceed to inquire into the conditions which regulated the management of estates,
let us look somewhat closer at the process which
determined their increase in number and in power.   A
very prominent feature of the life of the later Empire is
its inability to perform directly by its own strength and
through its own functionaries the divers political func-

tions incumbent upon it. It is all it can do to look
to the external safety of the Empire by guarding its
frontier, to put down open rebellion, to collect in its
hands the necessary financial means for general administration, and to conduct the work of the higher tribunals :
it has not the time nor the wish to follow up the
details of local administration and justice. This latter
power, which carries little pomp with it, but is in reality,
perhaps, the most important of all, inasmuch as on it
depends the everyday life of a countless population
it is constrained to delegate to municipal corporations,
to men of mark and position, to the great landowners.[69]
Looking at these last, which concern us most, we find that
by the time of Constantine they are allowed a special
standing in regard to taxation, their estates ranking apart
from the rest on the rolls of the tax-gatherer and the
proprietors being entrusted with the power of municipal
decurions in regard to the collection of taxes from their
dependants, as well as being responsible for the payment
of them,—a tremendous power and responsibility considering the importance these fiscal functions had assumed
in the life of the Empire.[70] In the same way we find the
landlords entrusted with the calling up of recruits for the
army, and endowed with extensive patronage in regard
to the appointment of priests, and even bishops, on their
estates. It is to them, again, that the courts and the
police have to turn for the production of persons accused
or summoned to appear in litigation before the judges.[71]
This means that they have eventually the power and the
right to employ force, and that they are made responsible
for the escape of such people from appearing at the trial.
Indeed, the power of coercing the labourers and farmers
of the domains is expressly mentioned, and it is clear that
it was employed not only in cases where the Government
was interested and called for the support of the landlord,
but also in cases where the private interests of the latter
were at stake, for the enforcement of work and distraints
in cases when tenants or labourers were remiss in performing whatever duties were incumbent on them. In

fact, the proprietor and his stewards acted in a way as justices of the peace for the settlement of petty disputes between tenants and the punishment of petty misdemeanours on their part. If the estate was leased, the leaseholder entered into all the rights of the owners, and in practice the stewards on large estates exercised wide-reaching powers of a political kind which were the more pronounced on the domains of the Crown. The stewards of these estates, mostly freedmen, commonly behaved as if they were regular magistrates, and were not sparing in appealing to the help of armed force for the execution of their orders.[72] No wonder that in the shadow of these wide privileges private advantages grew up : we find already on these Roman estates the tenants paying fines on the occasion of the marriage of their daughters.[73] The surrender of governmental influence to private individuals expressed in these various traits created a very doubtful position, and as often led to encroachments and lawlessness as to useful support on the part of the magnates. The emperors often refer to these evils and make fruitless attempts to check them ; but the policy of fitting out the landed aristocracy with political power over their tenants and even over their neighbours goes on developing nevertheless, and is certainly produced quite as much by the unavoidable necessities of the period as by a mistaken policy of this or that particular statesman. In the Celtic districts there was a special stimulus for its development in the tenacious traditions of clientship,[74] and we may be sure that in Britain particularly the action of great men in administering justice and protection, calling up to answer charges and inflicting punishment was not deemed strange or unusual : it would merely appear as the continuation of a similar action on the part of clan-chieftains. However this may be, the growth of political privileges of the great landowners, and the influence of this growth on the development of their private rights, appear as two of the best established facts of the later history of the Empire.

These observations have been taken to mean that the system of territorial lordship had been formed by the later

Empire, and had only to be borrowed by the barbarians when they took up the inheritance of Rome. But that is going a good deal too fast, and, indeed, at the same time when we notice a considerable increase of the political influence of great men, we have to record their very characteristic helplessness in economic matters ; and as the outcome of these two tendencies which counteract each other—a process of readjustment of rural relations which yielded results as yet very different from those which obtained in the feudal ages.

To prevent any misunderstanding, let me **Economic advance of Peasantry** say again that the growth of patronage of great men, as fostered by the Empire and as directed against its Government, is a phenomenon of first-rate importance ; it gives expression to the fact that society was getting disintegrated into local units after the strain and glory of existence as a huge, highly-organised whole. People seek protection where they find force, and they look for efficient force near at hand rather than in the exalted institutions of the Empire.[75] But this same regressive process of the formation of new local bodies has another aspect in which not the great men but the small people appear as the necessary agents in the work of rescuing society from ruin. It is not only protection and some order that are needed, but also cultivation, the work of feeding society and keeping up its material intercourse. And in this direction the great landowners, and even the government, can do very little by themselves, in spite of the apparatus of laws and decrees, of soldiers and police, of exactions and prisons. The evidence of the fourth and fifth centuries is unanimous in showing us a great economic and social crisis, a State armed with all the resources of enactment and coercion, and powerless to check depopulation, dereliction of duties, fraud and concealment in evading public burdens, to fight against the squalor and barrenness of deserted soil and ruined husbandry.[76] What had most to do in producing these results—whether it was the harrying by barbarians, the exhausting taxation, the drain of conscription on productive population, the heartless methods of mechanical bureaucracy, the sense of insecurity and the despair called forth by the fruitless toil of generations, the moral enfeeblement of people who had lost the fibre of manliness, the transference of hope and faith to another realm which is not of this world—it is impossible to estimate with exactitude ; but the results stare us in the face on every page of the Theodosian Code, not to speak of historical narratives.   And in this connection arose another great movement : by the side of the growth of political patronage in favour of the great goes the growth of economic self-government in favour of the small. I use the expression " self-government " on purpose, because not independence, but a power of directing efforts and seeking profits by the energy and insight of the labourers themselves, rather than by management from above, appears as the only anchor of safety in this time of great difficulties.

Scholars who have made a special study of the condition of the later Empire have come from different points of view to the same conclusion, namely, that the great landowners were quite as much hampered in their power over their tenants as the Empire itself was hampered in its power over land-owners.   It was not sufficient to have all manner of legally-established rights and powers when the ability to put all these rights and powers into practice was paralysed by the lack of vital energy in the local body. The great landowner owed the thriving condition of his estate not so much to the fulness of his control over it and of his authority over his dependants, as to the number of these dependants, the steadiness of their work, and their energy in prosecuting the economic advantages springing from local conditions, on the possibility of applying capital to cultivation with a sufficient guarantee of interest, and on the possibility of appealing to resources outside the estate in case the resources of the estate failed. The position got awkward and uncomfortable, when one had to depend almost entirely on the local supply of labour and materials, when there was very little guarantee as to the proceeds of any capital sunk into the land, when taxation

was at the highest pitch, and the available number of
cultivators very small by reason of unsatisfactory political
circumstances and physical depopulation. All the weight
had to be thrown on the *quality* of the work of the labouring
population. There could be no hope of great profits ; in
fact between the necessity of treating his dependants fairly
and paying heavily to the government, the rent of the landowner must have been very low.[77] And undoubtedly it was
not the great estates but the smaller possessions which had
the better chance of weathering the storm, because they
were more modest in their aims, nearer to actual life in their
employment of capital and labour, more fitted to call forth the
untiring and unflinching energy of the labouring household.[78]
In accordance with these initial facts we notice characteristic
deviations in the course of development of Roman law
itself, curious attempts to modify it under the pressure of
overwhelming financial and economic difficulties. Wonder-
fully hybrid forms of possession arise. The 'Επιβολή provides
for the compulsory distribution of deserted and uncultivated
land among those who hold estates that are still in cultivation. It is enacted that if anybody takes upon himself to
manage a farm which has been left by the former owner, and
assumes the payment of taxes for it, even the occupation
of a couple of years will carry the right of possession with
it.[7] Different practices which resulted in the legislation in regard to ἐμφύτευσις, the betterment of land and
the privileged occupation of it, and which were accom-
pained by remissions of rents and taxes, arose on the soil
of Imperial domains, and then spread into the possessions
of private lords.[80] And there can be no doubt that these
practices were more efficient in fostering cultivation in sick
spots, if one may use the expression, than the methods of
mere compulsion mapped out by the Codes. The most
important corollary of this practice of melioration was that
it tended to strengthen small proprietors. It worked in the
same direction with the increasing difficulty of living under
the immediate pressure of fiscal and administrative exaction
in the cities. There is a marked reflux of " plebeian "
population from town to village, and a marked increase of

the class of " *vicani* " holding small plots as " if they were proprietors " (*quasi domini*).[81]

Colonate But the most important and significant feature of this process is the rise and development of the *colonate*.   This institution has drawn upon itself the attention of several generations of scholars, and has been subjected to a most searching and controversial enquiry.   Still there is an aspect of it which, though not entirely overlooked, has remained as it were in the background by the side of other elements, and, from our point of view, it is the aspect which merits most attention.   The *coloni* are farmers, originally free farmers, bound by agreement, and free to recede from that agreement after having satisfied its conditions ; ultimately farmers attached to the soil, which they cultivate in consequence of a permanent and hereditary tie, although protected by law in their personal status, the use of their holding, and the fixity of their rent.[82]   The work of modern investigators has been for some time chiefly directed to show in what way and for what reasons the State altered the condition of free contract underlying the institution into a condition of hereditary dependence.[83]   Then the economic processes by which the legislative changes of the fourth century were prepared in the course of the second and third centuries came to be discussed, and the dependence of small farmers on capitalists, of settlers in great estates on regulations laid down by owners, especially in the case of Imperial domains, was analysed.[84] But there is a third aspect of this process which also deserves careful study—it is the part played by the *colonate* as a meliorative institution, as a means to keep up and to improve agriculture in the Empire.   This point of view has been to a certain extent made use of when the passage from slavery to the ascription of rural serfs to the glebe had to be considered, although even in this respect attention was chiefly drawn to the public side of the process, the inscription on the census roll.[85]   Still, it was understood and explained that there was a gradual change from work in gangs under the supervision of overseers using the whip and the irons to enforce obedience to their orders, to the state of a domiciled serf (*servus casatus*) endowed with

interests and a *peculium* of his own, and with time to look
after them, and that this great revolution was a necessary
consequence of the need in which the landowners stood to
heighten the personal concern of labourers in their work
and well-being.   The compulsory methods were not entirely
rejected, and the margin of personal authority over the
serf by no means got rid of.   But the emphasis came to lay
on the conciliation of labourers by a direct and personal share in the cultivation of the land : it was not a
question of humanity or even of best policy — it became a question of necessity in face of the great crisis
which threatened the political existence of the Empire as
well as the continuance of its economic basis—the cultivation of the land.   But the enormous extension of the
colonate, as an institution of free farmers and free labourers,
the probable prevalence of *coloni* over the domiciled serfs
(*casati*) in regard to the cultivation of the land,[86] show that
it was not less necessary to conciliate the free cultivators
than to conciliate the slaves, and here current historical
theories have mostly failed to account for the course of
events, and it is only lately that what may be called the
emphyteutic aspect of the *colonate* has begun to be realised.
It has been urged in a rather one-sided manner that the
status of free cultivators was, as it were, lowered to meet
that of the rising slaves, and that out of the upheaval of one
class and the decadence of the other the intermediate condition of the Roman *colonus* and of the mediæval villain was
evolved.   Now this does not seem to square well with the
initial observations in regard to the desperate agricultural
crisis, the allowances which had to be made to cultivators of
servile stock, and the incitements to cultivation expressed
in the treatment of desert and emphyteutic lands.   Why
are we to suppose that the farmers and the free labourers
were the only class which had to be kept to their work by
bare force, while advantages had to be found for everybody
else ? [87]   I believe that the frequent enactments about the
pursuit and the penalties of runaway *coloni*, and the
undoubted extension of the police authority of landowners,
have more or less blinded investigators to the fact that free

labourers could not be drawn and kept on the lands of great men merely by highhanded treatment and compulsion, but had to be conciliated by substantial advantages as well. They got land, and the patronage under which they had to place themselves was probably rather a boon than a burden to them : it had come to be preferable to look to the protection and police of a great man in the neighbourhood than to the far-off power of the Emperor and to the cumbersome but exacting action of his officials—an inference not very complimentary to Imperial administration, but hardly to be avoided in the face of the evidence.

The balance of profit for which we have to look in the case of free tenants is the more necessary to explain the situation, as the stringent compulsion brought into view by the legislation of the fourth and fifth centuries must have been very shortlived in the West, the Empire itself having collapsed at the end of the fifth century, and in some cases, as notably in Britain, even at the very beginning of it. And still the *colonate* condition did not disappear : on the contrary, it developed, though there were no tribunals to uphold the laws of Constantine and Valentinian as to runaway *coloni* and as to landlords who had exceeded their powers in regard to fixed rent.[87a] It seems also clear from this point of view that the institution was formed and prospered, not through the devices of " gross " legislation, as one of the investigators expresses himself,[88] but through an economic advance in the condition of the free peasantry on great men's estates, which made it worth their while trying to keep up cultivation in spite of overwhelming odds—of the constant harrying of the country in times of war, and of the excruciating burden of taxation in time of peace. There could be no less propitious time for the assertion of the claims of great landowners and the constructive or organising activity of great property than the fourth and fifth centuries. The field belonged to the small farmers and peasants in so far as there was any field at all, and the constant decrees against their going away and leaving their houses and work must be taken primarily to mean, not that the time had come to bereave them of their legal rights, but that it was exceedingly difficult to carry on productive agriculture under given conditions—so difficult that it got to be a matter of common occurrence for the peasants to disregard not only the rights of the landlords but even their own interests, in so far as these were bound up with their houses and farms. And there is hardly any room for doubt as to the meaning of this revival of cultivation under the influence of the *colonate* at the very time when the *coloni* were losing the private rights they had been enjoying as Roman citizens : as neither the barbarian rover nor the tax collector are likely to have altered their behaviour, the peasants must have been compensated by considerable allowances at the hands of those very landowners to whom they were to be subjected. Low rents, economic self-government in the management of their farms, and efficient protection and help in case of need, must have been the attractions which had more to do with their holding out on the land than threats of fines and imprison ment.

African coloni Concrete facts are not wanting in support of these general considerations. Among the oldest records which have been rightly taken to bear on the question of the transition from separate contracts between landlords and single tenants to a system of holdings based on general settlements and custom, are the inscriptions of the African *saltus*, and in these the peculiarities of the privileged position of the *coloni*, the wish on the part of the owners to conciliate and to attract them, appear on every line. Two of those documents are emphatically based on the policy of melioration which reached its climax in emphyteutical legislation. The inscription of Henchir Mettich embodies regulations revised in the reign of Trajan, for an estate which had been a private *saltus* and subsequently passed into the hands of the Emperor.[89] The main point of these regulations is that the owners do not find it advantageous to manage their lands on the system of a general lease to a " conductor," and let them to a number of farmers. The husbandry methods are evidently calculated on a scale of extensive cultivation with a minimum appliance of labour to carry it on. The rent is paid as a part of the produce, mostly one-third, which leaves a very moderate net rent for the landlord, about one-seventh, because, as far as one can make out, one-fifth was swallowed by the tax. The eventualities of melioration of culture are especially considered with many details, and in each case considerable bounties granted in the shape of remitting the rent for some years, usually five. The occupation of waste and deserted land for purposes of cultivation gives rise to a possessory right, a *jus colendi,* on the part of the occupant. Work on the home farm is mentioned, but it is restricted to very few days in the year, six days in fact. So that it is quite clear that the *coloni* in question were anything but overworked or overburdened, and that the home farm did not depend to any considerable extent on their work. It was not large, it seems, and slaves must have been kept for its cultivation. This is a very important point. The *coloni* of the third and second centuries are farmers holding for a money rent or a share in the produce, and this second species of tenure seems to have acquired more and more importance in course of time.[91] The prevalence of these two kinds of leases points to self-sufficient and separate farming and to a very slight connection between the tributary farms and the demesne farm. This latter must have consisted sometimes in a counting house (*mensa*) and stores.[92]

When it was found that African inscriptions mentioned six and in some cases twelve days of work of the *coloni* on the demesne farm it was tempting to jump to the conclusion that the manorial system of dependent servile holdings supporting the home farm was already in force in Roman times.[93] But some reflection on the number of workdays shows that either there was hardly any demesne farm to support, or that it supported itself, independently of the customary labour of *coloni.* The plan was, for ages, to start separate self-sufficient holdings of *coloni,* and to get money or produce from them, not to organise cultivation on the home farm by help of labourers drawn from them. It is remarkable that even in the Codes, which bear witness to the practice of the fourth and fifth centuries, customary work (*operæ*) is mentioned only once.[94] We get another glimpse of the same system of melioration through the creation of small free farms on advantageous terms, in the fragments of an inscription found on an altar in Aïn Ouassel, which contained a statute of Hadrian on the occupation of wild and derelict soil (*Lex Hadriana de rudibus agris*). The *coloni* who take up the cultivation of such soil are promised different privileges, and we may surmise that their rents were light and their *status* well protected.[95] Of course, notwithstanding this consistent policy in favour of raising and strengthening a stock of free peasant farmers, frequent transgressions and oppressions were inevitable on the part of *conductores* and stewards, and, on private ground, on the part of the lords themselves. But the peasants were by no means inclined to endure such oppression passively. We know nothing of the actual lawsuits which they may have had with their private lords, but several notices exist as to their standing by their rights and customs in the way of complaints on Imperial demesnes The rescripts of Commodus found at Souk el Khmis and Gasr-Mezuar testify to the extension of the characteristic status of customary *coloni* on large tracts of land in Africa, and to their successful vindication of their usages against the Imperial stewards ;[96] and recent discoveries show us a similar population on Imperial estates [97] in Asia Minor, while the rescripts of Philippus for Araguene in Phrygia and of Cordianus for Scaptaparene in Thracia disclose the same readiness and ability on the part of the peasants to defend their cause against encroachments and abuses.[98] It has been conjectured with great felicity by Professor Ramsay that the very name of one of the Rural colonies on Asiatic domains—Hadriana—must have been drawn from the application to the spot of Hadrian's enactment *de rudibus agris*. The point is not without meaning, because it shows that the phenomena described were by no means confined to this or that particular locality, but extended in analogous forms all over the Empire.

Besides the equitable character of the settlement, and its avowed object of carrying through an amelioration of agriculture by an improvement of economic conditions, one feature strikes the observer very forcibly in these arrangements. If the standpoint of private settlement between landlord and tenant gets abandoned in favour of regional and hereditary custom,[99] individual claims had to be merged into common claims, and many of the advantages derived from communal associations accrued in this way to the peasantry of the extra-municipal lordships. There are many traces not only of organisation for the management of local affairs by the rural settlements within the territories of the *Saltus*,[100] but also ot economic intercourse on the lines of the so-called open field system. It was the natural result of the ties of neighbourhood, frequent co-operation, common management of pasture and wood, and common interests in upholding the same standard of customs.[101] The *coloni* act and complain as a body, the replies and decrees of the Emperors are addressed to them all. We may even get a glimpse of a commonwealth of farmers and labourers which enters into a compact with a neighbouring city in order to prosecute its petition at the Imperial court. It would be rash to attempt to define the precise degree and meaning of this evident growth of rural associations, but as one finds such associations unmistakably alive, the extant evidence may at any rate be taken to prove that the spread of the *colonate* was by no means accompanied with a complete surrender of rights on the part of free settlers as regards the landowner. Even if it amounted to an increase in the legal fixity of their condition and of the influence of private patronage or lordship, it must have carried many redeeming features with it, especially a fair assessment of rents and the welding of the separate farms into rural associations with definite customary rights and usages. This seems to be the fitting complement to the great modification of society brought about by the substitution of innumerable holdings of *coloni* for great and small estates,[102] and to furnish, as it were, the key to many phenomena which otherwise would have remained a matter of unfruitful contention between representatives of different nationalistic leanings.

Summing up   In looking back on the rural arrangements which probably obtained in Britain, we have, as it seems to me, to think of the process of Romanisation in this field neither as of a thorough remodelling of life and institutions nor as of the superimposition of a layer of Roman culture of varying depth over a subdued Celtic population. I should like to compare it rather to the influence of a stream which makes its way in several channels through the country, fertilising the plain around it and materially influencing the immediate surroundings, but not succeeding in entirely altering its general aspect. Behind the protecting lines of military occupation there was room for all sorts of conditions, from almost exact copies of Roman municipal corporations and Italian country houses to tribal arrangements scarcely coloured by a thin sprinkling of Imperial administrative formulæ. An agricultural settlement had been undoubtedly effected, or, rather, the germs of an agricultural settlement already existent in the southern shore of tribal Britain have developed into a considerable growth, and have been brought near, as much as possible, to the example of Gaul, but this settlement had still to conform in different degrees to primitive conditions in the distribution of population, and in its vernacular habits.

The country was to some extent rendered vertebrate by towns, villas and high roads. The individualistic southern system of single farms, with a more or less self-sufficient course of husbandry and separate plots, was especially inappropriate in the conditions of Britain. How far the settlement in large villages had progressed already during the Imperial era it would be difficult to say : it is not unlikely that it made its appearance in places where there existed special attractions for the gathering of people : in the neighbourhood of cities, by the stations on the roads, in connexion with the villas, and there can be no doubt that it began to spread earlier in the level east than in the hilly west. But although there is no reason for making this mode of settlement peculiarly and exclusively Teu-

tonic it had hardly yet attained any wide diffusion.[103] Its
proper development falls into a later period. However
this may be, one thing is sure : the prevailing husbandry
of the period was constructed on lines which did not admit
of an energetic cultivation of the soil, and therefore precluded a strong organising pressure from above on the
cultivators. It has been said rightly that the Italian field
system, as connected with the *fundus*, is individualistic in
its cast. Its most complete expression is that astonishing
building up of a rectangle cutting right through natural
accidents of the soil, and almost independent in their
mainstay on the plans and management of neighbouring rectangles.[104] The same ideas of absolute ownership
were embodied in a more pliable form in the provincial delimitations of the *fundus*. In its essence the *fundus*
ought to be a self-sufficient private property described
and enrolled as such in the cadastre. The great formal
value of the inscription did not consist merely in the
fact that it serves as a basis for the repartition of fiscal
burdens, but also in the notion that the *fundus* was self-
sufficient and did not depend in its main characteristics
on any connection with other bodies of the same kind.
But these views as to property, taxation, and husbandry
were quite unsuitable to regions where it would have been
ridiculous to keep on obstinately ploughing and manuring
in particular places, where waste stretched all round, inviting people to appropriate it by an easier grasp, where
pastoral pursuits yielded better profits and could be combined with agriculture by simpler methods, where labour
was not expected to be persistent or skilled. In such
circumstances systems of extensive cultivation arise of
themselves ; they have been called rather inaccurately open
field systems. The most important points to be noticed are
the primitive rotation of crops dependent on the fact that
the fields have hardly begun to emerge permanently from
the waste, the importance of pasture on the stubble, the
intermixture of strips of neighbouring claims, the dependence
of the cultivation of every share on the general requirements of the whole in regard to communication over the

fields, the time and the place for raising the different crops, the modes of depasturing the different kinds of animals, the regulation of uses of the waste of wood and water. All these forms of co-operation and eventualities of dispute appear to some extent in the settlements by hamlets, but greatly increase in importance in settlements by villages. In both cases, but especially in the cases of villages, they must have led to some kind of organisation on the basis of the multifarious communalistic incidents of rural life. And so communal usages, as distinct from the clan or the private estate, arise, not as the outcome of a definite national current or the production of the organising power of the landlord, but from the requirements of extensive agricultural settlement, and in a variety of shades and forms— both in Celtic and in Romanised districts, as, later on, in Germanised regions, in free groups of settlers as well as in gatherings of servile population, among farmers and peasants, under the immediate supervision of municipalities as well as under the protectorate of the Emperor and of magnates, or in districts where old tribal forms still prevailed.[105] According to these eventual varieties many traits might be different in these communities—the part played by the home farm, the amount of mutual dependence or independence of adjoining plots, the forms of co-operation and administration, the strength of tribal motives and arrangements, etc., varied undoubtedly from case to case, and altogether the forms of development were as yet very flexible and plastic. But some fundamental features went through the whole—the extensive half-pastoral character of the agricultural settlement, the barbarian habits of the labouring population, the social claims inherited from a tribal system based on personal freedom, the necessity for providing rural self-government for the co-operating and conflicting elements tied up in the social knot of the village settlement. Let us not forget that the forces at the disposal of Rome in the far-off province of Britain were of a very peculiar conformation, and that, as time went on, it became more and more difficult to conduct business on the basis of private enterprise and effort, while the necessities of culture threw more and more weight into the scale of economic self-government and on the conciliation of labouring masses. The part played by lordships and villas must not be overlooked, as, in conjunction with old traditions of chieftainship and clientship on the one hand, official and unofficial practices of patronage on the other, these elements must have provided natural and powerful centres to the process of settlement and organisation. But it must not be overrated either : the process is neither called forth nor entirely guided by private lordship, being in fact a general movement towards agricultural colonisation ; many factors have to be taken into consideration in regard to its progress besides that of private sway, especially the acute agrarian crisis and the peculiarities of the barbaric material from which rural organisation had to be constructed. It seems pretty clear from what has been said, that at that time rural affairs were, to say the least, much more complicated than theories which would account for the facts by the establishment of a simple domanial or manorial system would lead one to suppose. The explanation mapped out for Gaul by Fustel de Coulanges and his followers hardly suits the case of Gaul and certainly does not suit the case of Britain. The organising absolutism of the landlord is a fiction, dangerous in the sense, that it blinds the observer to the powerful counter-influences of tribal habits, of the great variety and frequent incompleteness in the application and the exploitation of labour to the soil, of the growth of half-dependent culture on a small scale. The assumption that there was no other tie between the inhabitants of villages than the will of the lord and the command of his stewards is at variance with evidence as to the activity of village associations.[106] Altogether it is as rash to suppose, on the strength of the usual division of great estates into the parts of the lord and of the tenants, that the relations between lord and tenants were already thrown into a mould resembling later villainage, as it is to contend that the legal institutions of the later Roman Empire are to be constructed on the clear lines of individualistic jurisprudence. The theory of

Mr. Seebohm's early book seems also one-sided inasmuch as it starts from the idea of a complete and unique organisation of the Roman villa, which is made to repeat itself through the ages like the " hexagonal cells " of the beehive.[107] But this one-sided theory has undoubtedly brought into strong relief the points of similarity and of contact between the British and the continental development on the one hand, and English institutions and their Roman antecedents on the other. Besides, the same writer, who began with an exaggerated simplification of the historical process, has provided us in his subsequent works with materials and observations which go far to supplement his earlier theories —I mean, of course, his remarkable analysis of Celtic arrangements in the light of Welsh custom. On the whole, and to put it shortly, the rural arrangements of the Roman period seem to have been to a great extent determined by Celtic antecedents. They were much less absolute and individualistic than the formulæ of Roman law would lead one to suppose, and under cover of the extensive lordships of the Emperor, of senatorial magnates, and of central cities, a crop of vernacular peculiarities and communalistic practices came up which prepared the ground for the coming in of new barbarian tides.

NOTES

CHAPTER I

1. *Elton*, " Origins of English History " (2nd edition, 1890), has done most to draw attention to pre-Celtic antiquities. The contrast of two ethnological types in Wales speaks powerfully to the eye. See the photograph of the big Celt and of the small Iberian given by *Mr. O. M. Edwards* in " Social England," edited by *H. D. Traill* and *J. S. Mann*, i. 2. The reconstruction of Iberian or Pictish institutions and manners is, however, a thorny task, and leads to doubtful results. Few scholars will follow *Mr. Gomme* in his attempt at delineating the local influence of pre-Aryan arrangements in England (" Village Community," 1890, 69 ff.). A more cautious attempt to disengage pre-Celtic facts is made by *Rhys* and *Brynmor Jones*, " The Welsh People."

2. *Skene*, " Celtic Scotland," iii. 331. Women are in the clan, but their position is derived from the standing of the men by whom they have to be represented and protected, fathers, sons, brothers, husbands, uncles, cousins, etc.

3. " Calendar of State Papers " (Ireland), 1603–6, p. 554 and 1606–8, p. 492. The fact is quoted by *Seebohm*, " Village Community," 219.

4. For example: *Carnarvon Extents*, Record Comm., 1: *Glodeyth.* Eadem villa libera est et sunt in eadem villa tres Wele, vidilicet Wele vocatum Wele Jorwerth ap Madoc, Wele Blethyn ap Madoc, et Wele Gwyn ap Madoc Et sunt heredes predicte Wele de Wele Blethin ap Madoc Lewelyn Wheith et Kenwricke ap Madoc ap Heilin et alii coheredes sui etc. All the population of Glodeyth traces its pedigree to a certain Madoc, and it falls into three communities of kinsmen which claim descent from the three Sons of Madoc.—The descriptions of the Bangor extents (following the Carnarvon Extents) differ somewhat in details, but point to the same system. For instance, p. 97: *Lannistyn*, Libere tenentes ; Primus lectus : Meuric ap Iorwerth, Lywelin ap Madoc, Meilir ap Iorwerth, Iorwerth ap Ade, Philip ap Iorwerth, Cade ap Heilin, Lywelin eius frater, Iuore ap Iorwerth, Heilin ap Madoc, Jeueran ap Lywelin, Gweulle filius Gruff, Gorun ap Made, Nest uxor Gruff, Howel ap Tenerin, Gweulle filius Eynon, Kynoc ap Philip, Iorwerth ap Lywarch, Madoc eius frater tenent 20 mesuagia et 6 bouatas terre, etc.

5. For instance : *Seebohm,* " Tribal System in Wales," app. 61 : Et sciendum est quod est quedam progenies liberorum tenencium in isto Commoto que vocatur progenies Rand' Vaghan ap Assere, que quidem progenies tenent in diuersis villis istius Commoti ; et tenuerunt tempore principum ante conquestum, videlicet totam villatam de Dennante, totam villam de Grugor, totam villam de Quilbreyn, totam villam de Penplogor et totam villam de Pennauelet, medietatem ville de Hendreuennythe, terciam partem ville de Prestegot, terciam decimam partem ville de Petrual. Et omnes illas villatas et parcellas villatarum predictarum tenuerunt in quatuor lectis, videlicet Wele Ruathlon ap Rand', Wele Idenerthe ap Rand, Wele Daniel ap Rand, et Wele Kewret ap Rand, unde primum Wele diuisum est in quatuar gauellas, videlicet Gauel Guyon ap Ruathlon, Gauel Blethyn ap Ruathlon, Gauel Kewret ap Ruathlon et Gauel Madoke ap Ruathlon. Secundum Wele diuiditur in quatuor Gauellas, vidilicet Gauel ap Iorwerth ap Idenerth, Gauel Madoc ap Idenerthe, Gauel Allot ap Idenerthe, et Gauel ap Tegwarat ap Idenerthe. Tercium Wele diuiditur in duas gauellas, vidilicet Gauel Eignon ap Daniel, Gauel Cadok ap Daniel, Et quartum lectum, quod est ultimum, diuiditur in duas Gauellas videlicet Gauel Griffri ap Kewret et Gauel Kenewrecke ap Daniel. And still further : *Villata de Dennante.* Kenwrecke ap Blethyn Vaghan, Iorwerth ap Lewelyn ap Blethyn, Kenwrecke ap Lewelyn ap Blethyn, Ken ap Blethyn Loyd, et Howel ap Blethyn Loyd tenent inter se duas gauelas de primo lecto integro, videlicet Gauel Guyon ap Ruathlon et Gauel Blethyn ap Ruathlon.—The commentary on these entries is given by *Seebohm,* o.c. 33 ff, 43 ft, who has been the first to utilise these remarkable data for the proper understanding of tribal organisation. I may point out, however, in regard to the example just quoted, that the kin of Rand' Vaghan ap Asser is termed a *progenies* and not a gwely, that the lecta or gwely are reckoned from his sons, and that the actual holders are partly his descendants in the fifth generation (for instance : Iorwerth ap Lewelyn ap Blethyn ap Ruathlon ap Rand'). We shall have to speak of these degrees by and by. At present I want only to show to what extent the whole arrangement of society was governed by relationship and descent.

6. *Seebohm,* " Tribal System in Wales," 78, 79.

7. *Arbois de Jubainville,* " Études sur le droit Celtique," 185 ff. *Skene,* " Celtic Scotland," iii. 177, 181, 183 ; *Atkinson,* " Glossary to the Brehon Laws," s.v. Fine. The *Finè* seems to comprise a man and his sixteen nearest relatives. This being so, the fine corresponds to the circles of relationships formed within the clan and its subdivisions around every member of it, which are especially conspicuous in cases of blood feud. The gwely, on the other hand, is one of those objective subdivisions. The formation of personal relationship is not rendered superfluous by the fact that social organisation is built up on the basis of kinship.

The recognition of this fact might have removed some of Heusler's and Maitland's doubts.

8. *Rhys and Brynmor Jones,* " The Welsh People," 51.

9. For example : " Ancient Laws of Ireland," ii. 356, 380, 390.

10. *Seebohm,* " Tribal Custom in Anglo-Saxon Law," 68 ff.

11. I lay stress on this point, because, on the one hand, it has become almost customary to treat the agnatic arrangement as if it precluded all rights on the part of women and all transmission of right through them : it is described in this way, for instance, in the well-known construction of Greek and Roman family law in *Fustel de Coulanges's* " Cité Antique." On the other hand, German scholars, more especially *Julius Ficker,* in his " Untersuchungen zur Germanischen Rechtsgeschichte," and *Andr. Heusler,* in " Institutionen des Deutschen Privatrechts," have argued that the admission of juridical effects of relationship through women and of rights, guaranteed to married women, necessarily dissolves the agnatic organisation. *Prof. Maitland* has adopted this view as to Teutonic antiquities (*Pollock and Maitland,* " History of English Law," ii. 7), and urged it even in regard to Celtic customary law in a review of *Seebohm's* " Tribal System in Wales," in the " Economic Journal," v. His position is tersely summarised in the words : " When we see that the wives of the members of one clan are themselves members of other clans, we ought not to talk of clans at all." (" History of English Law," 2nd edition, ii. 239). It is best to clear up this point when it meets us in the light of the circumstantial Celtic evidence as to clans.

12. Scandinavian laws make a fundamental distinction between children born in lawful wedlock originating in agreement (*maldagi*) and the offspring of irregular unions. The first are privileged in every way as *Árborenn,* rightly born, and their better status depends on the treaty between the two kins to which their father and their mother belong (see, for example, Gulathingslov, 25, 27, 115). In Celtic society marriage arrangements must have been often facilitated by endogamy within the same clan, as clans were very large, but the contractual element in marriage is very conspicuous. *Seebohm,* " Tribal Custom," 32.

13. Compare the review of a new edition of *Skene,* in " Revue Celtique," 1902, 358 ff.

14. *Seebohm,* " Tribal System in Wales," 104.

15. The tenants mentioned in the Welsh Surveys as active members of the tribal community are nearly all men. The Welsh laws recognise maternity " as transmitting inheritance in land " only in exceptional cases, more especially in the case of a marriage of a Welsh tribeswoman with a stranger. " Vened. Cod." ii. 15, § 1: " According to the men of Gwynedd a woman is not to have patrimony (inheritance from her father), because two rights are not to centre

in the same person, these are the patrimony of her husband and her own (they would have centred in her son) ; and since she is not to have patrimony, she is not to be given in marriage, except where her sons can obtain patrimony (a share by their father's right) ; and if she be given (in marriage to a man bereft of rights on his father's side), her sons are to have maternity." As separate property in moveables was certainly allowed to women, patrimony applies here evidently to rights in land. The claim in land by maternity arises only when the father is a stranger. " Vened." ii. c. 1, § 59. The Gwentian custom already recognises, in a general way, claims as to land on the part of the mother, but postpones them to the claims of all males in regard to the principal homesteads. " Gwentian Code," ii. 31, § 6.

16. " Tribal System in Wales," 31 ff.

17. *Seebohm,* " Village Community," 239, 240 ; *Meitzen,* " Wanderungen, Anbau und Agrarrecht," i. 184 f.

18. *Giraldus Cambrensis,* " Descriptio Walliæ," i. 17.

19. Many enactments of the Welsh laws can be explained only on the supposition that several tyddyns were clustered together in some of the villages. We hear of the smithy of a hamlet standing at nine paces from it, of a hamlet's kiln and of a hamlet's bull. If a fire breaks out in a hamlet by accident, only the first two houses on both sides of the street have to be paid for. " Dimetian Code," ii. 1, § 12 ; 8, § 33, § 36.

20. *Meitzen,* " Wanderungen," etc., i. sees in the " Einzelhof " a national feature of Celtic history. It cannot be denied that Celtic settlements might be locally recognisable by this trait in contrast with Teutonic settlements, for instance, on the border of Wales, or in Westphalia, but the fact of living in separate homesteads is not necessarily characteristic of the Celtic race, wherever it went, nor incompatible with Teutonic colonisation ; it does not proceed from ethnological peculiarities at all, but from topographical conditions and traditions of local history. Among Scandinavians, the Norwegians settle in " *gaards,*" or separate homesteads, and the Danes in " *by's,*" or villages.

21. See, for instance, " Vened. Cod.," i. c. 43, §§ 6, 7 ; " Dimetian Cod.," ii. 8, §§ 1, 2, 3. Compare *Seebohm,* " Tribal System in Wales," 45, 46.

22. *Cæsar,* " De Bello Gallico," v. 12.

23. *Seebohm,* " Village Community," 221 ff. *Meitzen.* " Wanderungen," i. 192 ff.

24. *Skene,* " Celtic Scotland," iii. 369.

25. For instance, Carnarvon Extents, 10 *Doloythelan.* Et sunt in eadem villa 10 havotri, vocata havot Penenmeyno, Partheosk, Havot Boyth, etc. Et predicta hauotrev de havot Penenmeyno vult sustentari per annum 120 animalia. Et predicta havotri de Partheosk 60 animalia, etc. The mode of using these mountain

pastures and summer hamlets (havotrevs) may be illustrated by
the practices of Alpine Sennhütten and of the Sæters in Norway.

26. Cf. *Pollock and Maitland,* " Hist. of English Law," ii. 242.

27. *Skene,* " Celtic Scotland," iii. 379, 380 ; *Gomme,* " Village
Community," 144 ; *Meitzen,* i. 208 ff.

28. " Vened. C.," ii. c. 24, and the commentary of *Mr. Seebohm,*
" Village Community," 120 ff. Comp. "Vened.," ii. 22, 1 ; iii. 24, 1 ;

22. In the typical instance, adduced in note 5, the progenies of
Rand Vaughan ap Asser is said to hold (tenent et tenuerunt)
the villages and fractions of villages described in the " Extent."
All the persons enumerated as holders in the lower divisions, the gwelys
and gauels, are said to hold as " Coheredes," in want of a better expression. " If a tribe-stock be adjudged to lose land, and some of its
members be in a border county, and they be not awaited for law,
they are entitled to law after they return " (" Gwent." ii. 30, 11).
" Bangor Extents," 98, *Abererch.* Ieueran ap Iorwerth et 83 alii,
tenent libere 12 carucatas terrae in communi 99 : Lannbedrok
Eynon ap Tegen (et 14 alii) in uno alio lecto. Et tenent in communi in villenagio 8 bovatas terre. The communalistic character
of the tenure is noted in the same way all through the Denbigh
extent. How easy it was for clergy and lawyers accustomed to
English feudal practices to slide from such an accurate description
to vaguer terms may be exemplified from the Record of Carnarvon.
It mostly omits the name of all but the elder tenant in each subdivision, but mentions coheredes. Then instances occur when only
the one elder tenant is named, and if we were not so copiously informed as to the constitution of the gwely, we might be easily led into
considering him to be the only tenant and to attribute to him a
private right to the land. The process of transforming the rights
of elders or chieftains into private lordships and single tenancies
is naïvely described by Sir John Davies in a letter to the Earl of
Salisbury (*Seebohm,* " Village Community," 218) ; cf. *Maine,* " Village
Communities of the East and West," 157.

30. A good deal of confusion seems to have been created by
Aneurin Owen's translation of trev gevery, as "registered
trev." Trevgyvryv means " joint account " village, as I am told
by Prof. Anwyl.

31. I may point to the following enactments to illustrate the
meaning of tir gyvriv. Lgg. "Walliae," ix. 32, § 1 (Miscellaneous
laws) : "there is to be no joint possession in any place, except in a
gyffriff trev," and in such a trev " every man is to have as much
as another, yet not of equal value." "And in such a trev sons are
entitled to land in lifetime of their father, but the youngest son
is to abide the death of his father, because he is to settle in his father's
place," v. 2, § 52. " There is one son who is not necessitated to wait
the death of his father to be invested with his inheritance, the son
of a man upon tir kfyrif ; " since his share of the erw of " his

father is not more than that of the most distant man in the trev. The youngest son, however, must wait, since he is to take his father's place," lx. 32 § 2. "Any person who shall demand land in tref geffry; is to choose his tyddyn in any vacant place he may wish, which has not a house thereon ; and after that to possess jointly with the others, xiv. 32, 2. A claim of equality only takes place in a " tref gyfrif," for every one is to equalise with another, as if they were brothers, § 3. The law of "tyr cyfrif " is, that no one's share is to be greater than that of another ; and therefore, there is no extinguished erw therein, for each is to have as much as another, 6. There a son is to have land while his father is alive, and that is the reason his brother no more shares land with him than the farthest in the trev, § 8. No one in a " tir cyfrif " is to go from his tyddyn if there be sufficiency of land in the trev to locate the claimant.

32. The question as to the relation · between trev-gyvriv and trev-veloghe is obscure, because there are no means of distinguishing clearly between later and earlier customs in this respect. We find, for instance, that the extents, which date from the time after the English Conquest, e.g. "the Record of Carnarvon," mention trevgifrif only as an incident of trevs peopled by villains, and though there is a vast difference between the position of the Welsh villains or taeogs and that of their English compeers, it seems that the admission to rights in the land of all members of a tribal community on equal terms was more adapted to practices where the power of the lord and the decisions of his maer or steward played a great part, Cf. Seebohm, " Tribal System," 18, 20. But Trev-gweliaug is not peculiar to free tenure, and is frequently to be found on villain land. Comp. " Record of Carnarvon," 40 (Gest.) with 25 (Bodellock). And there is nothing in the arrangement itself to make the try kivriv peculiar to taeogs. On the contrary, it is treated as a mode of holding in which persons of any condition may be interested. In this general sense it would occur even in cases of dadenhudd or hereditary claim. Comp. Seebohm, "Tribal System," 67, 68 and 73, 74, 92. The course of development seems to have been that originally a tribesman could claim settlement (a tyddyn) and a certain share in the common management of such agriculture as there was, and of pastoral rights according to the standard of 4, 5, 8 or 12 erws or strips to join in cultivation and grazing pursuits. In course of time, as land became more scarce and more valuable, hereditary rights sprang up in regard to it which, though they did not destroy the communal basis of ownership, led to restrictions and gradations in its working ; people got their shares in the use of the land not so much according to standard requirements of condition, but according to organic rights of succession. As I said, we cannot argue for more than probability in this respect, but what is above dispute and very material is the fact that *both modes of holding land described in laws and surveys,*

whatever their historical relations may have been, present two variations of communal ownership on the basis of agnatic groups.

33. " Gwentian Code," ii. 30, § 8 : A dadenhudd is the tilling by a person of land tilled by his father before him, Cf. " Venedotian Code," ii. 14 § 1 ; " Dimetian Code," ii. 8, § 107 ; " by three modes is a suit of dadenhudd to be resolved between heirs—if heirs of *equal degree* come together, such as brothers, in respect to their fathers' land, or cousins, or second cousins, in respect to their fathers' land, which their *fathers held unshared*, in succession, until they died." All the cases of tir gweliaug, the most common tenure in the extents, arise out of dadenhudd. The chief enactments on the shares in tir gweliauc are Venedoin C., i. 12, and Dimetian C., i. 23.

34. Dim. ii. 23, § 19 ; after there shall have been a sharing of land acquiesced in by co-inheritors, no one of them has a claim on the share of the other, he having issue, except for a sub-share, when the time shall arrive.

35. Comp. the interesting description of Irish gavelkind by Sir John Davies. Fermanagh, the County of the Maguires, was a classical place for it, the greatest part of the inhabitants claiming to be free-holders, and holding not at Common law, but by the custom of tanistry, the eldest claiming chiefry over the sept, and the inferior sort dividing their possessions according to gavelkind. Almost every acre had a several owner, who termed himself a lord and his portion of the land his country. *Skene,* " Celtic Scotland," iii. 186, 196 ; *Meitzen,* " Wanderungen," i. 183, 205.

36. " Dimetian," ii. 23, 14. If there be land in a family unshared (gwelygord), and they should all die excepting one person, the person is to have all the land in common. Cf. " Record of Carnarvon," 25, 40. Mr. Seebohm looks on the subject in the same way, and his opinion is conclusively proved by the manner in which escheats are apportioned. " Tribal System," 41. The Denbigh Extent sometimes expressly mentions that the tenants of a wele hold their land " ad invicem." See e.g. the description of the villa de Kelkenneys in the MS. of the Extent in Mr. Seebohm's possession.

37. Lgg. Walliae (Miscell. laws), v. 2. § 131.

38. The right of maintenance, coupled with the sole ownership of the chief of the household, plays a conspicuous part in Mr. Seebohm's theory in regard to Welsh land tenure, a theory which has been accepted by Messrs. Rhys and Brynmor Jones.

39. " Gwentian Code," ii. 31, § 2. " Dimetian Code," ii. 21, § 4, goes the length of calling the eldest brother the sole proprietor, but this extreme statement is counter-balanced by the descriptions of the Extents and by such passages as " Gwentian Code," ii. 30, § 8, etc. In the stage of a tribal community coupled with the assignment of shares according to gavelkind the elder would be the tanist of the wele, but not the only heir to it in the usual sense. Comp. *Paul*

Viollet, de la Tanistry, " Mémoires de l'Académie des inscriptions,"
xxxii, 275 ff.

40. I cannot agree with Seebohm as to the position of the
penteulu—" Tribal System," 91 ff., and Rhys and Brynmor
Jones, 195. The penteulu as *major domus* appears, e.g.,
" Dimetian C.," i. 8, § 1 where his saraad is equated to a third
of the King's saraad. In regard to the penteulu, as father of a
family, see n. 76. Mr. Seebohm is constrained to go back to the
ancestor of a wele (Lauwarghe ap Kandelik) to substantiate his
contention as to the patriarchal chief and sole proprietor of the wele.
But Lauwarghe must have been dead long ago when his great
grandsons held the land, and there is nothing to show that anyone
in particular had taken his place.

40*a.* E.g., Misc. laws, xi. 5, § 7, land that shall be sued by kin
and descent from the original share onward, is to be determined in
the sovereign court, but into the third descent land is to be sued for
in the Court to which all the land pertains, as between brothers,
cousins, and second cousins. Cf. xii. 1; " Gwent.," ii. 31, § 23.
The third descent leads to the fourth generation and the land to be
shared between brothers, cousins and second cousins is tyr gwelyaug
held by dadenhudd, which thus obtains precedence over claims by
kin and descent.

41. *Giraldus Cambrensis,* who knew Wales so well and has left
us such interesting descriptions of its condition in the twelfth
century, points repeatedly to the intimate connection between
military and social arrangements in this country. Two passages from his " Description of Wales " are especially worth
quoting.

I, 8:—Gens armis dedita tota. Non enim nobiles hic solum, sed
totus populus ad arma paratus tuba sonanti, non segnius ab aratro
ruricola, quam āulicus ab aula prorumpit ad arma. Non enim hic, ut
alibi—" Redit āgricolis labor-actus in orbem." Solum quippe Martio
et Aprili solum semel aperiunt ad avenas: nec bis in aestate,
tertioque in hieme, ad tritici trituram terras vertendo laborant.
Totus propemodum populus armentis pascitur et avenis, lacte,
caseo et butyro. Carne plenius, pane parsim vesci solent. II. 8.
Kambri nimirum, quia nec laboriosis oneribus opprimuntur, nec
servilibus operibus atteruntur, nec dominorum exactionibus ullis
molestantur, hinc eis ad propulsandas injurias ceruix erecta, hinc
ad patriæ tutelam audacia tanta, hinc armis semper et rebellionibus
gens parata Nihil estenim quod adeo corda virorum ad probi-
tatem excitet erigat et invitet ut libertatis hilaritas, nihil adeo
deprimit et deterret ut servitutis oppressio.—Every trait in
these paragraphs, which remind one of *Tacitus*' " Germania,"
ought to be studied carefully. There is some glamour of rhetoric
about them, but minute observation has provided the author
with their foundation of fact. A nation always ready to take up

arms, because not bowed down by heavy agricultural drudgery; no deep contrast between toiling villains and military nobles; a rude spirit of liberty, engendered by the fighting condition of the mass; on the other hand a participation of the warriors in such pastoral and agricultural work as had to be performed. This is a picture of primitive conditions which does not quite correspond to some modern ideas about the monotony of primeval serfdom.

42. " Gwentian Code," ii. 40, § 23.

43. " Gwentian Code," ii. 5, § 31, 32.

44. *Skene,* " Celtic Scotland," iii. 139.

45. *Rhys and Brynmor Jones,* " The Welsh People," 13, 39.

46. *Hildebrand, Knapp* and *Wittich* have tried to show that any attempt to represent ancient Teutonic Society as constructed on a democratic basis would lead to misunderstanding barbarian life and misinterpreting the account of Tacitus; in their view, barbarian warriors do not work and live by the labour of their dependents; ancient society is based on the leadership of a few chiefs and landowners and not on any supposed rights of common freemen. *Fustel de Coulanges* has spent much energy and ingenuity in France in trying to explode notions which in his mind gave too honourable a place in history to Teutonic invaders. *Seebohm* has thrust into the foreground in England the idea of manorial lordship as the organising institution of the Middle Ages, and has transplanted it partly into the domain of Celtic tribal antiquities by assigning to the chiefs of households the position of landowners and allowing other tribesmen only rights of maintenance. (Cf. " Tribal System," 88, 91). Messrs. *Rhys* and *Brynmor Jones* (e.g. 397), and *Palmer* see the necessary substratum for Celtic aristocracy in a numerous class of non-British villains toiling for them.

47. Weles of free *priodarii* or landowners interchange with weles and communities in trevgevery of *taeogs* or *nativi* and it would be difficult to say which were more numerous. In the Black Book of St. David's, *the free tenantry are left alone on the scene.* (See its recent edition by Mr. *Willis Bund*). Surely, a mere look at a Welsh Survey is sufficient to show that we have in them something entirely different from the English feudal arrangement, or from any system based on the superimposition of a free class on a population of servile labourers. The picture of a society in which the people are divided into two sets, both paying tribute to the princes and chiefs, is as clearly before us as could be wished. The *taeogs* and aillts (not to be confused with the alltuds), are often considered not in their individual capacities, but as the dwellers of distinct trevs E.g. " Gwentian Code," ii. 35, § 5, " Dimetian Code," ii. 8, 28. Very often the free trevs are designated as trevs of Grandsons " Werion." E.g., " Carnarvon Ext.," 22. *Dynthle.* " In eadem villa sunt septem wele libere, vocate

' Wele Werion Eignon,' ' Wele Werion Mourgene,' ' Wele Werion Rand,' " etc. Cf. " Record of Carnarvon," p. i. " Penruyn. Eadem villa libera est et de natura Werion Eden." Even in the highly manorialised estate of Aberffrau, which ought to stand not as a typical example but as an extreme instance of the influence of territorial lordships, the taeog-trevs are kept apart from the free trevs.

48. " Denbigh Extents " (Appendix to *Seebohm's* " Tribal System "), 75 : de duabus partibus Wele quod uocatur Pridithe Mough non fit nisi una gauella liberorum . . . Et de tercia parte ejusdem Wele, que constitit in tenura Nativorum inferius inter Natiuos.

49. Taeogs of uchelwrs occur in the Codes and in the Extents. E.g. " Record of Carnarvon," 3 (Cf. *Palmer*, " Land Tenure in Wales," 101). But these last show that as a rule, the Taeogs stood directly under the princes and the great lords who in English time had taken up the position of the old tribal kings and chieftains.

50. I will just quote a few passages (f. 180) from the MS. of the Denbigh Extent, which I had occasion to study through the courtesy of Mr. Seebohm : Villa de Petrual continet 1170 acras, consistit in 13 lectis liberorum. Priodarii de progenie Raud Vaughan quorum nomina patent in Deunant (cf. n. 5) tenent hic tantam partem in 5 lectis, quantum tenent superius in Deunant tE tenent hic quasi pro uno lecto quod vocatur Wele Wiryon Raud terciam decimam partem istius Ville—Villata de Hundregeda, que continet 1,299 acras terre consistit in tenura liberorum in 2 lectis, Unde liberum lectum partitur in six gauellas, que quidem gauellae partite sunt inter progenies fratrum, de quorum nominibus plenius patebit in posterum.

51. " Venedotian C.," ii. c. 18, § 12, 12, *Rhys and Brynmor Jones*, " The Welsh People," 218. The territorial subdivisions mentioned in the Laws are very artificial (*See* e.g. Gwentian, c. ii. 33, § 4. There are to be thirteen trevs in every maenol, and the thirteenth is the supernumerary trev, § 5 ; in each free trev, there are four randirs, three for occupancy, and the fourth pasturage for the three randirs ; § 6, there are two randirs in the taeog trev ; there are three taeogs in each of the two, and third pasturage for the two ; § 7 : there are seven trevs in the maenol of the taeog trevs. " Dimetian C.," ii. 20, § 9 : there are to be 7 trevs in a lowland maenol and 13 trevs in an upland maenol." The grouping into maenols is evidently a later one and contrived for the distribution of the tung ground tax. (*Seebohm*, " Tribal system, 159, 160). Similar artificial subdivisions of territory are reported from Ireland, where 184 Tricha-ceds were reckoned to comprise the whole country, each Tricha-ced consisting of thirty bailebiataghs, the bailebiatagh falling into twelve ploughgates, and the seisrigh, or ploughgate containing 120 acres.

Skene, Celtic Scotland, iii. 154. Cf. *Arbois de Jubainville,*
" Cours de literature celtique," vii. 101. In both the Welsh
and the Irish cases we come in this way across attempts of
central authorities to estimate and to arrange the natural divisions
for the repartition of taxes and other burdens. But, apart
from that, tribal arrangements always suppose a good deal of
artificial tinkering within the natural groups themselves—admisson
and adoption of strangers, alltuds, to make up full numbers
in groups which for some reasons had suffered a decrease in their
personnel, and reclaiming of land, splitting up into parts, and emigration in cases where the groups were overburdened with population.
Symmetric schemes are, altogether, very characteristic of tribal
Society. Compare the elaborate Athenian and Roman schemes
of gentes. See also *Meitzen,* " Wanderungen," etc., i. 187.

52. Bangor Extents, 109 : Maclure. Et nota quod omnes recog-
noscunt quod debent esse cum principe in exercitu suo pro domino
Episcopo exceptis Clericos. Dimetian C., ii. 23, § 9 : If an owner
of land have an heir without bodily blemish, and another who
is blemished, the unblemished is to be heir to the whole land,
whether he be legitimate or illegitimate, for no one who is blemished
can fully accomplish the service of the land due to the king in
the courts and in the armies.—We find instances where villains
are mentioned as bound to go to the war and to do suit of
court, but probably the term villain is used in such cases not for
mere taeogs, but for tribesmen who had got into subjection in
consequence of the English conquest. Bangor Extents, 99. Lann,
bedrok, Eynon ap Tegwaret (et alii) in alio lecto. Et tenent in
communi in villenag io 8 bovatas terre. Et debent ire in exercitum domini et facere sectam. Cf. *Rhys and Brynmor Jones,*
" The Welsh People," 445 : *Skene,* " Celtic Scotland," iii. 151, 188.

53. The assessors of the Welsh local courts are gwrdas, free
householders.

54. In the normal scheme of the cymwd mentioned above only
ten treys out of the fifty are described as set apart for demesne
cultivation. Maertreys occur seldom in the extents. *Record
of Carnarvon,* 2, Gannow. Eadem Villa est de Natura de Mayr-
dreue. " Venedotian C.," ii. 20, § 9.

55. The gwestva of the king or chief is described at length in
the " Vendotian Code," ii. 21, 1 ; 26, 27. *Seebohm,* " Tribal System,"
160, 161. " Venedotian C.," ii. 19, 5 : Neither maer nor canghellor
is to be imposed on a free maenol, nor progress, nor dovraeth, nor
youths, except the great progress of the household in winter.
" Dimetian C.," ii. 11, § 9 : The minstrels of another county are
to have a progress among the king's villains, while waiting for
their gifts from the king, if he give any.

56. " Vened.," ii. 19, § 9 : The aillts of the king are not to support
him, nor to support his household, and since they are not to support

him, they are not to retain their corn, nor their fish, but are to send them to the king's court ; and he may, if he will, make weirs upon their waters, and take their lines.—The meaning of the enactment seems to be that the food tribute of the aillts or taeogs is to be sent to the central offices, and not to be spent on the spot in the feasting of the king during his progresses.

57. " Dimetian C.," ii. 11, § 7 : If it chance that a maer shall not be able to maintain a house, let him take any taeog he will in his maer-ship for a year, and let him enjoy the milk of that taeog during summer, and his corn at harvest, and his swine in winter, and when the villian quit the maer, let him leave him four large sows with a boar, and all the other live stock, eight erws of spring tilth and four erws of winter tilth. The second year and the third let the maer act in like manner with other villains, and afterwards let him support himself during three other years upon his own property ; and then let the king relieve him by giving him other villains in the same mode. Cf. " Gwentian C.," i. 35, § 13.

58. *Seebohm,* " Tribal System," 127 ; *Rhys and Brynmor Jones,* " The Welsh People," 207 ; *Skene,* " Celtic Scotland," iii. 190, 321, 322.

59. *Seebohm,* " Tribal System," 168.

60. " Misc. Laws," v. 2, § 123. Alltuds and aillts are not sufficiently distinguished by *Seebohm,* o.l. 121. Cf. *Rhys and Brynmor Jones,* 124. The villains de advocaria and hospites de advocaria of Bangor Extent, 98, 99, are undoubtedly alltuds.

61. " Misc. Laws," v. 2, 126, 144.

62. *Sir Henry Maine,* " Early History of Institutions," 157 ; *Skene,* o.c. iii. 146, 172, 173 ; " Arbois de Jubainville," vii. 124, 126.

63. " Vened. C.," ii. 18, 8 ; " Dimetian C.," ii. 23, § 34. He is described as the leader of the kindred to the 9th degree by " Misc. Laws," xiii. c. 2, but this seems only a later and artificial limitation. " Vened. C.," ii. 18, 18 ; " Dimetian C.," ii. 23, § 34 ; " Vened. C.," ii. 19, § 2, 3 ; 31, § 18.

64. " Vened. C.," ii. 31, § 19, 20.

65. *Skene,* o.c. iii. 324.

66. *Skene,* iii. 390.

67. *Skene,* iii. 169, cf. 161.

68. As to the way clan holdings were turned into feudal holdings in Scotland, see *Cos. Innes,* " Lectures on Scottish Legal Antiquities," 157.

69. *Skene,* iii. 319.

70. Dimetian C., ii. 23, § 55.

71. Dimetian C., ii. 8, § 15, § 110, 114.

72. *Seebohm,* Trib. system, 65.

73. Misc. Laws, viii. 11, § 34.

74. Arbois de Jubainville, vii. 105 ff. *Skene,* iii. 142.

75. *Rhys and Br. Jones,* 191 ; *Seebohm,* 107.

76. Venedot. C., iii. 1, § 29, 30, etc. The separate position of the man with a family—gur-ar-teylu (deulu)—has to be well noticed, but it is a very different matter from the supposed position of a penteulu enjoying the patriarchal rights of the chief of a wele and the sole proprietorship of its land. *Seebohm,* " Tribal System," 90.

CHAPTER II

1. *Hübner,* " Das römische Heer in Britannien, Hermes, xvi." Cf. *Jung,* " Die romanischen Landschaften des romischen Reichs," 301. Similar observations have been made in a very instructive article in regard to Eastern Switzerland by *F. Keller* : " Die römischen Ansiedelungen in der Ostschweiz," Abhandlungen der Gesellschaft für Erforschung vaterländischer Alterthümer, Zürich, XV. 53, 57.

2. *Prof. F. Haverfield,* though drawing a more favourable general estimate as to the strength of Roman influence (" Romanization of Roman Britain, Proceedings of the British Academy," II, 192, 193), has repeatedly insisted on this point, e.g., " Victoria County History of Worcestershire," p. 201. " Edinburgh Review," 1899, April, " County History of Warwickshire," article on " Roman remains." Cf. the description of the southern hundreds of Surrey, especially of the hundred of Godley, in the Victoria History of Surrey.

3. *Pitt-Rivers,* Excavations in Cranborne Chase, near Rushmore, 1887–1898. Professor Haverfield remarks in his paper on the Romanization of Britain that similar customs have left traces in Italy. The barbarism of backward Italian settlements can hardly be made an argument, however, against the derivation of barbaric customs in Britain from primitive Celtic life.

4. Even Somerset, Dorset and Wiltshire form a part of the Welsh region in the time of Alfred, if one may judge from his locating his estates in these counties in " Wealhcynne." Alfred's will, *Thorpe,* " Diplom.," 488.

5. *De Courzon,* " Prolégomenes a Cartulaire de Redon," XIV, XVIII, CCXXVII. *Loth,* " Émigration bretonne en Armorique," 71, 183, 191–4. " Mots Latins dans les langues brittoniques," 21. *De la Borderie,* " Histoire de Bretagne," i. 288. This last writer is not inclined to admit a violent conquest, but is at one with De Courzon and Loth as to the thorough change effected by the influx of emigrants from Great Britain. As to the Romanization of Armorica before the overflow from Great Britain cf. *Desjardins,* " Géographie historique de la Gaule."

6. It may be noted as a significant fact that a whole crop of Christian sepulchral inscriptions, written in Latin, but characteristically Celtic in the shape of the monuments and in the names of the people mentioned in them, appears after the lapse of the Roman power in those very parts of the island from which Latin inscriptions

of the Imperial period are all but absent. *Hübner,* "Inscriptiones Britanniæ Christianæ, Introduction," vii.

7. *Procopius,* iv. 20, gives the Imperial version of these events, ascribing them to over-population. It is clear from his account that the emigrants left the island every year in large parties with women and children. The lives of the Breton saints show that the exiles often came over under the guidance not of military chiefs, but of ecclesiastics and monks. All the numerous saints of Brittany except five hail from Great Britain. The chief epochs of the emigration correspond to the turning points of the Saxon Conquest. There is especially a great overflow in consequence of the Saxon raid along Watling Street after Natanleag (511) and after the victory of Cerdicesford (519). *La Borderie,* i. 216, 255, 337 ; *Loth,* "Émigration," 163, 168, 169.

8. According to *M. de la Borderie,* the territory of the Osismii in Brittany was colonised by Cornovii, "Histoire de Bretagne," i. 309. Cf. *Loth,* "Émigration," 158, 165. It is not impossible, nevertheless, that in later documents, such as the lives of Breton saints, Cornovii means simply emigrants from Cornwall.

9. *La Borderie* (310) makes St. Brieuc come from Valentia, and thinks that Quimper (Corisopitum) was colonised by people from Corisopitum-Corbridge, near Newcastle. It may be remembered in this connection that in Celtic tradition Cunedda is made to come from the country adjoining the Wall. We need not, however, attach too much importance to such identifications. The general theory can afford to dispense with them.

10. *Mommsen* has indeed expressed his belief that if in modern England, apart from Wales and Cumberland, the old native language has disappeared, it has given way not to the speech of Angles and Saxons, but to the Roman idiom. "The Roman Provinces" (Engl. trans.), 194. Preface to "Gildas," 9, 10. In corroboration of this thesis, Herr Pogatsher has tried to show that the Latin words borrowed by the Saxons from their predecessors on the island have been affected by the phonetic changes which characterise Vulgar Latin, and that, therefore, these Romance loans testify to an extensive use of Latin among British natives. ("Zur Lautlehre der griechischen, lateinischen und romanischen Lehnworte in Altenglischen," Strassburg, 1888.) But there seems to be but slight foundation for these assertions. If Bede (ii. 1, iii. 6) mentions Latin as one of the languages spoken in Britain, nothing could be more accurate, as it was the language of the numerous clerical class ; but the same remark would have applied to Bede's own time, as is shown by his very writings. And when Gildas inveighs against British chiefs, he is bound to give somewhat awkward Latin renderings of their vernacular names. (Cf. *De La Borderie,* i. 269). As for Vulgar Latin, according to French scholars, the reverse of Pogatsher's contention would be true.

There is no trace in the words borrowed by the Teuton conquerors from their British predecessors, either of assibilation or of the weakening of *tenues* between two vowels which are characteristic of the Vulgar Latin of the fifth and sixth centuries. And some of the topographical names which have come over from the pre-Saxon period testify rather to the prevalence among the British population of Celtic speech than of Vulgar Latin. Kent, for example, proceeds from Cantion, which is Celtic, and not from Cancion (pronounced Cantsion), as it would have been in Vulgar Latin. The name of the River Trent supposes an ellipsis of the original *s* in Trisanton, and an intermediate form, " Treanta," is actually given by Bede in conformity with Celtic phonetic habits, whereas people using Vulgar Latin would have kept the *s* and probably spoken of the Trisant. Such observations, if they are correct, would tend to show that Latin was not spoken by many on the island, and that the bulk of the population kept on speaking Celtic dialects, while no Vulgar Latin of the same kind, as that which spread on the Continent gained firm ground. *Loth,* " Les mots latins dans les langues brittoniques, 20 ff., 29 ff.

11. The juridical aspect of the degeneration of Rome is well illustrated by *Blumenstock,* " Entstehung des Immobiliareigenthums."

11*a.* Professor Haverfield's interesting paper on the Romanization of Britain seems deficient in this respect, and yet the legal aspect of life can hardly be disregarded in Roman history.

12. *Mommsen,* " The Roman Provinces," 192 ; *Yung,* " Die romanischen Landschaften," 298.

13. *Loth,* " Les mots latins," 39 ff. Loth's list must be checked by a comparison with Rhys, " Archæologia Cambrensis," iv. series, vols. iv. v. vi. Cf. *Pedersen,* Vergleichende Grammatik der Keltischen, Sprachen, pp. 20 ff.

14. *Kluge* in " Paul's Grundriss der Germanischen Philologie," i. 309.

15. " Giraldus Cambrensis," i. 17, says of the Welsh ploughing : boves autem ad aratra vel plaustra binos quidem jungunt rarius, sed quaternos frequentius ; stimlatore perambulo, sed retrogrado. The Welsh laws, as we have seen, speak of the ploughteam of eight oxen. As to the four- and eight-oxen ploughs in use in Saxon England, see *Seebohm,* " Village Community," 62, 74. The Rhaetian big plough, described by Pliny, " Hist. Natur.," xviii. 48, was a combination of a plough and a cart (*plaustraratrum* has been suggested as a probable correction for the *plaumorati* of the MS.).

16. Roman agriculture was characterised by a lavish expenditure of human energy. *Mommsen,* " Roman History," Dickson's transl., i. 24 ; iii. 77. *Meitzen,* " Wanderungen," i. 276. Meitzen's attempt to fasten on the big plough as an invention characteristic of Teutonic psychology is not likely to carry conviction, o.c. i. 281 ff. *Peisker,* " Zeitschrift für Social und Wirtschafts-geschichte," v. 18 ff. has given a most learned description of ploughs in use in Central and Eastern Europe. He comes to the conclusion

that the big plough with broad ploughshare and a "sech" (soc) was borrowed by the Germanic tribes from the Slavs. Though he cannot be said to have proved this contention, he has shown convincingly, as it seems to me, that the development of the big plough was chiefly produced by the requirements of soil and of husbandry, and not by national traditions. See especially pp. 22, 31, 32, Victoria County History of Surrey.

17. *Mitteis,* "Reichsrecht und Volksrecht im römischen Kaiserreich," 4 ; *Blumenstock,* "Entstehung des Immobiliareigenthums im römischen Reich," 31, 95.

18. *Mommsen,* "Schweizer Nachstudien," Hermes, xvi. 474 ; *Blumenstock,* 99.

19. *Kuhn,* "Städtische und bürgerliche Verfassung des römischen Reichs," ii. 451. There was in Africa a procurator Augusti ad curam gentium, *Renier,* "Inscr. Afr.," 4033, and we hear of native chiefs, princes, ἄρχοντες, *Kuhn,* O. C., ii. 453.

20. *Kuhn,* O. C., ii. 245.

21. *Mommsen,* "Schweizer Nachstudien," 479, 485. In the history of Italy itself the transition from country divisions to cities was but gradual, but we are especially concerned with the contrast between the city of civilized Rome and the rural settlements of barbarians. The fact that the Romans could draw on Italian examples to define it does not alter the main point, which is that the Roman conquest did not do away with the customary grouping and institutions of conquered tribes.

22. *Mommsen,* "Römisches Staatsrecht," iii. f. 21 ; *Blumenstock,* 52, 116, 117, 130.

23. On the movement from the cities to the villages, *Weber,* "Agrargeschichte Roms," 263, 264.

24. *Plinius,* "Hist. Nat.," iii. 4, 37 ; Vocontiorum civitatis fœderatæ duo capita Vasio et Lucus, oppida vero ignobilia xix, sicut xxiv Nemausensibus attribuita. *Mommsen,* "Römisches Staatsrecht," iii. 719.

25. *Jung,* "Ueber Rechtsstellung und Organisation der alpinen Civitates in der römischen Kaiserzeit," Wiener Studien, xii. 99 ff. *Salvioli,* "Sulla distribuzione della proprieta fondiaria," Archivio Giuridico, N. Ser. iii. 225.

26. *Schulten,* "Die Landgemeinden im Römischen Reich," Philologus, liii. 634 ; C.T.L. ii. 2632.

27. *Schulten,* "Landgemeinden," 635, 642.

27a. Mr. Haverfield has published in the *Athenæum* (26 Sept., 1903) a most interesting fragment of an inscription from Caerwent drawn up "ex decreto ordinis respubl(icae) civitatis Silurum." It shows that the Tribe of the Silures continued its life as a *civitas* and was administered by an *ordo*—probably by sessions of the chief men of the tribe held in Caerwent.

28. Respublica Pagi : *Orelli Henzen,* iii. 5215 ; *Blumenstock,*

132 ; cf. 118 ; *Schulten*, "Landgemeinden," 645 ; *Kuhn*, ii. 279. *Flach*, " Origines de l'ancienne France," ii. 37.

29. " Ulpianus Dig. L.," i. 30 : qui ex vico ortus est eam patriam intelligitur habere, cui reipublicae vicus ille respondet. *Blumenstock*, 114.

30. " *Festus* sub voce *vicus* : Ex vicis partim habent rempublicam et jus dicitur, partim nihil eorum, et tamen ibi nundinae aguntur negotii gerendi causa et magistri vici quotannuis fiunt."

31. *Gaius :* vicis legata perinde licere capere, atque civitatibus, *Blumenstock*, 120–3. *Curiales* of *vici* are mentioned ; for instance, " Cod. Theod.," xi. 24, 6, 5 ; *Salvianus*, " De gubernatione Dei," x. 18.

32. *Schulten*, " Landgemeinden," 657, 658.   The population of the Saltus Burunitanus is grouped, for instance, into a sacral community, which acts as substitute for a social and political commune.   *Mommsen*, " Das Dekret des Commodus für den Saltus Burunitanus," Hermes, xv. 393 ; *W. Ramsay*, " Geography of Asia Minor," 178 ff.

33. *Schulten*, Libello dei Coloni d'un domani imperiale in Asia, "Mittheilungen des deutschen archæologischen Instituts in Rom," xiii. 226.   *W. Ramsay*, " Geography of Asia Minor," 173.   The προάγων of Hellenistic districts corresponds to the praepositus of Romanised provinces.

34. The inhabitants of the Saltus Burunitanus had obtained a redress of their grievances from Commodus, and it is to this successful opposition to the exactions of the procurator that we owe the celebrated inscription of Souk-el-Khmis.   C. T. L. viii. 10570. For the commentary to it, see *Mommsen*, " Das Dekret des Commodus," Hermes, xv., and *Fustel de Coulanges*, " Recherches sur quelques problèmes d'histoire," 25.

35. As to the functions of Imperial procurators and of *conductores*, farming Imperial estates, *W. Ramsay*, " Cities and Bishoprics of Phrygia," i. 281.   The administration of the estates of the Church of Rome, as described in the correspondence of Pope Gregory the Great, is based on a powerful bureaucratic organisation. *Mommsen*, " Zeitschrift für Social und Wirthschaftsgeschichte," i.

36. *Schulten*, " Landgemeinden," 630 ; *Blumenstock*, 188.

37. The Breton *plou* comes from *plebs*, and indicates the civil parish, whereas *lann* means the ecclesiastical colony and parish. The use of the Romance derivation (plebs-plou) is significant ; it shows that the village districts or civil parishes existed among the Armorican population in Roman times.   *La Borderie*, " Histoire de Bretagne," 282 ; *Loth*, " Émigration Bretonne," 228, 229.

38. *Gierke*, " Deutsches Genossenschaftsrecht," iii. 134 ff.

39. *Beaudoin*, " Les grands domaines dans l'Empire Romain," Nouvelle revue historique de droit, 1898, 82.

40. *Weber*, " Agrargeschichte Roms," 22 ff. ; *Pauli-Wissowa*,

" Realencyclopædie des Klassischen Alterthums," s.v. Ager.

41. *Paul-Wissowa, voce* Ager ; *Blumenstock,* 177.

42. *Weber,* " Agrargeschichte," 43.

43. *Blumenstock,* 71.

44. *Daremberg et Saglio,* " Dictionnaire des Antiquités," s.v. Latifundia (Lécrivain).

45. "Ulpianus," Dig. L. 15, 4 : Forma censuali cavetur, ut agri sic in censum referantur ; Nomen fundi cujusque ; et in qua civitate et in quo pago sit ; et quos duos vicinos proximos habeat. Et arvum, quod in decem annos proximos satum erit, quot jugerum sit : vinea, quot vites habeat : olivae, quot jugerum et quot arbores habeant, pratum, quot intra decem annos proximos sectum erit, quot jugerum ; pascua, quot jugerum esse videantur ; item silvae caeduae. Omnia ipse qui defert, aestimet. Hyginus, Gromatici scriptores, p. 205 : certa enim praetia agris constituta sunt, ut in Pannonia arui primi, arui secundi, prati, siluae glandiferae, siluae vulgares, pascuæ.

46. " Syrisch-Römisches Rechtsbuch aus dem v Jahrhundert," ed. by *Bruns and Sachau,* 37 : 5 jugera of vineland were equated to 20 jugera of best arable, 40 jugera of second-class arable, and 60 jugera of third-class of the same.

47. *Seeck,* " Die Schatzungsordnung des Diokletian," Zeitschrift für Social und Wirthschaftsgeschichte, iv. 338.

48. *Seeck,* 277. Cf. *Arbois de Jubainville,* "Fundus et villa," Revue historique de droit for 1900, 213.

49. *Seeck,* 280, 1282.

50. "Cod. Justinianus," xi. 59 : de omni agro deserto et quando steriles fertilibus imponuntur, especially 5, 8, 9.

51. Eumenius, gratiarum actio, 11 : septem millia capitum remisisti, quartam amplius partem nostro. Eum censuum remissione ista septem millium capitum viginti quinque millibus dedisti vires, dedisti opem, dedisti salutem. Cf. *Sidonius Apollinaris,* "Carm." xiii. 19 ; " Cod. Theod.," xi. 28, 13 ; " Nov. Valentiniani," iii. 33, 2 ; *Marquardt,* " Staatsverwaltung " (2nd ed.), ii. 230 ff. Sometimes the alleviation could be effected by reducing the taxation of every single jugum. Ammianus Marcellinus, xvi. 5, on the lessening of the taxes of Gaul by Julian.

52. " Dictionnaire des Antiquités," s.v. fundus. *P. Viollet,* " Histoire du droit français," i. 39, n. 2. *Bloch,* in Lavisse, "Histoire de France," i. 437. The chief work on the *fundi* is *Arbois de Jubainville,* " Origines du droit de propriété." But one must also take careful note of the criticism of his theory by *Flach,* " Origines de l'ancienne France." I need not say that the fundus plays a great part in F. de Coulange's thoroughly individualistic theory, e.g., " L'alleu et le domaine rural," 17 ff.

53. *Flach,* " Fundus, villa et village," in Revue Historique de droit for 1900, p. 385 ff.

54. *Lécrivain,* " Mélanges de l'école de Rome," **v.**

55. *Flach,* " Origines de l'ancienne France," ii. 32.

56. *Weber,* " Agrargeschichte Roms," 120 ff.   *Voigt,* " Ueber die *Agri Compascui,*" Abhandlungen der K. sächsischen Akademie Phil. hist. Classe X.

57. *Hansen,* " Agrarhistorische Untersuchungen, i ; zur Geschichte der Feldsysteme."

58. Mr. Seebohm has devoted to the subject of the affinity between the open field practices of England and France an interesting paper, read before the Cymrodorion Society, but hitherto unpublished.   He traces those common practices to Celtic antecedents as well as to Roman influence, and I can but follow his lead in this respect.   It seems to me that not so much the unity of Roman influence fashioning barbarian agriculture, but also the close resemblance of the primitive agrarian habits of northern barbarians, be they Celts, Germans or Slavs, has to be insisted upon in order to explain the features of the so-called open-field system.

59. *Salvioli,* " Sulla distribuzione della proprieta fondiaria," iii. 503 ; *Mommsen,* " Ostgothische Studien," 494.

60. *Mommsen* was the first to point out their exaggeration in an article on the " Italische Bodentheilung," Hermes, xix. 393 ff.

61. *Salvioli,* iii. 221, 231 ; *Seeck,* " Schatzungsordnung," 288. The provision made for starting the veteran as a landed proprietor is mentioned in C. Th. vii. 20, 38.

62. *Bloch,* in Lavisse, " Histoire de France," 440 ; *Salvioli,* iii. 502.

63. The Codex Theodosianus gives a whole series of enactments calculated to protect independent communities of peasants.   The most remarkable apply to eastern *Metrocomiae,* "C. Th.," xi. 24, 6 ; i. 16, 12 ; viii. 5, 35.

64. *Frontinus,* " De controversiis agrorum," p. 53 (*Lachmann*) ; frequenter in provinciis . . . habent autem in saltibus privati non exiguum populum plebeium et vicos circa villam in modum munitionum.

65. On the Roman villa and its dependencies, see *Lécrivain,* " Latifundium " in the " Dictionnaire des Antiquités grecques et romaines," ii. p. 2962 ; *Meitzen,* " Wanderungen," i. 352. As to Britan in particular, *Mommsen,* " Roman Provinces," i. 94.   I need hardly mention that an appreciation of their probable social influence forms one of the chief aims of *F. Seebohm's* " English Village Community," 78 ; *Lécrivain,* " Latifundium," 957.

66. *Varro,* " De lingua latina," v. 36 : quos agros non colebant propter silvas aut id genus, ubi pecus possit pasci, et possi debant, ab usu salvo saltus nominarunt. *Aulus Gellius,* " De verborum significatione ap. Festum," 320, b, 20 ; saltus est, ubi silvae et pastiones sunt, quorum causa casae quoque. Si qua particula in eo saltu pastorum aut custodum causa aratur, ea res non peremit

nomen saltui, non magis quam fundi, qui est in agro culto et ejus causa habet adificium, si qua particula in eo habet silvam.—Ulpian is still coupling the saltus with pastures : saltus pastiones que (20 ad Sabinum D. xxxiii. f. 8, § 1). See on the subject *M. Voigt,* " Ueber die agri compascui und die staatsrechtliche *possessio* der römischen Republik in the Abhandlungen der Sächsischen Gesellschaft der Wissenschaften," Historisch - Philologische Classe, **x.** 225. *Mommsen,* " Das Dekret des Commodus," Hermes, **xv.** 409. The original sense of saltus was gradually extended, and the expression may have been employed in a looser way to indicate all manner of great estates concurrently with *latifundium.* But the meaning of exempted territory was technically characteristic of it, and as a matter of fact, most *saltus* must have been tracts of primitive and insufficient cultivation.

67. *Schulten,* " Die Grossen Grundherschaften der römischen Kaiserzeit " ; *Rostowtzew,* " Die Kaiserliche Patrimonial-Verwaltung in Aegypten," Philologus, lvii. 565.

68. *Beaudoin,* " Les grands domaines dans l'Empire romain," Nouvelle Revue de Droit, 1897, 555 ; *Lécrivain,* " Latifundium," 958, 962. *Pelham,* " The Imperial Domains and the Colonate," lays stress on the rise of special agrarian customs such as the Colonate on the estates of the emperors, and on their gradual spread to the practice of private estates. It seem most likely that Imperial domains did play a leading part in the evolution of social customs and of social legislation, but it must not be forgotten that the effect of their influence as leading examples must have depended chiefly on the fact that their condition was very much like that of any private *saltus.* Cf. *Seeck,* " Die Pachtbestimmungen eines römischen Gutes," Zeitschrift für Social und Wirthschaftsg., vi. 334. As to Gaul, *Blumenstock,* 94. Our best information as to the management of *saltus* is drawn from African and Asiatic inscriptions, and this may be explained by two considerations. To begin with, Africa and the Eastern Hellenistic provinces are particularly rich in inscriptions, and the output of Britain in this respect is insignificant when compared with them ; evidently it was more the fashion in Germany and Britain to trust to unwritten custom. Secondly, Asiatic, and possibly Egyptian, evidence points to the maintenance in those parts of ancient traditions as to the treatment of rural districts administered as royal and, later on, imperial estates. I shall have to come back to the peculiarities of their condition, and it may be sufficient at present to refer the reader in regard to the estates of Pergamene kings converted into imperial saltus, to *Ramsay,* " Geography of Asia Minor," 178 ; " Cities and Bishoprics of Phrygia," 284 ; *Rostowtzew.* Studien zur Geschichte des Kolonates (1910). As to Egypt, *P. Meyer,* " Philologus," lvii. ; and from another point of view, *Rostowtzew,* op. cit., cf. De Zulueta in my " Oxford Studies in Social and Legal History," i. Traces of rural

holdings and buildings probably connected with *saltus* are not
wanting, however, in the western half of the Empire, f.i. *Schumacher*,
" Römische Meierhöfe im Limesgebiet," Westdeutsche Zeitschrift,
1896, 1 ff. 17.   *J. Naher*, " Die baulichen Anlagen der Römer in dem
Zehntlanden Karlsruhe," 1883.   *Saltus* are sometimes mentioned in
inscriptions of the Germanic provinces.   See C. T. L. xii. 2250, 2251,
2272, 2604, *Pelham*, " The Imperial Domains and the Colonate "
(1890), p. 27.

69. *Beaudoin*, " Les grands domaines dans l'Empire romain,"
N. Revue historique de droit, 1898, 90, 95, 550.   *Henri Monnier*,
" Études sur le droit byzantin," Revue histor. de droit, 1900, 87 ff.

70. *Blumenstock*, 124 ;   *Seeck*, " Schatzungsordnung Diocletians,"
317.

71. *Lécrivain*, " Latifundium," 965, 966.

72. *Beaudoin*, " Les grands domaines," Nouvelle Revue hist. de
droit, 1897, 596, 599 ;   1898, 104.

73. *Beaudoin*, 1898, 211.

74. *Blumenstock*, 53.

75. The practice of illegal patronage (patrocinia) is growing fast,
and calls forth a number of prohibitive enactments, *H. Monnier*,
l. c.

76. Salvioli and Seeck have laid especial stress on this aspect
of historical development.

77. *Seeck*, " Die Pachtbestimmungen eines römischen Gutes, on
the Lex Manciana," iv. 37–40.

78. *Salvioli*, " Distribuzione," 533, 534 ff.

79. *Blumenstock*, 152, 184 ;   *Seeck*, " Schatzungsordnung Diocletians," 287.

80. *Salvioli*, " Distribuzione," 509.   It would be difficult to
exaggerate the social importance of " emphyteutic " practices and
customs at this juncture of the world's history.   We must not
merely hold on to the technical ἐμφύτευσις as sanctioned by
Zeno and Justinian, but also take into account the crop of emphyteutic tendencies in the constitution of hereditary and privileged
tenant-right in return for colonisation and cultivation of the soil, in
regard to small farmers and peasants."   *Mitteis*, " Zur Geschichte
der Erbpacht im Alterthum," 31 47, 61.

81. *Salvioli*, " Distribuzione," 508, 512, 518.

82. Some of the legal enactments as to the status of coloni are
collected in C. Just. xi. 48.   I have treated this subject at some length
in a Russian work on the " Origins of Feudalism in Lombard
Italy," Petersburg, 1881.

83. This side of the question has been mainly discussed by
Savigny, " Ueber das Colonat " (Kleinere Schriften, i.); *Huschke*,
" Ueber den Census des Augustus " ;   *Kuhn*, " Städtische und
bürgerliche Verfassung Roms," i. ; *Rodbertus*, " Ueber die Adscrip-
titier, Colonen und Inquilinen in die Jahrbücher für National-

ökonomie und Statistik," ii. ; *Heisterbergk*, "Entstehung des Colonats."

84. *Fustel de Coulanges*, "Le colonat" in the Recherches sur quelques problèmes d'histoire ; *Mommsen*, "Das Dekret des Commodus," Hermes, xv. 408 ; *Beaudoin*, "Les grands domaines," i. 693 ff. ; *Pelham*, "The Imperial Domains and the Colonate," 1891 ; *Schulten*, "V. colonatus" in the Dizzionario epigrafico of Ruggiero ; and Seeck, "Colonatus in *Pauly-Wissowa*, "Real-Encyclopædie des Klassischen Alterthums.

85. These points of view have been especially urged by Rodbertus, op. cit.

86. *Bloch*, in *Lavisse's* "Histoire de France," i. **444.**

87. In a sense the ascription of the coloni to the glebe was only one side of the universal process of ascription of the different classes of society to their callings and duties, as carried on by the later Empire. See especially *Kuhn*, "Städtische und Bürgerliche Verfassung Roms."

87a. Cf. my paper.

88. *Seeck*, "Die Pachtbestimmungen eines römischen Gutes in Afrika," Zeitsch. f. Soc. und W.g., vi. 368.

89. Commentaries on these most interesting inscriptions, first published by *M. Toutain* ("Revue historique de droit," 1897, and "Mémoires de l'Académie des Inscriptions," i. Série xi. 1 ff.), are given by *Schulten*, "Abhandlungen der Göttingener Gesellschaft der Wissenschaften," Ph.H.Kl., ii. ; *Beaudoin*, "Les grands domaines de l'empire Romain " ; *Seeck*, "Die Pachtbestimmungen eines römischen Gutes in Africa," and *Cuq*, "Le colonat partiaire en Afrique," Mémoires de l'Académie des inscriptions, is. xi. 87 ff. Cf. *Mitteis'* "Zur Geschichte der Erbpacht im Alterthum," 29. Cf. now the inscription of *Ain-el Djemala. Rostowzew*, "Studien zur Geschichte des römischen Kolonates." *Corcopino*, "Mélanges de l'école de Rome," 1906, and Klio, 1908 ; *Mispoulet*, "Nouv. Rev d'hist. de droit," 1907.

91. *M. Cuq* has made this out convincingly against Fustel de Coulanges, who tried to show that the *partiarius* was a peasant settled on the land without agreement, and legally at the mercy of his lord. Mém. de l'A. des Inscr., sér. xi. p. 117. The coloni of the African inscriptions are certainly leaseholders, though their lease may be formed by the very fact of their living on the land of the emperor or of a great man, and thereby submitting to the rule of the "lex saltus," the "perpetua forma," which was decreed for the cultivators of this land. The passage from explicit agreement to tacit acquiescence in a condition to which one succeeded by inheritance, and with which all one's means of subsistence were bound up, seems to have been the intermediate step between free leases and ascription to the glebe, and it is in this sense that I should like to interpret the suggestion that it is on the imperial

estates that the first germs of a colonate fixed to the soil appear.
From the legal point, the colonus of a great estate, as is shown, for
instance, by the Gasr Mezuar case (C.T.L. viii. Suppl. 14, 428), had
a lease, and was originally free to leave.   In reality he submitted to a condition which was framed for him and for his successors
once for all, unless they preferred to commit a kind of economic
suicide, and thus he became gradually the subject of the
landowner, whether emperor or a great man, or a city, and
this condition was legalised by general enactments in the fourth
century.

92. *Schulten,* "Libello dei coloni d'un domanio imperiale in Asia,"
Mittheilungen des deutschen archaeologischen Instituts in Rom,
xiii. (1898), p. 227.

93. *Fustel de Coulanges,* "Recherches sur quelques problèmes
d'histoire," 129 : Le propriétaire n'a pas distribué le domaine entier.
Il a fait de ce domaine deux parts : l'une qu'il a concédée aux colons,
l'autre qu'il s'est réservée.   La part des colons est subdivisé en
petits lots que chacun exploite pour son compte.   La part reservée
aux propriétaire est cultivée à l'aide des bras de ces mêmes colons "
L'alleu et le domaine rural, 85, 87.

94. "De colonis Illyricianis," C. Just. xi. 53 (A.D. 371).   Comp.
Seeck, "Pachtbestimmungen," Z.S.W.g., vi. on iv. 23-27 of the
Lex Manciana ; *Weber,* "Agrargeschichte," supposes that in the
fourth and fifth centuries there took place a general change from
payments in money and kind to services (Frohnden), but there is so
little evidence to support that suggestion that he is obliged to go
back to a passage of Columella de re rust., who advises the landlords
to look more sharply after the performance of work by the coloni
than after rents.   But Columella's work belongs to the very period
when rents in money and in kind were the rule, and it is hardly
proper to draw arguments from him as to a modification of the
conditions of tenure which is thought to have taken place in the
fourth and fifth centuries.   Besides, what Columella had in view
must have been a stringent supervision of the whole husbandry of
the coloni, who had to deliver part of the produce to the landlord.
As a matter of fact, such a supervision had to be carried on systematically.   Roman landlords did not take up the point of view that the
farmer's self-interest was a sufficient guarantee for the proper management of their plots, and the consequent profits of the landowner.   They used *custodes* and *exactores* to supervise the *coloni*
of their estates " (*Plinius,* "Epist." ix. 37 ; "Lex Manciana," iii.
15-17 ; *Cuq,* op. cit. 114).   Altogether the question as to the time
when the passage from farming for rent to cultivation burdened
with labour services was effected must remain open, but in making
conjectures on this subject we must not forget that a system based
on the employment of semi-servile labour has two sides.   If it
corresponds to an overbearing power of the lord over his subjects

and a state of natural husbandry on the one hand, it entails the rise of very extended and complex home-farm organisations on the other. Mommsen, with his usual profound insight, has in passing noticed the fact and the reason in his article on the management of the estates of the Roman See under Pope Gregory I. in the " Zeitschrift für Social- und Wirthschaftsgeschichte," i. 59. Gregory's correspondence gives us a welcome clue to the economic system on Italian soil at the close of the sixth century. And the main feature is quite clear —the land is parcelled out to small farmers for rents in money and in kind : labour services do not play any part in the arrangement. Of course, it would be wrong to generalise this instance and to apply it to Roman countries in general. But it would not be less wrong to generalise the few indications there are in regard to labour services in Roman times. The transition to services and home-farm cultivation must have been effected at an earlier date north than south of the Alps, as is shown, for instance, by the enactments of the Bavarian law. But even there it does not seem likely that a general advance towards the formation of great home farms was made at a time when economic culture and public order were rapidly sinking, and landowners had to use all sorts of inducements to keep up cultivation anyhow. It seems more probable that the tremendous social change involved in the process described was mostly achieved in the epoch of gradual reconstruction of European society which began with the Carolingian and kindred reforms, and culminated in the feudal system, although in that work of economic organisation leading institutions, such as the Church and Monarchy, largely drew on examples and traditions going back to the time of Imperial Rome. Cf. *Gummerus*, Die Frohnden der Kolonin. Helsingfors, 1906.

95. C.J.L. viii. Suppl. 1487. *Brunns-Mommsen*, " Fontes juris Romani Antiqui " (sixth ed.), 382. Commentary of *Schulten*, " Die Lex Hadriana de rudibus agris," Hermes, xxix. Comp. *Seeck*, " Die Pachtbestimmungen," Z.S.W.g. vi. or iv. 15–22 of the L. Manciana.

96. C.J.L. viii. 10,570. viii. Suppl. 14,428.

97. *W. Ramsay*, " The Historical Geography of Asia Minor," 173 ff. as to Ormeleis and the Cyllanean Estates in Phrygia. Rescript of Philippus to the κοινὸν τῶν Ἀραγουηνῶν παροίκων καὶ γεωργῶν τῶν ὑμετέρων. *J. G. C. Anderson*, " Journal of Hellenic Studies," xvii. 418 ; *Schulten*, " Libello di coloni d'un domanio Imperiale in Asia, Mittheilungen des deutschen Archaeologischen Institutes in Rom, xiii. 225 ff. ; *Haussoulier*, " Revue de philologie," 1901, 18 ff. It is out of the question in a book treating of English social history to go at any length into the remarkable but complex investigations of Rostowzew (see more especially his " Studien zur Geschichte des römischen Kolanates, 1910). It may be pointed out, however, that they establish conclusively the importance of Hellenistic precedents in the history of the colonate. The author shows, to begin

with, a large population of half-servile tenants (λαοί βασιλικοί) on the domains of the Ptolomies in Egypt and of the Seleucidæ in Asia Minor. He traces, secondly, the practice of compelling agriculturists to abide in their ἰδία, their place of origin to fiscal and administrative measures of these Hellenistic rulers. But it is hardly necessary to point out that we have to do in such a case only with one of the currents which made for serfdom during the Imperial period. A study of the Digest, especially of D. XIX, 2, shows that the lawyers of the second and third century A.D. considered the conditions of the *coloni* as governed in the main by the law of leases (*locatio conductio*), and therefore the problems as to the passage from free contract to servile status in the course of these and subsequent centuries still holds good. The process on private estates must have been influenced by the evolution on the estates of the Emperor, but it was not subordinated to the latter, and we have to account for it in connection with many other causes besides Hellenistic precedents. These and similar limitations do not detract, of course, in any way from the value of Professor Rostowzew's investigations.

98. The coloni of Araguene complained against fiscal officials (καισαριανοι), soldiers and city magnates, who seem to have worried them by quartering themselves on them, and exacting carriage services. *Schulten*, " Un libello," 243 ff. The *vicani* of Scaptaparene in Thracia seek redress in an exactly similar case through a certain Pyrrhus, miles compossessor. " Zeitschrift der Savigny, Stiftung für Richtsgeschichte, Romanistische Abtheilung," xii. p. 246. It is curious to hear that they openly threaten the patrimonial administration with a wholesale exodus : ἐπεὶ οὖν οὐκέτι δυνάμεθα φέρειν τὰ βάρη καὶ ὡς ἀληθῶς κινδυνεύομεν ὑπὲρ οἱ λοιποί τόδε καὶ ἡμεῖς προλιπεῖν τοὺς προγονικοὺς θεμελίους . . . Ἐάν γε βαρώμεθα, φευξόμεθα ἀπὸ τῶν οἰκείων καὶ μεγίσταν ξημίαν τὸ ταμεῖον περιβληθήσεται.

99. *Fustel de Coulanges*, Recherches, 40 ; *Schulten*, s. v. colonatus in *Ruggiero's* " Dizionario epigrafico."

100. *Schulten*, " Libello dei coloni," 232. Tне κοινὸν τῶν Ἀραγουηνῶν γεωργῶν καὶ παροίκων has already been mentioned. The villagers of the Cyllanean estates in Phrygia formed colleges for the worship of Ζεὺς Σαβάσιος, and it is not likely that these associations should have been restricted to purely sacral purposes. *Schulten*, " Libello," 239 ; *Ramsay*, " Cities and Bishroprics of Phrygia," i. 283. In the light of these facts, the statement of *Beaudoin*, " Les grands domaines," N. R. Revue de droit, 1897, 566 : " la plebs saltus ne possède aucune constitution municipale ni magistraux locaux," seems inadequate. Comp. 1898, p. 745. The elected local magistrates were called magistri in the West, and προάγοντες in the East.

101. *Siculus Flaccus*, " De conditione agrorum," 157, 9 : compascua, quod est genus quasi subsecivorum sive loca, quae proximiquique vicini, id est qui eorum contingunt pascua communiter

habent. Id. 150, 12 : quorundam vicinorum aliquas silvas quasi publicas, immo proprias quasi vicinorum esse comperimus, neque quisquam in eis cedendi pascendique jus habere, nisi vicinos, quorum sunt. *Isidor*, " Origines," xv. 13, 9 : compascuus ager dictus, qui a divisionibus agrorum relictus est ad pascendum communiter vicinis.

102. Cod. Theod. quoted in n. 63. Considerable stress has been laid in the history of the Eastern Empire on a supposed contrast between the settlement of individual coloni (πάροικοι) in the VI. century, as exemplified by the Novellæ of Justinian, and the communal organisation of the peasantry, as recognised by the Νόμος γεωργικόε of the Iconoclast Emperors and by later charters. Russian scholars have tried to explain this change by the influx of Slavonic tribes. *Ouspensky*, " On the Slavonic Community in the Byzantine Empire." Journ. of Ministry of Public Instr. vol. 225, p. 30. More moderately *Vassilievsky*, on the " Agrarian legislation of the Iconoclasts," Journal of the Ministry of Public Instruction, vol. 199, p. 258 (Russian). " Materials for the Social History of the Byzantine Empire," ibid., vol. 202, p. 160. Comp. *Zachariæ von Lingenthal*, " Geschichte des griechisch-römischen Rechts." The *vici* of the Code Theodosianus and the recent discoveries as to the organisation of the Asiatic *saltus* shows that in this case, as in the western instances, communal institutions arose independently of ethnographic causes on the soil of Roman provinces as well as on soil conquered or colonised by Germans and Slavs. These institutions were generated by several facts which recur in all the instances of which we have been speaking : tribal survivals, extensive semi-pastoral methods of husbandry, settlements which involved a good deal of intermixture of rights, the necessity for territorial lords to organise their districts and possessions, not on the principle of the steward's absolute rule, but on that of tributary self-government. No need to add that there were many varieties and gradations in these communal arrangements, but it would be difficult to attempt precise definitions and distinctions in regard to their obscure origins. Enough, if we may discern the general direction of development. Cf. *De Zulueta*, Patronage in the later Roman Empire in my " Oxford Studies in Social and Legal History," I, 1909.

103. The traces of hamlet settlements are still visible on the English maps of western counties. *Maitland*, " Domesday and Beyond," 16. These clusters are especially characteristic of Wales and Cornwall, or of parts freshly conquered from the Celts. See, for example, the description of the Welsh strip in the border of Gloucestershire, " Domesday," i. 162. Comp. *Taylor*, " The Domesday of Gloucestershire," 202.

104. *Meitzen*, " Wanderungen," etc. i. 288 ff. 320. See the map of the neighbourhood of Brescia, given and explained by *Schulten*, " Römische Flureintheilung," Abhandlungen der K. Gesellschaft

der Wissenschaften in Göttingen, Phil. hist. Klasse, N. F. ii. 7.

105. To illustrate the manner in which such institutions and customs are formed by the force of circumstances, in surroundings where it would be impossible to trace any marked influence of Teutonism, I should like to point to the very remarkable case of land arrangements in the Roussillon. They have been described with great fulness and exactitude by M. Brutails. Communal rights and institutions arise, as it were, by themselves for the regulation of a husbandry and of a land-holding largely dependent on pastoral pursuits and the temporary occupation of waste. See especially pp. 243–253. Comp. 262 : les mœurs agricoles du temps, la multiplicité des troupeaux, les complications résultant du droit de vaine pâture devaient entrainer journellement des différends au sujet des dommages causés par les bestiaux dans les propriétés particulières, sur les berges des ruisseaux, aux arbres, aux haies, etc. Ce fut pendant de longs siècles, c'est encore de nos jours dans les montagnes, la source de la plupart des procès. Comp. Brutail's remarks on the popular institutions, termed *subreposats de la horta*.

106. For example, " L'alleu et le domaine rural," 438 : " le droit du propriétaire est sans limites et sans réserves. Ni la foret, ni le marais, ni le sol inculte ne lui échappent," 172. " Pas une seule ligne qui mentionne un usage commun de terres ou une communeauté de village. Pas une seule fois avant le x. siècle un mot qui signifie communeauté. Pas une seule fois vous ne voyez les gens d'un village se réunir spontanément, délibérer entre eux, prendre une décision quelconque." I can but endorse the remarks of Blumenstock, 47, when he points out the " Kritiklosigkeit von Fustel de Coulanges überall, wo es sich um Bodenrechtsverhältnisse handelt, die sich von dem sogenannten vollen Eigenthum durch irgend etwas unterscheiden." The celebrated French *savant* directed a furious onslaught against the attempts of German scholars to vindicate a village community introduced into mediæval Europe by the Teutonic invasion, but he would have certainly resented even more the notion that village communities were living or forming themselves under Roman rule. He was clear in his mind about the origin of all property in land from private ownership.

107. Special quotations are not needed, as the whole book on the " English Village Community " is devoted to that theme. I will just point to pp. 267–269. The stress is laid on the power of organisation of the lord, which cuts short the assertion of individual rights, and welds the peasantry into a servile or semi-servile community for the purposes of the cultivation of the domain and of the imposition of burdens.

Second Book

THE OLD ENGLISH PERIOD

CHAPTER I

THE ENGLISH CONQUEST

I. General View of English Settlement

THE settlement of Saxons, Angles, Jutes and Frisians
in Great Britain modified considerably the history of this
The Course of country. It could not do away with all
the Invasions the acquirements of the Roman period,
it did not lead to a wholesale destruction or flight
of the provincial population and to the formation of
Teutonic communities on a clean slate. But no more
likelihood is there that the appearance on the scene of this
powerful new factor produced only a modification of the
upper stratum of society or the substitution of a few Teutonic masters for a few Romanised masters over the heads
of the British population, and that it did not interrupt the
continuity of provincial institutions, and especially of the
Roman estates. There are many indications of a very
thorough change in the habits and conditions of life and of
a very peculiar course of development at this historical
juncture. The main facts have been pointed out so often
that it will suffice for our purpose to recall them in a general
way to the mind of the reader. It is clear that the influx
of people of Teutonic blood must have been considerable.
The best warranty for such a conclusion lies, on one hand,
in the complete victory of Teutonic speech over Romance
and Celtic, a victory especially striking in regard to local
nomenclature,[1] on the other, in the extant historical information as to the protracted struggle and the very gradual
progress of the conquerors. The onsets of pirates against
the Saxon shore in the third and fourth centuries must already have left certain deposits of foreign settlers behind

them, in the same way as the analogous attacks of Franks, Goths, Burgundians, etc., on Gaul introduced *læti* and federated barbarians into the province long before the Roman Government gave way. Still, these preliminary colonies did not play an important part in the history of the island just because it was an island, and the silver streak rendered the wholesale introduction of entire tribes more difficult. But after the withdrawal of the legions, a real immigration began. The invaders had again and again to draw on the support of their kinsmen on the continent, and, on the other hand, the northern Germanic tribes, which had stood too far back to take an active part in the looting and the land-grabbing in the West and South, poured in one population wave after the other into the opening which presented itself in the north-western corner of the Empire. It has been conjectured that women and children were often brought over; and it is significant, in regard to the number of the invaders and the character of the movement, that Bede mentions specifically that the home of the Angles on the continent was left desolate and empty in consequence of the migration of its population to Britain.[2] This remark, although certainly not based on careful census returns, gives testimony which is sufficiently weighty and definite for our purpose : it shows that our best informed and almost contemporary witness considered the invasions in the light of a migration of entire tribes, and not as the foundation of stray colonies by reckless adventurers. Nor can there be any doubt that there occurred much direct destruction of property and uprooting of institutions. The Chronicle preserves traditions of several cases of sacks of towns, which ended in their complete ruin for a time or even permanently : the cases of Anderida, Uriconium, are well known, and the ruins of Roman walls and houses on the sites of Verulam, Rochester, Lincoln, York, etc., speak as loudly as the chance entries of the Chronicle.[3] It has been noticed, also, that in most cases when Roman villas come to light, traces of fires show that they had been ruthlessly destroyed and pillaged. And, apart from the direct damage done to

the products of Roman life and civilisation, we have to
take even more into account the indirect effect produced
by such inroads and catastrophes, the loosening of social
ties consequent upon them, the decay of institutions which
had sprung into being in an entirely different atmosphere,
and required some order to fulfil their destination... It was
not easier to uphold an advanced cultivation of the soil and
intricate relations between landlords and coloni than it was
to proceed with a satisfactory coinage, lively trade intercourse, or fine literature. It has been noticed already that
the political strain of the later Empire made itself felt
in a universal lowering of standards on all sides, in a very
perceptible barbarisation of Rome and of the provinces.[4]
There can be no doubt that the actual downfall of the
Imperial power and the effect of the appearance of barbarian conquerors and settlers led to a rapid reduction of
the requirements and means of culture. And, if it is rightly
urged, on the other hand, that the barbarians had not the
power nor the interest to destroy entirely the commodities
accumulated in the provinces and that, on the contrary,
they must have tried to possess themselves of goods and
men, of capital and machinery, of useful arrangements
and skilled labour, this observation will go to explain
the passage from one period to the other, but will
not lessen the importance of the catastrophe itself;
because, quite apart from ill will, brutality, and wanton
destruction, the disruption of the old order of things
was an indirect consequence of the change in the main facts
on which political and social existence depended. It is
not necessary to burn a man in order to kill him : a thrust
through some vital part of his body may be sufficient to
destroy an organism, and the social dismemberment consequent on the invasions was by itself fatal to ancient institutions, and necessitated new departures : people had to gc
back, as it were, to a more primordial condition of society.
Again, the fact on which we have been laying stress in the
preceding chapter—the fact of the very incomplete
Romanisation of the Britons—must have played an important part in determining subsequent development.

Instead of having to cope with a society which was romanised to the core, and which no amount of disruption could bereave of its Romance character, the English conquerors fell upon a mass of people many of whom still talked Celtic, still kept up many Celtic views on kinship and clanship, on the appropriation of land and the modes of its cultivation, on tribute, etc.

The result was a much more thorough predominance of barbarian customs and institutions than that which obtained **Teutonic Stamp** in neighbouring Gaul. We shall never learn to **of Old English** what extent the English race, as founded in **History** those days, is in actual descent by blood the product of Teutonic or of Celtic forefathers, any more than we can say in what precise proportion the blood of Teutons, of Slavonic Wends, of Lithuanian Prussians, and Baltic Finns is mixed in the bodies of the present citizens of Prussia. It would be also a hopeless task to trace in what way the psychological traits of the English people have been affected by the mixture of its component parts in one mould. Happily, these unprofitable disquisitions are not necessary to understand that in the beginning of the Old English period the predominating population of the island was very much alike in its habits and institutions to the tribes of Germany on the right bank of the Rhine,[4a] and that it was gradually drawn away from them on a new and independent course, not so much by the admixture of Celtic and Roman blood, as by the peculiar aims and conditions of its history. Renouncing speculations as to the number of Britons which survived under the sway of the Saxons and Angles, we may rest satisfied with the undoubted fact that they increased in numbers towards the West and were most numerous in the territories acquired by the West Saxons in the seventh and eighth centuries and in Strathclyde. Let us merely take note that the England of the eighth century is a Teutonised country, forming a marked contrast with Gaul, which, though conquered, was developing Romance speech and true to many Roman customs.[5] In both countries the downfall of Imperial power and of the centralised and powerful bureaucracy proceeding from it

led to the subversion of the financial system, which had
played such a prominent part in the life of the provinces :
it came to be paralyzed if not actually abolished in the
hands of the barbarians.   At the same time, the confusion
of political and private interests, and the introduction of
numerous institutions of public and private law peculiar
to the barbarians, produced profound changes and necessitated a thorough remodelling of society.   But the stamp
of the Teutons is laid in a very marked manner on the
language of England, on her political and legal institutions,
even on her ecclesiastical life, in which Christianity had to
be engrafted afresh after the cataclysm of the invasions.
No more likelihood is there that in the economic arrangements of society the traditions of the Empire should have
flowed on without disturbance, though one may be prepared to come across all kinds of remnants and survivals
of them.

Besides all the facts which may be adduced from
the sources of the early English period in support of
Danish Invasion the above conception of the Anglo-Saxon
invasion there are valuable indications as to
its character to be obtained from later occurrences,
if they are interpreted with sufficient caution.   The
invasions and settlements of the Angles, Saxons,
Jutes, and Frisians had hardly ceased when a new
series of migrations began—the migrations of tribes coming
from still more northern parts—from Jutland, the Danish
isles, and Norway.   The raids and settlements of these
people in the eighth, ninth, and tenth centuries do not
seem to have differed materially from those of their predecessors of the fifth, sixth, and seventh centuries.   If anything, they were less obstinate and less successful.   But
still their course and results disclose not chance onslaughts
or successes of stray adventurers, but a continuous flow of
Scandinavian immigrants and settlements, which transformed the social aspect of the north-east of England.
As the difference in speech and customs between English
and Danes was not great, they amalgamated easily into
one whole, which showed no discordant features and no

violent change. But there cannot be any talk in regard to
the tract of the Five burghs, or even of the wider Danelaw,
of a mere substitution of one set of lords for another and
of a slight modification of the surface of society, leaving
untouched its deeper layers of economic organisation and
working populations.[6] ᕁ Even less reason is there to assume
such unruffled continuity in the case of the more thorough
inroads of the Angles and Saxons.

II. RANKS AND CLASSES

The first question which requires consideration in regard
to early English society applies to the distinctions to be
drawn between its classes. We must try to make out in
what relation the conquerors of Britain stood to each
other and came to stand to the conquered population ;
whether there arose an aristocracy among them, and, if so,
on what lines ? On the other hand, what indications
are there as to the position of subjected and dependent
people ?

A very valuable glimpse as to the initial arrangement of
Anglo-Saxon society is afforded by the laws of Æthelberht,
Kentish Laws of Kent, the king who took the first step to
introduce Christianity among the heathen
invaders. These laws, though directly applying merely
to one, or possibly to two, of the little States created on
British soil by the invading tribes, reflect a condition
of things which may be fairly taken as an example of
similar arrangements in the neighbouring tribal States, if
details are left out of the account.

This statement of Kentish customary law of the close of
the sixth century records a division of the people which
falls in a striking manner into line with the recorded
characteristics of German, especially Low German, legal
custom. In this State, containing a mixed population of
Jutes and Saxons, we find a threefold division of the people

into *earls, ceorls, læts,* besides the slaves, a division exactly
corresponding to the threefold division which formed a
distinctive feature of the Saxon, Frisian, and Thuringian
system on the Continent, in contrast with the Frankish and
the High German (Bavarian, Alemannic). The three orders
were termed in the vernacular German dialects *ethelingi,
frilingi, lazzi.*[7] The privileged position of the aristocratic
class in Kent was expressed by the fact that fines for
transgression against them were twofold in comparison
with those of the free,[8] while the price paid if an earl
was killed seems to have been three times greater than that
of a freeman : the ceorl of Kent was paid for with 100 gold
solidi to his kindred and the earl with 300 solidi, at least at
the end of the seventh century.[9]

This reminds one most of the Frisian scheme, in which
the noble, however, got only twice as much as the freeman all through, and of the Thuringian, where he got a
threefold wergeld. Besides the price paid to the kindred, there was a fine for the infraction of peace (*fredus*)
rendered to the king, and in the case of the freeman it
amounted to one half of the payment to the kindred and
to one third of the whole wergeld, exactly as with the
Franks, bringing up the entire wergeld to 150 solidi in
gold.[10] Within these chief distinctions of rank there were
many grades, three varieties of læts being mentioned
expressly, while there is also some indication of several
degrees among the ceorls.[11] This feature may again
be illustrated by a reference to the Alemannic and Lombard codes, which divide the free tribesmen into several
subdivisions, as best, medium, and minor men ;[12] in
this way we get instructive indications of the attempt
of the barbarians to appraise as exactly as possible differences of birth, wealth, and influence noticeable among
their kindreds.

The typical freeman of the Kentish laws is the *ceort,* the
man who has no special distinction to claim, but stands in
the middle rank of society : he is referred to when general
rules are laid down.[13] Without carrying any modern
notions of democratic freedom into the description of this

main class, we may well surmise that it owed its independent
and important position to the fact that the bulk of the
warriors who had conquered the Kentish shore belonged to
it, that it formed the mainstay of the tribe in the struggle
with the neighbouring states and tribes. Of the earls we
cannot tell much, unless we borrow our characteristics
from the analogous cases on the Continent, where we find
the ethelings to be a tribal nobility, risen to the top of society
through the predominant position of leading kindreds in
regard to government and religion.[14] The *læts* form a
very interesting item in this social arrangement, and,
although mentioned only in a couple of enactments, present
several well-established traits which are worth attending to.
The name speaks for itself. It was applied concurrently
with *litus, lazzus* and *aldio* to the descendants of conquered
tribes which retained personal freedom and certain tribal
rights, but were reduced to the position of tributary dependants of the conquerors. Some of them may have come
from over the sea with the freemen and ethelings, but we
have also evidently to look to that class to find the place
of the remnants of the Romano-Celtic population of Kent.
It must be noticed that some of these people appear to have
held a very tolerable position, as we find them provided
with the substantial wergeld of 80 shillings. These were,
however, the best among them; and by the side of these
we find representatives of the same order, marked by the
modest prices of 60 and 40 shillings.[15]

Altogether, the whole system, with its various social
degrees, gathered into three main divisions, appears primarily as an arrangement for estimating personal rank
and tribal qualifications : we do not perceive in it any
distinct elements of landed property, or special connection
with royalty.

Later laws present many memories and survivals of the
arrangements discovered at starting : it may even happen
that a king, speaking in general words of his
people, still refers to them as ceorls and
earls — the free and the noble.[16] In the
laws of Alfred the ceorl is still taken throughout as the

West Saxon and Mercian Wergelds

typical freeman,[17] and when wergelds and fines are mentioned without any direct reference to the rank of the person whose claims they are meant to satisfy, they apply primarily to freemen in the simplest signification of the term, and to the lowest rank, namely, to the ceorls. A mere reference to an increase of fines, according to the rise in social status, may have been deemed sufficient to guide the wise men of the courts in regard to other cases.[18] But the usual practice is to differentiate society into three classes, of which the two superior may be gathered into one main division. These classes are : ceorls, common freemen, with a were of 200 silver shillings, sithcundmen, with a were of 600 shillings, and king's thegns, with a were of 1,200 shillings.[19] The sums are given for Wessex and Mercia, and the actual value of the fines varies according to the difference of currency between these provinces, while Kent remains apart, with its ancient system based on gold currency, but the enactments of Ine and Alfred represent undoubtedly a later development of customary law than those of Æthelberht, and are chiefly interesting in that respect.[20] The new element introduced into the estimates of social condition is on the very face of it the element of patronage : it takes the place of tribal nobility, and creates an aristocracy of its own. Both the twelvehyndman and the sixhyndman are *gesithcundmen*, followers of chiefs, and enjoy their privileged position in regard to *were* and *wite*, and in other respects, by reason of the exalted patronage bestowed on them. These classes are commonly divided according to their very different appreciation, and, of course, it is important to know why they are divided. It has been suggested that the sixhyndman is in truth a man of the same *status* as the twelvehyndman, that is, a king's thane, but a Welsh one or of Welsh extraction, while the highest *were* is reserved to the thanes of English birth.[21] This may have been one of the cases in which 600 *were* arose, but hardly the only one. The 600 shillings division is mostly mentioned in connection with a scale of *weres* which starts from the purely English wergeld of

200 shillings for the ceorl, omitting the Welsh wergeld of 120 shillings, so that we are led to suppose that the higher rungs of the ladder are not meant in these cases for Welsh people, but for English. And there seem to be several classes which are naturally indicated for this position, namely, thanes, military followers of lesser rank than the vassals of the king, on the one hand; the sons and relations gathered round both, on the other—this last necessarily a rather numerous class; and the laws give us some indications that this was so.[22] The *læts* mentioned in the laws of Æthelberht disappear, but, instead of them, we hear of *wealhs* of different rank, the successors of the provincial population, of which those of lower degree took up a position not unlike the one formerly held by the Kentish læts.[23]

The remodelling of society under the influence of patronage is certainly a most characteristic and important process,

Patronage

and it is well worth while to point out the traits bearing on its course and origins. We find the mutual tie of protection and service spreading in all parts of society, among common people and among powerful people. On the one hand, the *hlaford*, the private lord, becomes an almost necessary protector in the case of freemen of lower degree, especially of those who do not own land : a definite part of the fine in case of murder is reserved to him by the side of the fine to the kindred, and he is looked upon in this way as supplementing the kindred for the defence of individuals against violence.[24] He appears also to help them in case of litigation, but, on the other hand, he is made to look after police and is bound to support the Government in watching the conduct of his clients, and producing them, if need be, before the courts of justice.[25] It is also clear that some service, either personal or pecuniary, has to be rendered by the clients in return for the protection and authority of the hlaford.[26] In like manner, in the higher regions of life, kings and great men look for the provision of effective military and administrative service, not only and not so much to the ordinary obligations of the fyrd and of suit of court, but to the special connections formed by patronage, to the service

of their followers, their gesiths and thanes. In principle
the tie is a personal one ; the follower may often live with
his lord or the king, take his meal in his hall, ride forth on
his expeditions, and fulfil his errands as a personal attendant,
provided for in regard to arms, horses, and other requirements
of knightly existence. But as this kind of service becomes
more important and systematic, the followers receive
land on conditions closely resembling the continental practices of beneficiary endowment, and, on the other hand,
those who hold land in larger quantity get drawn, whether
they will or not, into the class of followers, which develops
gradually into a professional organisation of officials and
knights. Besides the necessities of administration, the
marked changes in the methods of warfare had much to do
with this process. The specially equipped warrior, completely armed, expert in riding and ready to serve for
longer periods, was taking the chief place in warfare, while
the levy of the fyrd became more and more cumbersome
and inappropriate for pitched battles and protracted
expeditions. The freemen, of whom the bulk of the fyrd
was composed, had, in consequence of the increase of the
population and the permanent settlement on the land, become small householders encumbered with large families,
and by necessity more bent on tilling their fields than on
" earning wounds " and seeking booty in war. No wonder
that a special well-equipped force became necessary to
stiffen the unwieldy and unsoldierly gatherings of the
fyrd. The rise of the professional military class from
the large body of freemen is actually dealt with in a systematic spirit in enactments and customary law. Again
and again we come across statements that the rise in
social prosperity, the " thriving " of a person leads from
the condition of the common freeman, the ceorl, to that of
the sithcundman and king's thane, and the following stages
may be marked in this process.[27] The wealh gets to equal
the ceorl if he owns a hide, the normal family holding, for
which he pays the king's tribute (gafol).[28] His were still remains less than that of an English ceorl (120 shillings instead
of 200), but the condition of " gafol gelder," of the man

paying tribute from his land to the king, and bound to
come to the fyrd, the national levy, seems to be common
to both.[29] The next main division is marked off by
the holding of five hides, which entitles the Englishman
to a were of 1,200 shillings, and the Welshman to one of
600 shillings, and places them in the position of military
followers connected with the king by the ties of direct or
indirect patronage.[30] The case of the lesser wergeld of
600 shillings is not presented with sufficient clearness in
regard to born Englishmen, but must be assumed to have
formed a kind of minor subdivision within the group.

The Estate of   The relation of both classes to the land
the Soldier   was a matter of first-rate importance, not
only for themselves, but also for the government of
those times, such as it was.   The laws of Ine give
interesting glimpses of the internal life of the social
group formed by the estate of the professional soldier.
He is considered as a pioneer of economic progress and
colonisation as well.   When he gets his land he is not
merely looked to by the king for military support, the
maintenance of order, and the collection of such tribute
as might be incumbent on the hides passed to him, but he is
made responsible for the success of agricultural management
on his estate.   His land is more than a commodity for
himself : it is also the groundwork of political duties, and
therefore not to be considered simply in the light of private
ownership.   As a matter of fact, it may probably be *loaned*
by customary process, perhaps even booked according to
stricter and more solemn rules, but its possession carries
with it for the thane an obligation to *settle* it, to provide it with tenants for efficient cultivation, and certain
conditions are laid down, which make neglect to attain
this aim an offence against the king, who gave the land.
If a thane has received 20 hides of land, he ought not to
leave this benefice of his without showing that at least
twelve of them were provided with tenants, were settled ;
if he had but three, one and a half at least had to be given
back as settled.[31]

The same laws go further, and give some directions as to

the mode of treating peasant settlers on such estates ;
Ceorls and naturally enough, as the thane appears only
Geburs in the light of a conditional occupier of
land, and the settlement itself is effected not merely for his
private profit, but also in the lasting interest of the king.
In this connection remarkable rules are laid down, which
distinguish between two classes of *coloni* on those royal
estates : those who hold dependent land, but are not
provided with the very homesteads in which they have
to live are to pay rent, while those who get their dwellings from the lord, are also to perform work.[32] From
other sources we may surmise that the people who had
to take yardlands, generally quarters of a hide, and
to settle on them, the *gebúrs,* as they were often called,
became gradually attached to their holdings, not only by
the fact that they received a place of abode and land for tillage, but also because the stock they had to start with in
their farming was often provided for them.[33] But their
relation to the lord as described in Ine's enactments is one
of contract, and is placed under the direct supervision of
the government. All these details are full of interest and
meaning : they show that on the one hand the soil of the
kingdom was being pieced out in large patches to provide
for lay-thanes and mass-thanes, for people of the military and
administrative profession, and for people of the ecclesiastical profession.[34] The land-books supply evidence that in
consequence of these loans and grants vast numbers of freemen who had held their land directly under the king, had
paid tribute to him and attended the fyrd with his ealdormen and sheriffs, came to be placed under the intermediate
lordship of military or ecclesiastical magnates,[35] while other
freemen, who had no land of their own, or sat crowded
on their own land, entered into different arrangements with
the great landowners as dependent tenants. It would be
wrong, however, to generalise these observations, which disclose the working of important processes, but do not warrant
any exhaustive classification of ranks. Neither the existence
of thanes and churches, which owned land by scores of
hides, nor the occurrence of *coloni,* who, though personally

free, are placed in a condition of indebted dependants on great men's land, make it certain or probable that the ceorls as independent but small landowners burdened with public tribute had disappeared, or that the legal status of the ceorl as the common freeman, with rights analogous to those of the noble or of the royal follower, though smaller in amount, had become an anachronism.[36] On the contrary, even the administrative enactments that have been handed down to us in Ine's code testify in many ways to the elements of freedom and citizenship in the life of those portions of the peasantry which are directly concerned in the precepts as to the settlements of colonists. The districts mentioned are and remain virtually royal, and one of the aims of the series of enactments is to connect the peasants with the estates, and to place them out of reach of arbitrary exactions and sudden personal changes of the lords to whom the estates had been entrusted. A second feature has also to be noted, namely, that one important class of tenants is composed of men who do not get their dwellings and, probably, their outfit, from the lord. Evidently people are meant who live in their own " flets " though their land has been subjected to a neighbouring thane's superiority. Of course, such transitional conditions are apt to develop, and their development may lead far ; but what we witness in the laws of Ine is not the goal, but the beginnings, of such a development ; and by the side of the *gebúr* who has taken a yardland by contract, and of the ceorl who has to pay rent to a lord, we have to keep in mind the existence of the *ceorl* as a free husbandman holding a hide, and cultivating it with the help of his family and slaves, paying tribute only to the king, and fully able to thrive to the possession of several hides and to the dignity of a thane. The difference in his original position and in that of the *gebúr* and of the dependent ceorl would not be reflected in the wergeld, as all would be paid for with 200 shillings, but this is merely a proof that even the ceorl who had fallen into dependency had come from a free stock and retained very important characteristics of his descent.

The effect of this process is illustrated in a remarkable **Effect of Norse** manner by the third stage reached by **Invasion** class distinctions, a stage characteristic of what may be termed the Danish period of English history, ranging from the close of the ninth to the beginning of the eleventh century, and culminating in the rule of Canute.

The terrible struggle with the Norsemen undoubtedly contributed to deepen distinctions and to develop the peculiar attributes of the classes, because both tribute and professional military service became obligations of primary importance, which had to be enforced at all costs, and came to be regarded as the main features of social organization.[37]

Already in the undated laws of the North people, which most probably belong to Halfdan's kingdom of York, a characteristic attempt is made to bring Northmen and Englishmen together under the operation of one wergeld tariff; and the arrogant superiority of the Northern conquerors expresses itself in the fact that whereas the chief English ranks are appreciated in the usual manner in Northumbrian currency (thrymsas), the Northern Hauldr is reckoned to be worth twice as much as the English secular or ecclesiastical thane (4,000 thrymsas instead of 2,000, or in Wessex shillings 2,000 instead of 1,200). Thus a special distinction is created for the North people which towers over all other ranks.[38] The treaty between Alfred and Guthrum is more modest, in so far as it places the Northmen on the same footing with the English twelvehyndmen, that is the men of highest degree, the military and ecclesiastical followers of the king. Still, the main idea, that even the simplest Danish soldier is worth as much as an Englishman of high rank is quite clear.[39] Apart from the sense of national superiority, the reason for such an exalted estimate consisted in the fact that the Dane as member of the " Army " (here) was certainly not less a professional soldier than the West Saxon thane, although he was not provided for in the same way : he had to rely not on land-endowment and settled capital,

but on the power of exaction and domination which was
exercised by the army as a whole. But this equalisation
of the professional soldiers on both sides led to curious
consequences in regard to the internal class-divisions
of both nations. All the free Northmen taking part in
the army are assumed to be equal and *haulds*, although
in their home in Scandinavia there were quite a number of
distinct social groups, and the invaders certainly belonged to
very different sets. The "army" and victory had made them
equals and raised them to the highest standing, but as no
amount of victorious arrogance could achieve an equality in
wealth and consideration, it is quite clear that most of these
haulds with four mark wergelds were in truth petty people,
and likely to shrink even more when the army came to be dis-
banded. On the other hand, the social distinctions which
had grown on the soil of old custom among English
folk had to be rearranged in accordance with the rough
contrasts imposed by the treaties, and we find that the
intermediate shades of sixhyndmen and wealhs are disregarded, and one main distinction left standing : the
professional class on the one hand with its 1,200 shillings
were, and the tribute-paying peasant on the other with a
200 shillings *were*. These last are termed ceorls sitting
on tributary land, and freedmen, leysings, are equated with
them. The arrangement is a very rough one. and it would
not do to argue too much from it in regard to the position
of particular sections of the community. It is not clear,
for example, how the 120 shilling and the 80 or 20 shilling
wealhs would henceforth be taxed ; it is more than probable
that of the pesantry some would be raised to the value of
twelvehyndmen, at least in cases of reckoning with Danes,
while others would be placed on the footing of tributary
ceorls. But the general tendency to make a broad distinction
between warriors and peasants is unmistakable, and cannot
but be regarded as an ominous sign of the times and a powerful factor in the process of social differentiation. It is
kept up in later enactments. The compact between
Ethelred and Olaf Tryggvason (993) makes all free English
and Norse people alike worth twenty-five pounds, that is,

gives them all the high *were* of 1,200 shillings, but does not even mention the peasantry. Canute is more explicit : he addresses his people of different nationality, as all the twelvehynd and all the twyhyndmen of his kingdom, in this way insisting on the lines drawn by the former treaties.[40]

It should be noted that the more we advance in point of time, the less pregnant the meaning of the *weres* and *wites* becomes. On the one hand, tribal relations and kinship are more and more disarranged : the enforcement of fines and the liability to take part in paying or craving them get more and more uncertain and inconvenient, and even legislation itself sometimes turns its enactments against the fundamental principles of the system. King Edmund, for instance,[41] enters the lists against the practice of obligatory participation of kinsmen in the payment of weres ; and as weres were never designed to be paid by single individuals, the loosening of the responsibility of the kindred meant nothing less than the decay of the system of pecuniary compensation. On the other hand, capital and corporal punishment, imprisonment, exile, personal amercements and fines imposed on bodies of men knitted together in frank-pledge or territorial joint responsibility develop and increase with the rise of police supervision cn the part of the Government. And in the case of the Norsemen themselves, whatever their condition may have been at home, it would have been very difficult to arrange them according to were-paying and were-craving kindreds in England. In this way the high price came to be a terroristic measure and not a genuine estimate.

In consequence of the remarkable transformation of which we have been speaking, new terms arise and new definitions are sought for the different social groups. The sixhyndman disappears entirely, as I have already said. The ancient name of ceorl becomes rarer, while *gebúr* often takes its place, to indicate the dependent cultivator of the great man's land. And a famous expression of the feudal age makes its appearance. *Tunesman* points to the ceorl as member of the village community,[42] in opposition to the landowner moving in another and a higher sphere, the sphere of the king's court and of the king's riding followers. The position of these various classes and their actual importance in the general economy of the country, however, will become apparent only after we have examined the grouping of the population round certain centres, and its organisation for different purposes of social life.

CHAPTER II

THE GROUPING OF THE FOLK

I. THE KINDRED

IN any order of society the individual cannot live entirely by himself, is not self sufficient, but has to rely in many respects on the support and help of his fellows ; and though the forms of co-opera-

Agnatism

tion were not so varied and did not produce so many results in ancient as in modern times, the existing groups were more powerful in their action. The single man was weaker, in proportion to the deficiencies of his knowledge and skill, on the one hand, and to the scanty development of the State, on the other. It would be wrong to assume that communalistic and co-operative factors entirely subordinated individuality : it certainly had many opportunities and openings for asserting itself, but the share of natural groups, of associations arising and growing by themselves, apart from direct arrangement and contract, was very powerful in the life of the people.

The most inevitable and natural association of the kind was provided by the kindred spreading from the family. The kindred of the German tribes was more loosely con-stituted than that of the Celts, the Romans, or the Greeks ; it did not develop so consistently on the rigid lines of agnatic clan organisation ; we do not see it on British soil under distinct leaders or acknowledged elders. Still it entailed a powerful cohesion of individuals, and far-reaching limitations of their freedom of action in many important respects. It was agnatic in its main constitution. Every person belonged to his father's kindred ; even the lawfully married wife was not separated from it from the point of

view of social responsibility and protection, though her
marriage had brought her into a new economic sphere.
Her chief avengers and helpers in trouble were still her
father and her own agnatic relations, not those of her husband.[1]   Again, though a man expected support in case of
aggression and trouble from different quarters, calling his
lord and the fellows of his craft as well as his maternal kinsmen, sworn-brothers, foster-brothers, etc., to his assistance,
his mainstay for the exaction and the payment of fines, for
the swearing of oaths, provision in case of destitution, and
watching over the interests of his offspring after his
death, was found in his paternal kindred.[2]   In the most
striking instance of co-operation, in the payment and recep-
tion of the *were*, the relative importance of the support was
expressed in Anglo-Saxon as in Celtic law by the expedient
of allotting two thirds of the wergeld to the paternal kindred
and only one third to the maternal.   The maternal kindred,
we have to bear in mind, was an allied organised unit,
and not chance helpers drawn from all sides by relationship
through sisters, cousins, aunts, or nieces.   It is true that,
as time goes on, the idea of relationship, of ties spreading
from individual to individual in all directions, tends to
substitute itself for the idea of an alliance of organised units ;
but though we certainly witness a gradual dissolution of the
groups, there is no reason for assuming that they were dissolved
or did not exist at the very beginning ; and there are many
facts even in the course of this process of dissolution which
point to an increasing solidarity of grouping in proportion
as we get back to earlier times.   Even in the time of Æthelstan special provisions had to be made for cases where the
kindred of great men or of peasants were so powerful
that it was hard to get justice done in regard to their
members.[3]   The Anglo-Saxon laws of wergeld do not go
into the minute details presented by Norse laws in regard
to the ramifications of kinship and the sections into which
it was divided, but the wergelds were of the same kind
and approximately of the same amount, and there is every
reason to believe that the grouping of kinsmen went on
analogous lines.   This being the case, we must try to realise

what it means when we hear in Norse law of most elaborate provisions made for gathering and estimating the interests and forces of men within the degree of sixth cousins, grouped around a central agnatic kernel of second cousins (the vísendr of the Frostathingslov, the baugamenn of other Norse laws). These indications ought not to be made light of ; they were not invented at random, and they point to a state of society where the people, though not so neatly divided into gwelys and clans as with the Welsh, still settled closely enough together to maintain the idea of solidarity of wide groups constructed on the basis of far-reaching genealogical reckonings. Any one may try to gauge the difference between relationship, as it exists at present, and the ties of the ancient kindred, by trying to ascertain who his kinsmen are up to the degree of sixth cousin, and what practical effect such relationship may have. And if we take into account that in regard to early German society we learn expressly that kinship regulated the arrangements of the host, the protection of a person in regard to life, limbs, and honour, the responsibility for misdeeds, the participation in all important family affairs like marriage, wardship, inheritance, land settlement, management of property,[4] and provision in cases of extreme need, we shall get a dim notion of the extent to which a man was implicated in the life of his kindred in those days. And in realising it we ought to think more of the power of such a natural association than of the possibility of dissolving it into individual degrees of relationship. The importance and bearing of these ties was well understood by the Germanic tribes, as we can surmise from the very solemn and circumstantial enactments in regard to admission into the kindred and to dereliction of it which have been preserved to us in the Norse and in the Germanic laws, as well as from the rules on the growth of the kindred.[5] It formed in this manner a whole and not a mere plurality of persons ; the *genealogia*, the *fara*, the *mægth* were recognised associations for social purposes of all kinds, and not indefinite numbers of relatives, like our modern Smiths and Browns.[6]

In regard to the special Old English term, mægth, it has to be noted that it is characteristically used not only for the kindred but also for the tribe and for the province, that is, for groups which are treated primarily as ethnographic and territorial units and do not admit of being dissected into a number of persons.[7] In the compound term *mæg-burg* the unity of the mægth also finds adequate expression, and stress is emphatically laid in it on the *borgh*, the association for protection and joint responsibility.[8]

Mægth

How far was the mægth organised ? Some organisation was a necessity ; and we find traces of organisation among the Germanic peoples, though, in accordance with the very varying and pliable conditions of their existence, in very different stages. Not to speak of the closely united Frisian tribes, which in the case of the Dithmarschen develop a complete system of clans,[9] we find traces of organised kindreds among the ancient tribes of inner Germany as well as among the Scandinavians. Later on, and especially in England, there are no signs of a recognised chieftainship or ealdormanship of the mægth, and the many occasions when it had to transact business were evidently dealt with by meetings of its members or of its elders. We hear often of such occasions, though we are left without precise information as to. the modes of action involved in them.[10] The silence of our sources in this respect is by no means unusual : in how many cases are we not left to make inferences on the strength of a stray word or two in regard to the most important institutions of those times ? And it has to be noted that the assumption of some permanent organisation is not in any way disturbed by the right of every single individual to claim support for the exaction and execution of payments according to varying degrees of relationship. There is no inherent opposition between this practice and the settled organisation of kindred, because this last exists not for the apportionment of claims but for enforcing them by the authority and action of the whole. As in the case of claims for damages by English citizens against China, the payments would fall to the

aggrieved parties and to their relations, although the
enforcement of the claim has been achieved and could not
but be achieved by the power of the British Empire ; so
the way to bring home the claims of some Billing or some
Hocking was to raise the Billings and the Hockings
to action as a body, the solidarity of which was fitted
to support all possible claims, and not this or that
suit in particular, with its eventual bearing on the interests of men standing on different rungs of the ladder
of relationship.[11]

Scholars have been disputing a good deal about the
juridical character of the *Sippe* or the *mœgth* ; is it a corporation ? Is it an association based on the union of individuals ? Is it something between these two ? Is it a formless
chain of relationship shaping itself differently in accordance
with each particular case ?[12] It seems almost as if these
enquiries had been conducted with an exaggerated sharp-
ness of juridical definition and construction, and a certain
disregard of the peculiar setting given to juridical problems
by place and time. Already, on the strength of what has
been brought forward hitherto, it may be suggested, I
think, that the *mœgth* was not merely a chain of links of
relationship, or a web of rights and claims stretching from
a given individual in all possible directions ; it was a definite
body. Although every single person belonging to it was
in a way connected with the mægth of his mother, and this
double connection admitted of complications and conflicts,
still the preponderance of agnatic connection was sufficiently
clear, and made possible the formation of groups of kindred,
in contrast with indefinite relationship. The permanence of
a common aim and will ruling over the decisions and interests
of single members has been declared to be the test of the
corporate character of associations, and the mægth we are
describing possessed to some extent this qualification. It
was a body of natural growth and not of mutual consent ;
a body excluding strangers by blood and keeping access to its
membership difficult and dependent on certain stringent
formalities ; a body which could not be dissolved, and could
not be forsaken without a special and abnormal renunciation

of rights. Its aim was mainly political—protection and joint responsibility, and the carrying out of this aim involved some organisation and the possibility of taking decisions and putting them into execution. In this way, though it left a large margin for the action of every individual, of households and other forms of association, it had a distinct and most important range of action of its own.

But besides this political life the mægth and the families into which it was divided had a good deal to do and say in **Settlement of** regard to the settlement of property and the **Kindreds** conduct of economic affairs. It is clear from the place-names that the settlement of the Jutes, the Saxons, and the Angles in Britain was largely effected on the principle of allotment of territory to mægths. If we value the researches of Mr. D'Arbois de Jubainville in regard to the tradition of the names of private *fundi* in the topographical nomenclature of France, no less should we value the conclusive argument drawn by Kemble from the patronymic names of English villages, an argument the more remarkable, as it points to Kent, Sussex, and the East Anglian shires as the special homes of settlement by mægths. We should have expected so much from *à priori* considerations, because these counties were the abodes of the first settlers from Teutonic shores, of those who were more crowded in their tracts of debarkation, and able to transmit the peculiarities of their previous constitution in a purer and more thorough form.[13] The Æscings, Effings, Getings, Hoppings, Tootings, Wokings, Bletchings, Kennings, etc., of Surrey, for example, have left a marked imprint on the soil; and the constant recurrence of these forms is sufficient to convince us that even where the names are drawn from the peculiarity of the site, the occupation must have been effected largely on the principle of connecting the territorial division with a kindred.[14] This fact went a long way to provide each kindred with a real basis for its existence. If the kindred succeeded in keeping together for several generations in a particular place its ties would become more and more close and exclusive. The territory occupied by the kindred was subdivided between house-

holds which were intended to hold together and to stave off
divisions by common management and by emigration or
new settlement.

The unit of landed property is characteristically the
land of a family, the *hiwisc, hiwship, hide,* as applied to
land. These famous terms have been chiefly
Terra Familiæ considered from the point of view of taxation
and of the repartition of the duties incumbent upon
the land. But they are first evidence in themselves as to
the character of landownership in the early period of Saxon
occupation. It is not the individual who comes forward
here with his rights, but the family. The term *family land*
and the old English *hiwisc, hiwship,* which correspond to it,
are so peculiar that there can be no question of a borrowing
of foreign names, and still less of foreign notions.[15] Even
the *tributarius,* the *manens,* and the *casatus* assume a peculiar
signification in English charters : they are not to be taken
as pointing to the status of servile tenants, they apply
primarily to settlers endowed with normal rights and bound
to perform the normal duties of free householders in this
early period of English history.[16] Wealhs may also be
placed on the same footing by being recognised as free
gafolgelders of the king and being connected with a family
land, a hide of their own, though their personal estimation
will not reach that of Englishmen of equal social standing.[15]
This possible equation with the wealhs gives us also a clue as
to the probable constitution of the family settled on the
land. The equation could hardly have been effected if
the mode of ownership in both cases had been entirely
different ; and so we are led to infer that the Welsh *gwely,*
as the settlement of free gwrdas, and the Saxon Jutish,
English family holding, were probably not unlike each other.[17]
This conclusion finds support in the well-known peculiarity
of the ancient tenure of gavelkind which, though it was
sometimes contended in later times to be distinctly Kentish,
was not unknown in other parts of the country, and seems
to represent the original mode of hereditary succession
of free folk. It became a system of division, and so did
the succession in partible socage, which is the common

succession applying originally to free non-military tenure. Even such socage was sometimes held jointly, however, and as for gavelkind, its tangled intermixture of rights of ownership speaks loudly for the original preservation of the unities of holding, not only in the performance of duties, but also in cultivating the land.[18]   Indeed, gavelkind could not exist in a time of extensive agricultural husbandry without the corrective of the household community, which is also implied by the *gwely*.   It would be going too far to suppose that the special feature in the construction of the gwely, its community of offspring of a great grandfather, held good also in the case of the Anglo-Saxon family land : this principle and the consequences of it are marked by too peculiar traits to be assumed without positive evidence.   But it is important to notice that the family holding as a unity did play a prominent part in the occupation of the soil by the English ; and not only is there nothing to show that these holdings are mere combinations at will, liable to be dissolved by the wish of each single shareholder, every *Ganerbe*, as the German expression goes, but the continuance of these holdings among free settlers through centuries is a convincing proof by itself that the disruptive tendencies of hereditary divisions and endowments of single individuals were effectually kept in check by custom.   Division became necessary sometimes, but it was not the prevalent and ordinary result of succession.   The ordinary result must have been the keeping together of the holding and the provision for unruly and dissatisfied elements in side settlements and side callings.[19]

The family holdings, as units of property or tenancy rising above the individual interests of single members of **Folkland and** a family, and implying a kind of house-com**Bookland** munity for purposes of cultivation and the rendering of dues, seem to extend all over England in its Welsh as well as in its Anglo-Saxon districts, and to provide for the elementary grouping of society. The rules which governed family property of that kind were rules of popular custom, of folk-right, and the land which came under the action of these rules was *folcland*,[20] as opposed to land which had been exempted from them through the influence of the Church, the legislative action of king and witan, and the formal testimony of charters or books— to *bócland*.[21] This latter class of land was growing steadily ;[22] and the fact that it was based on express privilege and described in the books has made us well acquainted with the exceptional conditions of its existence, while the ordinary conditions of folk-right remain in the background. Still, it is not difficult to get at some of the more important rules in regard to them—partly by the help of the contrast which the recorded testimony of the privileged tenure lays stress upon.   To begin with, folcland was not to be alienated from the community of the kindred, and even when through the spread of bócland transactions in landed property came into use, the proper course was to obtain the consent of the interested relations of the actual holder, if it had to be given or sold, and still more if it had to be devised out of the natural course of succession.[23]   The chief feature of a book, on the contrary, was that it empowered its owner to dispose of the land at his will, to give or sell it, or to institute an heir to it.[24]   In the light of these arrangements, it is hardly possible to consider the *cwiðes* or donations on the death-bed otherwise than as exceptional proceedings supported by the Church, and intended to increase the custom of folkright by the strength of a deed or by the testimony of ecclesiastics.[25]

It is through the books and *cwiðes* that another exception to the common land law asserts itself, namely, that women are introduced to the holding of land.   As far as Anglo-Saxon evidence goes, there is no direct prohibition against their possessing land or ancient tenements as in Frankish and Thuringian law,[26] and no such restrictions as in the case of Frisian and Norse law ;[27] but there can be hardly a doubt that Anglo-Saxon law started also from the exclusion of women, and that it was by the help of the Church that they improved their position in this respect.[28]   The ground for this exclusion must have been the same as that which led to their later disabilities in regard to military tenure—they

were not fighters and could not be entrusted with the
defence of the social basis of family rights and property ;
even in respect of small agricultural plots it had to be taken
into account, that it is not with the plough and the oxen
a woman has to busy herself, but with dairy work and house
industry.[29]

There is nothing strange in the fact that the weaker sex
was deprived of rights in two different periods of legal
history, and came to assert them in two distinct periods
later on : the older custom excluding women from land
inheritance corresponds to a military arrangement of society
as well as the feudal one, though the feudal basis was
narrower than the ancient one. The emancipation from
restraints came in both cases from the progress of industrial
ideas of society, which in the earlier instance were transmitted by the Church, the representative of Roman industrial
culture, whereas feudal notions gave way before modern
industrial development.

However this may be, it seems clear that we have to
recognise in the early polity of the English in Britain a
marked tendency towards the arrangement of
Hundreds   society on the tribal system. The households
and the mægths are the groups with which it reckons in
dividing the land and in apportioning rights and duties.
It may be pointed out ultimately, that the political organisation of the territory started from the smallest of these units
—the household. This organisation had to provide for
three main functions of political life—for the gathering of
the host, for the collection of tribute, and for the administration of justice ; and to meet these three main requirements the hundreds arose all over the country. Even
where, as in the Danish shires, wapentakes and wards took
their place, the original English division must have been
one into hundreds, and the significant wapentake itself
points to a more recent form of the gathering of the armed
people of the district.[30] Now, recent researches into the
grouping of hundreds and hides leave no doubt as to the
fact that the district called a hundred was considered a&
a group of a hundred households, a hundred *hiwiscs*, as I

should prefer to say, in order to escape the double or triple
meaning of the word " hide." [31]   As a matter of fact, these
calculations supposed a good deal of rough reckoning,
rounding off, exempting, and overburdening of the actual
areas ; but the main idea runs through the whole of Old
English history, and the frequent remanipulation of the
map of the hundreds shows that the aim was not merely
to provide a fiscal fiction without relation to reality.[32]
Certainly the households counted were households *ad
waram* or *ad geldum*, as people used to say at the time of
Domesday ; there was land exempted from the reckoning
and there was land where the separate households had
disappeared to make room for larger economic bodies, but
whatever intricacies the system may present in its fiscal
calculations, it may be taken as an historical document of
the first magnitude.   Going back as it does at least to the
times of Bede, it testifies to the attempts of the English
invaders to build up their society by joining together in
symmetric order the households of their warriors.[33]   No
wonder that these households turn out to be more numerous
and more crowded in the shires which had been the first
vantage-ground and the strategic basis of the conquerors,
sparse and artificial in newly acquired districts. [34]

II.   The Township

The settlers had soon to learn that the material used
for the framework of their tribal society was in many respects inadequate, and must be supplemented
and strengthened by other contrivances.   It
was not a case of people who, like the Celtic
tribes, had come over to their places of abode in compact,
unbroken masses, and had remained sheltered from disturbing influences by their remote position or their mountains.   The Teutonic invaders came over by sea, in small
batches, had to fight their way across the island in a war
which lasted two or three hundred years, and got mixed
up among themselves and with the conquered population
in an endless, tangled strife, if one may use the expression.
Such a history strengthened their military organisation

**Artificial
Associations**

but loosened and dissolved the ties of kindreds and households. The latest comers, the Danes and Norwegians, though they came from countries with a developed tribal organisation, show in an especially striking manner the prevalence of military ties and the scattering of families.[35] The necessity for society and for the government to react against these disintegrating tendencies manifests itself in many characteristic facts : I will only mention the formation of voluntary and involuntary associations which have to protect individuals, and to stand pledge for their behaviour ; that is, to assume the very functions which formed the object of the kindred group.[36]

These phenomena are not of our domain, however, and interest us only in so far as they give the measure of the breaking up of old ties, and of the necessity of providing new ones. But we have to pay special attention to another side of the same process, namely to the growth of the *tún* as a social institution which, starting at least in part, from the settlement of the kindred, developed its own peculiar character and organisation. We have seen that among the Celtic tribesmen inhabiting Britain there was a tendency to disperse over the land in family groups, each of which either raised its common dwelling-house surrounded by sheds, closes, and stables, or a hamlet of a few houses, a *trev*, formed of some *tyddyns* in close connection with each other. As the agnatic family group grew and began to feel cramped in its original district, normally after a succession of three generations and on the coming in of the fourth to its full right, the original trev broke up or swarmed off into a number of distinct trevs or hamlets. It was not difficult to do so, because the husbandry arrangements were chiefly bound up with hunting, tending of bees, and pastoral pursuits, and such agriculture as there was did not make people strike deep roots into the soil. There was still enough of wood and waste land to enable them to occupy large tracts and to parcel them out at their convenience ; and as for the mode of building, it was well adapted to these migrations and changes of abode : the houses were light wooden structures which did not require much capital, care, or labour for their erection. The periodical swarming of the population from old hamlets into new was in this way the rule in Celtic territory. The Roman conquest does not seem to have brought about a radical change in the dispersion of rural population. It must have hampered, and perhaps arrested, the practice of clan redivisions. Villas appeared as centres of administration and cultivation. Agriculture progressed ; the hamlets struck permanent roots, and in many cases they grew naturally into villages, while in other cases large settlements may have sprung up in connection with the central knots of the system of roads and markets ; but still hamlets and separate farms continued by the side of the larger agglomerations, and there was no special reason for giving prevalence to the one or to the other mode of distribution of dwellings and population—each had its advantages, and each held its own in accordance with local incidents and customs.

The Teutonic invasions, on the contrary, had a decisive influence in bringing about a concentration of the people in villages, *túns*. The new settlers were bent on keeping together, for purposes of cultivation and defence ; the troubled times which began with their invasion and went on until the complete organisation of feudal monarchy were not propitious to separate homesteads and farms. The sway of the military class over the agricultural was made easier by the gathering of masters, foremen, and tillers in the same centres. Quite apart from the question whether the rural agglomeration was organised hierarchically around one lord, or composed of many more or less independent holdings,, the *túns*, *hâms*, *leys* and *thorpes* of the English and Northern settlements are mainly villages and not hamlets, groups of considerable size, and it is with this prevalent form that we shall have to deal in our review of the general features of rural life in Anglo-Saxon times,[37] though it has to be recognised that there were still many hamlets and separate farms by the side of these typical Old English *túns*. The Welsh border, and the counties which had been only slowly and partially reclaimed from the Welsh, presented all shades of transition from the pure Celtic *trev* or hamlet with its cluster of *tyddyns*, to the large congregations of homesteads and holdings characteristic of the midland and the eastern shires. In their case we can well perceive how much depended for the maintenance of the system on the abundance of wood and waste. And we find something of the same kind, namely a scattering of homesteads, in some northern districts, where the clearance of the wild waste was carried on by the individual efforts of scattered settlers.[38] A detailed account of settlement and colonization would have to make a careful estimate of all these variations and peculiarities. For our purpose it is sufficient to note that the prevalent form of the distribution of dwellers, dwellings, and holdings in the Old English period was their concentration in permanent villages of considerable size, and not their dispersion in hamlets or single farms. This is indirectly implied in the fact, that for administrative and judicial purposes the hamlets are ignored and thrown together into villages which, though they are artificial composite bodies, point to real villages as the common form of social grouping. The fiction becomes appropriate and even possible merely because there is a well-known reality by the side of it. Rural districts composed of hamlets or farms are called into being as villages, because they form the exception alongside of villages in the proper sense of the term. And it has to be noticed at the outset that the urban district, the town in the modern sense of the word, appears another variety of the *tún*. The fact that there is no special designation for the latter, before the borough came to the fore as a special form of town, is very characteristic. Evidently there is no fundamental difference in social composition and organisation between the village and the town of those times. London is a " wic " as much as the most insignificant " herdwik " on the Welsh border. Therefore we need not draw a distinct line of demarcation for the sake of supposed clearness where there was none.

As the present special use of "town" debars us from employing that otherwise convenient term, we

Township and Vill

have to speak of tún and township as the Old English did when speaking of the units of rural organisation ; while village can only appear a looser designation for describing the rural group.[40]   "Vill" does not do, though recommended by great authorities, because it is Norman, and slurs over the main feature in the history of local institutions, namely the primordial Old English character of the *tún* settlement.   A vill is the *tún* as accepted by the French conquerors, not as founded or resettled by English colonists.   It may be doubtful in regard to the vill, whether it should not be regarded as the product of the manor, or of an artificial system of fiscal and police arrangements ; the word *tún* is sure to keep well before our eyes the archaic character of the institution and its original and natural meaning of settlement.   We shall have so much to do with artificial arrangements and fiscal uses of terms and things, that it may be best from the outset to get hold of a kind of *totem* which may remind us that the world does not primarily exist for the sake of fiscal schemes, nor society for the sake of police arrangements.   With this preliminary caution, we may notice that the *túns* and the later vills proceeding from them, present the lowest administrative grouping of society, the hundred and the shire rising over them as higher and more comprehensive units.   Even in the feudal epoch when the manors had in so many respects made good their influence, the vill remained the normal territorial division,[41] and there can be no doubt that it has even a greater claim to be reckoned with as a *tún* in Old English times.[42]

CHAPTER III

THE SHARES IN THE TOWNSHIP

I. THE GELD HIDE

THE proprietary and economic arrangements of the township are peculiar, and cannot be explained either on the well-known lines of private ownership and separate management of private interests, nor on those of seignorial sway, nor on the basis of strict communalism, treating individuals as subservient items, nor as a consequence of a system of kinship. It is an arrangement which has some traits in common with every one of those we have mentioned, but remains distinct from all of them. The term which may best indicate its main characteristic would perhaps be that of a community of shareholders. We are quite familiar with companies of shareholders nowadays, and the notion of the rights and duties connected with a share may be illustrated in many respects even from the present practice of such companies ; but there would be the fundamental difference between these modern companies and the Old English township that the rural groups of which we are speaking are communities and not companies, that they do not arise from a definite agreement or as a manifestation of the free-will of those who join them, but grow, and as natural growths have an independent existence as against the individuals attached to them, while the shares are not formed at random as indifferent arithmetical parts of the aggregate, but form organic units and stand in organic relation to the composite unity of the *tún*. The meaning of these limitations and attributes will be more clear if we look at the facts in which the rural system of Old England is expressed.

A *tún* is normally a social organisation composed not of
people with divers proprietary rights and economic pursuits,
but of households brought into definite and simple relations
to each other in regard to rights and duties.   For the sake
of simplicity we may suppose that it consists of a number
of equal shares called *hiwiscs*, *hides*, which render it possible
and easy to apportion rights and duties to the members of
the rural society.   As a matter of fact the population of
the *tún* was commonly arranged not on one plane as holders
of whole shares or *hides*, but as it were on steps, some
holding hides, some half-hides, some quarters of hides or
virgates, and half-virgates or bovates, and some again
scattered on the outskirts of the system with cottages and
crofts.   But this differentiation of the arrangement does
not destroy its fundamental idea—the proportional adjustment of rights and duties, though it be effected not on a
uniform but on a graduated scheme.[1]

The hide has been prominent in all inquiries as to
Anglo-Saxon social arrangements, because it is constantly

**The Hide not a
Measure of Land**

mentioned in the documents ; but the evidence
in regard to it has not been construed in the
same way by the different scholars who have
treated it.   There are several points which one must eluci-
date and keep well in view in order to understand the real
meaning and working of the hide.   To begin with, it has
to be noticed that hides are not measures, though often
expressed in measures.   We often hear of 120 or 160 or 180
acres, and the like, in the hide, or of parts of the hide
measuring thirty acres, etc. ; but it would be wrong to suppose that any thirty acres would form a virgate, or any 120
or 160 or 180 acres a hide, as one might say that so many
acres might go to the *furlong* (*quarentena*) or to the *leuga*.[2]

It could not even be said that the hide is a definite measure
of arable land to which proportionate rights not defined by
strict measurement were appendant in the use of pasture,
wood, water, etc.   Not only that the reckoning of rights
in a hide may have started from the possession of 120 acres
of arable in one place and from the possession of 160 in
the neighbouring village ;[3] in one and the same village the

allotment in the arable may have been taken to be one of 120 acres in one sense and of 144 acres in another sense, and may have been one of 136 acres up to a certain year and of 160 acres from that year to the next step in development.[4] The hide, the carucate and the sulung were evidently too elastic quantities to be regarded as measurements ; but they keep all through their characteristic as shares, because whatever their arithmetical variations they are always equal as against each other within the limits of one and the same *tún* at one and the same time.

The second point to be mentioned is the fact that our documents in speaking of these shares attach two different meanings to them.   In Domesday, in the Geld **Geld and** Inquests, in the Hundred Rolls and other docu-**Ware Units** ments compiled with a fiscal purpose, we mostly hear of them as fiscal units, as units for taxation and for the apportionment of other public duties.   This is certainly a most important aspect of the case, and it gives rise to exceedingly valuable calculations which carry approximately the weight of statistical estimates, and present a most welcome opportunity for arithmetical deductions in the study of epochs otherwise so barren in the elements of quantitative analysis.   But the value of these quantitative data may be exaggerated ; nay, they may even lead us into error, if we use them too confidently for our guidance.   It would hardly be safe to picture to ourselves the real world in exact conformity with the round numbers, the rectangular areas, and the neat symmetrical schemes towards which these fiscal units show a natural gravitation : it is impossible to believe that villages should be founded and kept developing in conformity with a scheme for providing them with ten or five twelve- or six-plough teams,[5] notwithstanding their countless varieties of position, agrarian advantages, facilities of intercourse and the like, or that their territories should stretch over the land in squares formed by so many miles in length and so many miles in breadth.[6]   Not that such schemes did not exist or that they had no relation whatever to reality ; some connection with it they must have had, but this connection has to

be ascertained through them and by the help of them and
not as already given in them ; almost as the real shape of
a continent has to be delineated across the degree of
the map and not along them.

Indeed the documents take sufficient care to warn us
of the artificiality of their calculations. They constantly
speak of geld hides and geld carucates, of ware acres or
acre-wares, implying that real hides, carucates and acres
are not identical with their fiscal namesakes. The object
of these last is to " defend " [7] the proprietary units in regard
to the requirements of the government, and the assumption
of round numbers, the proportionate increases and reductions are as natural to them as a fidelity to the natural
conditions of husbandry and to legal arrangements are a
necessary element in the constitution of real hides. One
might almost be tempted to compare these fiscal namesakes
of the agrarian shares, these geld hides, geld carucates
and acre-wares in their relation to field hides, field carucates
and field acres, to the mysterious *fylgias* of northern mytho-
logy—beings bound up with live creatures, but leading a separate existence as their weird double. These
" doubles " bring mischief, especially when hidden in an
unaccountable way in the body of their companions. Even
so the hide cannot be mistaken in its bearing when the
document frankly tells us that there are in truth a hundred
hides in a place, but that it will defend itself only as one,[8]
or if it is expressly mentioned that an estate pays geld
for one virgate although it contains sufficient land for five
ploughs.[9] But there are numbers of instances in which the
discrepancy between geld and field shares is not so clear,
and the inferences drawn from documents get to be dangerous in consequence.[10]

The first, although not the most important, set of questions which have to be put and answered relates to the
fiscal shares in the geld inquests. They are undoubtedly
units of taxation forming the basis of its repartition. By
burdening a certain district with so many hides, or lightening
its burden of hides, the government placed it in a certain
position in regard to fiscal requirements. It had to perform

services and to pay more or less in comparison with other
districts. It could be said, and the expression was actually
used in the Norfolk and Suffolk Domesday, that in the case
of a geld of twenty shillings being imposed on the hundred
a particular tún had to contribute sixpence or fourpence to
it,[11] but, instead of saying this the government could demand two or six shillings from the hide or carucate at
which a tún was taxed.[12]

We hear a good deal of the consequences of this
system of rating in the shape of resettlements of hidage,
e.g. of reductions of the number of hides in some districts,
and of an increase in others.[13] The larger units have to
be differentiated into fractions in order to appraise fiscal
and other duties with some detail. Indeed, we see that the
geld hide, as well as the geld carucate, is taken to correspond
to a certain number of virgates or of bovates, and these
resolve themselves generally into acres. To all these subdivisions the same character of artificiality is attached as to
the higher units : the geld virgate or geld bovate representing, as it were, a certain number of counters as against
other counters, may turn out to be different in its arithmetical composition from the field virgate and field bovate of
the district, while the acre may be either an entirely
unreal quotient, an arithmetical fraction, or one of a number
of real acres on which taxes and duties were charged while
other acres in the same place were left out of account.[14]

Now, it would be, of course, important to discover
traces of any constant reckoning as to the relations between
the large unit and the fractional units. And indeed,
though in field practice instances of six virgates to the hide,
and the like, do occur,[15] for fiscal purposes the hide and
the carucate generally divide into four virgates or into
eight bovates, and the sulung into four yokes.[16] The
artificial character of these divisions is well exemplified
when the virgate falls into four ferthings, because this
seems to be the unit designed to be at the bottom of the
scale : it would not easily break up into acres according to
the usual reckoning, and seems to render the division into

acres unnecessary, as it produces fractions of one-sixteenth
of the carcucate, which would be sufficient for all ordinary
fiscal purposes.[17] But the usual thing is to divide hide,
carcucate, and sullung into acres on the semblance of the real
agrarian shares. It is generally assumed now that the geld
hide, the geld carucate, and the geld sulung were reckoned
uniformly in the time of Domesday at one hundred and
twenty acres, and that this reckoning corresponded to the
main tradition of agrarian divisions. Reserving the question as to these last, I must point out that the case does not
look so cheerfully simple to me, even though scholars, justly
celebrated for critical acumen and for the power of reading
numbers, have expressed themselves emphatically in this
sense.[18] Domesday clearly recognises different modes of
valuation even in regard to every single fiscal term. The expression " hide " of Leicestershire is admittedly taken in a
different sense from the hide of Cambridgeshire,[19] and it
would be strange to suppose that the hide and the carucate,
which mostly exclude each other, and sometimes, though
rarely, meet on the same ground,[20] should be taken to
imply the very same thing and to divide in the same way.
As to the sulung, not only can it not be shown that it was
reckoned at one hundred and twenty acres, but there is
considerable likelihood that it was not, and comprised a
good deal more.[21] On the contrary, the repartition of
hides into a small number of acres, forty, has been distinctly made out in regard to the south-western counties.[22]
Those who assume the constant division of the hide and of
the carucate into 120 acres have to admit that there is a very
large number of cases which do not conveniently fit into
this equation ; and, though no other equation exceeds this
one in frequency,[23] still, in view of the many aberrations from it, there can be no question of its acceptance
as the unique hide or unique carucate of Domesday England.
It may, indeed, have been before the eyes of the Domesday
Commissioners and of the Royal Exchequer as the *ideal*
apportionment of the carucate, and of the hide when an
equivalent to the carucate, and this view must have reflected the average conditions of agrarian distribution ; but

if there is any point in Domesday where this ideal aspect
comes primarily to the fore, it is not in the divisions of the
fiscal hide and the geld carucate, but in the appraisement
of land fit for the plough.   There the ideal measure of the
plough-land could be conveniently resorted to, and has
indeed been made to play a part.[24]   As to any exact relation
of fractional counters, it was not imposed by the Treasury
of the Conqueror as a uniform standard on the whole of
England, and it certainly did not exist before the Conquest.
The Normans were as yet inexpert in needless centralisation,
and could well tolerate different modes of reckoning the
fractions of their geld-land, as is shown by the existence of
the East Anglian reckoning, of the Leicestershire combinations, the Devon and Cornwall distribution, the Kentish
system, the south-western reckoning, etc.   From their
fiscal point of view they did not lose anything by the fact
that a particular fraction of the hide was represented by
ten acres in Wiltshire and by thirty acres in Cambridgeshire, since ten is quite as much a fourth part of forty as
thirty is the fourth part of 120.

Of course, all this makes a very considerable difference
to us, as it discloses an even more confusing variety in the
actual conditions than we are accustomed to reckon with,
and renders the problem of getting at the real shares, as
distinct from the fiscal shares, considerably more complex ;
but the perplexities of future antiquarians have not been
taken into account by the awkward people with whom we
have to deal.

If we look at the Domesday hide as an artificial unit
of assessment, which has diverged considerably from the
team-land, the fact that it was often or even mostly subdivided into 120 fractions called acres, and, as we maintain,
sometimes subdivided into forty fractions, or perhaps forty-
eight, or even sixteen, loses a good deal of its interest.   It
has certainly to be taken notice of in order to follow
and sometimes to reconstruct the reckoning operations of
the assessing authorities, but it does not give the real
acreage of counties and townships or the true size of
holdings, or their actual uniformity or diversity.   North-

amptonshire, for instance, appears in three consecutive
valuations as containing [3,200], [2,663½] and [1,356] hides.
The reduction of its hidage is an important point, and can
be explained as a consequence of more exact assessment
and of a relative alleviation of its burden,[25] but it would be
very difficult to argue from these estimates to the actual
size and aggregate number of the rural holdings contained
in it. The relation of the geld units to the actual occupation
of the land would still remain a matter of complex inference.
The necessity for such inferences is indeed clearly expressed
in the general method of collecting evidence followed by
the Domesday Commissioners. If the relation of the hides,
carucates, and sulungs to the actual occupation of the soil
had been expressed on an average by the statement that
hide, carucate, and sulung (solin) contained about 120 acres
of arable, it would not have been necessary to make
elaborate inquiries about the number of plough-teams
which might be kept in a particular place and which actually
were there ; or, to state it in a different way, about the
extent of land which might be tilled by average plough-
teams in distinction from that which was actually under
tillage. This method of inquiry, which runs through the
whole of the Domesday Inquest, is evidently a result of the
fact that the geld-hides and the carucates of the Geld Rolls
did not correspond any longer to the actual features of the
land settlement. Certainly, the carucate and the sulung
had been originally meant as plough lands, possibly also
the hide, but they were not so any more in the sense in
which they were used for the assessment and the fiscal
" defence " of the land in Domesday. And so, if we
want to use that record directly in order to get at agrarian facts, it would be more to the purpose to look, not to
the *carucatæ* or *hidæ*, but to the entries as to *carucæ* and
terræ carucis,—ploughs " which are there " and " which
could be there," than to the entries as to hides, carucates,
and sulungs. If we want to know how many plough-teams
of eight oxen were, on the average, used for tilling the land
in England, we have to take the first series of entries, and
we shall get at the approximate number of full plough-lands

actually provided with stock, the *terra vestita*, the " geset-land," in England at the time immediately after the Conquest, and sometimes at the time immediately before it. In the case of districts which had suffered great devastation, these figures may serve as an index of their losses, whereas in the case of counties where the commotions of that period had been less violent, the number of the teams may give us an insight into the constant aspects of cultivation.[26] If we want to know what was the quantity which could be used as arable, apart from its actual stocking and direct cultivation, we have to take up the second set of figures, and they ought to tell us on the average of 120 acres *per* plough-land, how many acres lay in the shots and furlongs of the rural England of 1086, or in places which had been used as arable within living memory, or at least might be used in this manner. Such questions need not have exercised too much the experience of jurors thoroughly conversant with the features of the husbandry of their districts. The information about the number of hides, carucates, and sulungs came in as third item, and applied to the units of assessed land, which did not coincide with the units of area or cultivation. In this way we may say that the Domesday inquiry in respect to land was directed primarily to registering the extent of arable in general, of arable stocked, and of arable assessed.

II.   The Field Hide

As for the assessment itself, there can be no doubt that, as described in Domesday, it followed a course of repartition from above. The whole amount of the geld was divided in round numbers of hides and carucates between the shires, and in each shire between the hundreds or the units corresponding to them ; the hides of the hundred again were assigned to the different townships as much as possible according to a scheme in which the larger townships got ten and the smaller five hides (or twelve and six carucates respectively) assigned to them ;

Assessment

the separate tenements had to take over their proportional share within these five- and ten-hide groups according to their size and financial capabilities, and their fractions were appraised in hides, virgates, bovates, and acres, or in some other similar fractions.[27] Similar systems of repartition of hides, as units for fiscal and administrative purposes, have left traces in older documents distributing the hides among the Anglo-Saxon shires, or assigning them to the boroughs.[28] There is even a list of a repartition of hides between the tribes, seemingly of Edwin's time, which starts from the same principle and seems to embody a general scheme, meant to serve as a basis for the repartition of duties, among tribes and hundreds, of which the occasional mentions of hides in Bede present the application to single instances.[29] The working of such a system leads to artificial equations and to schemes which it would be misleading to accept as descriptions of real husbandry. Still, the realities of life could not but be reflected even in these symmetrical schemes. In two respects these schemes of repartition lead necessarily up to a consideration of actual agrarian facts. Firstly, as the assessment was to be proportional, it had to take into account the relative economic strength of the different districts and tenements. Secondly, every tax has to conform to the actual revenue from which it has to be drawn, and must start from an approximate valuation of this revenue.[30] But, apart from these obvious connections between a scheme of repartition and the estimate of economic condition on which it had to apply, the hides, carucates, virgates, bovates, acres, etc., were not merely movable assessment counters, but actual units of land assignation, if one may use such a term. The acre was primarily used not as a fraction of an imaginary assessment unit, but as a square measure and a division in the field. In the same way, the bovate was not invented as a fancy name for the eighth part of a big rating unit, but as the share in the fields proportionate to the labour of one ox in the team of a plough, together with all sorts of rights appendent to this share in pasture, woods, watercourses, etc. And, although we sometimes have to take the

virgate as an appropriate expression for " one fourth part,"
it was primarily the Norman rendering of the yard of land
(rood of land), and even more often of the yard-land, that
is, of the holding starting from a rood of land as from its
base.[31] Even so the yoke pointed perhaps to the four oxen
abreast in a plough and to the acres tilled by them or
apportioned to them according to their work in a larger
team.[32] And the carucate and the sulung have surely to
be considered as the actual land allotments carved out for
the full plough. Lastly, the hide, the hiwisc of land, though
sometimes used as one of a number of counters, was
evidently primarily meant to represent the " tenement of
a household."

As a matter of fact, while the characteristic names of
things may point in our case to their more or less obscure
origin, they are not mere etymological clues for recon-
structing bygone conditions. They are constantly applied
in their obvious and primary sense. The acre was more
naturally a field measure than an Exchequer counter ; the
bovate and yard-land actually served to designate the
holdings of the peasantry ; and the hides and carucates
appear as actual units of land ownership. Not only the
later chartularies, which are not likely to represent a new
arrangement in this matter, distinguish clearly, as we
have seen, between assessment units and fractions, on the
one hand, and real holdings and measures, on the other, but
Domesday has itself not a few indications as to the difference between the two.[33] The proper formula for the assessment unit was " defendit se pro una hida," a formula in
which the fictitious element involved in the taxing operation
is sufficiently expressed. Indeed, as we have seen, the
terms " arable land " (terra carucis), " plough-land " (carucata), and " household land " (hide), represent in one sense
three stages of adaptation of the requirements of the State
to the conditions of the country, the two latter appearing in
turn to correct the discrepancies which had arisen in the
course of time between the primary apportionment and the
actual facts of ownership and husbandry. The estimate of
the amount of " arable " was rendered necessary even where

the land was appraised in carucates, because these geld carucates did not coincide with the real agrarian units ; values other than agrarian, e.g. salt-ponds, fisheries, markets, mills, were brought in to modify it ; [34] in many cases special favour for a monastery or a courtier, the encroachment of a magnate or a sheriff tended to lessen it ; [35] the fiscal habit of repartition in convenient round numbers, and the political habit of holding on as long as possible to traditional apportionment in spite of the flow of life—all these causes made it necessary to resort to a new estimate of the amount of arable and of the stock used in its cultivation, even in the case of those districts which had been apportioned in plough-land some 200 years before Domesday. The discrepancies were even more flagrant in regard to the more ancient form of assessment by hides or sulungs. The growth of fiction, and the readjustment of it in great emergencies on the strength of rough averages, were necessary features of a system which expressed the conditions of a whole country in the course of centuries in more or less symmetrical numbers of fiscal shares.

The most important point for us, however, is that this system of apportionment of taxes and duties was not the **Agrarian Units** product of a fanciful plan ; it followed the arrangements of real life in a limp and imperfect manner, but it was suggested by these arrangements and was dependent on them. The carucate got to be a unit of taxation because the chief divisions of the land were based on the grouping of plough-lands ; and to this side of the matter we have now to turn our attention.

The carucate, the sulung, and the hide, with their subdivisions, are used all along as units of agrarian occupation, as typical holdings.[36] We hear of hides lying in certain fields, representing certain tracts of land, limited by definite boundaries, containing a certain number of acres. In donations and sales the quantity of the land given or sold is expressed in numbers of hides, or sulungs, or carucates, according to the districts.[37] Inasmuch as all these units are more or less intimately connected with the land tilled by one plough, they tend to an average size of 120 acres of arable *per* piece,[38] but in later descriptions of actual economic condition we constantly come across larger and smaller numbers, according to local custom ;[39] and, indeed, a little reflection will show that the 120 acres for the hide, the thirty acres for the virgate, the fifteen for the bovate, are to be considered merely as averages, because, apart from local variations in the quality of the soil and the strength of the teams employed, we have to reckon with at least two factors of first-rate importance which modified such averages; namely, the diversity between the two-course and the three-course system of agriculture, and the difference in the importance of agriculture as compared with pastoral pursuits. In the first case it is clear that the three-course system necessitated a greater size of the holdings, while the two-field system admitted and demanded a smaller expanse.[40] This may partly account for the often recurring duplication of arable land as against actual stocking with ploughs in the north.[41] As for pastoral pursuits, they were still prevalent in the west and in districts covered with fens and marshes in the east ; and as the hide included both arable and pasture, its centre of gravity shifted, as it were, in the case of such regions as Devon, Cornwall, and the fens ; so that the holdings came to be very large in their surface, and small in the number of acres of arable assigned to them.[42] Still, the average reckoning is characteristic, at least for the later period verging on the Norman conquest, especially as it establishes a connection between the various units in use at the same time, and may serve as an index of their comparative antiquity : the hide being least in agreement with it, because it was the most ancient of all and the one which had undergone the greatest number of rearrangements.[43] Besides, the hide was not even originally designed as a plough-land, but as the land of a household (*terra familiæ*) settled on the land (*mansa, manens, cassatum*) and liable to tribute (*tributarii terra*). There are traces of ancient assessments which are largely different from the later practices illustrated by Domesday and the Geld Inquests. Bede and the document styled the Tribal Hidage speak of a greater number of hides than there were in the time of Domesday ; and this evidence which points to the existence of official lists of hides in the seventh century, leads us to assume that the country was divided into a greater number of political shares, and that in some well-known districts such as Kent, more particularly the Isle of Thanet, in the Isle of Wight, the Isle of Ely, in Sussex, the land was assessed in much smaller units than those in use at a later period.[44]   The discrepancy between the general numbers is striking, but there is hardly any ground for the desperate expedient of declaring the ancient assessment a product of gross exaggeration.   It is too well attested for that, and it goes too much into detail. It seems simpler to suppose that the primary repartition went really by the number of households and not by the number of big plough-teams provided on the average with 120 acres each.   In many cases, where the population was crowded on narrow strips of territory, this must have produced a considerable excess in the numbers of hides.[45] The decrease in the total number and in the repartition of hides must have been the result of a gradual adaptation to the standard of the big plough and of a corresponding consolidation of fiscal units.   Indeed, it would be strange to assume that the Angles, Saxons, and Jutes from the very first arranged their settlements on a uniform pattern and started everywhere from the eight-oxen team.   It would seem more natural to surmise a good deal of variety in the beginning and the use of less complicated implements.   As a matter of fact, the glimpses afforded by the evidence at our disposal point in this very direction.[46]

In some cases, however, it can be shown that the later apportionment of hides remains identical with that mentioned in early land-books ; but that need not disturb the general view, that the hide expanded as an agricultural unit, and that the number of hides shrank, the instances of undisturbed continuity being generally derived from endowments of churches and monasteries, which led to the most enduring and secure possession of those times, to an early application of high farming and to a good deal of colonising enterprise.[47]   No wonder that the big plough and the large unit appeared there at an early period, and that the economic tendency in such cases was towards comparatively rapid increase and progress, while the fiscal tendency on the part of the ecclesiastical owners to which the government must have to a great extent given way, went towards the lessening of duties, or, at any rate, towards keeping them at a fixed and immovable standard.   When the abbey of Crediton got a district which comprised more than an entire hundred, only twenty hides were reckoned in it.   In the time of Domesday it had to submit to an increased assessment, but even this increase could hardly have corresponded to the actual increase of wealth that had been achieved in the meantime.[48]   And if the sees of Winchester and of Bath went on estimating their possessions and contributing towards common duties according to the old standards of their endowments, this expressed not only the traditional continuity of their rights, but also the increased importance of their estates when compared with the shifting units of ownership and taxation around them.[49]

It was a tedious but necessary task to state with some clearness in what manner the handling of fiscal units by Royal commissioners and the agrarian distribution underlying it must be understood by us.   We may proceed now to the analysis of the part played by hides, carucates, virgates, bovates, etc., as units in the actual distribution and occupation of the land.

CHAPTER IV

THE OPEN-FIELD SYSTEM

I. AGRARIAN ARRANGEMENTS

THE formation of hides with their subdivisions was neither a mere fiscal expedient nor a casual distribution of the soil for the purpose of measurement. It grew up in connection with agricultural practices which made it necessary to apportion the rights and duties of the holders of land in a system which involved an intricate intermixture of claims and the necessity of constant co-operation between neighbours. It gave the measure of rights in dwelling and close, in arable and meadow, in pasture, wood and water, and the basis for the co-operation of householders in rural husbandry. It entailed a solidarity of the members of each household within the unit. Claims by the government and political duties of all kinds were apportioned according to it. Let us examine these different aspects of shareholding a little closer.

Commons

We may start from the following general outline of the economic position of the households of a township. They had the common and undivided use of the waste land, but this use could be limited and apportioned by the community. This waste land stretched usually over a great part of the territory assigned to the township, and the reclaiming of this land for purposes of exclusive cultivation and enjoyment was subjected to restrictive rules : the scarce and highly valued meadows were assigned under strict rules of proportionate division and redivision ; the arable, which formed the most important, and the most conspicuous portion of the whole, lay in scattered strips in the various fields and shots of the village, so that every holding presented a bundle of these strips equal to other bundles of the same denomination ; everybody had to conform to the same rules and methods in regard to the rotation and cultivation of crops, and when these had been gathered the strips relapsed into the state of an open field in common use. The homesteads and closes around them were kept under separate management, but had been allotted by the community and could in some cases be subjected to reallotment. If this is a correct general description of the main system in operation in the course of the thousand years from 500 till 1500 A.D., and extending many of its incidents to even later times, one can scarcely escape the conclusion, that whatever inroads the individual and the State may have made upon it, and whatever bias legal theory may have shown towards more definite and individualistic conceptions, the average English householder of the middle ages lived under conditions in which his power of free disposal and free management was hemmed in on all sides by customs and rules converging towards the conceptions of a community of interests and rights between all the household shares of a village.[1]

The waste included an enormous quantity of land, of the extent of which some estimate may be formed by looking at the Domesday entries concerning woods and pastures. Their area is generally described in quaranteens or furlongs and leagues with vague limits. Indeed, the delimitation of this space was so rough and approximate that the Domesday commissioners were satisfied with jotting down the size in rectangles of so many acres or furlongs or leagues in length and of so many in breadth,[2] and we may well think that where there was no natural boundary, such as a river or cultivated land, the boundaries between these waste spaces were difficult to define. Indeed, in districts with wide stretches of soil of this character there was for a long time no necessity and no wish to determine the respective boundaries, and the population of conterminous townships used the woods or the marshes concurrently.[3] We are told by the historian of the parish of Whalley that there were about 161 square miles in it, of which at least 70 miles formed the forests of Blackburnshire claimed by no township or manor in particular, while about 33,000 acres were appropriated as pasture and woodland by the different townships, only 3,500 being cultivated as arable.[4] The documents of Peterborough and of Ely show us the extensive intercommoning[5] of the population of the fen districts, and it has been lately made out by Mr. Round that the eastern border of Essex formed a sort of fringe often covered by the water, with no distinct delimitation of ownership between the villages adjoining it, and used by them as common ground for the pasturing of sheep.[6] There is hardly any need to mention that the south-western and north-western counties, with their sparse population, pastoral traditions and exposure to the inroads of the Welsh, were particularly adapted to that kind of indiscriminate use of the waste ; but there are distinct traces of wide tracts of woodland apportioned and used in a very rudimentary manner in the south-east itself.[7] The apportionment of claims, regulation of usages and supervision of their enforcement, were especially loose and superficial in these cases ; and referred chiefly to keeping the intercommoning restricted to the population of certain places,[8] to the performance of certain necessary operations for regulating the influx of water by ditches, canals and dikes ; probably at an early period—before the lords had fastened on the hunting rights—to some provisions as to the seasons and modes of sport.[9] In all such cases the necessity for a more careful definition of rights or even a complete division of them might arise sooner or later.[10] The parties to all such agreements, customary arrangements and delimitations, were often townships as undivided units, and thus in these cases of intervillar relations the unity of the township clearly asserts itself.[11] There is no sufficient ground on the other hand for ascending to the original ownership of a hundred. In some cases the waste not appropriated by a single township may have been considered as appertaining to the hundred, and many disputes in regard to it may have been decided in the hundred court. But there are also instances of the jurisdiction of the shire in such trials ; and if we examine the concrete examples of intercommoning which have come down to us, we see that in most cases it arose between two or three contiguous villages by reason of their natural position on the border of a large moor or a waste thicket.[12] This fact has a certain importance as illustrating the original vagueness of all legal distinctions in this respect. They start from a gradual appropriation of the soil, and proceed step by step to clearly defined and limited rights.

The treatment of wood, moor and pasture becomes more interesting when their quantity gets to be restricted, and floating usages have to be "stinted" according **Stinting the** to conceptions of proportionate rights. A com- **Common** mon entry in Domesday is that in a particular place there is sufficient pasture for the cattle ; sometimes, but more rarely, the mention of sufficient wood also occurs.[13] In these cases the quantity of waste land was not even practically unlimited, and the modes of appropriation of its benefits and proceeds had to be devised and kept up for the sake of the community to avoid destruction and to prevent unfair advantage being taken by some of the participants. In this connection the common appears as included in the territory of a definite rural community, and the right to use it is said in later legal language to be *appendant* to the holdings of this community, nor is there any reasonable ground for supposing that the principles on which these rights were apportioned and regulated were altogether different in earlier times. Without vouching for details, we may suppose that the customary jurisprudence of the feudal age fairly represents the main ideas which prevailed among the Saxons.

In regard to woods, it would be difficult to say how far the police regulations about the felling of great and valuable trees, which we find in practice in the feudal period, were already in use in Old English times : if we may judge from the legal enactments about the felling and burning of trees in private woods, some kinds of these were of sufficient value to call for special protection ; [14] and most probably there arose already in this early period some customary jurisprudence as to the rights of householders to cut trees for housebote and heybote, that is, for the erection and repair of houses and hedges, as well as for fuel, although we have no direct testimony on this point in Old English documents.[15] Indeed, the woods appear in the older evidence chiefly as places where swine get their food ! When estimates of their value are given in Domesday they are made from this point of view,[16] and the trees are characteristically appraised in Ine's laws according to their ability to give shelter to swine. If the use of common woods had to be limited in this respect, every tenement had to be entitled to send a certain number of their beasts to the mast-bearing wood.[17]

We hear much more of customs in regard to pasture proper, which already in Domesday times seems to have been in many cases rather restricted. The rural courts decided in later times what part of the pasture had to be used by horned cattle, what by sheep, and where goats were allowed to go. The seasons when this was to be done had also to be determined by common consent. The habits of all these animals and their wants had to be taken account of, and as for the concurrent rights of the villagers they might be determined by the size of the tenements. Sometimes the only restriction put on the use of the pasture was the requirement that the beasts should be owned by the villagers, should be *couchant et levant*, as was said by the Anglo-Normans, on the tenement, and not got over from abroad ; but there are many traces of the necessity in some places to reduce the number of beasts to be sent to the common pasture and to equalise or to apportion it according to the size of the holdings.[18] The same may be said about the use of waste lands for other purposes, e.g. for cutting turf as fuel (common of turbary). Altogether, the use of common was considered as appendant to the holding, and determined by a fair appreciation of its requirements and of the amount of commodities at hand. There can be no doubt that the idea of pasture rights as a valuable appendix to the arable of the tenement, and as commensurate with its position in regard to other tenements, was as ancient as

common pasture itself, and that the customs of later centuries in this respect, though they may have varied in regard
to details, represented in the main the same treatment of
these questions as the one which prevailed in Old English
times.   And it is important to take note that the rights of
using the common were all along directed and restricted
by the regulative power of the tun community.   Decisions
as to the quantity and the quality of commonable beasts,
the putting up of hedges and walls, the management of
drainage, regulations as to the cutting of grass, had to be
made by the community, and to be apportioned according
to the shares held in it by its members.[19]   Nor ought we to
think too lightly of the importance of the rights and interests
involved in this domain of rural custom.   In many cases
where pastoral pursuits were still much to the fore, this side
of life was hardly less important than agriculture itself.
The attempt of certain sections of Domesday to register the
numbers of the different animals on the estates points convincingly to the great importance of the subject.   Nor must
we forget that the pasture was more important in the same
degree as the habit of making and keeping hay was less prevalent.   Altogether it has constantly to be borne in mind
that the hide or any other tenement we are talking of is by
no means a measure of so many acres of arable, say of 120
acres ; but a quantity of arable *plus* the pastoral and other
common rights appendant to it.

A question of the utmost magnitude arose in regard to
the common waste ; namely, the question of reclaiming part

**Assarts
and
Inclosures**

of it for cultivation.   The reclaiming (" assarting ") of land went on from the very first settlements into later ages as one of the most
powerful processes tending to form society and to extend the
limits of its life.   The struggle against the waste and the
spread of cultivation gave rise to a change in the character of
commodities and a displacement of rights.   The men or the
man who turned portions of the common into arable fields
or enclosed them as private pasture, restricted the right
of other people to the use of the common, and sooner or
later these encroachments might reach a point where the

spread of cultivation came into direct opposition with the pastoral interests of other shareholders. The early history of the inevitable struggle is as obscure as it is interesting and important. We have in truth one great landmark in the setting up of a restraint on the approving tendencies of the lords of manors on behalf of their free tenants : later jurisprudence runs almost exclusively in the groove marked by the celebrated Statutes of Merton and of Westminster II., and it is clear that these statutes leave entirely in the shade a whole series of most interesting questions. What was the view of former generations on the rights of lords to approve ? Were the processes of colonisation and reclaiming carried on entirely at random in former days or were they shaped by some order and custom, etc. ? Still, even from the narrow point of view adopted by the Statute of Merton some significant facts appear which throw light on the general conception of the commons and of their uses. It is well known that the question, mooted in the thirteenth century, was decided in the sense that the lords had the faculty of approving if it could be shown that sufficient pasture remained on the common for the cattle of the free tenants. Now this right of tenants to " sufficient pasture " is highly characteristic. It is clear that it was taken to be the equivalent of that part of the share owned by the tenant which was not expressed in so many acres of arable, but consisted in the pastoral right appendant to it by reason of its being a share in a pastoral as well as agricultural community. As the amount of this pastoral right could not be expressed in acres, and yet was taken to represent something liable to legal protection, this amount had to be made out in each case. The sufficiency had to be tested by the custom of the village in regard to the kinds and the number of beasts allowed to take advantage of the common. The right of the free tenant, formally defensible in the King's Court against the lord, went back in its material contents to the custom of the village as to the use of the common pasture,[20] a custom which had not sprung up into existence in consequence of the Statute of Merton, but which had run on from Old English times, from the formation of the

settlements themselves, no doubt with many modifications
in details, but with the one main idea that the community
had to settle and to keep up by custom and decision the
modes of making good the general right of its shareholders
and members to their pastoral and other undivided rights.
And it is clear that originally these regulations did not have
in view any particular kind of tenant, but all those who
possessed land in the village, whether they were thanes or
ceorls, lords, free tenants, socmen or villains.   In this way,
even in the epoch governed by the feudal jurisprudence of
the King's courts, recourse was necessarily had to the
customs of a self-governing village community in regard
to the estimate of the *minimum* of pastoral rights; though
of course, at the outset, these customs did not arise with the
view of providing such a *minimum*, or for the sake of watching over the interests of the smallest class of the tenantry,
the freeholders.   Behind the *minimum* standard contemplated by the Statute of Merton lay a body of custom
devised for the ordinary routine in the management of the
common, and this ordinary routine applied quite as much
to the tenants in villainage as to the freeholders, and must
have applied even more uniformly to the ceorls of a Saxon
tún.   It is also to be noticed that in feudal times before the
Statute of Merton, the opposition of the tenantry to the
onesided reclaimings of land by the lord evidently went
further and hampered all kind of "approvement," of enclosing the land for private cultivation, whether it was carried
to the verge of endangering the economic welfare of the
free tenantry or not.   The Statute stopped so wide an
application of the right of shareholding tenants in the
common, but we have to reckon with the customary tendency towards such an application in the period preceding
the Merton enactment, and this by itself is significant
enough.[21]   The Norman lawyers took the line of treating
the whole question at issue as a conflict between the individual right of the free tenant in the use of the common and
the individual right of the lord in the ownership of the waste.
But it would be hardly safe to follow them so far in their
construction of the opposing rights as to suppose that the

position of the freeholder and of the manorial owner developed historically on a purely individualistic basis, and was rooted in undefined individual claims. The necessity of compromising interests and keeping some order in the regulation of such an important right as the right of approvement must have been felt all along, and, though irregular squatting and self-help in the matter of assarting may have been of usual occurrence, in cases of stinted common custom and agreement had to decide. We have not the evidence to show by what means such custom had the power to curb the members of the community in the Old English period, but certainly its force could not have been less than it was in Norman times, when we see constant traces of popular opposition on the ground of custom against attempts even of manorial lords to override the customary arrangement and to reclaim and enclose parts of the common for their several use.[22] A natural inference lies towards a more stringent application of the communal standpoint, at a time when the majority of peasant holders had not yet been juridically disenfranchised, and the law had not yet been systematically arranged on the basis of contractual obligation between individual parties. We may well suppose that in the case of wholesale approvement by villages, either while throwing off hamlets or while enlarging their own area of cultivation by the opening of new shots or fields, common decision had to be resorted to in order to shape the course to be adopted in detail.

In regard to meadows, communal rights are as conspicuous as in the case of waste land, although the motive for keeping
Meadows meadows under the constant and direct disposal of the community is an exactly opposite one. In one case communal rights naturally arose from the fact that there was a great deal of waste land and the drift towards individual appropriation was slight. In the other, meadows were jealously kept in the hands of the community because there were few of them, and the best provision for reconciling conflicting wishes was to arrange a temporarily and strictly regulated occupation. As a matter of fact, we find that the usual manner of making use of village meadows

was to put them under prohibition and enclosure until Lammas-day, and to distribute portions of them for the purpose of cutting the grass and making hay according to certain rules, either by lot or by rotation ; every household taking its turn in regard to every particular strip,[23]   When the grass had been mowed the land became the undivided pasture of the villagers. The one clear instance in which land owned by a community of ceorls is mentioned in an Old English legal enactment applies primarily to the duties of parceners in keeping up hedges for the protection of a meadow, and to the liabilities of those who had been remiss in keeping them up for damages occasioned by animals.[24]

In the important paragraph of Jne's laws we have just quoted, the meadow stands first, but along with it other **Shifting** " share-land " (Gedál-land) is mentioned, in **possession** which it is not difficult to recognise the strips **of Arable** of the arable which have to be protected by hedges for the time when corn grows on them, in the same way as grass has to be preserved on the meadow before Lammastide. The arable portion of the township has been considered chiefly as representing the open field system, and it has a right to the name inasmuch as there are only balks, thin borders of turf, to separate the strips assigned to the different house-holders, while hedges are raised merely as temporary enclosures until the harvest has been gathered, and taken down again until the new crop shows itself in the spring.[25] There are even cases in which the arable "share-land " gets distributed to single householders, on the same principles of rotation and assignment by lot which seem to have been the rule in regard to meadows. These cases of shifting occupation of strips of arable by members of the community occur chiefly in regard to fields belonging to urban settlements.[26] The practical reason of such a very communalistic treatment must have been that the fields in question had become an exceptional commodity, in the same way as meadows were an exceptional commodity in ordinary villages. Most likely they had been approved by communal action and under communal supervision from the waste land surrounding the town, and had never been allowed to lapse into individual ownership. These facts are not without importance, because most of the urban communities developed gradually out of purely agricultural or partly agricultural settlements, so that the practices adopted by them in regard to the management of the arable were hardly shaped on a model entirely foreign to the life of villages proper. The conception of communal ownership of the arable, which is so clearly expressed in the management of their fields, must be considered as the common stem from which both lines of management diverged, and it would be difficult to account for two entirely different conceptions of ownership in the two cases.[27] Indeed, in purely rural communities shifting occupation of strips of arable is not unknown. The so-called *runrig* or *rundale* system, which may be best illustrated by practices in Scotland, is based on it. Although it may very probably go back to Celtic practices in the Highlands, yet it is to be found in operation in Saxon communities in the Lowlands. In the townships of this region we often find a division of the arable into two parts—the inner part cultivated with greater intensity and with the employment of manure and other capital improvements ; and the outlying parts, which are tilled in a more perfunctory manner. The better, inner land is sometimes divided into strips, which are given over in turn to the several husbandmen, so that habits of constant occupation do not arise in regard to it.[28]

But undoubtedly in most cases which come under our notice in the later middle ages we find the open field system,

Intermixture of Strips coupled with a hereditary possession of the strips assigned to a share by the householder to whom the share belongs. The 120 acres, or any other number of acres contained in the hide, lie in different places, and are severed from the acres of neighbours by thin fringes of unploughed turf, the so-called balks. Even in this most common case there are many peculiarities attached to the tenure of these strips. The aim of the arrangement does not seem to have been to single out the land of a particular individual and to protect it from

encroachment and intrusion. Such precautions as are taken
in this respect are very slight. On the contrary, the close
union of the different holdings, their inclusion in one and
the same system, which is not devised by the will and
plans of any one of them in particular, but is carried on
by the whole group, is expressed in a variety of points.
The possessions are intermixed ; allotments are made,
not in patches set apart for the use of the different householders, but in strips assigned to every one in each of the shots
or fields occupied for tillage by the community.[29]   It is a
remarkable arrangement ; the more remarkable because
with all its inconveniences of communication, all its back-
wardness in regard to improvements, all its trammels on
individual enterprise and thrift, all its awkward dependence
of the individual on the behaviour of his neighbours, it
repeats itself over and over again for centuries not only over
the whole of England but over a great part of Europe.
Powerful influences must have been at work to originate
and to support it, and it is well worth while to dwell a little
longer on its social significance.   One thing seems clear :
although this system was not by any means the best for
furthering the progress of cultivation, it was particularly
adapted to the requirements of a community of shareholders
who were closely joined together in the performance of their
work, the assertion of their rights, the performance of their
duties and the payment of their dues.   On the supposition
that the basis of social arrangements was to be a repartition
of rights and duties according to the shares with which
people were endowed in the tenure of land, the complicated
open fields, intermixed strips and graduated holdings of
the *túns* would suggest themselves naturally ; and in this
cumbrous form the different obligations of economic and
political life would, as it were, strike root into the soil.   It
has been lately a matter of dispute among scholars whether
the scattering of strips in the shots of the open field system
was to be accounted for by a wish to equalise the advantages and the drawbacks, the conveniences and the difficulties of every economic combination between the shareholders of the village.   Some of our authorities hold the view

that a more natural explanation of the chequered proprietorship of the peasants in the open fields, would be found in the fact that the shots and furlongs were not occupied at once, but reclaimed gradually as the needs of the settlers increased, so that a householder came to possess widely scattered strips in the fields of his native village as a result of a long process of spreading cultivation.[30] But the proposed explanation does not seem to us to alter materially the conclusions which were previously admitted. It is irrelevant whether the shareholders A. B. C., etc., are thought to be endowed with strips lying in discontinuous neighbourhood to each other in three or in thirteen shots or furlongs. It is quite possible that they began by holding in three, and that only their great-grandchildren came to hold in thirteen. But in the early allotment within the first three shots and on subsequent allotments in the rest the strips were meted out in such a manner as to balance each other, and so we come, after a historical digression, to the same result, namely, that it was thought expedient to go on cutting parallel and scattered strips under approximately equal conditions, instead of turning the attention and the interests of every householder to one part of the soil and keeping it for his exclusive use.[31] Moreover, the cloven foot of rationalism is perhaps most apparent in the attempt to account for all the varieties in the construction of shots and strips by the growth of casual occupation and divisions among heirs. Nor does it seem very likely that in the case of migrations of considerable bodies of men and of occupation of the soil in close groups and not in small settlements, even the first colonists could avoid cultivating in several furlongs at the same time, and forming the holdings from strips scattered in several subdivisions of the common fields. And it is to such occupation by close groups that we have chiefly to look in the case of Teutonic settlements in England. What the exact relation of these modes of settlement to the former state of Celtic and Roman agriculture was it would be impossible to tell ; but one thing is certain—that the Teutonic conquerors had not to start entirely *de novo* in cultivating the island, and that therefore their bundles of scattered strips in the fields represented not so much a gradual adding of furlong to furlong as the allotment of extant arable on conditions which seemed fair and equitable to them. And the main trait in these conditions was, that every snare, whether a hide or virgate or bovate, had to get its strips in the shots of the open field in proportion to its place in the general scheme of the community.

A very graphic and instructive description of the process of allotment is afforded by a narrative of occurrences in the manorial court of Wahull, Bedfordshire, preserved in a cartulary of Dunstable Priory. The proceedings are comparatively early—they occurred probably in the time of Henry II, or of his sons—and notwithstanding their feudal framework, the presence of the lords of the manor, of a submanor and the like, the communal character of the whole process is well preserved, and there is no reason to suppose that these things were done very differently at a time when the manorial organisation of village life was not so rigid nor so complete.

In the time of the war (perhaps the rebellion of 1173) the eight hides in Segheho were encroached upon and appropriated unrighteously by many, and for this reason a general revision of the holdings was undertaken before Walter de Wahull and Hugh de Lege in full Court by six old men ; and it was made out to which of the hides the several acres belonged. At that time, when all the tenants in Segheho (knights, freeholders and others) did not know exactly about the land of the village and the tenements, and when each man was contending that his neighbours held unrighteously and more than they ought, all the people decided by common agreement and in the presence of the lords of Wahull and de la Lege, that everybody should surrender his land to be measured anew with the rod by the old men, as if the ground were being occupied afresh ; every one had to receive his due part on consideration of his rights. At that time R. F. admitted that he and his predecessors had held the area near the castle unrighteously. The men in charge of the distribution divided the area into sixteen strips (*buttos*), and these were distributed as follows : there are eight hides in Segheho, and to each two strips were apportioned.[32]

Thus the possibility of re-divisions, starting from the idea that the actual holdings in the fields ought to be commensurate to the shares which they represent in the village group, was not excluded, and it is natural enough that we should oftener get glimpses of such re-arrangements than of the original allotments following the conquest or the reclaiming of virgin soil. The possibility of these re-arrangements on the basis of the customary law of rural organisations proves the existence of the view that although the strips of arable held and cultivated by the different households were usually handed over from generation to generation and could form the object of legal claims, they constituted at bottom the shares of the households as members of a community, and could be shifted bodily from one place to the other provided their proportionate value was maintained. The strongest and most elaborate expression of this principle is found in Scandinavian legal customs ; and it may not be amiss to refer here to its rules, inasmuch as occasional instances of reallotment may, as we have seen, be supplied from purely English evidence, while the deep-rooted ideas of Scandinavian folk on the modes of land-settlement cannot have been without influence in a country the soil of which is thickly studded in the north and north-east with *bys* of Scandinavian origin.[33]

Apart from the processes of allotment and re-arrangement and of the intermixture of strips, communal features in the

Open Field Pasture

management of the arable are clearly marked in its reversion into common pasture after the harvest, and in the management of the course of agriculture by common and not by individual dispositions. The fact that the field became a united whole after the season of the crops is one of the most conspicuous traits of rural life, and it has several interesting consequences. Its importance lay, firstly, in the recurring illustration it gave every year of the limitation of individual rights in the fields to one season and one economic process, the raising of the

crop ; while the right of the community re-asserted itself at
other seasons and for other purposes.   There were certain
peculiarities in mediæval husbandry which gave to this
matter more than a theoretical meaning.   Let us remember
that it was conducted on the principle of maintaining
local balance between agricultural and pastoral pursuits.
The agriculturist was also a cattle breeder ; as a rule he
could not rely on foreign or distant markets to supply him
with his beasts ; he had to look for their maintenance
himself, and he was mainly dependent on pasture for
this purpose, because the cultivation of grass and even the
making of hay were, as we have seen, exceptional.   The
cattle fed on the soil in a literal and natural sense, and the
management of pasture for oxen and sheep became as
necessary and important a feature as the ploughing work
of the oxen and the shearing of the sheep.   Leaving the
question of sheep-farming in its relation to wool trade and
cloth manufacture on one side, as it would lead us too far out
of our way, we may content ourselves with dwelling somewhat on the part played by pasture rights in the usual
round of agricultural work.   Not only was it necessary to
get sufficient pasture, but it was exceedingly important to
get it close at hand ; the pasturing on the fallow in the
immediate neighbourhood of the village saved a good deal
of supervision, and was safer than the sending of cattle to
far off drifts ; a momentous consideration in those troubled
times.   In regard to the plough-oxen pasture situated near
at hand was a necessity during the ploughing seasons,
stretching over a good deal of the year.   It would have been
out of the question to send the oxen to distant pasturages in
the intervals between their work-days on the strips.   In this
way even in villages where the three-field course of agriculture was in use, the pasturing on the fallow was a most
important concern, and had to be looked to and maintained
by the peasanty, as one of the mainstays of their welfare.
And a great part of the country, though it is not known
exactly how much, lived under a two-course system, reserving half the fields for pastoral purposes.[34]   In some places
we come across even a greater predominance of pasture

over arable. But without dwelling on these last more exceptional cases, there can be hardly a doubt that the primary importance of rights of pasture must have been one of the reasons which gave the whole husbandry of an Old English village a decidedly communalistic bent.[35] We must not fail to take notice of the other side of the arrangement which I have characterised by the expression local balance between agricultural and pastoral pursuits. If the material support which cattle-breeding had to seek in pasture rights over arable land has to be insisted on, no less material was the support which agriculture found in the practices of cattle-breeding. The fields lying fallow were not only the most convenient pasture land in the village, they were also the means of providing the soil with manure. If the wild-growing grass was almost the only available forage for the village cattle, the refuse of this cattle was the only manure which was used for the improvement of the soil. And thus the question of bringing the cattle to pasture assumed a new importance. We hear a good deal about obligations to use folds for sheep, and there can be no doubt that the meaning of them must be sought in the value of the manure.[36] The free man of Old England was characteristically described as fyrdworthy, moteworthy and fold-worthy:[37] this expression calls for comment on many sides, but for our present purpose it is the right of a man to keep his cattle in his own fold or in the fold of the village that has to be noticed, because it illustrates the part played by the manuring question in rural husbandry, even from the point of view of the social divisions of these times. And it is the more significant that although the manuring power of cattle was well understood and carefully made use of, and though its management had the effect of drawing the cattle as much as possible to the fallow pasture, considerations of private interest were not strong enough in this case to provide for a division of the strips between the households in manuring time. The fallow pasture remained communal, though the fold may have been private property in some cases ; and if we may judge from practices followed in our own days, one of the duties of the village herdsmen was to look to a fairly equable driving of the cattle over the fallow, so that no one householder should be too much privileged or prejudiced through an uneven repartition of refuse over the field.[38]   These are not trifling questions : they deal with interests and welfare, and it is not of second-rate importance that they were managed on the communal and not on the individualistic principle.

The customary and compulsory rotation of crops gives also occasion for gauging the wide difference between the notions and habits of Old English agriculturists **Rotation of Crops** and our present ideas on the conduct of rural business. I have already spoken of the prevalent systems of cultivation ; the three-field system with its shift of winter seed, wheat, spring-seed, barley or oats and fallow ; the two-field system with its alternate change from crops to pasture ; the system of occasional cultivation with its temporary occupation of patches of land for the raising of a series of crops while the rest remained pasture ; cultivation in closes with special manuring and a more complex rotation of crops.[39]   Of these systems the first two were undoubtedly the most usual and we must turn our attention to them.   The main point about them was that the plan of the agricultural operations to be performed : the seasons for the commencement and the interruption of work, the choice of the crops to be raised, the sequence in which the different shots and furlongs had to be used, the regulations as to fencing and drainage, etc., were not a matter of private concern and decision, but were to be devised and put in force by the community.   Such was the general practice at the time when we can actually observe the working of rural arrangements by means of documents and descriptions, and there cannot be the slightest doubt that the same was the case at the time when the husbandry systems of Old England were settled on the chequered boards which the maps of the country before the enclosures present to us with such abundance of detail.   And it is evident that the gradations of the social status of the tenants do not make any difference in these respects.

Whether we have a half-servile community under a lord, or a village of socmen or other free people, the essential features of the map do not vary, and the customary arrangements are made and enforced by the community, possibly with more or less pressure from stewards and powerful people, but in the main on communal lines ; so communal indeed, that even the strips of the lord's shares were in many cases intermixed with the rest and thus bound to submit to the plan of management and the rules laid down by the common consent of meetings of the shareholders.

In regard to the house, and to the close or croft adjoining it, the householder had a right of private ownership which seems at first sight to be as well grounded as the freehold property of the present day. Already in regard to the ceorl, the Old English freeman of the lowest degree, it might be appropriately said that an Englishman's house is his castle. His *edor*, his hedge, was protected as well as the King's or the thane's burgh, though the penalty for breaking through it corresponded, as in all other cases of infringement of private rights, to his personal status. Within the precincts of the house, the *flet*, the ceorl had police authority and had to be compensated if anybody fought there.[40] The " weorthig," the homestead surrounded by a separate close, had to be protected against the inroads of strangers and animals by a fence which was kept up under the owner's directions and by his personal care.[41] Still, even in regard to house and close there was a superior power stretching over them ; not merely the power of the King, as chief of the government, or of the nation or tribe as a political body, bending all civil rights under the supreme requirements of its political existence, but of the village community in its entirety as against the separate households as its component members. The assumption rests in this case on inferences, but such as they are, they have to be considered in the absence of direct evidence either for or against. We know, to begin with, that the early Teutonic conception of the homestead ranged it in the category of moveable property,[42] and gave scope for frequent displacements in consequence of wars, migrations

Toft and Croft

and rearrangements of settlements. On all such occasions
the allotment of homesteads and closes as well as of other
elements of the holding was effected by the common action
of the association of the village, and could be modified in
consequence of some further change in the territorial occupation. Such changes must have been especially frequent
at a time when the boundaries between the tribes were
constantly shifting, and the invading Angles, Saxons,
Jutes, etc., pressed forward step by step on the soil of
Britain. But even when the movement of conquest had
more or less ceased, migrations and resettlements of rural
occupation remained frequent, because they were the
necessary outcome of the expansion of population and of
the reclaiming of waste land. The story of these molecular
movements has never been told, but distinct traces of
them exist still in the shape of recurring names which
may be found all over the country. It is clear that
Little Over is a colony of Mickle Over as much as
Lesser Nailsworth is an offspring of Great Nailsworth,
although we have no means of judging in what order and
sequence the branches grew from the stem.[43] Now the
formation of the new settlements was, of course, sometimes simply the outcome of the squatting of single settlers
in wood or waste, but it may also have been an occupation
by entire bodies of men, and in this case it involved a
division of allotments, a formation of homesteads under
the regulating influence of the community, which by itself must have kept present and alive the ideas and
practices of the superior entity of the village group.
And, in some instances at least, the sending forth of
these colonies must have reacted on the state of the mother
settlements themselves. We do not know enough about
the conditions under which the swarming off from an
established village was begun and conducted, and we need
not speculate about its definite methods ; but so much we
may take for granted, that in many cases the disruption of
the old group must have led to a remodelling of the old
tún, as well as to the formation of new *túns*.

Lastly, there were two subjects, which demanded a good

deal of attention and common action, but on which, not-withstanding their importance, we have scarcely time to dwell. I mean the drawing and keeping up of frontiers and the management of village streets, roads, ways and paths. The intermixture of strips, and the scattering of the bits of ground to which people had to find access in the course of their farming rendered this last subject especially momen-tous.[44]

II. ORGANISATION OF THE TOWNSHIP.

It is time to consider by what means this far-reaching and complicated shareholding arrangement was carried out. The documentary evidence at our disposal does not enter fully into the matter, and, naturally enough, this side of rural life has not left distinct traces on the ground itself. Again and again the student of these everyday occurrences is hampered by the fact that information about affairs which did not stir the passions, and were not productive of sharply defined changes in law and government, is not reflected in chronicles, or even in legal documents and memorials. Let us remember that our court rolls begin to run only from the end of the thirteenth century, that even continuous records of the King's Courts have come down merely from the close of the twelfth, that early manorial rolls hardly ever condescend to make entries apply-ing to field trespasses and economic administration, though these items appear conspicuously in later rolls ; and that the constitution of such a prominent court as the court of the hundred is merely glanced at in an enactment of Edgar, while for a somewhat fuller description of its work-ing, we have to rely on the late and private compilation of the so-called laws of Henry I. Even in feudal times we hear more of the fields and of the farming than of the agencies by which the latter was carried on. Still there is some weighty evidence to go by, if we supply the deficiencies of early documents by information cautiously drawn from later data, and if we allow inferences from the subject matter of rural life to its formal organisation. It seems clear from this latter point of view that some sort of constant and efficient organisation was needed to settle the many questions concerning the conduct of communal business in the fields, woods and waste. It does not help us much to say that these things were carried on automatically, because this could only mean that they were left to take care of themselves, and surely it is to men and not to things that we have to look for the making of plans, the settlement of difficulties and the enforcement of rules. Custom is a great force when it has been set going, but in order to get its motion it must start from arrangements or decisions of some kind. No more would the notion of " reality " help us without schemes to fasten the real obligations on. Because " reality " is only a name for a more or less constant division of rights and duties between the several shareholders, and in this case, as in others, the part could not exist without the whole, the customary division could not arise without some premeditation and care to make things fit and to keep them in order.[45] Besides, whatever the repetitions and memories of arrangements may have been, life was nevertheless a growing and changeful process, and never more so than at a time when people were looking out for new openings and struggling for conquest. Surely the open field system of Old England had not yet shrunk to the mechanical repetition of antiquated ceremonies and hampering arrangements which it assumed in course of time, when the real progress of agriculture got to depend not on " champion " practices but on individualistic farming. The very tenacity of custom in the shape of almost meaningless survivals testifies to its having been very full of meaning before. It would hardly have been needful to vindicate and explain with such insistence the necessity and influence of by-laws, of village regulations for the carrying on of the affairs of the rural community, if we had not been advised of late by high authority not to value too greatly their legal force and even their matter of fact importance. Now, I confess to being unable to understand how the whole series of operations of which we have been speaking could have been conducted, if there had not been binding rules and directions and managers or officers to look after them. Nor are we left in

the dark about the scope and action of by-laws. We find
every point of village husbandry that we have been describing illustrated by rules and prohibitions emanating from
the authority of village courts.[46]

Let it be noted that the authority of the by-laws is sometimes, as, for example, in the Durham books, expressly
deduced from the common decision of the members of the
village. The injunction of the lord may appear by the
side of it, but it is not necessary to establish the rule
which comes into force by common assent.[47] A difficulty
seems to arise in connection with this evidence. May we
draw inferences from these later cases to the working of rural
authorities in Old English times ? The evidence which we
get in feudal records is always more or less transfused with
a manorial element. It is not the court rolls of the villages
as such, but the court rolls of manors which give it ; it is
not the meeting of the village people, but the halimote of a
manor, which formulates the decisions : the influence of the
lord and of his officers makes itself felt in certain formulas, in the exaction of penalties, in the claiming of
privileges. To meet this difficulty we have to lay stress once
more on the fact that all the material arrangements which
made the working of the courts and the enactment of by-
laws necessary stretch right up to the epoch of the first
occupation of the land by the early English settlers. The
allotment, reclaiming, fencing in, ploughing, harvesting,
pasturing and manuring of the " gedál-land " of the hides
could not be carried on without by-laws similar to those
which begin to be enrolled about the fourteenth century in
regard to manorial land. And as in manors, as well as in
villages occupied by free settlers, practices connected with
open field and share-land were carried on, we must assume the making of by-laws and the enforcement of agrarian police regulations for the free, as well as for the
servile, villages ; probably even more for the first than for
the last, because in their case common advice and common
authority was unavoidable, and one does not see what else
could have curbed the individual householders to the
observance of so many and so awkward rules. The by-

laws were indeed a body of rural customary law, and all the
people in the village had to conform to them, although the
means of enforcing the conformity varied according to times
and according to different classes of persons.   How powerful
the strength of the common grouping was, may be gathered
from the fact that the free tenants of feudal times, who
through their direct connection with the royal courts stood
in one sense outside the manorial organisation of the
village, and had the juridical means of disputing and checking its influence, were nevertheless as a rule subject to the
operation of by-laws, took part in framing them and could
be forced to obey them.   The process against them was more
cumbersome than in the case of villains : they had to be
distrained with some caution when the latter were punished
in a more summary way.   But there were means of execution
against them on the basis of by-laws ; [48] and when, as was
natural in their position, conflicts arose and they applied
to the royal courts, these last, notwithstanding their
individualistic leaning and their habit of drawing a line
between the law of the royal courts and the customs of
manorial courts, did not question the general position as
to the obligation of freeholders to follow by-laws, but
merely reversed what they regarded as exaggerated assertions of the power of these subsidiary and self-imposed
laws. [49]

The regulations imposed on the villagers were of a two-fold
nature : they might be the result of explicit decision, or
else they might take the shape of custom.   The action of
the community in these two cases naturally took different
courses, though both these streams of rural law flowed
ultimately from the same fount—the lawgiving power of
the community.   In the first case we have to look for rules
elaborated and proclaimed by meetings or courts, in the
last to declarations of usage made by people who were held
to be versed in it, and to particular rulings and decisions of
officers entrusted with the carrying out in practice of customary arrangements.   There are traces of both varieties of
rural ordinances.   The first class is represented by the by-
laws proper, which are framed by manorial courts and have

left their records in the manorial rolls,[50] or, in some few
instances, have come down to us from villages whose organisation was, as it were, extra-manorial, and managed by
special meetings of the householders.[51] The action of the
manorial courts in themselves is characteristic enough, inasmuch as it represents in the arrangement of rural order, not
the interests or wishes of the lord and his stewards, but the
common necessities of the rural group in its peculiar management of champion farming. On the other hand, it is quite
usual for vexed questions in regard to village affairs to be
decided by an appeal to custom, to immemorial or ancient
usage ; and in such cases sworn experts are chosen from
among the householders and by them in order to declare
what the usage exactly is.[52] It seems fair to suppose that
questions of detail were settled by the officers or servants
who had to attend to the various needs of rural police and
administration, and that the action of these men was of
great influence in practice on the formation and inevitable
shifting of customs ; whereas it must have been kept in
check and made liable to revision and correction by the
court in more important matters, in cases of conflict and
protest.

And so we are led to ask : How was the current administration and police of the village carried on, and by whom ?
How were the rules of the community and the orders of its
officers and servants enforced, and by whom ? In both
cases the special enquiry which we are now carrying on as
to the state of these arrangements in Old English times, is
to some extent obscured by the fact that our evidence as to
these petty affairs comes almost exclusively from the later
feudal period ; and as to administrative and police arrangements, we have to suppose a good deal of change in the course
of development from one epoch to the other. We have
nothing else to do, however, but to put together the
slight indications which have come down to us from Old
English documents, with the full but somewhat distorted
details of the manorial age, and to lay especial stress amongst
these latter on those traits in which the stamp of manorialism
is least marked. Many points of detail must remain doubt-

ful, but perhaps we may be able to gather some guiding principles to go by.

In regard to special workers required in village life there will hardly be much matter for controversy. It is clear that the herdsmen [53] who had to attend to the cattle and to carry out the various regulations as to the use of pasture in its different kinds, were by the very nature of their duties more or less in the same position in the manorial and in the non-manorial organisations ; on the estates of great men and in villages occupied by groups of free ceorls. The shepherds and swineherds with their attendants had much the same thing to do in both cases, and the fact that the manorial servants had probably to attend to the collection of dues, such as pannage and grass-gafol, does not materially alter their position. It is worth notice, however, that this branch of village work might assume great importance and call forth the existence of special overseers of pasture-land. We hear of " greaves " of moors, officers who ordered the impounding of beasts in case of trespass, managed drainage, and probably exercised the police supervision over the moor district. We find them in later times on land belonging to sokes ; that is, in districts occupied by very free tenants ; they are elected by some assembly, but we cannot say precisely in what way they were distinguished from pettier officers in charge of similar duties in ordinary villages. Dyke greaves also appear in regions where the important duty of protecting the shore from incursions of the sea had to be attended to.[54]

In the same way the " woodwards " had to look after woods, the cutting of timber, the provision of housebote and heybote, the use of underwood, the gathering of brushwood, the supervision of wood-pasture, etc. The office of the " heyward " was also devoted to a kind of work connected with the incidents of the open-field system in all its varieties : the setting up of hedges, and the removal of them at the close of the season, was a consequence, not of manorial economy, but of open-field practices.[55] All these officers, and locally perhaps some others, were elected by the body of householders of a village ; and sometimes, as in the case of large moors and woods in which several villages intercommoned, by group meetings of these villages or of their representatives.[56]

All these branches of work covered, however, only the outskirts of rural life and some of its special applications. We may safely suppose that they were not always differentiated in the same manner, and that in many cases the differentiation was not carried very far ; there may have been many villages where a common herdsman with some attendants was deemed sufficient. In any case there were a number of matters in which, quite apart from manorial requirements, the village had to be represented by an officer for the carrying on of its economic and police business. There were meetings to be called and their resolutions to be carried out, cattle to be impounded, petty transgressions in the fields to be looked after ; the authorities of the hundred, of the shire, and eventually of the kingdom to be communicated with, taxes and levies to be gathered, matters of local police in street, way and field to be attended to, etc. Later on we find some of these functions specialised. We hear of elected coroners in especially privileged cases, and of elected constables in ordinary cases.[57] We hear also of elected Borg-ealdors in Kent which seem to go back to early times, and of tithing men as police representatives of townships in other counties.[58] But the most ancient and usual rural officer was undoubtedly the " reeve " gerefa, greave. Just because he was the general and principal representative of the village he came in later times to be much exploited by manorial administration ; his office got to be a downright burden, and had to be forced on the villagers. The duty of serving as reeve was even considered in some local customs as a sign of serfdom. But it could not have been so from the very beginning. Even if we had no direct proof to the contrary, it would be difficult to suppose that a man who had mostly to act as a petty authority was meant from the first to be selected from the lowest order of the peasantry, although that peasantry was in most places made up of different elements, and very free in some. The fact that the " gerefa " was commonly elected in feudal times does not necessarily imply a high position, because the heavy duties incumbent on him certainly made the choice not a favour and scarcely an honour. But in all cases in which the townships were called upon to act in political affairs the reeves appear as their necessary representatives. Whether the village appears before the King's court or the commissioners of some royal inquest by four or by six representatives, the reeve is always included in the deputation, and his closest companion is the priest, surely a representative of no servile institution.[59] Moreover, there are enough incidental mentions which show that the reeves were by no means always servile in status and duties.[60] It seems that in Old English times the reeves were considered from two points of view, which were not very clearly distinguished. Sometimes they appear in a special connection with a landlord, as stewards managing his lands and the dependent population on them.[61] The same name and the same office appear to apply to a person whose duties resulted partly from the concentration of the open-field group, and partly from the exigencies of the King and of magnates: In a sense this mixture of attributes was even more common in Old English than in Middle English times, because the contrast between the bailiff and steward on the one hand and the reeve on the other had not been fully developed as yet ; the reeve may have been a village headman and a steward at the same time ; though he was not necessarily both.[62] Without pretending to know exactly how these matters were arranged in the different stages of Old English history, we may nevertheless guess that the reeveship gained in importance as a rural agency at the same time and in the same way as it lost in point of social status. It presented, as it were, the knob, by which every kind of pressure from above was transmitted, and in proportion as this pressure became greater, the importance of the factor of transmission increased, though the personality of the holder did not gain by his enforced intercourse with the people in authority. In one sense we may even suspect that the reeveship became one of the earliest links in the manorialising process, inasmuch as it had to represent everywhere the requirements of the King, which were apt to assume in those times a proprietary tinge.   The element of landlordism came still more to the front in the later half of the Anglo-Saxon period, when the *landrica* became a recognised institution ; the reeve could be considered as the steward of the landrica, and we are unable to say to what extent these two varieties of the office, that of the great man's steward and that of the village headman, balanced or displaced one another.

The reeve appears in the political documents of the Norman age and of the constitution of the hundred as one of five or six representatives of the township.   They are *jurors*, and called up to give testimony as to questions of local custom, local affairs, local economic conditions.   We have to be especially thankful for the notice which informs us of the presence of this body of suitors in the hundred court, because it shows the use of such deputations to be something more than a Norman device.[63] The elements for working the inquest juries and the hundred court were evidently in existence, and more or less in shape, before the day when King Edward was alive and dead.   This supplies us with a connecting link for the important institution of wise men who have to give their verdict as to special questions addressed to them, and of trustworthy men who have to take notice of facts in order to be able to testify to them.   This institution, or rather these two institutions which may have acted either jointly or each by itself, fit remarkably well into the legal practices of the higher regions of Old English life.   The wise men, the authoritative thanes of the shiremote and of the witenagemot have commonly to express their views as to the customs of the shire or of the folk, and the testimony of such men is taken and attested as a means of settling controversies as to rights. It is to be noted as a significant fact that there were not only occasional deputations to the hundred court as well as to other higher courts, but standing committees of jurors formed for purposes of presentment and declaration of customs : the hundredors, the tenants attending at the court of the hundred.   An interesting glimpse into the working of this machinery is afforded to us by Edgar's enactment as to the witnessing of sales of cattle. Each " geburscipe," each township, has to provide for six sworn witnesses of such sales, and the " hundred-ealdor," the reeve of the hundred, has to apply to them in cases of doubt. The number itself is not without significance : it is the normal number of village jurors including the town-reeve and the priest.[64]

Unhappily our Old English evidence as to the composition and organisation of the township *moots* is scanty, though we cannot wonder at the indifference and reticence of our sources of information in regard to their humble doings. Still there are not a few traces of their existence, and we have means to judge of the general character of their work. In the Domesday Survey we come across mentions of *moots* collected by reeves for purposes of local management in different parts of the country. There can be no doubt that the halimotes, composed of free and servile suitors and transacting all kinds of local affairs which we find everywhere in feudal times, did not spring up into existence as an invention of Norman landlords, and we have to trace them in most cases to the halls which form the centres of Domesday manors. The grouping according to townships, and the connection of the reeve, the priest and the four representative villagers with townships, would lead us further to consider the *town moot* as the nucleus of rural administration.[65]

Besides, even if we had not possessed any direct information in regard to local meetings, the many affairs in which they had to exercise their influence in one way or the other, either by direct arrangement, by declaration of custom, or by the election of officers, servants and jurors to mind the interests of the village people, would have been evidences by themselves ; to understand the bearing of this evidence our best way is to look at the successors of the Old English moots, the manorial courts of the feudal age. They show us, if not the exact forms in which the old moots transacted their business, at least the general drift of it, and this seems sufficient for the rough purpose of historical understanding.[66]

I should like to add some questions, as the very putting of them may help us to look a little more closely into the working of the system, and to suggest some additional inferences in regard to it. The halimotes of the Middle English period were not merely assemblies or meetings for the sake of making agreements, but regular courts. Not only was their economic business transacted under substantially the same formalities as the juridical one, but they had power of jurisdiction in regard to transgressions and infringements of their regulations and prohibitions.[67] But was this power an expression of the communal element which they derived from the contingencies of the open-field system of shareholding, as practised from Old English times ; or was it imparted to the courts by the commanding element of feudal lordship ? Were transgressors punished, fined, distrained, because they were recalcitrant or offending members of the village community, or because they were subjects and possibly serfs of the manorial lord ? There are no direct answers to these questions, but there seem to be some clues for answering them. We have seen that freeholders were subjected to the operations of by-laws and of their restrictive provisions, though the process of enforcing obedience was more tortuous and uncertain in their case, because of their eventual recourse to the King's courts. And in the case of these freeholders it seems hardly possible to derive obligations analogous to the duties of less privileged tenants, from the feudal tie of tenure. As we observe in their case, which was a very common one in the North and East of England, a kind of double relation, a standing ground in rural jurisdiction on the one hand, in the public courts on the other, so we might be led to suppose that in the period before the Conquest in ordinary and petty cases the folkmote of the township not only gave its economic directions, but enforced them either directly through judgments and verdicts, or indirectly by the derived authority of its officers and servants. But then there was the other eventuality ; the possibility of prolonged protest, disobedience, resistance ; and in such cases the matter must have gone up to the courts of the hundred, of the shire, and eventually of the King ; which could always act in such cases by eliciting declarations of trustworthy local men, either on oath or without it, in regard to local customs and occurrences.[68]

On the other hand, it seems quite impossible to account for the entire conduct of the open-field affairs of the townships on the supposition that the hundred court had to look after the endless and minute incidents of agrarian practice.[69]

III. POLITICAL DUTIES

When the close agrarian grouping of the shareholders of a village has been realised, one comes to understand Scot and why all the requirements of the Government, Lot of the Church, and of the military aristocracy were charged to the townships, and why the repartition and collection of most duties remained a concern of the townships even when the country had been parcelled out into Manors and Knight fees. It was not a casual expedient that made the Kings and the National Councils turn to the townships for the collection of various dues in war and peace, but the fact that they were natural groups kept together not by the external pressure of threats and fines, but by the positive interests of everyday life. And it is to the strong vitality of these interests and groups that the revival of England after the Danish scourge and its firm settlement under the rule of the Norman Exchequer and of the Norman courts has to be ascribed more than to the various devices for exacting contributions. The shareholder who participated in the common husbandry of the township was also a participant in the burdens which were laid on it by the powers that be. He was *in scot and in lot* with the township,[70] and he had to face the township in regard to all sorts of requirements as the township faced the sheriff and the Royal Treasury. Tribute was imposed from above on the shires, then subdivided among the hundreds, and ultimately partitioned among the townships, leaving them to cope with their individual sums.[71] The hidage with

which the history of tribute begins was imposed in this way,
although the authorities began early to compound with
privileged persons and institutions for rearrangements and
exemptions ; [72] on the one hand, to look not only to the
block sums imposed on the districts, but also to the rough
capabilities of these districts and of their component parts,
on the other. Still, both the hidage and the Danegeld,
which came to be so crushing a burden, were imposed
primarily on the districts, and, what is more, the whole
district, and especially its lowest units, the townships in
town and village, were held responsible for the whole amount
of the tax under the joint liability and reciprocal guarantee
of the shareholders in scot and lot.[73] Changes in the
traditional impositions and the alleviation of customary
burdens were not so easy to effect, though they were effected
every now and then by the mere force of circumstances,
which even the harshest and most unwieldy of governments have to recognise, if they want to stop short of un-
bearable requirements. The cry for alterations testifies as
much to the persistency of customary claims, as to the
occasional deviations from them.

It is needless to say that the governmental requirements
of early times were based not so much on the collection
The Township   of money, though the Danish exactions show
In Hundred   a much greater stress in this respect than we
and Shire   might otherwise have suspected, but on the
gathering of resources of natural husbandry, and on personal services. The administration of justice, the whole
conduct of business in the higher centres of the hundred, the shire, the national councils was chiefly bound
up with the action of people who were made to appear in person, to do suit, as the feudal term was, and
we need not dwell on the burdensome character of these
enforced wanderings for political purposes. Originally
the attendance of all freemen of the districts was required,[74]
but in the later years of the Old English period we see
already the beginning of a system which reached its fullest
development in Norman hands, the change from an all-
round suit to a representative one, and the localisation

of this last into certain tenures.[75]   It is sufficient for our immediate purpose to point to the representative suit of the township at the hundred court, and to its liability to be called by representatives to the shire or any especial Royal court or commission of inquiry. As a matter of fact it is found that the hundred suit of the village is mostly performed by certain tenures, or more exactly by the tenants possessed of them, but the expedient of apportioning the suit by settling it permanently on certain holdings which had to receive a corresponding enfranchisement in other respects does not alter the principle of the duty.[76]   The reeve and four men come as the representatives of the township as a whole, and the township is responsible for their appearance because they are within its scot and lot territory.   The enforcement of military service, of the gathering of the fyrd, and of its substitutes, is more complex.   So much is clear, however, that the obligation got to be early graduated according to the size of the share held by a freeman in the land of the country, and in this way it was not quite independent of the township organisation.[77]   Still we have no direct evidence to show that the service of the fyrd was enforced through the medium of the village group or of its officers.   On the other hand, already in later Saxon times the township was being turned into a police unit of great moment. Whether the fact depended on the disruption and intermixture of the associations of kindreds or not, at any rate in the period of the last kings of English and Danish race we find the government introducing a system of personal frankpledge which was fitted on to the territorial groups, so that the township had to look after its arrangement, and sometimes even to perform its duties.[78] Besides supporting the system of frankpledge, the townships were made answerable for crimes committed within their territory when such crimes could not be charged to distinct malefactors, or when malefactors were not properly pursued.[79]   In an analogous manner the townships were made the chief organs for the collection of the heavy Church-scot.[80]   Altogether, the treatment of the township as a united group to which State and Church look for the performance of social duties appears as a natural result of the compact build of the township as an economic unit.

CHAPTER V

THE HISTORY OF THE HOLDING

HITHERTO we have been considering the township as a combination of shareholders endowed with rights as to land, carrying on a peculiar system of farming, and subjected to a set of duties in regard to the State and to the Church. But our survey would be not only incomplete, but misleading, if we did not pay attention to the constitution and life of the share itself—of the single holding entering as a unit into the combination. This unit presents some very remarkable traits. To begin with, the shares are not uniform or always equal. Not only did the acreage and the relation between the different elements of the share—close, arable, rights as to meadows, wood, pasture, water-courses, etc., vary a good deal according to local conditions, but, as we have already seen, in each given locality the shares were arranged as full, half, quarter units, etc. These fractions were not arbitrary, nor left to the casual working of individual wishes and chances. They arranged themselves according to certain natural degrees and divisions, which are easily grasped, because they started, in most cases, from the natural divisions of the plough-team, as the most important implement of a rural household. Land acquired its chief value as cultivated soil. Of course, the possibility of an appreciation of land on other than agricultural grounds was not excluded : it may have had great worth as a surface for grazing sheep, or as containing salt, or by reason of fishery rights attached to it, and the like. But the usual and normal mode of forming shares and estimating land was afforded by its relation to active agriculture as expressed in

The Plough-land and its subdivisions

the work of a plough-team provided with the requisite number of oxen for tillage. Now the normal English plough-
team with which the Domesday Survey reckoned was very
large. It worked, on an average, with eight oxen; though
the possibility of using smaller teams on lighter soil or in
exceptional circumstances is by no means excluded. Indeed,
we hear of smaller teams, and, curiously enough, ancient
pictures of ploughs represent them as drawn by four or even
two oxen.[1] But there is ample evidence of the fact that, at
any rate, from the eighth to eleventh centuries the eight-
oxen team was considered as the one best adapted to
the requirements of the soil and to the shape of the fields,
and that the general drift of farming development ran in
the direction of its introduction whenever possible.[2] It is
not easy to form an adequate opinion as to the origin and
merits of such a plough, but the facts are there, and they
must have been well grounded in natural conditions, because
the heavy cumbersome team held its own all through the
period covered by champion farming, and was in vogue in
some places even so late as in the eighteenth century. It
seems to have been an implement which supplied the
deficiency of individual exertion and skill by an accumulation of animal strength. However this may be, the fact of
the arrangement itself does not admit of doubt, and the
shares were graduated according to the main standard of the
plough-team and of its natural sub-divisions, the virgates
and bovates. Besides these, there was in every township
a number of smaller tenements which did not join in the formation of plough-teams, and were irregular in size, but the
main agricultural work was carried on by the regular units
and a corresponding social importance was attached to
them.[3] Originally the normal holding of the free moteworthy, fyrdworthy and foldworthy household was assumed
to be the hide, the land of the full plough-team, but in process of time this proportion could not be kept up, and we
find free people sometimes possessing more and sometimes
less ; in any case, the holding of virgates and bovates became
quite common among the free as well as among the servile
peasantry.

Before investigating the conditions under which these variations in the size of holdings were effected, we must

Population of the Holding look to the composition of the human group gathered on each share. Although one person, the chief of the household, was deemed juridically its owner or tenant, it was meant to supply the needs of several people, of a family of kinsmen and dependants.

In the earlier centuries of Old English rule the number of such dependents must have been considerable, even on the restricted shares of common ceorls : there were undoubtedly many slaves, prisoners of war and their offspring, people bought on the market or kidnapped in the borderland districts, even people who had fallen into slavery through crime or insolvency (wite-theows).[4] Undoubtedly most of these were to be found among the domestics and rural servants of the magnates, but they played also originally a part in the economy of certain of the freemen, inasmuch as those last were warriors capable of obtaining slaves by force or well-to-do men with means of buying and keeping bondmen. Still, even in the earliest stage of English life, it could not be said that English society was a slaveholding one in the sense in which it has been argued sometimes that ancient Teutonic society was slaveholding. The lesser people had very soon to look after a good deal of agricultural work themselves, and it was evidently not thought humiliating to lead a plough or to superintend the sheep-farming or cattle-breeding even for those who had the right and obligation of carrying arms and joining in the fyrd. Unfree labourers there were, but farming pursuits and work were not restricted to them or specialised by them ; they toiled alongside of their freeborn masters.[5] Indeed, we have to notice again, as in the case of the Welsh, that slavery turns out not to be a fit economic and social basis for a primitive, half agricultural, half pastoral society : the slaves are difficult to keep and awkward to deal with ; people have not yet learned to organise their work and to supervise it. They are led to allow the slave a good deal of liberty and economic independence, they prefer turning him into a subjected freedman and a tributary householder instead of exploiting his personality thoroughly and completely. Tacitus' words seem remarkably fitting in respect of the the slaves of Old England : they are mostly provided with small households of their own, used as *coloni*, rendering rents in kind and very often liberated from the stain of personal slavery.[6]

A striking illustration of the force of the social considerations tending this way is afforded by the fact, that the Danish invasions and conquests, which were characterised by such cruelty and reckless treatment of the vanquished, did not lead to the formation of any considerable class of slaves in the Eastern counties occupied by the Danes : such vestiges of slavery as there were at the time of Domesday point towards the West.[7] The fact is certainly not to be explained by a greater inclination on the part of the Saxons for enslaving the Welsh than there was in the case of Danes in regard to Saxons ; we have rather to attend to the development of larger complexes of property in the West, which afforded a more convenient field for the use of slave labour than the scattered and generally small households of the Danes.   Such slaves as there were within these last were distributed in small batches among the shareholders of the *by's*, and very likely were not recorded in the survey at all.   On the contrary, the class of *lysings*, or freedmen, is very noticeable in those very districts, and evidently was recruited from those who under different social conditions would have been or would have remained slaves.[8]

The point which we have to insist on now is. that the serfs employed in the household of a small shareholder were not the economic mainstay of this household, and were not distinguished by the quality of their work from its freeborn members   How far and in what cases the weaker of those members had to bear the brunt of productive work, and the stronger were able to indulge in loitering and military adventures, it is difficult to say with any degree of certainty.   In the course of invasions and raids, the tendency towards burdening the weaker people, women, old people, the offspring of younger brothers, etc., with more than their proportion of

work, must have been particularly strong. But, when all
this has been said, the facts remain, that the original hide
allotments of the ceorls were meant to represent the needs
not of a class which could afford to exact tribute, to abstain
from work and to specialise on military pursuits, but those
of a class which was meant to face both ways, to sustain
the fyrd arrangement of military policy, and at the same
time to perform the necessary farming labour of the community largely by its own hands. How far this arrangement
was tenable, and whether it was not doomed to degenerate
or develop into something else, are questions which will have
to be approached by and by.

   If a system of shareholding was to work at all, some
means had to be devised to keep up the unity of the
shares. And indeed, as the shares became identified with
Unity of   ploughlands or with natural subdivisions of
the Holding   them, arrangements were evidently at work
which prevented the partition of holdings according to
the infinitely varying chances of inheritance. Of course, in
the case of servile or colonary tenements the pressure
of the lord's power could regulate succession and restrict
it by admitting only one heir among many, the elder
brother, or the younger brother, or the person most qualified
in the eyes of the lord.[9] But as we see shareholding in
operation among free people and not only among serfs,
some other explanation is needed to account for the unity
of tenements.[10] And it may be noticed at the outset, that
the same causes which prevented irregular partition worked
evidently in checking partitions of any kind. The economic
unity of the hide was not a cunning artifice, it was an organic
arrangement based on a combination of live beings. The
ploughland could not fall into any given number of pieces,
and even when partitions became necessary it had to keep
to the simple divisions of two, four and eight subshares,
while "thirds," "fifths," "sevenths" would have been impossible fractions ; even so it could not go further than the sub-
share represented by the labour of one ox without destroying the ox, or in other words, without renouncing the essential condition of agricultural husbandry. And this means

that if there were more than eight heirs to a hide, more than four to a half-hide, more than two to a virgate, more than one to a bovate, something had to be done to satisfy their claims without destroying the value and even the meaning of the inheritable tenement. And the check which worked with such power in these cases, was felt to a great extent even in the case of other combinations. It is clear, that there was every inducement to preserve the unity of a larger holding, say of a hide or a half-hide, because its disruption, even if not amounting to physical absurdity, would mean the break-up of a customary working arrangement, a break-up disadvantageous in most cases, and simply ruinous, if the resettlements and subdivisions should follow each other quickly in the course of generations.

Indeed, we see many indications as to the expedients in use to counteract the harmful influence of the breaking up of the holdings. In Scandinavian and in ancient Teutonic law we find the well known marked disinclination to admit women to the inheritance of land, which goes so far sometimes as to debar them from any inheritance of the kind, but more often puts them in a position of disadvantage in comparison with brothers and even more remote male heirs. This, of course, was primarily meant to guarantee economic and military efficiency, but it tended also to diminish the number of possible claimants, and it seems probable that the older rules of folcland succession in England, and also some forms of artificial bookland succession, adhered to this course. The equality by right between male heirs of the same degree remained, however, and in this respect the customary development of land law seems to have proceeded on two different lines. We find socage tenure in the early feudal law both partible and impartible according to local custom,[11] and this shows that different rules were gradually elaborated in regard to it.

The case of partiblity is best represented by the Kentish tenure of gavelkind, which undoubtedly goes back to Saxon usage and, while it became singular in the feudal epoch, must have applied to a great, if not to the greater, number of free tenements in the Old

Gavelkind

English period. Now, its partibility must not be taken to
imply a constant or even a usual practice of hereditary partition. It amounts to a possibility of partition by right
and to an equality of claims between co-heirs which lead to
the admission of concurrent interests in the holding. As a
matter of fact, the holdings remained united as far as possible, but every one of them was saddled with a certain number of rights, which had to be harmonised by an apportionment of proceeds as long as the unity lasted.[12] It cannot be
said that the arrangement was a convenient one, notwithstanding efforts to get rid of a superfluity of claims by buying
out claimants and making provision for others on reclaimed
land and in new settlements. The Kentish tenements, as
they are described in later surveys, are covered with an
intricate network of rights before they get broken up into
irregular and sometimes exceedingly small fractions.[13]

In regard to the earlier period, we may surmise a greater
freedom in finding exits for the surplus of population and a
slower progress in its growth. But the main drift of this
mode of development consisted undoubtedly in keeping the
shares united, so far as possible, while admitting the
concurrent claims. It was a system resembling the practice
which obtained in Germany in so-called " Ganerbschaften,"
unions of coheirs carrying on husbandry arrangements on
shareland.[14] At the back of the whole system lies the eventual recourse to real partition, although we are unable to
say how far it was made compulsory on the claim of one, of
several, or of a majority of co-heirs, and what means were
employed to guard against too frequent an occurrence of
such partitions besides considerations drawn from practical
expediency. The actual working and the importance of
these unions of coheirs is further illustrated by the frequent
occurrence, before the Norman Conquest, of tenure in *parage*.
It mostly occurs in the case of thanes, that is, privileged
landowners standing outside the village communities, but they
had the same interest as the village people in keeping their
estates together even when equal claims were conceded, on
the strength of Old English custom, to heirs of the same grade.[15]
When we read of thirteen thanes holding a certain estate

in paragio, we must picture to ourselves the arrangement as a union for the purpose of the management of the estate, but with a recognition of the equal position of all in regard to the land. What is especially important, such unions appear not only as private and economic arrangements, but as a species of tenure recognised by the law and regulating the rights and obligations of the holders.[16] The demesne of peasant proprietorship presented evidently even a greater scope for the development of similar unions. The best proof of their vitality and importance consists in the fact, that the system of shareholding with its regular units did actually exist all over England, notwithstanding the prevalence through a great part of it of the rule of concurrent inheritance.

At the same time, the other line of development must not be lost sight of. It seems clear that even before the advent **Consolidation of Holdings** of the feudal age rules of primogeniture and junior right were forming themselves on the basis of local custom. Their practical value for the maintenance of the economic strength of holdings was so evident that it seems irrelevant to consider whether they came in first on servile tenements and by consideration of the interests of manorial lords or were developed independently on both sides—in regard to free owners and to tenants of all kinds. In any case, whether through parallel adaptation to circumstances or through a subsequent assimilation of free holdings to holdings of *coloni*, we find the customs of single succession arising in regard to tenements which cannot be traced either to a servile or to a manorial origin ; impartible socage and many varieties of burgage tenure are founded on these lines. The conception of service may count for a good deal in this process of the unification of holdings as regards succession, but it is not sufficient by itself to explain the facts of the case, and by its side, working in the same direction, stand obvious considerations drawn from the economic efficiency and convenient management, which applied quite as much to free as to dependent shares and estates, and the smaller the share or the estate the stronger must have been the tendency

against divisions. The historical result of this struggle
between the two tendencies at work—the striving towards
the maintenance of united shares on one hand and the growth
of population, on the other—is clearly expressed in the general fact that, though the idea of the hide, as the land of
the one household, had to be given up, and the virgate and
bovate became the typical household units, the parcelling up
of property generally stopped at this, and the system of
shareholding was kept up in the shape of these smaller
subdivisions of the ploughland. This rough result is very
characteristic in many respects, and we shall have to revert
to it again further on.   At present we must lay stress on the
fact that the most usual arrangement of rural land tenure at
the time of Domesday, whether in villainage or in socage, is
governed by the grouping into virgates and bovates, that
is, by an arrangement into small consolidated shares.

Thus, in matters of hereditary succession, we notice a
customary consolidation of shares called forth and kept up
Alienation of by farming requirements. A second question
Land has to be put in order to understand the
bearing of ancient law on land holding. How far was
the household share a commercial commodity, a unit of
value to be sold and bought, mortgaged and given away,
either as a whole or in parts ?   The opposition between
bookland and folkland is largely based on the treatment of
this question.   The owner of a popular holding in ancient
law was undoubtedly greatly restricted in the above mentioned respects. He could not break the holding up at
pleasure, give it away or sell it as he wished, because it represented not so much his own private concern as the allowance
of his family, and because his relations had expectant
hereditary rights in regard to it.   In fact, he was hampered by family considerations in this matter as much as he
was hampered by township arrangements in the matter of
the economic disposal of the holding.   But it was difficult to
preserve the standpoint taken up by ancient law in regard
to alienation.   There were powerful forces making for a
more complete private disposition as to land, besides the
natural tendency of every owner to get rid of restrictions,

besides the many occasions when the temptation arose
to treat land as having a commercial value, to barter or to
give it for this or that reason ; the Church appeared with its
never-ceasing claims, and the King, as a representative of
government, had to use land largely in remuneration for
services, an object which was better attained by assigning
the temporary use or the conditional use of it than by
alienating it once for all.

A certain mobilisation of lanled property became, as a
matter of fact, inevitable, and it was effected by two principal
methods. The bookland theory was developed in a sort of
barbaric imitation of Roman law practices. There arose
a species of land holding, guaranteed by book and not by the
witness of the shiremote, protected by ecclesiastical anathemas, royal authority, the solemn presence of witnesses and
the grudgingly given consent of relations against attempts
to traverse or to destroy deeds of alienation to strangers.
Land so held became the *terra testamentalis*, the *terra hereditaria*, the private property, which one could give and sell,
and sooner or later the same practices began to make their
way in the disposal of ordinary folcland, though as to this
last there remained more occasions for contest and complications.

The second way by which landed property was put into
the market and mobilised was the formation of *loanland*,

Loanland   the passage of a piece of land from the hands
of the owner into those of a tenant for a number
of years, or for life, or for several lives, or in hereditary possession in consideration of stipulated or implied services.
This category of landholding became especially important
at a time when the simple selling of land was not very usual
and not easily effected, and when, on the other hand, a number of great landowners had at their disposal vast tracts of
land which they could not utilise personally and directly.
Leases with a tendency towards protracted and hereditary
tenant right appear in use in all ranks and classes of society.
We find bishops endowing military retainers with estates
in hereditary succession, and for three generations,[17] kings
creating tenancies for their followers, without definite time

limits as to the use of the holdings,[18] landowners of great
and small size parcelling up parts of their estates among
rentpaying farmers, and starting colonies of dependent husbandmen in consideration of dues in kind and of labour
obligations.

Now, all the processes described could be applied to shares
included in communal groups as well as to estates em-

The Share and the Individual bracing entire groups or to land not occupied
by any groups at all. But in the case of share-
land the direct result of these transactions was
neither a disruption of the township community, nor a
severance of the ties connecting the alienated share with
the neighbouring allotments, but merely a change of its
personnel, the passing from the hands of one holder and one
household into the hands of another. The successor had to
submit to the general conditions and requirements of the
community in the same way as the ancestors, the buyer as the
seller, the leaseholder as the landlord. The system of reality
with all its consequences in the apportionment of rights and
duties acted in the same way as before, or ought to have
acted as before, and we sometimes hear of complaints that
it did not. In this way, we find in the life of the original
Old English settlements a curious combination of two principles—the individualistic principle in personal relations
and the communalistic in real relations. A man was not
held down or led by the township in his personal fortune;
he could freely thrive or decay, but the land which he possessed was fitted into the obligations and rights of the community in a way which was meant to be permanent, or at
least to alter only with the general growth of the community.
I mentioned the original settlements in order to distinguish
the townships created by popular occupation from the large
number of those which grew up under the colonizing influence of the King, of the Church, or of great men : in these
last the influence of private will and disposition was, of
course, very prominent from the very first.

Of course, the contrast in principle between these two
conceptions of the personal and of the real arrangement of
life ought not to be exaggerated. They necessarily reacted

on each other. The fetters of the open-field system hampered private enterprise and made it difficult for an ordinary villager to rise by mere agricultural industry and thrift. On the other hand, when the political and proprietary factors outside the life of the village enabled a man to thrive, they might sometimes carry him altogether out of his class, and in that case he might turn to be a very awkward member for the village community to deal with. But still, on the average, the system served to make the two ends meet, and it is to such average conditions that we have to look chiefly in the general review of the subject which the scanty means at our disposal enable us to make.

CHAPTER VI

MANORIAL ORIGINS

THE laxity of organisation which is characteristic of the state of Old English society, as arranged in townships and hundreds, gave free scope to the play of indi-

Individualistic Tendencies vidual forces making for more effective economic management and more consistent legal rules. We see in operation a set of causes which contributed powerfully to the spread of inequality in society. They may be summarised under the heading of spread of patronage. We have already had occasion to touch on some of the phenomena connected with it, but it is necessary to consider them yet from another point of view. One of the most striking political features of the time is the insufficiency of central power for the discharge of its governmental duties, and the consequent necessity for its subjects to seek private protection. As long as the tribal arrangement with its far-reaching family ties was in good working order, the supplementary protection was afforded by the families, agnatic and cognatic kindreds, etc., which encircled the individual and acted as political groups of great power and wide responsibility. But the influence of the kindreds soon began to fade in the new and complicated conditions of English life. The government still appealed to the action of kindreds in settling landless men, in looking after people who had left their ordinary surroundings,[1] etc. But it had more and more to take into account the shattered state of these primitive institutions, and to appeal to groupings of people designed to replace or to strengthen them. The voluntary association of the guild appears as a powerful substitute for kindreds in the case of men of all sorts, of traders, artisans, landowners, etc., and it is evident that what is sought is not merely or

chiefly social intercourse, but mutual guarantee and protection between its members.[2]

The patronage of powerful individuals and of the most
potent of social forces—the Church—has to be taken
into account even more than the rise of the guilds. The
lord (the hlaford) becomes at an early time an important
agent in the social order. A definite and very considerable part in a man's wergeld is assigned to him by the
side of the kindred.[3] On the other hand, he is made
responsible for the behaviour of his client, a fact which
implies a certain power of control and coercion.[4] The
relation of patronage, or commendation, as it is called in
later sources, is originally produced by free agreement
and may be dissolved under certain conditions by any one
of the parties,[5] but relations of mutual support could not
be trifled with and lightly thrown over ; and, on the other
hand, the hlaford had to be careful how he treated his
dependants, if he wanted to keep up and increase his social
influence and material profits. Such relations, once
started, tended to crystallise and to connect themselves
with all sorts of material obligations—loans, gifts, endowments, rents, tenancies, and the like. Complicated
settlements of claims were necessary in such cases,
and the government insisted on a certain stability
in these relations,[6] which assisted it in its administrative
task. In fact, by the side of voluntary commendation we
find at the close of the period an involuntary one. A man
could sometimes go with his land where he pleased, but
there were also cases when he could not ; a householder
commended to a great man had usually to stick to his
patron, or to put it in another way, patronage had a tendency to strike roots and to develop into a lasting lordship
over free men and their land.[7]

Commendation being originally a purely personal relation,
did not necessarily lead to the subjection of whole townships or districts ; on the contrary, it resulted
in a heterogeneous position of divers tenants in
the same locality.[8]   But there was another kind
of patronage growing up on Old English soil which assumed

**Soke and
Sokemen**

naturally a territorial cast. I mean the frequent grants of private jurisdiction made by the Anglo-Saxon kings. Public justice was at best cumbersome and onerous ; in a sense, it was a source of profits and exactions. Fines had to be imposed and levied, local means provided for the easy discharge of petty causes, and great men were considered the best local agents for enforcing obedience and taking up the settlement of local disputes. Small people were freed, on their side, from costly peregrinations and processes, while great people obtained new sources of income and influence. Many interests worked together in this way for the institution of aristocratic franchises on a territorial basis.

Even in the earliest history of Teutonic settlements in Great Britain germs of a patrimonial justice are discernible. Every householder possessed coercive power not only over his slaves, but also over other subjects (hiredman, geneat,) at least within the precincts of his house and private close,[9] and the importance of these rights grew in proportion as the subject population increased. When the greater part of the English rural population sank down into the condition of peasants, the settlements of disputes among them and the infliction of punishments for petty offences came to form by itself a very considerable jurisdictional area and in connection with the fact that the geburs or villains were not considered as mere serfs, but presented a mixed condition both in point of rights and as to origin, the vast domain of patrimonial justice and police assumed an importance approaching that of the public courts. Besides, the application of patrimonial jurisdiction became more and more frequent and more extended by virtue of the direct conferment or the prescriptive use of rights of sake and soke (cause and suit). The formulas granting such franchises vary in their wording, mostly dwelling, besides the two main terms, on *toll* and *theam, infangene-theof, utfangenetheof,* and *flymenfyrmth,* but sometimes embracing the grave cases of homefare, forestall and rape.[10] When the trial of such cases was made over to a private person, a court, necessarily grew out of it ; it was a kind of chip severed from the block of the public courts of the hundred, county, or realm, a court based on the participation of those free men who came under its soke, or had to do suit (*soke*) to it. Although in some cases personal considerations went, as it were, across these immunities, keeping some people out of them and joining other people to them in spite of their place of abode, on the whole the grants of sake and soke embrace districts and modify the position of the population of these districts in regard to the ordinary course of jurisdiction.[11]

At the same time, there were generally two accessory aspects of the situation created by the franchises : freemen were indeed given over to patrimonial courts, but in regard to them the courts of sokes, though held in virtue of private grants, were still considered public courts and liable to supervision, appeal from and restriction in the use of their powers. And in some respects these freemen still had to sue in the King's courts, and formed the bulk of the suitors of the hundredand of the county. In this way, though neighbours of the villains in the halimote of the estate, sokemen were still kept formally apart from the latter as members of the soke, and were called up to the hundred and to the shire on the strength of their personal states. In fact, the very designation of sokemen is broader than the group of men under private soke, and embraces a number of people who attend the regular courts. It arose seemingly from the contrast between the personal suitors of hundred and shire on the one hand, the peasants represented by the reeve and four men, the villains, on the other.[12] There is a second point to be noticed in regard to this group : namely, that jurisdictional subjection to a lord, settled as it was on a territorial basis, almost by necessity led, at a later stage, to some sort of economic subjection. The freeman under soke had not only to appear in certain contingencies at the lord's court as an assessor or a suitor and to pay amercements and fines to it, but he came to be considered as a paying dependant, and indeed as a rent-paying tenant of the lord.[13] This last turn taken by the subjection of men under soke may be either explained by the fact that a great number

of them had really taken up tenancies or converted
their independent holdings into tenancies, or else by the
degradation consequent upon the surrender of public rights
over particular districts by the kings. Those dues
which were formerly paid to the King as tribute became
rents in the hands of private lords to which the King had
passed his subjects. To put it more correctly, we should
nowadays have classified such dues under these two heads,
whereas it is very doubtful whether the Old English government and folk realised fully the contrast between both. At
any rate, kings are certainly found giving away powers over
districts as if they were granting estates. They subject
free families to dependence on lords by acts which are
framed as gifts, and carry alienations of public rights with
them. One of the consequences is the raising of interme-
diaries—the lords of sokes—between the King and his
former direct subjects.

In the Danish period we find already traces of a conception which reminds one of the celebrated feudal maxim,
" *nulle terre sans seigneur.*" There have come down to us
many enactments worded as if in every place there was a
landrica constituted over the free and servile population.[14]
It is more than doubtful that such an exhaustive parcelling
up of jurisdiction among private lords had already been
fully carried out before the Norman Conquest, but the
enactments I am alluding to were not framed at random,
and lead to the assumption that about the year 1000 the
normal Englishman was supposed to have a jurisdictional
lord above him, though in many cases that lord may have
been the King himself, in his capacity as a great landowner.

The attempt to carry out such a scheme shows to what
extent the necessity of an aristocratic superstructure to
the social order was realised at that time.
Rise of Military Class Such tendencies and the institutions arising
from them evidently do not owe their ori-
gin to superficial and arbitrary measures ; deep currents
must have moved in this direction. Some of these currents
have been noticed already—the desire for protection on

the part of the weaker members of the community, the
disruption of the ties of kindred, the policy of a government
conscious of its inefficiency in the discharge of secondary
duties and of its inability to enforce justice and police
in local matters.   But other currents of similar magnitude
have also to be reckoned with.   As in the case of patrimonial justice and commendation, we discern from the
very beginning in the life of Teutonic tribes the germs of
a military class. They are formed by the *comitatus*, Gefolge,
gasindi, *gesio*.   Kings and chieftains gathered a following
around them which did not concern itself with the arts of
peace, but lived for war and by war.   It did not coalesce
with the body of the nation in arms, the host, *fyrd*, or *here,*
but remained as a separate organisation partaking of the
characteristics of a court, a guard and a standing division of
the army.   The invasions and conquests took up a long
time, as we know, and all through this period of strife the
military followings played a conspicuous part.   But even
when the country became more or less pacified, the members
of these followings, although they were mostly endowed
with land instead of living at the court and table of their
chief, remained in close touch with him in regard to military
service.   They were called up and came with their retinues
when it was not considered necessary or possible to move
the fyrd.   And it is clear that this natural requirement of
a standing military establishment and of a professional
class to support it grew exceedingly in importance, and led
to a social transformation of a most decisive kind when the
offensive war ceased, and the English conquerors were
driven into a position of constant and wearisome defence
against the onslaught of barbarians who had not got their
share as yet, and pressed on from behind.   Positions
were reversed.   Frankish, Italian, English society, instead
of assailing the Roman world, had to desist from its peaceful
work in order to repel the Arabs, the Avars and Magyars,
the Saxons, the Slavs, the Northmen.   England had to
deal with those last, and every page of the chronicles of
this time testify to the strain, the danger, and the havoc of
the contest.   People had to fight, to work, and to pay in

face of inroads which brought home to every household the necessity not of gain or conquest, but of self-preservation. The fyrd was not the proper institution to carry on such warfare. It was not composed of invaders seeking booty, but of householders and labourers called off from their homework. The profound change was expressed in the very fact that the great majority of its members did not possess the hide holdings considered to be sufficient to provide for a household and to maintain a warrior at the same time. They were holders of virgates and bovates, of small tenements barely sufficient for scanty peasant life. The fyrd was still pressed from time to time to go to war, but it had mostly to act by local divisions, to protect the more immediate neighbourhood of threatened districts, and when he had to hobble about the country in pursuit of the " *here* " of the Norsemen, it was more a burden to the people than a protection to them.[15] Indeed, the necessity for a more efficient, more professional and better equipped force made itself felt in every respect, and the materials for such a force were evidently to be found not among wretched virgaters with their bows and arrows, but in the military followings which could be required to appear on horseback with helmets and coats of mail, with well forged swords and axes, and which could be made to do garrison duty in fortresses. Even the old hide holding was found insufficient to enable a man to do all that, and five hides are considered by custom as the tenement necessary for the proper outfit of a knight, that is, a tenement which made him independent of township arrangements and personal work, which raised him, in fact, to the condition of a squire and contrasted him with the peasant virgaters around him.[16] This contrast between the five-hide estate of the thane and the virgate of the peasant is highly characteristic of the time. It implies, to begin with, that the thane was to find means of sustenance not merely for himself, but for his retinue,[17] the heavily armed warrior being as a rule surrounded by a few lightly armed henchmen. Secondly, the distribution of thanes' estates and the corresponding obligation of ecclesiastical and lay magnates to maintain fully equipped warriors implied more and more the subordination of the common people, of the virgaters and holders of bovates to the specialists of war, the growth of private dues and duties to support the members of the military class. Thirdly, the social differentiation between the two layers of society had as its result that the lower freemen lost more and more the character of settled warriors and assumed the position of *coloni* and labourers ; their weapons glide out of their hands, as it were, and with their weapons disappears their main claim to freedom. We have to keep in mind that the whole process followed its course by slow steps, apart from any attempts to systematise its results by comprehensive schemes. No knight fee theory more or less akin to that which found so complete an expression in the documents of the Red Book of the Exchequer was elaborated as yet, the land was not parcelled out into military units deemed more or less equal and forming the basis of governmental claims ; this part of its process was left to be achieved by the Normans.[18] In fact, by the side of the ordinary endowments of five hides and the cumulative agreements with cities and great landowners, we find a number of small military tenancies of one or two hides, and even less, whose holders are characterised as thanes. Two explanations of this fact suggest themselves. In the Eastern districts the large number of small freemen testifies to the recurrence under Danish influence of a state of things similar to that which obtained all through England in the time of Saxon, Anglian, and Jutish conquests ; the thanes and freemen in question are the members of the " here " just settled on the land, still numerous and still in a condition which may be termed appropriate for light troops and offensive purposes. As we have seen, the members of these hosts are formally equated by the treaties in point of wergeld with the military landowners of English districts, though they correspond historically to the ancestors of these landowners. But in the West also we find a good many small thanes, and in this case we have to think apparently of single soldiers to whom small endowments had been assigned, and not of officers with small retinues, as in the case of the five-hide thanes.[19] Indeed, in accounting for the rise of the military class we should go wrong if we lost sight even for one moment of the more humble representatives of it, of the sergeants-at-arms as they were sometimes called during the feudal period, geneats, rodknights, as they were termed in Old English phraseology, drengs, as they were designated by the Danes.[20] This class is an important one from the manorial point of view, but it has undoubtedly its military significance too : the rodknights, riding servants provided with horses, were not only used for carrying orders and summonses : these geneats and drengs had to follow their lord as a military leader, and must have played a conspicuous part in the expeditions of the professional soldiery. A few of them stood in direct connection with the government, but most were included in the estates of great men and thanes and recruited for military purposes through the medium of their lords. In a word, though the system of knights' fees had not been formed, the differentiation of the military class from the labouring class was already carried out in substance before the Norman Conquest, and it is in what may be called, for want of a better word, the Danish period of English history that this differentiation has to be located, although its germs appear even in earlier times.[21]

I have laid stress on the military aspect of this process of social differentiation because it is a very important one, but, of course, it is not its only aspect. The thane did not merely act as an officer and a man-at-arms. In possession of a special military position, he became also the natural representative of government. The people around him were made to support him by payments and services, and this meant that they had to look up to him as a lord in greater or lesser degree. He was in a way an agent of the central government, and he became himself a small potentate through the fact of possessing various powers delegated or derived from the central government. He had to rule his dependants and peasant neighbours in matters of justice and police, he became the *free man par excellence*, while they sank into the position of villains or, at best, socmen. His estate was tending to become a unit of police and jurisdiction on the basis of governmental claims. In this way the political changes which followed the rise of the military class and the extension of commendation and franchise led in a considerable degree to the formation of a lordship as a superstructure of the township. To appreciate this last process in all its bearings, we have now to take into account the set of *economic influences* making for it.

From the very first stages of the English occupation of the island we have to reckon not merely with small landowners joining in townships on the shareholding system, **Stock on Estates** but also with great landowners, possessed of large tracts of land and utilising them according to their wishes and notions. The tradition of Roman estates, for one thing, could not be entirely swept away. Notwithstanding all the havoc and perturbations brought about by the conquerors, notwithstanding the tremendous changes in habits and speech as testified by the complete alteration of local nomenclature, it would be preposterous to suppose that Roman landmarks and arrangements were wilfully destroyed and no advantage taken of the existing stock and labour arrangements. There is happily no need to deny the survivals in many places of practices connected with Roman estates in order to account for the preponderating Teutonic stamp of rural life in Old England. The King got to be and always remained a great landowner. The Church with its various institutions and corporations soon became a great landowning power, and borrowed its methods to a great extent from Roman antecedents and continental examples, although it must be kept in mind that not one of the English churches could trace its pedigree as a land-owning institution from the time before the English Conquest. Great men of different origin, ealdormen and royal reeves, earls and thanes came forward as great landowners who had to deal with scores of townships, wide tracts of waste and numerous serfs and clients of all kind. In ordinary husbandry and in the spread of colonisation capital was needed, and capital was provided by the wealthier people, with the consequence that those who accepted help frequently lapsed into a condition of dependency on the borrowers.   An estate, as well as a holding, did not consist merely of land, but also of meat, men and oxen necessary to make it work.   As we know more definitely about the plough-teams of eight oxen, the mentions of the corresponding outfit will be readily made out, as, e.g., in the case of a legacy by Abba the reeve, who supplies half a sulung of land with four oxen.   But cows, sheep, swine, are also provided, and corn to start with.   In a curious document of the beginning of the tenth century, bishop Denewulf tells us of his exertions to colonise and raise the value of an estate at Bedhampton.   When the bishop received it from the King it was deserted and devoid of outfit, but he succeeded in providing stock and settling farmers in all its holdings, and he mentions expressly, that after the last severe winter there were 420 swine and seven slaves and ninety sown acres, evidently on the home farm.[22]   But we have to start from the fact that the lords did not introduce in their policy views and methods of a kind entirely different from those which prevailed in the case of free settlements, but adapted and modified the same methods for their own benefit.   A township created on ecclesiastical land was not materially different in regard to its constitution, in the arrangement of its agriculture, its pastoral rights, its treatment of the waste from a neighbouring township on folcland, nor was this last entirely free from duties and dues derived from the occupation of the land, though these duties and dues were exacted by the King's officers.   And a simple act of the King, a grant attested by a book, could place the freer district substantially in the position of a private estate, and, as we have seen, such grants became very usual in consequence of the development of a military and governing class.   Then again there were still many steps between the heterogeneous dependency of the freeholders of a township on various lords for commendation and soke and the unification of soke and, probably later, of commendation in the hands of one lord.[23]   In fact, the arrangements in both cases followed the accustomed groove of an open-field community with a system of dues and duties superimposed on it.   This fundamental resemblance of both arrangements in regard to their economic basis made it more easy to slide, as it were, gradually from one variety into the other and to combine tenures of different origin and different degrees of dependance under one and the same lordship.

The development of the manorial system, as it is called forth by economic evolution, presents several features of interest and importance.   It is chiefly ex-

Feasting and Feorm pressed in the growth of the demesne on one side, of rents and services on the other.   Territorial lordship did not necessarily imply the existence of a demesne, that is of a special appropriation of one part of the soil to the use of the lord.   Not only is it possible to imagine a state of things in which the lord, without making any portion of the soil particularly his own, would come or send to a district or township to levy the tribute imposed, but we actually catch glimpses of such customs in many places.   We know that it was the prevailing system for the collection of rents in kind or of tribute among the tribal Celts.   Indeed it is so much the natural organisation of tribute in a tribal state of incomplete subjection, that we find similar customs among many other nations in the same stage of development, e.g., among the Scandinavian folk.[24]   A chieftain comes with his retinue to feast on his subjects for a certain number of nights or days ; a temporary house is erected for him, if he does not take up his quarters in some headman's farm ; provisions flow in from the district according to a customary standard ; the henchmen of the chief, his horses and dogs are quartered and feasted by other local people.   We still find examples of such feasting progresses in Saxon,[25] and indeed in Norman times,[26] and there is hardly any room for doubt that these customs represent the most ancient forms of tributary subjection, running in an uninterrupted sequence from Celtic tribal arrangements.

Even more frequent is the modification of these feasting dues which occurs when the provisions are not con-

sumed by the chief or lord in the course of his customary
progress, but have to be reserved and accumulated for his
use. The allowance of bread, cheese, honey, ale, flitches of
bacon, meat, will be a customary one, and though it would
come by bits from a number of tributary households the
lord would be primarily interested in getting the aggregate,
while the repartition and collection of dues would be left to
the tributary community. It will be reckoned as the farm,
the provender of a night or half a night, or a week, as might
be, and of such farms we hear a good deal both on royal
and on ecclesiastical manors.[27]

This modification of the crudity of the feasting immediately leads to some material consequences. The farm will
Manorial have to be accumulated in some central place
Centres which may be properly called a dominical
house or mansion. The *mansus iadominicatus, the curtis
dominica* of continental customs, appear by the force of
the same circumstances in English surroundings. The *barton*[28] and the *berewick*[29] are settlements connected with
barns for the collection of corn and other produce
with no special agricultural plots attached to them.
The *herdwick*[30] presents another variety in places with
pastoral pursuits; in the centre of dwellings of herdsmen and the storehouse for the gathering of cheese, butter
and the like. It need not be provided with any
domanial exploitation. The expressions berwick and
herdwick are indeed found commonly as sub-divisions
of manors, as subsidiary centres for groups of holdings
under manorial sway, but there is nothing in this subsequent co-ordination of terms which need astonish us. In
many cases, the mansion itself may not mean more than a
counting house or a storehouse,[31] and there may be, on the
other hand, a piece of demesne attached to the barton or
the berewick.[32] Still it is not without importance to note
the varieties of arrangement indicated by the shades in
terminology.

The next step is the most common and significant one.
It is represented by a domanial farm round which dependent
holdings are gathered. The central holding, the *heafod-*

botl,[33] becomes a hall in which the business transactions between lord or steward, on the one side, and the tenants, on the other, take place, and in immediate connection with this centre of organisation stands the home farm, *dominicum*.[34] In this large category of estates, subdivisions may also be noticed ; the case of a domanial close cultivated entirely by labourers attached to it, leading its separate economic life, as it were, and drawing from its environment of tributary manses only or chiefly rents in money and in kind,[35] the opposite case being that of domanial strips scattered among those of the tenants and cultivated entirely or chiefly by the peasantry, while the produce of these strips is gathered for the benefit of the lord : the term characteristic of this variation is " gafolearth." [36]   The great majority of instances is supplied by cases when a separate home farm with some servants and labourers attached to it is supported by a systematic concentration of work of different kinds to be performed by the tenants.[37]

Inland and Warland   Before we proceed to the examination of the rents and services connected with these demesne arrangements, we must glance at one fundamental distinction which covers all these various cases, namely, at the general distinction between demesne and tenant land, as expressed in our sources. It is rendered in Old English terminology by the opposition between *inland* and *warland*. Now, this terminological observation leads up to a curious complication in the arrangement itself.   Inland by itself means directly the inner land—the central farm, and suggests as its opposition outland,[38] which is actually used, though seldom, at least in the sense of tenant holdings. *Geneatland* and *reeveland* [39] appear in its stead with the very meaning required, and *gesettland* [40] alternates with geneatland to indicate stocked holdings, dependent tenancies provided with cultivators and means of cultivation. Then, *gevered land* and *warland* appear, and there is a considerable number of instances which fix the meaning of these terms. *Warland, gevered land* is the land which defends itself or defends some local division in regard to the requirements of the government, more especially in regard to taxation. Inland would on the contrary

be land freed from those requirements or not directly subjected to them, and sometimes this is expressed in as many
words.[41]   Now this is remarkable :—we are led to the
conclusion that the brunt of taxation was borne by the
land of the tenants, while demesne farms were as a rule
exempted from it.   Some qualifying remarks have to be
added to prevent misconceptions and to meet certain peculiarities of our information.   When Norman terminology
was, as it were, extended over the English, " *demesne* " did
not fit exactly with inland.   The first term was mostly
used in a narrow sense, it did not cover the whole
portion belonging to the lord of the manor personally—as
inland did—but only the home farm, cultivated for the use
of the lord and excluding plots which may have been leased
on different conditions out of the inland.[42]   In some cases
the term " inland " was applied to those very leased or
detached plots of the lord's land which were not included in
the demesne—this seems to be the narrower sense of inland.[43]
But it cannot be doubted that these niceties of distinction
were occasional, and that broadly inland and demesne were
two names for the same thing in the two languages which
were spoken in England after the Norman Conquest, the
word demesne ascending in its low Latin form of *dominicum*
even to earlier Old English times, when *inland* was prevalent in English terminology.   There is sufficient evidence
of a system of taxation omitting the inland and bearing with
all its weight on the. dependent holdings. but this system
could not be kept up ; and the demesne lands had to undertake part of the liability, probably because otherwise the
burden would have proved quite incommensurable to the
strength of the dependent population.   To a certain extent,
the settlement of the *wara* was a matter of private arrangement between the lord and his dependants, so that in some
cases he may have taken over part of the fiscal liability and
required more in the way of rent and labour, and in other
cases levied lighter dues for his own use and burdened the
tenant holdings with all the responsibility in regard to
fiscal exactions.[44]   But still the settlement of this question
was not entirely left by the government to private interests.

The tenantry and the demesne came to answer not only
jointly but also separately—we hear of requirements addressed directly and merely to the villains of such and such a
lord, of defaults and breach of duty by them, and the fact
that these cases are not concealed from our view by the
guarantee of the lord shows that each party had special dealings with the king's officers.[45] A reasonable explanation of
the original exemption of inland may lie in the idea that the
privileged part of the estate, the *inland*, was burdened in
another way; as the particular endowment of the upper class
it had to bear the primary responsibility for the work of
government, the professional military organisation and the
spiritual care of the Church.[46] This explanation, if accepted,
would bring into stronger relief the decisive influence of the
political reorganisation of the country on an aristocratic basis
in the course of the Danish period and in connection with the
Danish wars. From the purely fiscal point of view a great
deal seems to speak for such a reading of the evidence. The
geld was the tremendous burden with which people had to
reckon in these arrangements, and the geld was primarily
a Danegeld after all. There is no likelihood that taxation
should have been so stringent and so burdensome in the
earlier times and under the easier sway of Saxon and Anglian kings. Indeed the history of all barbaric governments
begins with a very insufficient organization in this respect,
and when taxation has to be increased and becomes a corner-
stone of policy, a point is reached which opens a vista of an
entirely new social development. The hide, the land of the
household, becomes more a unit of taxation than an agrarian
entity, and society at large from being a rather loose aggregate of more or less independent communities and individuals gets to be arranged in view of stringent and even
crushing military and fiscal obligations.

Reverting to the organisation of the estate, we have to
notice on its home farm a number of officers, servants and
Manorial   labourers, who have to take care of the lord's
Officers   interests, to perform the special work of the
demesne, supervise the services and to exact the dues from
the peasant population. We have met them already in the

character of an executive staff in independent townships, and it is not difficult to picture to ourself, how their position would be affected by the tacking to it of domanial duties. We may take the reeve as an example, because we know most about him and there is even a special treatise on his office dating from the eleventh century.[47]

The reeve of this treatise, though his office is termed *scire*, is not the sheriff, but, as we can judge from his attributions, the steward of an estate. He has to mind and to direct all the details of husbandry, from the repairing of buildings and the regulation of ploughing and harvest down to the setting of mouse-traps. He has constantly to mind his lord's interests, and to carry out his commands, but, characteristically enough, he is reminded no less of the necessity of knowing and following the custom of the folk, as it is expressed and kept up by wise men. Thus folk-right has to be combined in the management of affairs with lord's craft. The details, the economic prescriptions which follow on the general exhortations of the treatise, embrace the routine of all kinds of farm work : ploughing, sowing, harvesting, threshing, manuring, setting up of hurdles and fences, taking care of cattle, sheep and swine, repairs of dwellings, stables, house furniture and agricultural implements, etc. The supervision of the different services performed by the peasantry is not expressly mentioned, but self-understood, though we cannot say with certainty in what way the officers employed on the estate, the *wicneras*,[48] divided the different tasks between themselves. Altogether it seems clear that whenever there had arisen a powerful central organisation, one of the regular manors, as mentioned in Domesday, the life and the work of the peasantry attached to it came to depend a good deal on the views and habits of the steward of the estate. At the same time we must not lose sight of the facts that even in such regular or average manors defending themselves for five or for ten hides, the usual arrangement of husbandry and dues was not a matter of caprice and arbitrary disposition, but very much the outcome of popular custom. And, secondly, it should be remembered, that there are innumerable instances when the manor is yet rather a name and a beginning than a complete arrangement, and that in these cases rural affairs must have been regulated by agreements and meetings between parties of approximately equal strength and had to follow in the time-honoured grooves of township practice. In these cases we cannot find a proper basis for the display of such craft as is described and recommended by the eleventh century treatise, and we must assume that the gerefa was still mainly an elective local officer, a headman, possibly dependant on the *landrica* of the district, but hardly to be considered merely as his personal steward.

Another important feature of the demesne organisation is the presence of a certain number of labourers living

Labourers on the Domain on the home farms or in crofts attached to it, and forming, as it were, the kernel of the cultivation of that part of the estate which was reserved for the needs of the lord. There can be no doubt that these labourers were mainly slaves to begin with, and, as we have seen, in the Old English charters which mention the stocking of estates such slaves appear by the side of the oxen and the outfit in seed. Sometimes, as in the case of Selsea,[49] their numbers were considerable, But in course of time a number of free people appear as workmen on the estates, and we get glimpses of a resident population of such " boor-born " labourers dwelling on the land of great lords in a kind of hereditary dependence.[50] Although there does not arise a special legal status of servitude of the glebe in connection with such arrangements, a current of economic development is disclosed which leads to the establishment of a condition very similar to such servitude from a matter of fact point of view. There was plenty of material for the formation of this group of " boor-born " labourers among the numerous " broken, kin-shattered " men who were constantly thrown out of the ranks of society by war, disaster and crimes, and indeed the documents mention expressly " wite theowas," as one of the elements of the class. Besides, we may assume that the increase of population rendered it necessary for a good many younger brothers and descendants of younger brothers to seek settlement and employment on the land of well-to-do neighbours.

The rise of this class of labourers may account to a certain extent for the decrease and decay of slavery and pure serfdom on the estates. As the wants of demesne farms in respect of labourers directly managed by the stewards came to be provided for by the "boor" class, there was less call for the employment of downright slaves, and the intermediate status of economic serfdom with some Christian and legal personality recognised in the labourer, gained ground in the manorial arrangement. One of the advantages of this way of providing workmen for the demesne consisted in the fact that the owner of the estate could pay some of the men employed by granting them plots for their own use free of charge.[51] As there was more land than money or provisions, this seemed a convenient mode of hiring labourers. The practice spread from the free workmen to slaves, and we often hear of manumissions accompanied by the surrender of farms for the use of manorial workmen.[52]

One of the conditions of the process described was that manorial husbandry could draw on the resources of dependent holdings, and that the "hall" became the economic centre around which virgates, bovates and cottages of tributary peasants were grouped, as satellites around a central planet.

Rents

Rentpaying tenancies are exceptional at this time. Agreements were made sometimes about "loans" (læn) of land to people of some position "on the basis of money rents[53] and *censores*,"[54] rentpaying peasants are mentioned sometimes, but these practices were unusual at a time when money was not easily procurable and such as there was flowed into the royal treasury to meet the requirements of the war establishment and of heavy payments to the Danes. As it has been pointed out several times, and from different points of view, the gafol land of this period is the *warland*, the land answerable for the King's gafol and the geld.[55] Of course, this implied a distribution of this rent between the townships, manors and holdings, and probably the absorption of a good deal in the way of money by the intermediate instances. But the Old English period is still pre-eminently one of natural husbandry, and it is to the incidents of such husbandry that we have chiefly to look in order to explain its working. Rents in kind were common enough, and any one of the numerous statements as to the collection of a " feorm " tells us about the quantities of bread, butter, cheese, eggs, bacon, fish, honey and ale, which the tributary holding had to send in.[56] A negative point to be considered is, that cultivation by farmers on the principle of sharing the produce with the lord is never mentioned—a curious contrast with the methods of Roman landlords. Produce in kind is estimated in fixed quantities and not in shares of the harvest.

The most striking feature of the manorial system, as it begins to form itself, is the concentration of tributary services, of work performed by the villager for **Services** the profit of the lord. Sometimes the special obligations are not expressly described, and it may be stated that two or three days per week are required for such work as may be wanted and ordered by the steward. But customs are rapidly forming themselves in regard to the quantity and the quality of the services imposed on the holdings, and in their aggregate these customs cover all varieties of rural work.

The best way to get an insight into the organisation of an Old English manor, and to form an estimate of the part **The Manor of** played by the different classes of its popula- **the Rectitu-** tion, is to analyse the description given in the **dines** so-called " Rectitudines Singularum personarum," and to compare it with some other Anglo-Saxon documents, describing rural services and dues.[57] The " Rectitudines " belong to the later years of the Old English period, and have been drawn up presumably some time in the eleventh century, perhaps about 1025, thus disclosing arrangements which lead up directly to the statistical data of the Domesday Survey in its entries devoted to Edward the Confessor's time (T.R.E.). The fulness of detail and the wide range of social ranks embraced by the description show that we have to do in this case with a treatise for the use of royal stewards, perhaps of sheriffs,[58] or of the administration of some bishop or secular magnate. The lord of the estates on which the classes of men enumerated in the treatise are dwelling was, in any case, a person of great power and of the highest standing, but, of course, the indications given might apply in a certain measure to manorialised estates of different size and kind.

The treatise starts with a characteristic of the thane, thus including tenants of military rank dependent on a great lord, for the King, a bishop, or a secular potentate of Godwine's or Leofric's stamp, had to deal with many military tenants of this kind. The thanes are supposed to hold bócland estates, as a rule, from which the *"trinoda necessitas"* of the fyrd, the maintenance of fastnesses (burghbote) and the repair of bridges is still due ; besides various forms of occasional guard duties, the keeping of fences in the king's hunts, etc. Special military service in distinction to the fyrd is not mentioned, and this means that the measure of the thane's services in the fyrd was given by the size of his estate or, to put it differently, by the number of hides he possessed. He was called up more often and went in better armour than the ordinary ceorl because he held five hides or more, while the ceorl had one or less.

Next comes a class to which the term *geneat* is applied in the English original. The chief incidents of its tenure are

The Geneat the payment of rent, and riding services, The *landgafol* stands foremost, and no further distinction is drawn between tribute due to the King as an original tax (cyninges gafol, the *gafol* rendered from folcland) and rents as an outcome of private agreement or private subjection : the tributary character of the land (gafol land) is the one point attended to.[59] Riding and carrying services and errands of all kind are also conspicuous, whereas agricultural work is only occasional and consists in help during harvest, in mowing or reaping. This is characteristic of a well-known class of tenants on later estates—the

drengs and radmen, but many of the so-called socmen were
also performing services of the same kind.[60] Indeed, if we
are to judge from the Latin translation which renders *geneat*
by *villains*, and from the analogy presented by the ceorls
sitting on gafol-land, we should say that for those of the
twyhyndmen who had been converted from the status of
direct subjection to the King to that of tribute paying dependants of great men, the *geneat* class of the Rectitudines
presents the most natural position.

Then come cottagers (*cotsetle*) holding plots of about five
acres each, while the geneats were evidently assumed to
hold ordinary shares on the plough team standard. It is
pointedly noticed that the cottagers do not pay *land gafol*,
and this exemption once more substantiates the intimate
connection between the rent and the normal holdings in
the fields. On the other hand weekwork appears as a
feature of the cottager's condition. They have to work one
day in the week for their small tenements. They are expressly stated to be personally free.

In the case of the *gebúrs* the weekwork gets to be the
characteristic trait of the tenure.[61] They are, as a rule,
The Gebúr peasants possessed of yardlands, and the outfit
of their yardlands is provided for them by the
lord. It consists of two oxen, i.e. the fourth part of a
ploughteam, one cow, six sheep and seven acres of sown
land. This last seems to imply that a case of cultivation on
the three-field system had been taken as a pattern, and
that seven acres out of the ten which would come under
winter seed in a virgate of thirty acres have been provided
with seed by the landowner,[62] while the remaining three acres
represent the usual "gafolearth." It is recommended
to give such a peasant provided with land by the lord, a
horse in addition to the ordinary outfit of his land, but this
was evidently a recommendation which could not be carried
out in all cases,[63] whereas it was one of the chief traits in
the condition of the geneat to be able to ride and to drive.
The peasant in the condition marked off by the term *gebúr*,
was actually a *colonus* who had brought his personal strength
and labour on the land and had received his outfit as well

as holding and dwelling from the lord. After his death the property found on the holding had in strict law to go back to the lord which had lent the outfit. Still there could be some " free " property along with the stock provided by the landlord and this did not fall under the rule of resumption after the death of the tenant : this point shows that the precarious and burdensome condition of the *gebúr* is to be explained mainly by his economic dependence on the landlord as a rural capitalist, and that even this overburdened class has not lost all vestiges of a status of personal freedom.

The work which is to be performed in consideration of the farm is heavy and begins to assume the shape of the ordinary servlices of villains as described in later surveys. The main obligation is the " weekwork," the performance of labour on the domain of the lord and at the bidding of his stewards during some days in the week.[64]   The chief example of the Rectitudines " is taken from a case where the gebúr has to work two days in the week for most part of the year and three days during the spring and the harvest season. The choice of the kind of work to be done is left to the steward. Besides, the gebúr has to do additional ploughing work of different kinds—to plough one acre a week in the autumn, three acres as " gafolearth," providing the seed for those from his own barn, three acres as " benearth," and two as payment for making hay.[65]

It may be said, that the condition of the Old English gebúr, as described by the " Rectitudines," compares favourably with the status of later villains. There **General course of evolution** is in particular no trace of a progression from an unlimited amount of work to a restricted amount. It is clear in regard to the *gebúrs* that the expression to do work " as they are bid " refers primarily to the possibility for the stewards to select one kind of service instead of the other, the number of work-days remaining fixed nevertheless. And in the test case of the " Rectitudines " this number does not exceed two or three days in the week, while later on it was sometimes extended to four or five, and three was considered as quite the *minimum*. There was undoubtedly, a great number of additional duties, but these also did not get less on later manors.

The clue to an explanation of this gradual increase in the burdens of the peasantry seems to lie in the fact that the class from which villainage arose was evidently drawn to a great extent from an originally free population. If we were right in assuming that old English society was not a slaveholding society in its main composition and in the arrangement of its labour, the line taken by social evolution lay chiefly in the direction of a spread of labour-discipline and subjection over a class of free tribesmen, as their means of sustenance grew smaller, while military and fiscal requirements became heavier. And it is obvious that such a process entailed a gradual increase of burdens.

On the whole we are, perhaps, warranted to conclude, firstly, that the manorial system arises at the end of the Old English period mainly in consequence of the subjection of a labouring population of free descent to a military and capitalistic class, and, secondly, that the personal authority of the lord of the manor is gradually gaining the mastery over a rural community of ancient and independent growth.

BOOK II

NOTES TO CHAPTER I

1. Celtic names seem to have mostly survived in the greater, eastern half of England in the case of rivers (Thames, Usk, Avon, His, etc.), and in a few instances of ancient town centres, like London itself. There are also many traces of Welsh nomenclature in the names of the hundreds in Worcestershire, Shropshire, Herefordshire, Somersetshire, etc. Roman traces are chiefly visible in *cesters* and *streets* (strata). The overwhelming majority of names of settlements is Old English. *W. H. Stevenson*, "Engl. Hist. Rev.," iv. (1889), 356 ff.

2. Bede, i. 15.

3. *Green*, "The Making of England" (edition of 1900), i. 161, 162.

4. Cf. my "Roman Law in Mediæval Europe," 1909.

4a. *Stubbs*, "Constitutional History" (Libr. edition), i. 11, 12, *Maitland*, "Domesday and Beyond," 222, 232, 327, 337. I need hardly mention that *Freeman* was an ardent, probably too ardent an advocate of Teutonic influence in English history.

5. In this sense I cannot but endorse the remarks of *Mr. Haverfield* in the *Antiquary* for 1897, although I differ from him as to the previous influence of Roman civilisation, and plead for a greater affinity and continuity between Celtic and Teutonic life in the island.

6. It may be said that the condition of North-eastern England, as described in Domesday, represents a more primitive formation than that of South-western England. This enables us to a certain extent to use the first in order to reconstruct the history of the latter. Cf. my "English Society in the Eleventh Century," 1908.

7. I have treated of the gradations of rank in the continental laws of the tribes in an article on "Wergeld und Stand," in the "Zeitschrift der Savignystiftung für Rechtsgeschichte," Germ. Abth. xxiii.

8. Æthelberht, 13, 14, 15.

9. Hlothere and Eadric, 1, 3. I am unable to agree with *Seebohm's* explanation of these texts. ("Tribal Custom in Anglo-Saxon Law," 468 ff. and 462 ff.) See my review of "Tribal Custom," in the "Vierteljahrsschrift für Social- und Wirthschaftsgeschichte," i. 137. Compare *Dr. Liebermann's* rendering of the passages in question in his edition of the Anglo-Saxon laws.

K. Maurer, " Angelsächsische Rechtsverhältnisse, Kritische Ueberschau," 1853, p. 60, thought that the payment mentioned in the
laws applied to the half of the wergeld which had to be paid by the
murderer himself, the half for which the kindred was responsible
not being mentioned. *Haddan* and *Stubbs* translate *medume* by
" half." But these attempts seem to have been prompted by the
wish to bring up the Kentish common wergeld to a sum of 200
shillings in order to make it correspond to the West Saxon and
Mercian payments. This consideration falls to the ground, however, if we accept *Seebohm's* theory that the Kentish wergelds
were reckoned in gold and the West Saxon in silver.

10. There would be the fundamental difference, however, that
the Frankish fine is a fraction of the whole wergeld, and therefore
increases and diminishes with it, while the Old English king's
fine seems to have been constant. The sum itself, 150 solidi, reminds one of the Gothic and Burgundian wergelds.

11. Ætheberht, 75 ; 27. The " medume " leodgeld, the medium
or average wergeld, seems to point to the possibility of different
estimates in regard to ceorls.

12. *L. Alamannorum*, " Pactus," ii. 39 ; iii. 27. Liutprand, 62.

13. *Seebohm* draws a distinction between the ceorl and the freeman. " Tribal Custom," 483.

14. Wergeld und Stand, 178 ff.

15. Æthelberht, 26.

16. Alfred, 4.

17. Alfred, 35, 25, etc.

18. Alfred, 11, 77 ; comp. Ine, 35. It is noteworthy that Eadward and Guthrum, 7, 1, use frigman in opposition to theowman.

19. Ine, 45, 30 ; 63 ; Alfred, 10, 18, 29, 39.

20. *Seebohm*, " Tribal Custom," 361 ff. His observations as to
the differences between the currencies, on the one hand, and the sums
of wergelds and fines on the other, are very instructive, but his
attempt to draw an exact equation between the Kentish ceorl and
the West Saxon twelvehyndman is based on a misconception,
as it seems to me. The very passage of the Leges Henrici I. 76,
which notices the provincial varieties of wergelds, speaks of Kentish
villani, and contrasts them with the *barones*. There is no reason
why the sums should coincide, and the fiction of a coincidence is
merely produced by a strained interpretation of the texts as to
Kentish wergelds which raises that of a common freeman to 200
shillings in gold.

21. *Seebohm*, " Tribal Custom," 397.

22. Ine, 51, draws a distinction between the *gesiðcundman land-
agende* paying 120 shillings for non-attendance at the fyrd, and
the *unlandagende*, who gets fined with 60 shillings, exactly half
the first ; in both cases, the fines are one-tenth of the wergeld.
The landowner loses his land besides. Comp. Ine, 35. There can

be hardly a doubt that twelvehyndmen and sixhyndmen are meant. Gesiðs not owning land might exist in many different positions, as minor followers of the King, who had not been endowed with land ; as followers of high thanes, as members of the family of a landowning thane. The fragments of customary laws treating of the " thriving " to higher rank, make a distinction between men of gesiðcund blood and actual thanes.

23. Ine, 32, 33, etc. Comp. *Schmid's* "Glossar" v. Wealh.

24. Ine, 63.

25. *Pollock* and *Maitland*, " Hist. of Eng. Law," i. 6.

26. The obligations of the *geneat*, the follower, towards the lord are stated with some exaggeration and a scriptural tinge in Eadgar, iv, 1, 1.

27. This seems to be the meaning of the oft quoted text as to the thriving of a ceorl to the dignity of a King's thane ; " and gif ceorl gepeah þæt he hæfde fullice fif hida agenes landes, cirican and kycenan, bellhus und burhgeat, setl and sundernote on kynges healle, þonne wæs he þononforð þegenes rihtes weorðe." (As to the meaning of the terms burhgeat and setl, *Stevenson* in " Engl. Hist. Rev." 1897, p. 489.) The version in the North People's law is more explicit in some respects : 9. And gif ceorlisc man gepeo þæt he hæbbe 5 hida landes to cynges utware and hine man ofslea, forgilde man hine mid ðwam þusend þrimsa. 10. And þeah he gepeo þæt he hæbbe helm and byrnan and golde fæted sweord, gif *he þæt land nafað* he bið ceorl swa þeah. 11. And gif his sunu and his sunu-sunu þæt gepeoð þæt hi *swa micel landes habban* bið se ofsprinc gesiðcundes cynnes be twam þusendum. The stress lies clearly on the possession of 5 hides of land, though *Seebohm* has tried to construe these paragraphs to mean that a ceorl had no full kindred, and that therefore only in the third generation would his de-scendants become thanes. " Tribal Custom," 363, 369, 412.

28. North People's ranks, *Liebermann*, i. 460. And gif Wilisc man gepeo þat he hæbbe hiwisc landes (another version : þat he hyred and eht age) and mæge cyninges gafol forðbringan, þonne bið his wergeld 120 scill. And if he ne gepeo buton to healfre hide, þonne si his wer 180 scill. And gif he ænig land næbbe and þeah freoh sy, forgilde hine man mid 70 scill. Cf. Ine, 32 : gif Wylisc mon hæbbe hide landes, his wer bið 120 scill., gif he þonne hæbbe healfe 80 scill., gif he nænig hæbbe 60 scill.

29. Ine, 23 : Wealh gafolgelda 120 scill., his sunu 100. The position of gafolgelders is extended to English geburs, which in these cases appear as equivalent to ceorls, by Ine, 6 : gif hwa on ealdorman-nes hus gefeoht oþþe on oðres geðungenes witan 60 scill. gebete he and oðer 60 geselle to wite. Gif he þonne on gafolgeldan huse oþþe on gebures gefeohte 120 scill. to wite geselle and þæm gebure 6 scill. It is not quite clear why the wite should be twofold in the latter case, but the contrast between the witan in high authority and

the geburs and gafolgelders is marked and supposes an exhaustive classification of the folk ranging the twyhyndmen or ceorls under the second heading as people who had to till the land (gebur — colonus) and to pay tax. The gafolgelder would be the English for *tributarius*, which we see so often mentioned in the land books, and which points originally to a householder charged with public and not with private tribute, with *cyninges gafol* and not with *rœdegafol*.

30. The 5 hides held to the King's *utwaru* are, as we shall see later on, taken as *tributary* units in opposition to real agrarian measures. It would be tempting to take the King's utwaru as a military obligation, and it has been taken in this sense (e.g., by Liebermann), but the term seems clearly connected with *wara* and *gevered*. It corresponds to the gafol of the ceorls.

31. Ine, 64 : Se þe hæfð 20 hida se sceal tæcnan 12 hida gesettes landes þonne he faran wille. Cp. 65, 66. Ine, 68, provides for the case of a gesiðcundman being driven off from his holding. It enacts that he is to lose his *botl*, his dwelling, but not his *setene*. This last expression has given rise to many comments. *Prof. Maitland*, for example, thinks that the personal relations which the gesið had organised around him were to remain undisturbed. But if this had been so, the driving off would amount to very little. I am inclined to interpret the setene of this paragraph as the outfit, the capital of the gesið himself. He was, after all, " settled " by the King quite as much as his tenants were settled by him, and he either was provided with an outfit by the King or brought it of his own ; in both cases it was fair that it should be guaranteed to him.

32. Ine, 67 : gif mon *geþingað* gyrde landes oþþe mere to *rœdegafole* and geereð, gif se hlaford him will þæt land aræran to weorce and to gafole, ne þarf he him onfon, gif he him nan botl ne selð, and þolie þara æcra. The thane is menaced with the loss of his authority over the land if he subverts the conditions which have been agreed upon with the peasant farming the land or settled on the land.

33. *Seebohm*, " Village Community," 139.

34. Bede's letter to Archbishop Egbert of York, c. 11 : quod enim turpe est dicere, tot sub nomine monasteriorum loca hi, qui monachicae vitae prorsus sunt expertes, in suam dicionem acceperunt . . . ut omnino desit locus, ubi filii nobilium aut emeritorum militum possessionem accipere possunt.

35. The conversion of public *tributarii* or gafolgelders into householders dependent on the Churches is what the land books generally tell us about. Private gafol sprang in those cases from public tribute, either through being surrendered by the kings to the use of the monasteries and of sees, or by growing gradually as an

addition to the original public burden. It is doubtful whether the fundamental change in the condition of gafolgelders was rightly realised in the beginning, either by them or by the government which gave them away, but in course of time it came to mean a good deal. In the light of these ecclesiastical donations, the assignment of hides to secular thanes mentioned in the enactments of Ine almost looks like the institution of hlafords over districts rated at a certain number of hides : these hlafords were answerable for a certain proportion of actual settlers on the land they had received ; and there is nothing to show that only new colonists were meant : customary gafolgelders must have made up a good part of the people with whom the hides were "settled." The colonists attracted by agreement, by *ræde*-gafol, in contrast to cyninges gafol, appear as an important adjunct. Comp. *Maitland*, "Domesday and Beyond," 232.

36. *Seebohm* has repeatedly tried to show that the typical ceorl of Alfred, and even of Ine's time, was a gafolgelder (for example, "Tribal Custom," 355, 373, 395), and I should have nothing to say against it if *gafolgelder* were taken as the *tributarius*, the ceorl householder, rated at a hide for public obligations, and in many cases surrendered to a monastery or to a thane. But the aim of *Seebohm's* explanation is different ; it would entirely dispose of the "masterly independence" of small landowners and reduce them to the position of private tenants on great men's land, and for this there is no warrant in the evidence, and no likelihood in the general course of development. The ceorl or twyhyndman is still and very distinctly the small freeman of Alfred's laws. I should like in this connection to adduce two significant passages from Æthelred's laws, vii, 2, 4 : Si quis ieiunium suum infringat, servus corio suo componat, *liber pauper* reddat 30 denarios et tainus regis 120 solidos, et dividatur haec pecunia pauperibus. In viii. 3, there is an English rendering of the terms : *bunda* mid 30 pen., þræl med his hide, þegn mid 30 scill. Whatever the exact sums may have been, and notwithstanding the extraordinary increase of the fine in the case of the higher order, the social contrast is clearly presented, and the *bunda*, evidently drawn from the Norse *bonde*, is valuable as an indication of the status of a peasant householder.

37. As to the tremendous burden of the Danegeld and its influence on the history of English social distinctions, see *Maitland*, "Domesday and Beyond," 4.

38. "North People's law," *Schmid*, "App." ch. 2. Comp. *Seebohm*, "Tribal Custom," 363, who, however, does not take notice of this preposterous privilege of the victorious nation, and builds his theory on a supposed exact parallel between Norse and English ranks.

39. Ælfred and Guthrum, 2 : eal we lætað 8 healf marc Engliscne and Denisce efen dyre, buton þam ceorle þe on gafol lande sit and

heora lysingon, þa syndon eac efen dyre, 200 scill. The ceorl keeps his ancient wergeld ; he is still a twyhyndman, and the fact of his being equated with a Danish lysing does not make him more a freed-man, than the fact of every Danish soldier being reputed a 12 hynd-man renders this soldier a great landowner. As for the Leges Henrici, I. (i. 70, 6 ; 76), of course their *liber homo* is the thane and the twelvehyndman, while the ceorl is termed *villanus*, but this is already the well-known terminology of Norman feudalism.

40. The heriot laws of Canute throw light on the gradations of the official aristocracy (Can. ii. 71). His enactment of 1020 begins : Cnut Cyning gret his arcebiscopas, his leodbiscopas, and Thurcyl eorl and ealle his eorlas and ealne his þeodscipe, twelf-hynde and twyhynde.

41. Eadmund, 1.

42. *Tunman* or *tunesman* is very rare, however.—Eadg. iv. 8, 13 are the chief texts.

NOTES TO CHAPTER II

1. Leges Henrici, I. 70, §§ 12, 13, 23, and the fragment on marriage, *Schmid*, " App." vi. § 7. In the " History of the English Law," 239 ff. these passages are made the starting point of an analysis on the lines of Heusler's and Ficker's theory, which dissolves the conception of the mægth as an organised group.

2. I have tried to illustrate the problems of ancient Teutonic kinship from Norse law in an article on " Geschlecht und Ver-wandtschaft im Altnorwegischen Recht," in the " Zeitschrift für Social und Wirthschaftsgeschichte," vii.

3. Æthelstan, vi. 8, 2 : Gif . . ænig mægð to þan strang sy and to þam mycel . . . xii hynde oððe twyhynde, þæt us ures rihtes wyrnen and þone þeof foren forstande (of the London Dooms). The Latin versions of iii. 6 and iv. 3, render mægth by *parentela* and *cognatio*. The text (Æthelstan, vi. 8, 2), is instructive in yet another way, as showing that twyhynd people were supposed to form mægths, and occasionally even very strong mægths.

4. *Amira*, in Paul's " Grundriss der germanischen Philologie," ii.[2] 138 ff. *Brunner*, " Deutsche Rechtsgeschichte," 110 ff. The subject of the mutual obligations of the members of a kindred is treated in great detail and with clearness in *Amira's* " Nordger-manisches Obligationsrecht."

5. On the ættleiðing of Norwegian law, see Gulathingslov, 58 ; Frostathingsl. ix. 1. Although it was chiefly used as a means of legitimation of children not born in lawful wedlock, there is nothing in the archaic ceremony described to restrict it primarily to that

particular act. In old Swedish law the " Aetleþa " applies chiefly
to cases of introduction of freedmen into a kindred. " Vest-
göthalag," Arfþær B. 23 ; " Ostgöthalag," Ærfa B. 20, 25. As to
leaving the kindred, see especially Lex Salica, 60, De eo qui se de
parentilla tollere vult.

6. Genealogiae holding land. *L. Alamannorum*, " Pactus," 26.
Brunner, " Deutsche Rechtsgeschichte," i. 84 ff. *Pollock* and *Maitland*, " History of English Law," ii. 242, 243 ; *Heusler*, " Institutionen," i. 260, does not go so far as the " History of English Law,"
but ascribes the collegiate character of *genealogiae* and *farae* to the
fact of their being communities holding land.

7. Bæda, iii. 20, and *Plummer's* note to it, ii. 174.

8. Ælfred, 41 : Se mon se ðe bocland hæbbe, and him his
magas læfden, þonne setton we, þæt he hit ne moste sellan *of his
mœgburge*, gif ðær bid gewrit oððe gewitnes, ðæt hit ðara manra
forbod wære þe hit on fruman gestrindon and þara þe hit him
sealdon, þæt he swa ne mote, and þæt þonne on cyninges and on
biscopes gewitnesse gerecce beforan his mægum.   An interesting
case of a mægth claiming land is mentioned in a book executed
by Bishop Werferth of Worcester (872–915).   *Thorpe*, " Diplomatarium," 167 : Đa æfter Eastmundes forðside, bereafode seo
mægð þæs ilcan londes ge þa gastas þara forðgewitenra manna,
ge þone bisceop and þa cirecean at Weogornaceastre. At the Witenagemot at Saltwich the bishop craved the land on the strength
of the testament : spræc ic on þa magas mid þe erfegewrite, and
wilnade me rihtes.   Đa beweddode me Eadnoð, and Ælfred, and
Ælfstan þæt hio . . . oððe hit me ageafon, oððe on hira mægðe
þone mon fundon þe to þam hade fenge and to lande. . . . Đa
Eadnoð þe þæt land hæfde gebead hit ealre þære mægðe hwæðer
hit ænig swa gegan wolde. The Church had eventually to surrender the land for a certain rent to Eadnoð, as the representative of the mægth.

9. The chief sources for a study of these curious organisations
which attracted Niebuhr's attention, are *Neocorus*, " Chronik des
Landes Ditmarschen, hgg. von Dahlmann " (Kiel. 1827) ; for
example, pp. 206, 575, 619, etc. ; and *Michelsen*, " Sammlung
altditmarscher Rechtsquellen " (Altona, 1842) ; for example,
" Landrecht von 1447," i. § 7, 9, 69, 71, 72, etc., 111, 112, 113, 146,
164, etc. " Landrecht von 1539," 81, 92.

10. The lawsuit of Eadnoð's mægth with the See of Worcester
could not have been carried out without several meetings.   An
instance where common action and decision was also unavoidable
is presented by Æthelstan, ii. 2, cf. 8, which obliges the mægth to
find a settlement for one of their members who has got no land, and
to provide him with a lord. As it is an obligation, and a very cumbersome one, the mention of the mægth, as a body (þæt mon beode ðær
mægðe, þæt hi hine to folcryhte gehametten and him hlaford finden

on folcgemote) cannot be treated as vague talk about relations. The unity of the mægth is personified in a certain *forspreca* in the constantly recurring and important case of the settlement of a marriage contract between two kindreds. *Schmid,* " Anhang," vi. 1, 6. Comp. the cases arising from guardianship—Hlothere and Eadric, 6 ; Ine, 38.

11. The preamble of the Frostathingslov speaks of blood feuds waged between whole kindreds and producing great slaughter among the chief men of the kindreds, quite apart from their degree of relationship with the men who had called forth the feud. The Sagas tell us that a common expedient was to pass over the leadership in a feud to a chieftain.

12. *Pollock* and *Maitland,* " History of English Law," ii. 243.

13. *Kemble,* " Saxons in England." Comp. *Green,* " Making of England," i. 46.

14. It has been suggested that the place-names in *ing* may be derived from the personal name of the first settler or of the person to whom a particular place was assigned at the Conquest. *Stevenson,* " Engl. Hist. Rev." iv., in a review of Earle's " Land Charters. This may be so in many cases, but the use of the *ing* suffix for the formation of names of kindreds and tribes is so well established and so widely spread among Germanic nations, that it seems hardly likely that the English place-names which contain this suffix should go back in most cases to names of single settlers. The Aescings or Getings are surely patronymics in the same sense as the Scyldings or Scylfings, and in all these cases the dominant idea seems to be that a number of persons are held together by ascertained or supposed descent from a common ancestor. The place-names which appear as mere plurals, without the adjunct of *ton* or *ham,* are especially characteristic.

15. The personal basis of the hiwisc is very clear in the translations from Scripture. For example, Exodus xii. 3. On the other hand, it is commonly used instead of hide and sometimes hiwscip appears in the same sense. (*E.g.* Ða onféng héo ænes híwscipes stówe.) *Higid* appears as the fuller form of *hid.*

16. The expression *terra unius familiae,* which alternates with hide and *hiwisc* in the Anglo-Saxon charters is not to be found in the same sense in continental documents ; and when a special departure has to be sought in such cut and dried formulae as the expressions of charters, there must be a weighty reason for such a deviation. The usual *mansus* of continental documents must have been deemed insufficient to express the meaning of the vernacular term, and nothing more adequate than *terra familiae* could be found. The *tributarius* of English books seems to me not so much the equivalent of the tributarius of the Salic law as a translation of *gafolgelda.* The *casatus* was probably accepted as corresponding to the *set* and *gewered* of Anglo-Saxon terminology.

17. Hired and æht stand characteristically in the North People's law, and hide in Ine, 32. Thus the intimate connexion of the hide of land with family and kindred is once more illustrated.

18. As to the means by which the unity of the holding might be preserved, we shall have to speak further on. I would only call attention at present to such cases of voluntary agreement between brothers as the one described in King Alfred's will.

19. A similar tendency is manifested in the customary rules as to oðal succession in Norway. *Brandt*, " Forlæsninger om Norske Retshistorie," 161. *Boden*, " Das Odal " in " Zeitschrift der Savignystiftung für Rechtsgeschichte," Germ. Abth. xxii.

20. The three well-known instances where folcland is expressly mentioned are Edw. I. 2 ; C. D. 281, and C. D. 317. In all three cases folcland is opposed to bocland, and two different modes of holding land are meant ; in fact, the two principal modes. This is made clear by the enactment Edw. I. 2. To these instances we may without doubt add two charters of Cenwulf of Mercia's time in regard to estates in Kent, described as "terrae sui propriae puplicae juris " and as " reipuplicae [jur]e conditionis." *Thorpe*, " Dipl.," 57, 58 ; and *Earle*, " Landcharters " (C. D. 199), 90. The facsimile of this last charter has been published in the " Ordnance Survey Collection," i. 6. The terms of the first help us to supply almost with certainty a lacuna of three letters in the second ; and there can be hardly any doubt that we get here a Latin rendering of folcland, namely *terra reipublicae juris*, a very valuable rendering, as it lays stress on the main characteristic of folcland—on its being land held as it were by a public title, proceeding from the folc, under special obligations to the State and to the King. This being so, we may well suppose that in most cases, where grants are mentioned, the land, which became bócland, in consequence of these grants, had been folcland before. In this connexion one very remarkable feature, illustrated by the deed of exchange of 863 (C. D. 281), seems interesting. I mean the fact that the same land, while it is folcland, is subjected to multifarious duties in regard to the King, and is liberated from these duties when it gets to be bócland. It has already been mentioned that it is impossible to construe most of the early donations of the Codex Diplomaticus, otherwise than as grants of superiority and profits. The point of view which I am trying to make out in regard to folcland, as the collective designation of the so-called family lands, which also were tributary lands, would allow us to widen the circle of our observations in regard to folcland. We should have to look for it not only to the three or five cases, where the term is expressly mentioned or clearly translated, but to the whole range of deeds telling of the subjection of ordinary holdings, which used to be called *ethel* by the old school, to the *trinoda necessitas*, the King's gafol, the obligations as to Fæstingmen, Royal progresses,

etc. When folcland was turned into bócland, it was very often
exempted from many, and in some rare cases from all, such duties
towards the King, and had henceforward to serve chiefly or entirely
the Church or even secular grantees. The idea underlying these
exemptions is well expressed by Bede, iii. 24 : Rex Osuiu,
pro conlata sibi victoria gratias Deo referens dedit filiam suam
Aelfledam, quae uixdum anni aetatem inpleuerat, perpetua
ei uirginitate consecrandam ; *donatis insuper xii. possessiun-
culis terrarum, in quibus ablato studio militiae terrestris, ad
exercendam militiam caelestem, supplicandumque pro pace gentis
eius aeterna, deuotioni sedulae monachorum locus facultatesque sup-
peteret.* The Anglo-Saxon version has : " þa twelf *bócland* him
gefriode eorðlices camphades and eorðlicre hernesse to bigongenne
þonne heofonlican camphad and to munucstowum gesette," etc.
Ealdorman Alfred's will (C. D. 317) discloses another important peculiarity of *folcland* : it is land subject to a course of
succession entirely different from bookland. Whereas the bóclands are freely given away by the Ealdorman to his wife,
their daughter and some followers or friends, the folcland is not
included in this testamentary disposition, but has to go by right
to a son whose legitimacy and right to receive this part of
the inheritance is not incontestable and has to be confirmed
by the King. Should there arise lawful issue from the legitimate
marriage of the Ealdorman, all other dispositions fall to the
ground. The same conclusion as to the special privileges of land
bestowed by book is supported by many other facts, but Ealdorman's Alfred will has to be especially attended to, because both
terms, folcland and bócland, occur in it. On folcland, see my
article in " Engl. Hist. Rev.," 1893, January. *Maitland,* " Domesday and Beyond," 244 ff. *Lodge's* paper in the American Essays on
Anglo-Saxon Law, has still value on account of its careful analysis
of the charters, although some points in it are out of date.

21. It is hardly necessary to make special quotations as to the
constitution of bócland, as most of the charters of our diplomatic
collections are devoted to them. I will just point out *Th.*
" Dipl.," 54, 104, 148, as instructive instances. As to the formu-
laries, their development and significance, see especially *Brunner,*
" Zur Rechtsgeschichte der römisch-germanischen Urkunde,"
and *Maitland,* " Domesday and Beyond." But I should like to
call the attention of the reader to some especially characteristic
and important points. One of the principles of the Old English
law of real property seems to have been, that all individual property as opposed to the customary use of land in family holdings,
must have been bócland instituted by a legislative act. This is
so much the case, that all transactions regarding landownership are not only sanctioned and corroborated by books,
but the possession of the original grants or books establishes

a presumption as to ownership.   Books are given, withheld, stolen
and forged, in order to establish such presumptions.   See, for
instance, the curious cases, *Th.* 478 ; 40, 202, 207.   A complete
set of books going up to the original grant is, of course, the
best proof of title, but even the possession of one or other
link in the chain is not without value in a suit, even apart
from its tenor.   From the same point of view, the legislative
machinery of King and witan is made to intervene in private
transactions in order to originate the privilege of bookland, or to
give it a renewed sanction.   A bishop may be brought to make a
donation of land to a powerful magnate from his own land ; but
the King will appear on the scene to convert the land into bócland,
and to endow the owner with the right " to geofene and to syllanne,
ær dæge and æfter dæge, sibban oþþe fremdan þær him leofost wære "
(*Th.* "Dipl." 375).   In a very ancient instance, King Ine is made
to grant to a monastery land which the previous owner wants to
convey to it (C. D. 71 : ego Ini rex Saxonum pro remedio anime
mee aliquam partem terre donans impendo, id est decem cassatos,
Hengisti abbati . . . consentiente Baldredo qui hanc terram
donauit ei per petitionem Sergheris ; per me donatio hec imperpetuum sit confirmata).   At a certain period the legislative character of the creation of bócland is expressed in a formula mentioning not only the enactment of the King, but the consent of the
witan.   For example, *Th.* "Dipl." 124, 128.   *Maitland*, " Domesday and Beyond," 247.   It may be added that under-kings
were held to be unable to constitute bócland.   But the most
striking consequence of the construction of bócland as land endowed with express privilege, lies in the fact that the King himself, although the chief agent in the creation of bócland, cannot
dispense with express enactments in regard to his own individual
or private property.   This is already indicated by the deed of
exchange of 863 (C. D. 281), in which the bócland of the King
is turned into the folcland of the King, and *vice versa*, which I
am inclined to interpret as an exchange of land held by the King
as private owner against land which had been subjected to him
as sovereign, with the right of craving taxes and services incumbent on that land.   Instances of bóclands held by kings, and disposed
of by them in their capacity of private owners, are common, and
the most famous are, of course, those in King Alfred's will (*Th.*
"Dipl." 487).   But besides, we have a whole group of charters which
tell us of proceedings instituted to create bócland for the King.
An excellent instance is afforded by Archbishop Æthelheard's claims
(A.D. 798) in regard to Church property which King Offa had appropriated : the monastery of Cocham is said to have been held all along
" sine litteris," and to have been left to Offa's heirs *absque litterarum
testimonio* ; but in the case of some other land, he, the King, had taken
care to have it secured to him and to his heirs by book (quas scilicet

terras ibi viventi conscribere fecit suisque heredibus post eum). *Th.*
"Dipl." 42, C. D. 258, is a charter of Æthelwulf of 847, booking to
himself, by the advice and leave of his great men and bishops,
20 hides in Dorset as inheritable property (cum consensu et licentia
principum et episcoporum meorum aliquantulam ruris partem
viginti manentium mihi in hereditatem propriam describere
jussi). A charter of Eadward the Elder (between 901–909, *Th.*
"Dipl." 157) mentions land which has been booked to the King by
the West-Saxon witan in private inheritance (on ece erfe).

22. The contrast between the five hides of folcland and the
innumerable bócland estates of Ealdorman Ælfred is characteristic
enough. Abba's the reeve's will is also interesting, because in his
case the bócland estates had probably been gathered chiefly by his
own exertions, *Th.* "Dipl." 469. On the view that most grants of
bócland did away with the direct connexion between ceorls sitting
on folcland and the King, and created private lordships, the
spread of this class of estates gets to be an ominous sign of social
transformation.

23. We have to rely on indirect evidence in this respect as a
downright rule forbidding alienation of folcland has not come
down to us. Still the indirect evidence is not scarce, nor, as it seems
to me, obscure. To begin with, there is the usage of introducing
relations as corroborative witnesses giving their consent (*Lodge,*
" Essays on Anglo-Saxon Law," lays great stress on this). Then,
we find that there is a constant stream of feeling and custom running
against the power of alienating and devising land out of the kindred,
and a large number of cases arise wherever the best established
bócland rights of the Church and of devisees are attacked by mægths.
I will just point to C. D. 143, 156, and to *Th.* "Dipl." 96–98, as
examples. Indeed, this popular opposition is so strong that in
Alfred's time the tendency to restrict succession to the kindred,
and more especially to the father's kindred, gets formulated even
in regard to bócland. It is expressed by the King, with certain
restrictions, in his will, and, what is more, it is made the subject
of a special enactment : bócland which has been inherited from
kinsmen ought to remain in the kindred, Alfred 41. *Th.* "Dipl."
491. *Brunner* has rightly recognised in these bócland entails
a reflection of the rules holding good as to the *ethel,* that is,
according to our construction as to folcland. " Urkunde," 192.
What is brought forward against this view in the " History of
English Law," does not convince me. I fail to understand in what
way family ownership has to be taken as the outcome and not the
origin of intestacy ("H.E.L." ii. 247). The same problems arise all
over Western Europe, and everywhere we may notice the gradual
and awkward process of development from family ownership towards rights of private ownership and power of individuals to
alienate and to devise. *Blumenstock* has devoted to this theme

in regard to Frankish law the second book of his work on the " Entstehung des Immobiliareigenthums." Cnut ii. 79, though it applies
to the special case of land acquired by the characteristic process
of paying the taxes which the rightful owner did not pay, seems
to indicate that by Cnut's time land in general had come to be
devisable and capable of being given and sold.

24. " History of English Law," ii. 252. Bócland was sometimes
called terra hereditaria, terra testamentalis, and a book might be
called a testamentum, even if it did not contain any immediate
disposition as to inheritance, C. D. 90 (*Earle*, 40), *Thorpe*, "Dipl."
291. The term *erfeland*, which occurs in a few instances (*Th.*
"Dipl." 475, 476), seems to correspond to terra hereditario jure
possessa, that is, to bócland.

25. The action of the Church is an important " material " factor
by the side of the " formal " enactments of kings and legislative
bodies in the creation of bócland and of cwides. *Maitland*,
"Domesday and Beyond," 242. The cwide was not bound up
with any of the formalities necessary for the creation of bócland,
and, indeed, it was very much given over to the discretion of the
representatives of the Church. A priest might swear that a dying
man had bequeathed some land to the Church, and a bishop might
swear for more. *Brunner*, "Urkunde," 201 ; *Pollock* and *Maitland*, "History of English Law," ii. 315. But we have in this
matter a curious case of conflicting legal tendencies. While the
Church strove for formless testamentary dispositions, and carried
her point in many cases by help of anathemas and by her influence
with the kings, and while customary feeling spoke strongly against
the disinheriting of kinsmen, and came forward as a social force
with which even the Church had to reckon, there was a third line
of legal development which, as it were, cut the two others at angles—
I mean the tendency to try testamentary dispositions from the
point of view of bócland right. From this point of view a man
might freely dispose of his land if the power of testamentary dispositions had been granted to him or to his ancestors by book,
not otherwise. If this was not the case, or if the case was doubtful
or opposition in prospect, it was safer to ask the King that one's
will might stand, or to beg him to make one worthy of devising
estate by will. *Th.* "Dipl." 499, 505, 512, 540, 562, 575. A very
full formula in regard to testamentary disposition is given in a
charter of Edward the Confessor. *Th.* "Dipl." 576. Cf. *Pollock*
and *Maitland*, "History of English Law," ii. 318.

26. L. Sal. de alodis : de terra vero [salica] nulla mulieri hereditas non pertinebit sed ad virilem sexum quot fratres fuerint tota
terra perteneat. L. Rip. substitutes hereditas aviatica for terra
salica. The paragraphs ought to be considered in conjunction
with Edictum Chilperiei 3, which points to a time when there was
no inheritance except the direct succession of sons, failing which

the land reverted to the village community (vicini). The Thuringian law is very explicit as to the connexion between landholding and the use of arms, i. 6 : ad quem hereditas terrae ad eum et vestis bellica, id est lorica, et ultio proximi et solutio leudis debet pertinere. Only in case of a failure of heirs male in the sixth generation, the land may lapse from the spear to the spindle.

27. On the baugrygr, see my article, " Geschlecht und Verwandtschaft im Altnorwegischen Recht," Zeitsch. für Social- und Wirthschaftsg. vii. *Ficker*, " Erbenfolge," has started the idea that there was no archaic rule against women owning land, and the " History of English Law " has adopted his theory in regard to English legal antiquities, ii. 241. But *Brunner* has, as it seems to me, presented a convincing defence of the common doctrine against these views. " Zum Erbrecht der Weiber," in " Zeitschrift der Savignystiftung für Rechtsgeschichte," Germ. Abth. xxi. For my part I find it difficult to believe that the exclusion of women from inheriting and holding land can be the product not of primitive conditions and of an undeveloped state of landholding, but of a gradual restriction of women's rights. The supposed later restrictions would appear in a very archaic guise, and with too remarkable a concordance among nations which could not have had any direct influence on each other.

28. The spear and spindle distinction seems to have been deeply engrained in Old English usage, to judge from King Alfred's will. Th. 491, 492. Another variation of this same view meets us in the precedence given to the father's over the mother's kindred, Th. 480–483. In course of time, and chiefly through privileged legislation in regard to bócland and cwiðe, woman-right as to land undoubtedly obtains recognition. See *Thorpe*, " Dipl." 201, 288, 337, 459, 462, 465, 466, 524, 593. Women even have part in oaths in regard to land ownership, Thorpe, " Dipl.," 289.

29. Compare the remarkable customs in regard to the division of property in the ancient Germanic laws. The proper inheritance of the woman is her *gerade* (Geräth), the household furniture. Norse law puts women back in regard to land inheritance, and points to " loose money," *lösa öre*, as a natural outfit for them.

30. *Stubbs*, " Constitutional History," i. 107. As to the wapentake, see especially North People's law, 57 ; Æthelred, ii. 32, 7 ; Lgg. Edw. Conf. 30 ; and *Vigfusson*, " Icelandic Dictionary," s.v. Vapnatak.

31. *Corbett*, " Tribal Hidage," Trans. R. Hist. Soc., xiv. 210.

32. *Pollock* and *Maitland*, " History of English Law," i. 543 ff. Comp. *Napier* and *Stevenson*, " Crawford Charters " (Anecdota Oxoniensia), 44.

33. A direct enactment in regard to hundreds appears only in Edgar's time, Edg. I. 1 (Comp. Lgg. Henr. I. 70). But apart from the fact that hundreds and hæreds are too common

in the early history of Western and Northern Europe to
be considered as later and casual expedients, Alfred's laws can
hardly have meant anything but the hundreds and kindred divisions, when they speak of boldgetæl (Alfred, 37), a general term
admirably adapted to the reckoning of districts by round numbers
of settlers. I can only agree with Mr. Corbett when he insists on the
remarkable concordance between Bede's mode of estimating land
and the round numbers of the so-called "Tribal Hidage," "Trans.
Hist. Soc.," xiv. 191, 207 ff.   Instead of attributing these large
and round numbers to preposterous exaggerations, and testing them
by the 120 acres standard drawn from Domesday Book (*Maitland*,
"Domesday and Beyond"), would it not be more cautious to suppose that Bede knew what he meant, and that his estimates of the
different districts was based on lists of the *boldgetæls* of these districts ?   His regional estimates may all be reduced to hundreds, and
our uncertainty as to the identification of the position of different
tribes, or as to the reasons why the estimates do not conform to later
data in regard to the size and importance of various counties, ought
not to interfere with a recognition of the importance of such estimates
and lists.   But, of course, in order to do this we must renounce the
notion that the terra familiæ (hiwisc, hide) is everywhere, and at all
times, to be taken as approximately 120 acres of arable.   The
hiwisc implies merely the settlement of a family without indicating
its size, and the *boldgetæl* implies a reckoning of homesteads without
deciding as to their agrarian attributes.

34. The hundreds are smallest in Kent and most extensive
in Devon. *Stubbs*, "Const. Hist.," l. c. *Napier* and *Stevenson*,
"Crawford Charters," as to the hundred of Crediton.

35. A Norseman was allowed by usage to have two wives, one
at home and the other in the land where he lived during an expe-
dition. How many wives would be allowed in case of several
expeditions we cannot tell. In any case, such a state of things
does not indicate much certainty and fixity, at least in regard to
mother's kin and "nefgildi."

36. The gilds are an interesting subject of study. The part
they played may be gathered from Alfr. 27, 28 cf the statutes collected
in *Thorpe's* "Diplomatarium." Their history would have to
be made out in connexion with the interesting facts relating to
Norse gilds. In the later period, which may be called Danish
for the sake of brevity, the institution of the frankpledge or free-
borh makes its appearance, an institution which, though it has
given occasion to much idle talk and exaggerated speculations,
still is of an incontestable importance, and evidently goes back
to Old English antecedents. Comp. *Pollock* and *Maitland*, "History of English Law," i. 544. It sprang up naturally when the
system of mægborh had spent itself.

37. *Maitland*, "Domesday and Beyond," 16 ff.

38. Examples of " nucleated " villages are very common. As scattered farms or homesteads form rather the exception, a few instances from the documents at our disposal may illustrate their position. On the fringe of Cheshire bordering on Wales, and recently acquired from it at the time of William the Conqueror, we find, for example, the following Domesday descriptions. Dd. i. 269 : Manerium de Roelent : Ad hoc manerium jacuerunt hae bere-uichae Dissaren, Bodingam, Chiluen et Mainmual. In his est terra unius carucae tantum et silua una leuga longa et dimidia lata. Ibi unus francigena et 2 villani habent 1 carucam. Item Widbulde, Bloiat, Dinmerieh et Brenuuen. Terra est 1 carucae quam habent ibi 2 villani et 1 serviens comitis. Altogether the 269 folio of the first volume of " Domesday " supplies many instances of small settlements scattered among forests and moors. Dd. iii. 221 (Cornwall) : Comes habet unum mansum quae vocatur *Wescota* quam tenuit Ulnodus die quo R. E. vivus fuit et mortuus— 1 fertinus et reddit gildum pro dimidio fertino. As to Devon, " Crawford Charters," 71. Some of the Yorkshire descriptions in Domesday apply also evidently to scattered hamlets. For instance, Dd. i. 324. In Aldenburg habet Ulf 9 carucatas terrae ad geldum, ubi possunt esse 10 carucae.—Ad hoc manerium pertinet soca hæc : Wagene 1, Melse 2, Benincol, Rugheton 2, Scherle 4, Duuetorp 3, Meretone 1, Fosham 1½, Buirench 6, Niuuetone 1, Ringheburg 2 c. 5 b., Wassum 2 c. 2 b., Totele 5 c. 6 b., Otrege ½ c. Simul adgeldum 41 carucata terrae ubi possent esse 40 carucae. As to the causes which might determine the settlement in " nucleated " villages or in hamlets, see *Flach,* in " Histoire des habitations en France," ii. 74 ; and " Origines de l'ancienne France," 97. Comp. *Brutails,* " Roussillon," 34, 35.

39. *Maitland,* " Domesday and Beyond," 330. This point has to be kept well in mind when we want to form an idea of Old English local institutions, and we shall have to revert to it by and by.

40. Bishop Stubbs used *township,* and the American practice supports such an employment of the term, while it is not difficult to make the necessary reservation, that *tunscipe* or *geburscipe* in Old English was taken to designate the population of the town, while *tún* was used for the settlement and the district.

41. This has been brought out with complete clearness by *Pollock* and *Maitland,* " History of English Law," i. 547 ff. Cf. *Prof. Maitland,* " Domesday, and Beyond," 129 ff.

42. I need not repeat that I am considering the most usual and prevailing forms of village organisation, taking notice of exceptions only in so far as they illustrate the rules, or afford a substantial modification of the normal state of things. This being so, we shall have especially to deal with the nucleated village. Settlements in hamlets and scattered homesteads differed materially in their arrangements, but the practices which obtained in them do not indicate the prevailing principles of rural settlement in England.

CHAPTER III

1. "Villainage in England," 237, 258, 340, 344. *Meitzen* has dwelt much on the idea, that mediaeval rural arrangements proceed from the same principles as those embodied in the share-holding of modern joint stock companies, but his construction has the drawback of laying too much stress on the elements of artificial association, and throwing the organic growth of the rural community into the shade. Starting from it, we would be naturally led to deny the very existence of a village community as a natural corporation or, at any rate, to minimise its influence in actual life. In this direction lies the trend of thought followed by *Maitland*.

2. *Seebohm's* statement in "Village Community," 395, must be taken with a corresponding reservation. *Maitland*, "Domesday and Beyond," gives an instance of a hide reckoned in so many real acres and roods, from the Cambridgeshire Hundred Roll (ii. 575), but considers it a late and isolated case. The hide is made to contain "not only arable, but meadows, pastures, crofts, gardens and messuages," which certainly looks like a late attempt to bring order into the conception of the hide by making it a measure of land. Still this instance is not without meaning and value. It is not quite isolated, most of the Cambridgeshire descriptions of holdings adjoining this following a similar scheme. Secondly, it is clear that this measured hide contained much less than 120 acres of arable : that seems odd if we take our standing ground on the assumption that the normal holding started from 120 acres of arable *plus* all the adjuncts in meadows, pastures, crofts, etc. One would expect the measured hide in such a case to be one of 200 acres, like the Kentish sulung, or 180, or 240, or something of the kind. If the hide as a superficial measure could be reckoned at 120 acres, the hide in the arable fields must have been con siderably less. Lastly, it should be noticed that only the "pastura separalis" can have been included in the reckoning by acres, to the amount of only six acres in the Lawston instance. The common pastures remain outside. On the subject of the hide cf. my "English Society in the Eleventh Century" (1908) pp. 148 ff.

3. "Villainage in England," 239.

4. Ibid. 245.

5. For this reason *Mr. Round*, who has done most to bring out the principle of Domesday assessment by re-partition of units of 5 hides and of 6 carucates between the villages, considers the Domesday hide merely as a *geld hide,* and strongly insists on its being

entirely independent of area or value. " Feudal England," 63.
Prof. Maitland, who has also realised the artificial character of
many fiscal computations, does not, however, give up the idea
of an average relation between fiscal hides and real acres. In
his view : " We do not think that there would in general be much
difficulty in finding 120 arable acres for every fiscal hide " (" Domesday and Beyond," 501).

6. For example, Dd. i. 302, d : (Scireburne, Yorkshire) In toto
manerio 350 a. prati.   Silva pastura 8 levas longa et 3 levas lata ;
Silva minuta 4 levas longa et 1 lata.   Terra plana 5 levas longa
et 1 lata et 1 quarantena.   If such estimates were applied to the
United States of North America, they might mean that the land
was divided by rectangles on the map ; in Norman England they
are not based on topographical divisions, but have to be taken as
approximate valuations of the size of the manor and of its lands
lying waste.   When it came to fixing boundaries, people were either
careful to follow natural lines of streams, moors, hills, etc., and
striking local indications, such as old trees, rocks, watch-towers,
etc., or they merely indicated rights of intercommoning in woods
and pastures, according to the number of swine to be sent to the
mast, the wagonloads of wood, and the like.

7. On the *acreware*, " Villainage in England," 242.   They are the
acres which count in the fiscal reckoning, and " defend " themselves and the rest of the land in regard to fiscal requirements.   As
to the *wara* of the Burton Cartulary, which is certainly connected
with acreware, we shall have to speak hereafter.   *Werian* for *de-
fendere* in the sense of acquitting, answering for, is a well established
Old English term.   For example, C. D. 1323 (*Earle*, 237, A.D.
1035) : Cnut cynge . . . ic cyðe eow ðæt ic wylle ðæt Æðelnóð
arcebiscop werige his landáre nú ealswá he dyde ær Ægelríc wære
geréfa, and siððan he geréfa wæs forð oð ðis, C.D. 1057 (*Earle*, 349) :
þæt wæs þæt mon ælles ðises freolses are æfre for ane hide werian
scolde   A curious instance of a transfer by deed of two
bovates ad geldum Domini Regis is afforded by a confirmation
by H. de Scruby in 1237, of a donation of Ivo de Catrinesby, his
grandfather, in a Cartulary of Coton Nunnery. MSS. " Top. Lincolnshire " (Bodleian Library).

8. *Th.* "Dipl." 226 (Eadgar's charter, 963–975).

9. Dd. i. 100 (Somerset) : Halgevilla, quam tenet Brictricus . . .
reddit gildum pro 1 virga, et hanc possunt arare 5 caruce.

10. Perhaps the most remarkable instance of intermixture of
reckoning by geld hides and geld virgates with real hides and virgates is afforded by the Middlesex entries in Domesday.   The sums
are evidently given in geld hides, while the particulars point seemingly to the distribution of real hides and virgates among the tenants.
The consequence is that these latter items when added up
usually do not square with the sums, although not a word is said

to explain the divergence, and the terms used are identical in both sets of numbers. It is to be noted, however, that in some instances, for example, in regard to Westminster, the numbers are concordant (Dd. i. 128). This would serve to corroborate the idea that the estimates of fiscal hides did start from real agrarian occupation after all, but commonly swerved from it.

11. *Round*, " Feudal England," 99 ; *Maitland*, " Domesday and Beyond, 429."

12. For example, Dd. iii. 7 : Warnerius autem retinuerat geldum 1 hidae, scilicet 6 solidos. Turstinus vero, homo G. Maminot retinuerat geldum 3 virgarum, scilicet 4 solidos et 6 denarios. I take this typical instance from the Geld inquests of 1084 relating to the south-western counties. The numbers are often confused in these documents, and therefore it would be difficult to use them for statistical purposes. But nevertheless they give first-rate evidence in regard to the terminology of those times, and their general arrangement is sufficiently clear.

13. *Maitland*, " Domesday and Beyond," 450, 451 ; *Round*, " Domesday Studies," i., 98 ff. ; " Victoria County History of Surrey," 277.

14. For instance, Dd. i. 272 (Derby) : In Asseforde cum Bereuicis Rex Edwardus habuit 22 carucatas terrae ad geldum et 1 carucatam terrae sine geldo. Ibi nunc in dominio habet Rex 4 carucas et 18 villani habent 5 carucas. Terra 22 carucarum.

15. " Villainage in England," 239.

16. *Round*, " Feudal England," 44.

17. E.g. Dd. 22b : Bercheham.

18. *Seebohm, Round* and *Maitland* support this view.

19. *Round*, " Feudal England," 82. As to Lancashire and Yorkshire hides, ibid. 86, 88.

20. *Maitland*, " Domesday and Beyond," 395. On French carucates, *Guérard*, " Prolégomènes au Polyptique de St. Père de Chartres," clxviii. ; *Delisle*, " Agriculture et classe agricole en Normandie," 538.

21. My paper on Sulung and hide, " Engl. Hist. Rev.," 1904, April. The sulung of 200 acres seems to have originated in attempts to assign a definite acreage to every sulung, including messuages, tofts, and perhaps separate pasture, as in the case of some Cambridgeshire hides.

22. *J. A. Tait*, " Engl. Hist. Rev.," 1902, p. 280.

23. *Maitland*, " Domesday and Beyond," 393.

24. The ploughland of 120 acres has been chiefly advocated by *Eyton*, " Domesday of Dorset," 23 ff. *Maitland's* doubts as to the possibility of finding the necessary soil for teamlands of 120 acres (" Domesday and Beyond," 431) are connected with his conception of the *terra carucis* as arable which had been under actual cultivation. It seems to me, however, that even

on this hypothesis the necessary land could be found on the strength of the figures given by him. Certainly it would exceed the present cultivated area ; and no wonder that it should, if we take into reckoning the peasantless condition of contemporary England, the concentration of agriculture in the hands of large farmers, the spread of accommodation for industrial undertakings, and the large areas occupied by parks and sheep pasture. But we are not even reduced to this one explanation in regard of the *terra carucis*. In some places commissioners and local jurors may have understood the inquiry as to land sufficient for ploughteams in the sense of a direction to find out how many ploughlands there were or had been in a place, apart from actual tillage by existing ploughs. But the formula, " how many teams there might be," admits of a broader construction, and seems to have been actually understood to apply to all the land which could be turned into arable. Should this be conceded, there would be much less difficulty in locating the hypothetical ploughteams. I may add that this part of the enquiry had an important bearing for purposes of colonisation and melioration.

25. *Round*, " Feudal England," 153 ; " Eng, Hist, Rev.," 1900, p. 78 ff.

26. For instance, Dd. i. 299 : In Walesgref (Yorkshire) sunt ad geldum 15 carucatae terrae quas possunt arare 8 carucae. . . . Sunt ibi villani habentes 2 carucas. . . . T.R.E. valuit 56 libras modo 30 solidos. . . . Ad hoc manerium pertinet soca . . . inter totum sunt ad geldum 84 carucatae quas possunt arare 42 carucae. In his fuerunt 108 sochemanni cum 46 carucis, modo sunt 7 sochemanni et 15 villani et 14 bordarii, habentes 7 carucas et dimidiam. Cetera sunt wasta. Cf. ff. 300, 301, passim.

27. *Round*, " Feudal England," 44, 71, 75 ; " Victoria County History of Worcestershire," 236 ; *Maitland*, " Domesday and Beyond."

28. " Domesday and Beyond," 502.

29. Ibid., 507, 508.

30. The Domesday mentions of *Valet*, though by no means clear to us, were evidently meant to sum up the valuations of profits for the Exchequer. *Pearson*, " Early and Middle Ages," has made a special study of them.

31. *Round*, " Feudal England," 108 ; *Seebohm*, " Village Community, 36 ff."

32. *Seebohm*, " Village Community," 120.

33. We sometimes get the contrast between carucata ad geldum and carucata ad arandum. *Round*, " Domesday Studies," i. 199 ff.

34. Dd. i. 10 : Ore.

35. *Maitland*, " Domesday and Beyond," 466. Examples of arbitrary proceedings on the part of sheriffs abound in the statements of grievances. I will refer to one illustrating the meaning of hides as shares in fiscal organisation. Dd. i. 181 (Hereford) :

In Niware sunt 2 hidae et dimidia quae in Bremesese hundred conveniebant et operabantur, sed Rogerus de Pistes divertit illas ad Gloucestershire.

36. Domesday provides many instances in which the hide appears seemingly as an expression bound up with the levying of geld, so that when no geld is paid no hides exist. For example, Dd. i. 269 : Nunquam geldavit neque hidatum fuit (Cheshire) ; iii. 29 : has tenuit Rex Eduardus in dominio et nescitur quot hidae ibi sunt, quia non reddiderunt geldum, T. R. E. Dd. i. 76 : (Sherborne) nunquam per hidas divisa fuit neque geldavit. Cf. *Round,* " Domesday Studies," i. 107 ff. Sometimes *carucates* are made use of to supply the absence of hides on estates or portions of estates which were exempted from geld ; *Eyton,* " Key to Domesday," 18. But it would be wrong to draw too sweeping conclusions from this use of expressions in Domesday. By the side of them appear other passages mentioning hides and virgates which do not pay geld and yet are hides and virgates. Altogether the independent agrarian value of these terms is too well ascertained to admit of doubt. In this way the true meaning of such Domesday notices as those quoted above seems to be, that certain portions of territory had not been assessed in hides for the payment of geld, although hides in the sense of ploughlands for " domestic " use—" ad inwaram " one may be tempted to say—may well have existed there. In the case of newly conquered or newly reclaimed land, the ambiguous term hide may have been avoided on purpose, and the carucate as ploughland may naturally have been substituted.

37. It is so important to realise this point clearly, that I take leave to appeal to several examples. Cart. Sax. iii. 129 (A.D. 956) : Đis sind þa landgemæra þara 20 hida æt Hannige þe Eadwig cing gebocede Ælrice his mæge on ece yrue (cf. iii. 134). p. 133 : æt Bitelanwyrthe an hiwisce and æt Bromleage an hiwisce. *Earle,*" L.C.," 234 (A.D. 1003-1023) : Đis syndon þære halfu hide lond gemæru up æt þære pirian. C. S. iii. 139 : þis sint þæs hywisces land gemæru æt Udding. *Crawford,* " Ch." 20 : aliquam terre particulam . . . i.e. 7 tributariorum et dimidii, non tamen in uno loco, sed in tribus uillulis, etc. *Earle,* " L. Ch.",322 (C. D. 369) : Unam mansam ubi rustici uocabant toppesham . . . þis synd þære *anre gyrde* landgemæro at æsc hyrste þe gebyrað into þære hyde æt toppeshamme (Cf. *Earle,* 326, 327). Cart. Sax. iv. 38 : Dis is ðære twegra hid boc and anre gyrde æt Norrtune and ða feower æceras ðær to of ðæðe styfycunge (clearing) into ðam twam hidan and ða mæde. *Thorpe,* " Diplom." 541 : ic gean of Purlea into Nutlea healfre hide landes on east healf stræte. " Crawford, Ch. " 77, boundaries of a yardland which seems to lie in a heap. *Thorpe,* " Dipl." 580 (A.D. 1050) : and ic an Lefquene 15 acras at Palegr. and an toft—and Alfwald habbe mid ton þe he her hauede 16 acres mid tofte mid alle—Ulwine and his brother 20 acres at Reydon. Cf. Th. 590 (A.D. 1050).

38. *Seebohm,* " Village Community," 37 ff. ; *Maitland,* " Domesday and Beyond," 490. Once a hide mentioned in an Old English land book is said to contain 120 acres. *Thorpe,* " Dipl." 508 (A.D. 958): ic Aðelgar an an hide lond þes ðe Aeulf hauede be hundtuelti acren, ateo so he wille.

39 " Villainage in England," 239, 240.

40. The treatise on husbandry ascribed to Walter of Henley makes two different calculations for the ploughland on the two course and on the three course system, bringing up the first to 160 and the second to 180 acres. The size may be suggested by an exaggerated estimate of the capabilities of a ploughteam (*Maitland,* " Domesday and Beyond," 378), but the method is characteristic inasmuch as it supposes two different standards. If we therefore get only one in the case of the hide of 120 acres, we must either take it as an average, and assume that it was rather less than a three-field ploughland and rather more than a two-field ploughland, or make a choice between the two, and suppose that it fitted in reality only the cases of a three-field rotation or only those of two-field rotation. *Mr. Seebohm* seems to have taken it to apply to the three-field system, although the problem is not stated clearly by him.

41. *Is. Taylor* has constructed a theory on the foundation of instances from the East Riding of Yorkshire. He thinks that the carucata ad geldum is the quantity tilled every year in one arable field by one plough. " Domesday Studies," i. 157. Critics have rightly protested against the sweeping character of his conclusions (see, e.g., *Round,* " Feudal England," 87 ff.), but there seems to be a good deal of weight in the initial observations from which it starts. It is clear that there could be no attempt to subject the three-field system to a heavier burden of taxation than the two-field system, but the matter of fact inquiry by the Domesday Commission may have been conducted in such a way as to elicit in some cases, especially in the North, the diversity between the area under actual cultivation and the gross extent of arable land estimated as land for the ploughs, while, as a rule, no attempt was made to express this contrast.

42. *Seebohm,* " Tribal Custom," 424. We hear of a Cornish acre equated with 64 English acres. " Testa de Nevill," 185, 204.

43. If the charter C. D. 18 (*Earle,* " L. Ch." 281) should be genuine or based on a genuine one, the documentary evidence as to hides as agrarian units would go back to the time of Cædualla and the year 680 : hanc libertatem sub estimatione 70 tributariorum taxauimus in illo loca qui dicitur Pecgam aliisque locis circumquaque adjacentibus. The statement in itself tallies exactly with Bede's expressions. Cf. C. D. 1006 : de terra juris mei aliquantulam portionem juxta mensuram scilicet 10 familiarum. It is worth notice that when the hiwiscs and sulungs lie in separate patches they are called lands, and get their names from possessive patrony-

mics as the villages. For instance, C. D. 195 (*Earle*, 82): Donabo terram trium aratrorum mee propriae juris in regione Easterege, quae inibi ab incolis folcwinning lond uocatur atque iterum in eadem regione Easterege meae proprie hereditatis ruriculum unius aratri illis tribus adhaerens . . . sed illud aratrum unum on liminum . . . id est ðæt wynnhearding lond and babbinglond and an iocled on uppan ufre etc. *Thorpe*, " Dipl.," 109 (A.D. 854). . . . cassati in loco qui dicitur Heregeardinge hiwisc. Cf. Proceedings of the Suffolk Archæological Institute, iii. (1860), Extenta de Hadleghe, Suffolk, pp. 232 ff. : liberae terrae Gloucestreslond, Heestmanlond, Bonleyslond, Goddingefrelond, Knaptonsland, Edrichesfrelond, Corsfordeslond . . . (Custumarii) Aldhamelond, etc. In the last case, as will be noticed, the names, with a few exceptions, have nothing to do with persons or kindreds.

44. Baeda, i. 25 : Tanatos insula non modica familiarum sexcentorum, etc. A. S. version—Donne is on eastwardre Cent micil island, þæt is syx hund hida micel æfter Angel cynnes æhte, ii. 9 ; iv. 16, 19 ; iii. 4 : neque enim magna est (Iona) sed quasi familiarum quinque iuxta aestimationem Anglorum. In some cases the numbers are based on exact and local knowledge. For example, v. 19 (A. Sax. transl. ed. *Schipper*, 662) : Alchfred . . . geaf he him sona and sealde tyn hiwisca landes on þære stowe, þe cweden is Stanford and æfter . . , . sealde him mynster þritiges hiwisca on stowe, seo is gecyged in Hripum. In one case the familiae of the Latin text is rendered by folc in the Old English Version, iii. 24 (*Schipper*, p. 314). Oswio se cyning gef and sealde þam foresprecenan Peadon, Pendon suna þæs cyninges . . . Suðmercna rice, þa syndon, þæs þe menn ceveþað, fif þusendo folces (qui sunt, ut dicunt, familiarum quinque millium).

45. The cases of Thanet and of the Isle of Wight (iv. 16), as well as of Kent and Sussex, are especially conspicuous. Cf. *Maitland*, " Domesday and Beyond," 512.

46. " Domesday and Beyond," 358.

47. Ibid,, 494.

48. " Crawford Charters," 43.

49. " Domesday and Beyond," 228, 229.

CHAPTER IV

1. The late *Professor Maitland* admitted that the economic interests and affairs of the householders of a township were inextricably intermixed, but he thought that the legal consequences of this intermixture were slight and that there was not much of a village community to speak of. " Domesday and Beyond." 347 ff. Cf. " History of English Law," i. 691. On the open field system and the village community, cf. " English Society in the Eleventh Century," pp. 277 ff., 391 ff.

2. Cf. " Domesday and Beyond," 371.

3. *Thorpe*, 122 (A.D. 363), . . . et 4 carris transductionem in Silba regis 6 ebdomadas a diis Pentecosten, et ubi alteri homines silbam cedunt, hoc est in regis communione, hec sunt pascua porcorum que nostra lingua Saxonica denbera nominamus, hoc est Husneah, Efreðingdenn, Herbedingdenn, Wafingdenn, Widefetingdenn, Bleccingdenn, C.D. 364 (*Earle*, 171) . . . ðis synt ða denbera ðe to ðissum londe mid rihte belimpað, etc.

4. *Whitaker*, " History of Whalley," i. 263.

5. " Liber Ecclesiae de Burgo " (Society of Antiquaries), 192 ff. ; " Tilncholt est pastura Communis." Cf. *Blomfield*, "History of Norfolk," 72.

6. " Victoria County History of Essex," 369.

7. *Thorpe*, " Dipl.," 65 : In Ondrede pastum et pascua porcorum et armentum seu caprarum.

8. " Northumberland Assizes," 21 (40 Henry III.) : juratores dicunt, quod predictus J. disseisivit pred. R. de propria communa sua, . . . quia ipse antequam Ric., pater predicti Johannis aliquam terram habuit in predicta villa, solebat idem R. de Buttleston communam per totum annum in predicta mora (habere) . . . dicunt quod nunquam tempore ipse Johannes solebat ibi communare nisi tempore aperto et post blada asportata, scilicet quando vestitura campi ex parte illius morae asportatur. " Rot. Hundr.," i. 519 (Suffolk) : Prior de Shuldham . . . appropriavit sibi quandam pasturam communem in Sh. que vocatur Brithemorefrith, que debet et solet esse omnibus communis tempore aperto, et capit ibi de qualibet bestia ibi veniente unum obolum.

9. We know very little of the regulation of hunting rights in Old English time, as the only authentic Old English regulation which has come down to us applies to woods in private possession, but it is clear that the stringent regulations favouring private landlords were mainly the product of Norman legislation and usage and felt to be a grievance from the point of view of previous custom.

10. A good example is supplied by the accounts of trials (A.D. 825) at the Synod of Clovesho. *Thorpe*, 70, and A.D. 896, *Thorpe*, 139.

11. The frequent notices in documents of the feudal age, though dating from a later time, are very characteristic and undoubtedly go back to old customs. For example, *Dodsworth*, " Yorkshire Arch. Journal," x. 367, 547.

12. This is the basis of what was termed in later law " Common pur cause de vicinage." "Notebook of Bracton," 1194 ; Rot. Hundr. ii. 605.

13. Dd. i. 127, 128, etc. Silva ad faciem das domos, i. 38b ; Silva ad clausulam, i. 5, 16, 17, etc.

14. Ine, 43. *Thorpe*, " Dipl.," 140. Cf. *Andrews*, " Old English Manor," 225.

15. " Villainage in England." 276. Of course, the origins of the so-

called common of estover of later law must also be sought in older customs which arose, as it were, by themselves as soon as this definite appropriation of rights in the woods begins.

16. Dd. i.   Cf. *Round*, in the "Victoria County History of Essex," 374; "Victoria County History of Surrey," 291.   Cf. C. D., 204 (*Earle*, 95).

17. *Thorpe*, "Dipl.," 70 : "hit aræded was on Æðelbaldes dæge þrim hund swína mæst."

18. *Thorpe*, "Dipl.," 580 (A.D. 1050) :   And ic an Lefquene mine neue and J. and W., 20 acres at Reydone and þe mor þe ic and þo monekes soken ymbe min del, fremannen to note (for the use of freemen).   "Villainage in England," 262 : In support of the contention that the usages as to common are prefeudal in their main principles, it may be pointed out that the individualism of mediaeval Common Law makes itself felt as a current which has to struggle against ideas of ancient right and custom.   It is still with the township more than with the private owner or the single tenant that we have to reckon in this respect in the thirteenth and fourteenth centuries, although Common Law begins to introduce doctrines of individual usage.   The second argument rests on the notion of the holding as a centre from which rights in all the different spheres of rural life radiate, as it were, according to its share of interest in the whole.   In short, rights of common, as illustrated by later practices, must have originated in ancient custom, because the *tún* and the *hide*, with which they are connected, belong to ancient custom.

19. *J. Williams*, "Rights of Common," 37.

20. "Villainage in England," 272 ff.   I do not see why the "History of English Law" i, 612, treats the supposed original rights of the single freeholder to oppose approvement and enclosure as an instance of extreme individualism.   The argument which is put in his mouth in support of his claim does not seem to suit the case.   The imaginary spokesman of individualism is supposed to defy any and all the members of the community to restrict or infringe his rights to the use of the common wherever it stretched : there may be enough land for all purposes and you may be all agreed to approve one part of it, but I intend to use the common as before, and oppose any attempt to restrict or localise my rights, he is made, in substance, to say.   But the rights of the free tenants were asserted not against the community of the township or the majority of the townsmen, but against the will of the lord, which is altogether a different matter, and there is no evidence nor any likelihood that a single member of the community could arrest its regularly formulated decisions in regard to approvement or enclosures.   I may remark in passing that the support which is sought in the chapter *De migrantibus*, of the Lex Salica, is illusory.   This celebrated enactment ("L. Sa." xlv.) treats of a special case, namely of the intrusion of a stranger in the territory of a

village community. Against such an intrusion every single member
has a right to protest, although another member may have given
his consent. The case of a decision to admit the stranger by the
village *in corpore* is not considered, and there is nothing to show
that a single villager could override a decision of the village meeting
(*conventum*) or defy the majority of its members. The question
as to the mode of formulating such decisions and of the respective
rights of majority and minority in these ancient assemblies is a
distinct one and need not be discussed here.

21. This seems to lie at the root of the interesting case reported
and annotated in the " Notebook of Bracton," 1662.

22. For example, Eynsham Cartulary f. 74, " Villainage in
England," 260.

23. Meadows are mentioned, for example, C.D. 253, " Crawford
Charters," 73. The practices of the meting out of Lammas meadows
are well illustrated by the Eynsham case, " Villainage in England,"
259, and the Aston and Cote Case, 259 ; *Gomme,* " Village Community," 162.

24. Ine, 42 : Gif ceorlas gærstun hæbben gemænne, oððe oþer
gedálland to tynanne, and hæbben sume getyned heora dæl, summe
næbben, and etten hiora gemænan æceras oððe gærs, gán þa þonne
þe ðat geat agan, and gebete þam oðrum, þe hiora dæl getynedne
hæbben, þone æwerdlan þe ðær gedón sie ; abidden him æt þam
ceape swylc ryht swylce hit kyn sie.

25. The normal condition of an open field in "defence " time, protected by light hedges is further illustrated by Ine, 42, § 1 : gif
þonne hryðera hwelc sie þe hegas brece and ga in gehwær, and se
hit nolde gehealdan, se hit age, oþþe ne mæge, nime se hit on his
æcere mete and ófslea, and nime se agenfrigea his fel and flæsc, and
þolie þas aðres.

26. Arable open fields belonging to Malmesbury are described by
Gomme, " Village Community," 186, Arable open fields belonging to
Cambridge, *Maitland,* " Township and Borough," 55 f.

27. *Professor Maitland* has criticised the attempt to treat these
instances as survivals " of primitive communalism." " Law
Quarterly Review," ix. Of course, there is a special feature
in the instances quoted by *Gomme* and others—they are drawn
from the economic practice of towns which utilised the fields
in their immediate neighbourhood in this way instead of
letting them to farmers, and do not seem to have had a very
clear conception of corporate property. Nor is it admis-
sible to see in these instances typical examples of the general
management of open field arable in former times. But,
nevertheless, several characteristic points remain which ought
not to be slurred over. The fields in question are undoubtedly considered the property of the town community, and
the notion of such corporate property is evidently derived

not from new fangled arrangements but from ancient custom; the most natural account of the peculiar repartition of the strips is suggested by a comparison with Lammas meadows on the one hand, hereditary shares in the arable on the other, and there does not seem to be a need or a probability of a special derivation ; the transition from town to village community is very gradual and, indeed, both are varieties of the one *tún* or township, as has been very properly insisted upon by *Professor Jas. Tait*, " E. H. R," 1897, p. 774.

28. *Seebohm*, "English Village Community," 226, 439.

29. The Anglo-Saxon charters contain numerous references to practices and terms connected with the open-field system. For example, *Earle*, " Land Ch.," 208 : . . . anbutan þone garan (gore, strip stunted into a triangular shape), eft on þone weg, of þæm wege a be þæm heafodlande (headland, strip perpendicular to the acres of a shot and used by the ploughmen to turn back their teams and to get access to the field), eft in þæt oþer heafodland ane hwile, þænne in þa furh, þæt and long fyrh anbutan þæt *heafodlond* þæt swa on Cyneburgelond gemære, þæt andlong gemæres on þæt *heafodland,* of þæm *heafodlonde* eft on þone weg on hlydan (?) andlong hlydan on þone heafodweg . . . of þære fyrh a be þæm *hœfdan* to breoduninga gemære . . . of þæm *hœfdan* to þam *heafodlonde.* C. D. 1276* (*Earle*, 390). Ðis sind da land gemæro to Cyngestune *œcer* onder *œcere* . . . on ða *heafodœceras* . . . on tone *ealdangáran. Thorpe,* " Dipl.," 494 : Londes gemæro to Aweltune . . . þonne on þam *gemœnan garan* be uton ðæm dic . . . þonne and lang rode on þone *littlan garan* middeweardne . . . and se *heðfeld eal gemœne.* C. D., 8vo. *Earle*, " L. Ch.," 394 : Ðis sind ða landgemæra to Sandforde on ðám *gemánnan* lande. C. D., 658, *Earle*, 363 : þonne licgaþ þa þreo gyrda on oþære healfæ fromæ at F. on *gemœnum* lande.

30. *Knapp*, "Grundherrschaft und Rittergut," 107.

31. The peculiarities of the prevailing arrangement are even more brought into light by the fact that there were cases and regions in which the concentration of territory was aimed at. The ploughlands (*sulungs*) of Kent lay originally in separate patches, as is evident from their names, and the advantages of concentration are well expressed, for example, in the following document. C. D. 195 (*Earle*, 82): insuper etiam addidi on Eostorege quintum aratrum fratribus nostris concedendum, quod a reacoluensæ ecclesiæ prius transmotaveram, quod dunwalinglond dicitur. Has itaque terrulas ideo colligere et simul ita in unum coniungere eximiae caritatis industria curaui, ut facilius elaborare ac desudare sua propria in illis potuissent quas, adunati unius termine intra septa conclusi. This applies to an estate of several ploughteams, but the considerations expressed in the charter would hold good quite as much in the case of small holdings. Cf. " Domesday and Beyond," 338. *Meitzen,* i. 370. *Seebohm,* " Tribal Custom," 519.

32. MS. Cart. of Dunstable Priory ; Harl. MSS. 1885, f. 7, d.
* Villainage in England," 233 ff. Cf. *E. Bateson,* " History of
Northumberland," ii. 129. Map of the Manor of Rock of 1599.
" This map appears to have been made to illustrate a partial division
of the township. Before the division the township seems to have
contained a parcel of demesne (170 acres) in severalty, a separate
demesne moor, three fields, viz. Arksley, Rockley and Earsley fields,
and a town moor. A division of the township was desired by both
lord and tenants. The lord desired to throw together the scattered
portions of the demesne which lay intermixed with the tenants'
land, and, as the township is a large one, the tenantry of the village
found themselves too far away from their lands in the north of the
township. So the whole was divided for agricultural purposes into
two parts, as had been done at Long Houghton about forty
years before. There were twelve farms, and each consisted of
approximately 83 acres in all, i.e. 43 acres of arable meadows
and pasture, and 40 acres of waste. At the time of the division
five of the tenants took the Arksley field and the old demesne,
and the other seven took the remainder of Earsley field and Rockley
field, after the lord of the manor had been compensated for the
demesne. . . . Within the limits of each half township the common
field system probably went on as before. There is nothing on the
map or schedule to suggest that land was allotted to every farm in
severalty, but an effort was made to adapt the existing boundary
to the new state of things. Each of the new half townships could
be divided by the existing hedgerows into three fields, as the old
township had been." Cf. 155 ff. The interest of such instances
lies in the fact that they arise from an assumption of original
equality.

33. The Danish customary law of which the Schleswig agrarian
practices present one variety, recognised four different modes of
holding land : (1) common land, *fællesjord,* (2) private property
marked off by definite boundaries, *ornum, stuf* ; (3) share land,
held on the ground of regular assignation, according to a share in
the village, *rebdragen jord,* with the uses appendant to it, and (4)
land held by occupation without formal title, *gribsjord* (cf. *Haff,*
" Die dänischen Gemeinderechte," Leipzig, 1909). These contrasted species are illustrated by the following documents published
by *Stemann,* Schleswig's "Reichs- und Gerichts-verfassung im
XVII Jahrhundert " (Schleswig und Flensburg, 1855), 85, p. 93.
" Coldinger Recess," 28 : gribsjord (which has not been from ancient
times laid out in a holding) p. 249. gribsjord in contrast with " Stuf
and Særmark " ; iv. 24, p. 108. The character of land allotted as a
share in the village may be gathered from the following judgment
in a case of April 20, 1691 (*Stemann,* o.l. 122, p. 111) : enhver sin egen
lodschiffte jord herefter selffver at minde, haffve og beholde, saa
vit hannem efter sin gaardspart med rette tilkommen eller og kand
lodde og tilfalde, dog bör först for grande at udlægge til Foerte og

Gade (may every one henceforward use, have and keep for himself the land allotted to him by division in so much as falls to him according to the share of his holding or may hereafter fall to it or be allotted to it, but firstly the community of neighbours must get its village green and ways). The process of occupation and assignation is well described in *Stemann's* document, 105, p. 102 (March 24, 1684) : 6 Mand udneffened til at schiffte Kollebye March—ved et reb, som var afmerket til 8 Schar afmaalet og deelt, hvis iord som for det förste schal indtages til at plouge og saw udi, eftersom loddet er tilfalden ; Astrup og Synderins mænd samt G.P. i Holm at haffue öphoff og ligge y derst paa den vesterside; da haffuer de gjort öffverslag paa den Sonderwang, udi hvilcken Vang er afmaalt til 30 Aggere hver Agger 8 Schar, og desforuden 4 Schar aflagt hil V eien, at vilche A. og S. Mand samt G.P. tager först af Vester 2 Reebs Bredde som er 16 Scharjord, og de Scherebech Mand det tredie Reebs Brede med 8 Schar. (Six men appointed to divide the fields of Kolleby by a *Reeb* [cord], which was marked off to contain eight "Schar," measured and divided, whose land should be enclosed to begin with for ploughing and reaping according to the fall of the lot. The men of A. and S. and G.P. in Holm have to make the beginning and to lie farthest to the West. Thereupon have they made a computation in regard to the Southshot, in which shot there are measured 30 field strips [cf. acre-strips], each strip of 8 schars, and besides 4 schar are marked off for the way, of which the men of A. and S. as well as G. P. take first from the west to the width of 2 Reebs, that is land to the extent of 16 schar, and the men of Scherebech take the third Reebs width with 8 schar.)

In course of time encroachments and disputes might arise which led to redivisions on the basis of the shares, as seen in No. 158, p. 127 (March 3, 1710) : Lodseierne udi Brön haver varet paaklagende, at deres Agger og Eng sampst Tofftejord er urigtig delt og deres Mark dog er en reebt Mark, saa enhver efter sin Ottings anpart bör at have lige meget (undtagen hvad Ornum og Stuf er angaaende, det beholder enhver ubeskaret) . . . 6 Mand paa ligning giort en begyndelse 6 Allen eller 2 skar lang overmaalt, og paa 54½ Ottinger, som udi byen findes, fordelt. . . . A. Sörensen österst til Ophaf. . . . A. Simonsen vesterst til udfald . . . fordi han ligger yderst og nest til veien, saa er ham samme overlads Jord tillagt til aabœd. Shareholders in Broris have been complaining that their arable and meadow as well as Toft-land is not divided properly, although their fields are fields allotted by the Reeb (cord) in such a way, that everyone should have as much as everyone else according to his Ottingshare (the share of his holding), with the exception of private land of ancient assignation (ornum) or approved land (stuf) . . . Six men have initiated an equalisation of the shares by measuring six "Ells," equivalent to two Skar in length, and distributing strips on that scale to the 54½ Ottings which are found in the township. . . . A. S. received the easternmost strip to start with. . . . A. S. the westernmost to close up ; and as he lies at the fullest extremity towards the road, the land in excess has been allotted to him).

As an example of by-laws the following may be quoted (Agreement between the " Grande og Naboer " of Branderup ; No. 15, p. 138, A.D. 1672) : " They have decided that every man shall go out to mow grass on St. Waldborg's Day, and that it should be laid out by Ottings, so that everything should be done in accordance with right and equality. 2. Every year before the breaking up of the soil, they shall collect the stones, each on his field and remove them in carts. 4. All the men of the township (alle mend udi byen) shall appear at the village meeting (grandesteffne), when it is summoned, and whosoever does not appear will be at once fined four shillings. 5. No one shall go on his strips of arable or meadow to reap or mow before they have held a meeting about it and settled what day they will harvest, etc.

A description may be found in the " Scriptores rerum Danicarum," viii. p. 41, in regard to a " Solrebning " in Öster Höisted in Schleswig of 1513. Firstly the areas were measured out for the tofts on an average of 40 roods in length and 6 roods in breadth, with allowances to make up for casual disadvantages. Then the twelve representatives of the township apportioned every shareholding its strips in the fields, " in the damp and in the dry," in meadow and in pasture, etc. The principles on which these assignations were performed are clearly expressed in the Danish provincial laws of the twelfth century. Jydske lov, i. 55, and Eriks Sjællandske lov, II. 55, 56. According to them the toft appears as the " mother " of the holding in the fields, and the strips in these have to follow the order in which the house tofts are situated in the village according to the course of the sun (solskifte, solrebning). The same practices are found to have obtained in Sweden and Finland. *Schlyter*, " Sveriges gamle love," iii. 339 ; iv. 337 ; xiii. 257. " Upl. Lag." ib. 2 §1. *Schybergson*, " Finland's Historia," ii, 198. In a most interesting and suggestive paper by Laurid sen (" Aarböger for Nordisk Olakyndighed," II. Series, vol. xi. 1896), from which I have taken the last references, the author considers the enactments and instances just mentioned to apply to a process of general regulation of landholding which began in the twelfth century or even earlier and went on spreading from west to east. After the redivision arable and tofts became private property, while before the redivision we have to surmise more ancient forms of settlement and customs of land-holding (the forniskipt of Swedish sources) to which the regular arrangements of the Solrebning does not give any clue. As far as the description of Solrebning goes, *Mr. Lauridsen's* remarks are eminently worthy of attention, and the treatment of all questions relating to the disposition of the housetofts and the plans of village settlements is especially good. At the same time the author does not seem to have quite realised the importance of some traits which he mentions in passing without laying much weight on them. To begin with, though the distribution of the *solskifte* was undoubtedly meant to be a lasting one and any attempt at redistribution was obstructed by the necessity of unanimous consent on the part of the villagers, it is too much to speak of a passage from communal ownership to private ownership in this case. All the communal practices which we have been describing in regard to open fields of England—compulsory rotation, rights of common pasture, incidents of common appendant, of approvement on common land, etc., continued to hold good. Besides, the very fact that most of our recorded examples of Solrebning date from the sixteenth and seventeenth centuries testify to the frequent occurrence of redistributions of land on the basis of customary claims. It is clear that the assignation of the thirteenth and fourteenth centuries did not render those of the sixteenth and seventeenth superfluous or impossible. In this way it would be safer to speak of the Reebning as fixing in a definite manner the claims of each shareholder instead of assuming that it created private property. The second thing to be noted is that although the details of agrarian practices preceding solskifte are not clear to us, it is quite certain that they started from the conception of equalised shares and of a communal overlordship over them. Indeed the equalised share, the *ból*, or *mansus*, is quite as characteristic of ancient Danish landholding as the hide is of Old English landholding (cf. *J. Steenstrup*, "Studier over Kong Valdemars jordbog"). The *bóls* lay, in some cases, in separate plots, but consisted mostly, as in England, of bundles of strips apportioned to the tofts and scattered in the fields. To judge from indications in regard to Finlandish practices, the original mode of assignation may have consisted in the allotment of strips in yearly possession (*Kreüger* "Studier rörande de agrariske fór, hællandenas utvecklung i Sverige," Lund, 1882, p. 17, quoted by Lauridsen). However this may have been in Denmark, the whole process of subsequent division by Solrebning starts from the principle that all the *bóls* and *ottings* confer on their owners rights of equalised shareholders. And the communal overlordship has to be taken for granted in order to explain the whole process of redistribution. Lastly, the Northern practices, ranging as they do through the whole domain of Scandinavian open-field cultivation, appear as a forcible illustration of the idea that no seignorial compulsion or manorial organisation is needed in order to produce the system of township shareholding; they are directed by the action of strictly communal authorities. It is evident in their case that the equilibrium of open-field holdings may be produced by the concurrent interests of peasant neighbours and by the sense of household solidarity on one hand, of township organisation on the other, quite apart from any discipline and exploitation carried into village life from the outside. I cannot help thinking that this is emphatically a case for comparative study and for checking *a priori* assertions in regard to what was likely to happen in free and unfree settlements. The German system of *Feldgemeinschaft* has been often made the subject of comparison, but the Scandinavian evidence seems even more to the point.

34. *Andrews*, " Old English Manor," 117.   Cf. *Maitland*, " Domesday and Beyond," 336.

35. *C. S. Taylor*, " Analysis of Gloucestershire Domesday," and *Maitland*, " Domesday and Beyond," 436, assume a very marked prevalence of agriculture over pastoral pursuits, at least in the purely English counties, and compare the present acreage of arable land with the Domesday acreage, not to the advantage of our times. There is a good deal to be said in favour of this latter observation which, after all, seems a consequence of the fact that there is, properly speaking, no peasantry in modern England, while in the time of Domesday the peasantry was the most numerous and economically important class.   But the calculations on the basis of the ploughteam of 120 acres are not safe, because, as I have suggested elsewhere, the *terra carucis* most likely included land which had never been under tillage but was considered convenient for cultivation. The fact that pastures belonging to townships are seldom mentioned in the " Gloucestershire Domesday " can in no way prove that there were none, it seems that by one of the many unaccountable local aberrations from the common type of the inquiry, the Domesday commissioners and jurors of Gloucestershire did not attend to this matter or that the notices bearing on it were left out during the process of compilation.   There can be no material reason for the contrast which is presented by Gloucestershire and Somersetshire in this respect.

36. Dd., ii. 181, 187, 188, *et passim*.

37. *Earle*, " Land Charters," 343 (C.D. 853).

38. I am indebted for this information to Mr. Seebohm.

39. Feudal documents speak of *inhoc* (" Villainage in England," 226) where Old English charters employ the term *haga*. Earle, " Landch." 97 ; Thorpe, 46.

40. Æthelbirht, 27.

41. Ine 40 : Ceorles worðig sceal beon wintres and sumeres betyned ; gif he bið untyned and recð his neahgebures ceap in on his agen geat, nah he æt þam ceape nan wuht : adrife hine ut and ðolie æfwerdlan.

42. *Amira* in *Paul's* " Grundriss der germ. Philologie," 2 ed., iii. 173.

43. *Maitland*, " Domesday and Beyond," 365 ff.

44. *Meitzen*, I, 66.

45. E.g. " History of English Law," i. 609.

46. I will just refer to some passages from " Court-Rolls," containing economic regulations.   Especially valuable for the understanding of the working of the open-field system and of its importance in rural life are the Court Rolls of Manors belonging to the Chapter of Durham.   They date from the fourteenth century and are distinguished by the great care with which they enrol the agrarian transactions, but such transactions in themselves are, of course, only a specimen of what took place all over the country, and there can be no reasonable doubt that in substance they were as ancient as the open-field system itself.

Even in later times, however, the village assembly was not a mere ceremonial performance, as may be gathered, for example, from the Court Rolls of Hitchin printed at the close of *Mr. Seebohm's* volume on the Village Community. Mr. and Mrs. Sidney Webb have given many illustrations of the later practices of village and town communities in connection with the Open Field system (" English Local Government."—The Manor and the Borough, 76 ff.).   Cf. my article on Great Tew in the " Economic Quarterly Review."

" Halmota prioratus Dunelmensis," ed. by *Longstaffe* and *Booth* (Surtees Society, vol. 82), 123 (A.D. 1374): iniunctum est omnibus tenentibus villae, quod quilibet eorum veniant pro frethis, *birlaws* et aliis comodis et proficuis dictae villae ponendis ad praemunicionem dictorum praepositorum, p. 138 (A.D. 1377) : injunctum, etc., quod veniant ad praemonitionem messoris ad loquendum pro comodo domini et vicinorum.   Cf. p. 70, 103 ; p. 82 (A.D. 1370). Ordinatum est communi assensu quod quilibet tenencium veniat ad praemunicionem praepositi ad tractandum de communibus negociis et quod teneat hoc quod inter eos ordinatum fuerit, p. 17 (A.D. 1345).   Praeceptum est omnibus tenentibus villae quod servent frithes in bladis, pratis, pasturis et semitis et quod nullus eorum sit contrarius aut rebellis vicinis suis, p. 23 (A.D. 1358) ; ordinatum est ex communi assensu quod quilibet tenencium mundet partem suam prati quod vocatur Bradeenge, p. 24 (A.D. 1358): ordinatum est quod omnes husbandi non depascant pasturam cotmannorum cum pluribus averiis quam fecerunt ante mortalitatem, et quod quilibet cotmannus habeat partem suam pasturae . . . prout tenet p. 38 (A.D. 1368).   Ordinatum est ex communi assensu quod nullus lavet nec alia enormia ponat nec faciat infra placeam que vocatur Holowpoill et quod reservatur tantum pro aquacione averiorum et ad alia necessaria infra domos tenencium facienda p. 41 (A.D. 1365) : ordinatum est ex communi assensu quod nullus eorum permittat pullanos, vitulos, stickettos seu aliqua averia infra campum in quo frumentum seminatur a festo Natalis Domini usque blada sit messa et asportata sub poena dimidiae marcae solvendae per illum qui in defecto reperitur, p. 67 (A.D. 1368): injunctum est omnibus tenentibus villae nequis eorum permittant vitulos exire villam sine custodia ad depascenda blada ; injunctum est omnibus tenentibus villae quod nequis eorum succidet (sic) les

Calkes citra proximam curiam, p. 144 (A.D. 1378): ordinatum est ex communi assensu quod nullus husbandorum vel cotariorum habeat plura averia pro tenura sua quam ordinatum fuit ab antiquo seu alibi depascant quam antiquitus depascere consueverunt.—Ordinatum est ex communi assensu quod ad cornacionem messoris veniant pro collectione pisas et cum iterum cornaverit recedant de pisis predictis sub paena 6 den. ; et eciam quod nullus colligat nisi in pisis suis propriis exceptis pauperibus, etc., etc. p. 65 (A.D. 1367): injunctum est . . . quod quilibet eorum faciat arrare exteriores partes campi et eciam interiores partes p. 94 (A.D. 1370) Ordinatum est . . . quod quilibet tenens veniat ad facturam feni communis prati cum praemunitus fuerit sub poena amissionis partis sue et eciam sub poena gravis misericordiae, p. 122 (A.D. 1373). Ordinatum . . . quod quilibet eorum tenet terram suam in cultura ita quod quilibet seminat terram suam prout campi jacent et warectat in campis prout antiqui solebant.

W. O. Massingberd, "History of the Parish of Ormsby-cum-Ketsby in the Hundred of Hill and the county of Lincoln" (1899), 275 (A.D. 1410): it is enjoyned to all the tenants of the township of Ormsby that each of them shall cause a certain sewer, called Stercroft, to be repaired against their own land.—Enjoined to all the tenants of O. that they cause to be repaired all the ditches.

47. Examples of the interchanging of the expressions " injunctum est tenentibus villae " and " ordinatum est ex communi consensu " in exactly similar passages have been given in the preceding note. Sometimes both are united in one sentence, as for example 33, 174. There does not seem to be sufficient ground for the distinction drawn by the " History of English Law," i. 615.

48. " Durham Halmote Books," 23 (A.D. 1358): " Presentatum est per firmarios molendini quod tam libere tenentes quam alii depascunt per aucria sua quemdam locum qui vocatur le milndam quem ipsi firmarii clamant pertiner et esse separale domini. Ideo preceptum est eisdem firmariis quod distringant liberos tenentes illam depascentes. Et eciam injunctum est aliis tenentibus quod non depascant sub poena 13s. 4d., p. 51 (A.D. 1366). Praeceptum est distringere omnes liberos tenentes ad coperiendum molendinum et injunctum est omnes alii tenentes quod coperiantur citra proximam curiam praedictum molendinum, p. 61 (A.D. 1366) ; ordinatum est ex communi ; assensu tam liberi quam alii tenentes domini quod nullus intret campum pro balkys metendis nec permittant equos, porcos, bidentes nec aliqua averia sua exire villam sine custodia. p. 73 : praeceptum est distringere liberos homines ad reparandum molendinum aquaticum sicut in pluribus halmotis eo quod husbandi fecerunt per partem suam. *Massingberd,* " Court Rolls of Ingoldmells," 100 : ordered to distrain the rector of the Church for many trespasses made on the lord, also because he entered on bond land of the lord without the licence of the Court. Whereas the homage at the preceding Court had respite concerning a wall raised by the

same rector, now comes the homage and says that the said rector
raised the said wall on the bond land of the lord by the length
of 5 feet and the breadth of 1½ foot, therefore the rector in
mercy.

49. The term by-law " means the law of a *by*," of a township.
In " The History of English Law," i. 613, two or three cases
on the application of by-laws are quoted, with the remark : " Some
small power of regulating the rights of common belonging to freeholders we may allow to the manorial Court and its by-laws, but to
all seeming it was small." One cannot help reflecting on the relativity
of expressions like " small " and " great." The by-laws dealing with
the everyday transactions of thousands of townships may be a small
matter when compared with the " great " cases which came before the
Royal Courts, but for the bulk of the population, including the
freeholders owning land within reach of these by-laws, they were
hardly unimportant. As for the interesting trial reported vol. i. 623,
624, it shows a good deal of attention on the part of judges in regard to
the details of by-laws and a great latitude of local custom in formulating them. The fact that the judges recognised a sort of pre-
scription in the interest of the parson and a stretch of privilege on
the part of the lord in destroying ripe corn does not militate against
the validity of reasonable by-laws enforced at the proper time and in a
proper manner. I may add, in passing, that there is nothing to show
that the community had no notion of communal cultivation, because
it admitted certain rights of approvement on its waste. As we
have seen, the waste was treated in a very different manner from
the land in the fields (terra in campis). A good instance of the
recognition of executive measures taken to enforce common of
pasture by a Royal Court is presented by Northumberland Assize
Roll, 45 : " juratores dicunt quod praedicta placea . . . fuit
commune pasturae predicti Roberti et aliorum, et venit idem Al.
de C. et voluit sibi appropriare 60 acras de predicta pastura,
et fecit fossare ibidem. Et predictus Robertus et alii statim,
sine aliqua seisina quam idem Alanus inde habuit, pro-
strauerunt predictum fossatum et utebantur communa sua.
Consideratum est quod predictus Robertus et alii inde sine die.   Cf.
Massingberd, "Court Rolls of Ingoldmells," 44.

50. The rules quoted in notes 46 and 47 are examples of by-laws
proper. Most extents and custumals are drawn up on the basis
of verdicts of local juries. An example of an indenture of this kind
is given by the Crondale inquest of October 10, 1567 (p. 160).
The late date does not detract from its value, as it only follows a
general and archaic practice.

51. The regulations in regard to the apportionment of meadows
in the combined meeting of the tenants of Aston and Cote is the
standard case in point. Besides, as it has been so convincingly shown by Professor Maitland in " Domesday and

Beyond," the further we go into earlier periods the more common becomes the mixed township, consisting of freemen standing in various degrees and forms of dependence on great men. And in these cases the management of the thousand and one questions concerning the open fields had to be transacted by extra-manorial meetings. What must have been very common before the feudal epoch became the exception after the establishment of manorial feudalism. A curious instance of an apportionment of pasture by agreement between three baronies represented by eight men is given in *Weir*, "Historical and Descriptive Sketches of the Town and Soke of Horncastle co. Lincoln," 1820, p. 115. On regulations as to Open Fields, cf. my "English Society in the XIth century," 578 ff.

52. "Durham Halmote Books," p. 82 A.D. 1369: "Sunt electi jurati Willelmus Ibbi . . ., et Johannes Fermour electi sunt ad ordinandum villae, videlicet de frethis ponendis et ordinacionibus pro communitate villae et ad certificandum curiē ad proximum. p. 11 (A.D. 1296) [compertum] est per juratam quod homines de Dalton non debent habere communam ab inferiori parti del Welleleche versus fossatam pomerii (sed ?) aliquo anno, scilicet, quolibet tercio anno habebant fugam suam cum animalibus suis ad moram. Item juratores dicunt quod homines de D. solebant habere communam cum animalibus suis a porta manerii usque viam de Hesilden. Item juratores dicunt quod dicti homines solebant habere Communam in C. Greenside quando terra citra le Grenside jacuit Warectata. Item dicunt quod dicti homines non debent habere communam in le Cotwallis si claudentur, aut sepe uel fossato includentur.

53. *Andrews*, "Old English Manor," 206 ff. "Durham Halmote Books," 68 (A.D. 1368). De W. J. quia noluit pascere communam porcariam, prout turnus suus postulabat; p. 103 (A.D. 1370) injunctum est . . . quod conveniant ad mandatum prepositi pro comune proficuio et quod habeant unum communem pastorem." An elective smith and an elective "messor" are also mentioned.

54. *Massingberd*, "Court Rolls of Ingoldmells," xix. 47.

55. *Andrews*, "Old English Manor," 231.

56. The Court for the dens of the lowy (leucata) of Tonbridge, the ancient wood of Andred, was of that character. *Twysden*, quoted by *Kemble*, "Saxons in England," App.

57. For example "Rot. Hundr." i. 3.

58. "Rot. Hundr." i. 212. The Kentish borgh was a local body.

59. *Stubbs*, "Constitutional History," i. Let it be noted that the reeve and priest and their companions represent the township and not the manor. Cf. The characteristic way they are entered in Domesday, i. 133, Begesford (Herts), Presbiter et prepositus hujus villae cum 22 villanis habent 15 carucas. This is one of the indications that the reeve got to be unfree when the villain was transformed from a free ceorl into a bondsman, that is in the age of feudalism.

60. "Rot. Hundr." ii. 14: Willelmus prepositus de Apethorp, soke-

mannus domini Regis. *Suckling*, "History of Suffolk," i. 272
(Customs of Mutford, temp. Edw. I.) : Quidam illorum (soke-man-
norum) erunt prepositi per turnum suum. . . . Et prepositi eligentur
per sokemannos circa festum Sti Petri ad Vincula per turnum ut
dictum est. *Blomefield*, "History of Norfolk," i. 171 ("Customs of
the Manor of Gissing," A.D. 1327) : The praepositus and the messor
are chosen from the tenants without distinction of classes. Customary of the soke of Rothley, "Archaeologia," xlvii. 125 : Balliuus
domini Regis facit prepositum de quocunque voluerit tam de Rol.
quam de omnibus aliis ville soke, nullo excepto preter Stephanum
de Rol. It is quite common for sokemen to undertake some
of the duties of supervision in regard to agrarian arrangements.
They have to ride with their staves while superintending work in the
fields ("Villainage in England,"453). They are also called up for police
duties. For example, Survey of the hundreds of West Derby, Lons-
dale and Amounderness in Lancashire (three Lancashire documents
ed. by J. Harland ; "Chetham Soc." lxxiv.), 30. Villata de Ditton.
. . . ibunt cum balliuis comitatus et wapentakii usque ad proximam
villatam ad testificandum districciones quociens per cursum suum
acciderint cum aliis vicinis suis.

61. The gerefa, the smith and the child's nurse are considered by
Ine's law, 23 to be personal dependents of the thane, and may be
taken with him, if he leaves the manor. Testators often speak of
their reeves in their wills and make legacies to them, *Thorpe*,
"Dipl." 521, 581 ; *Earle*, "Land Charters," Cf. *Andrews*, "Old
English Manor," 130. The tract called "Geréfa," ed. by Lieber-
mann (Anglia, viii., now published in "Gesetze der Angelsachsen,"
I.) has the personal steward in view.

62. The "gerefa" of the tract just mentioned has not only to act
in the interest of his lord, but to mind the rights and obligations
imposed by "folcright," that is the customary common law. Cf.
Andrews, "Old English Manor," 140.

63. "History of English Law," i. 346.

64. Edgar, I. The jurors are distinguished in later times from
other village authorities. "Durham Halimote Books," p. 82
(A.D. 1369) : Johannes Fermour electus est in praepositum
et juratum. Et eciam isti sunt electi jurati ; Willelmus Ibbi,
Willelmus Tut, Willelmus Randolf et Johannes Teddi.—Ricardus de
Heworth, Thomas Perkinson, Willelmus Randolf, Willelmus Pouer,
Hugo de Joilton et Johannes Fermour electi sunt ad ordinandum
villae, videlicet de frethis ponendis et ad ordinacionibus (sic) pro Communitate Villae, et ad certificandum Curie ad proximum. It may
be noted that the reeve, John Fermour, appears on both committees,
p. 155 ; ordinatum est ex communi assensu tam liberorum quam
tenencium domini Prioris quod Willelmus Pouer, Gilbertus Randolf,
Rogerus Losse, Johannes Redworth, Willelmus Tolson et Thomas
Parkinson ad ordinandum et ponendum freth et omnia pertinentia

praedictae villae, sub poena dimidiae marcae.—*Whitaker*, "History of Whalley," 265. In the Court of three Manors in Clitheroe Castle, the "greaves" of the manor make return of jurors, for Worston one, for Pendleton two, for Chatham three, and so after proportion until a full jury be returned. "Court rolls of the Honor of Clitheroe," ed. by Farrer, 1897.

65. In view of the importance of the subject I may be allowed to give some details. The duty of attending local moots called by the reeve, and distinguished from the county assemblies and the hundred courts, is expressly mentioned. Dd. I., 269, *b*. (Lancashire—between the Ribble and the Mersey): qui remanebat de sciremot—per 10 solidos emendabat. Si de hundredo remanebat, aut non ibat ad placitum ubi prepositus jubebat per 5 solidos emendabat. Cf. ib. Si constrictus justitia prepositi alicui debitum solvebat, et si terminum a preposito datum non attendebat (one of the six cases when the Lancashire freemen had to pay customary fines). The English for *placitum* would have been *mót*, and it is clearly contrasted as such with meetings of the shire and of the hundred. In the light of this terminology we come to understand better the expressions of the Confessor's writ to the Berkshire thanes in favour of Abingdon (C.D. 870, *Earle*, "Landchart." 342); frigelice habban and wealdan Horneméres hundred on hyre ágenre andwealde . . . and swa sðaet nán scyrgerefe oððe mótgerefa ðar habban æni socne oððe gemót buton ðes abbudes ágen hæse and unne" (nullus vicecomes *vel praepositus* ibi habeam aliquam appropriationem vel placitum). The entire hundred had been granted to the Abbey, but it consisted of two large manors—Comenore of 50 hides (T.R.E.), and Bertune of 60 hides—and it seems natural to suppose that at least the meetings of these manors were included among the gemots to be held at the Abbot's bidding, while the praepositi styled mótgerefas must have been both hundred reeves and local reeves. On the other hand, the common freeman is described in a remarkable passage of another Old English charter as moteworthy, fyrd-worthy, and fald-worthy. (C.D. 853, *Earle*, 343.) The mention of the fold leaves no doubt as to the fact that local standing was meant as well as participation in the host. The mótworthiness certainly included the meetings of shire, hundred and wapentake (Aethelred iii. 3, 1), but it must have included also the rural meetings called by the reeve. The King's reeve mentioned in connexion with the *folcgemót* in Aelfr. 31 as a "mót-reeve," is a local steward of the King, in this case probably one appointed to watch over his interests in a market or port town. But the machinery was similar in other localities. Again, the frequent prohibitions to attend *gemots* on Sundays and feast-days (for example, Aethelred, vi. 22), evidently applied to all kinds of meetings for transacting local business even of the humblest kind. Cf. Edgar, i. 7; Schmid, App. xi. To return to the Domesday Survey, the

duty of tenants and sokemen to attend *moots* held in the manors of
great men is not unfrequently mentioned (Dd., i. 87 c ; 105 b ; 175).
The *gemót-hus* is mentioned in a charter of 900/901 ; *Birch,* "Cart.
Sax." ii. 246. (*Andrews,*" Old English Manor," 138.) But, what is more
interesting, these meetings were not considered to be necessarily
bound up with the halls ; indeed, to judge from one entry, at
least, a *halimot* seems to have been rather an exception. Dd., i.
265 b ; ("Actune ") : hoc manerium habet suum placitum in aula
domini sui. The village meetings were probably held originally in
the open air. A curious survival of this custom is afforded by the
interesting fourteenth century Register of Stoneleigh. The Sokemen
of Stoneleigh held their court in a place called Mot-Stowehill,
"Villainage in England," 430. We find a *tunscipesmót* mentioned
in a charter of Richard I.—*Eyton,* Shropshire, iii. 237, quoted
by *Stubbs,* "Const. H.," i. 90.

66. An important argument in this connexion is to be derived from
the fact that the original halimote is not differentiated into several
courts for the needs of free and unfree, for ordinary business and
criminal or police purposes, but forms one whole and transacts all
kinds of business.   (*Maitland,* "Introduction to Pleas of Manorial
Courts " (Selden Society). Cf. *Massingberd,* "Court-rolls of Ingoldmells," xv. xvi.   Evidently the basis of the court is the meeting
of villagers who have to settle their open-field arrangements irrespectively of rank in society and personal status. This does not
exclude the notion that at least some of the members of the Court
were to be freemen, fully moteworthy men, because in so far as the
meetings had to deal with legal matters this element of freemen
formed a necessary link with the higher Courts. The notion is
well authenticated for the feudal organisation of the manor.

67. For an example, I will refer to the entries in the Court-rolls
of Ingoldmells, 17, 27, 36, 44, 72, etc.   "Court-Rolls of the Honour
of Clitheroe," ed. by W. Farrer (1897), 6. William le Barker for an
open " gappe " in the Bull's stall, contrary to the by-law (in mercy),
7. Ib. 60 ; The jury say, that . . . C. M. . . . exceed their stints
on the common pasture in Chatburne, that Th. Talior does not repair
and make good his "Renghard" (a hedge). Cf. the editor's explanatory
note with a reference to a by-law of 11 Henry VII. (Cf. " East
Riding Memorial Rolls," published by *Boulder* in the " Yorkshire
Archaeological and Topographical Journal," 71.)

68. Instances of cases when rural transgressions were brought to
the notice of the hundred courts and of the hundred officers. " Rot.
Hundr." i. 446. Cf. "Court-rolls of the Hundred and Manor of
Crondal," ed. by Baigent (London, 1891), 142, 145, 146, etc.

69. This is the solution of the difficulty suggested by Prof.
Maitland.

70. The terms and practices alluded to are best illustrated by
feudal documents. For example " Rot. Hundr.," i. 216 : Priorissa

de Scapeia . . . appropriavit sibi tenentes suos qui solebant locare, lottiare et scottare ad villatam de Middeltun, et non faciunt ad dampnum patrie per annum 6 den. i. 210 : fratres domus Dei de Osperenge . . . subtraxerunt se de scotto et lotto que facere consueverunt ad borgham de Satameleford ad dampnum patrie per annum 12 den.—Et quod tenentes Templariorum subtraxerunt se eodem modo de scoto et lotto ad borgham de Esture—ad grave dampnum istus borghe. Cf. i. 238 (hundredum de Goscot, Leicester), i. 276 . . . omnes tenentes de villa de Spaldinge debent ad reparacionem pontis illius, quilibet pro rata porcionis terrae sue contribuere, ita quod quaelibet acra erit par alterius, i. 468 : quidam homines manentes in Reydone qui sunt de homagio de Brisigham, solebant stare in communis de Reydone, videlicet ad scot et lotte et ad omnes misas domini Regis, et extrahuntur a tempore Wydon le Verdun usque nunc ad libertates et misas de Brisigham. *Gage*, " History of Thinghoe Hundred " (1838), p. 85, Gilbert of Clare grants to the monastery of St. Edmund's two " liberos homines. Ulwinum . . . et Ulmarum de W. cum terris suis . . . nec aliqua consuetudo eis alia imponatur, quam soliti erant facere qui eas sub me tenebat—*excepto scottum regis* quod solvant cum suis vicinis in hundret, quando per totam Angliam currit."—The repartition of scot and lot among the twelve "letes," and the twenty-one townships of the hundred of Thinghowe is given in a Survey of the Hundred, A.D. 1184 (V.C., p. xii., etc.). The English terminology and the apportionment by townships leave hardly any doubt as to the development of these features from Old English origins. Cf. *Thorpe*, " Dipl.," 368 (Edward the Confessor to the Oxfordshire thanes, A.D. 1053) : ic habbe gegifan Cr. et Sᶜᵉ Petre into Westminster þet cotlif ðe ic wæs geboran inne . . and ane healfe hide aet Mersce, *scotfre* and *gafolfreo*.

71. The remark that the *villani* of such and such a place—we should say the township—have failed to make their joint contribution, is a frequent one in the Geld-roll of 1084, which is certainly based on earlier practice. (Dd., ii.) *Thorpe*, 305 (Canute—A.D. 1018) : Swa fela syðe swa menn gyldað heregyld oððe to scip gylde, gylde se *tunscipe* swa swa oðre menn doð to þaere muneca neode. The charter is spurious, but probably almost contemporaneous. As to the methods of subdividing the tax, see *Round*, " Feudal England," 49. From the point of view of taxation and other requirements, a place might be termed in Norman times a full township, *plena villa*. Liber Niger ecclesiae de Burgo (Society of Antiquaries), f. 167, d.

72. For example, *Thorpe*, " Dipl." 229, *Earle*, 100 (C.D. 216), *Earle*, 272 " Cart. Sax." iv. 23, Ibid., ii. 27, etc.

73. This point is clearest in later documents, " Rot. Hundr." i. 6 : Cum dicti sokemen omnes teneantur solvere duas marcos annuatim ad tallagium conjunctim, et non divisim, uno vel duobus

per domino absolutis a predicta solutione, nihilominus tota pecunia integraliter a residuis hominibus exigitur. "Rot. Hundr.," ii. 8 : Prior de Dunstaple impetravit domui sue 2 hidas terre et dimidia virgata—et ab illo tempore se subtraxerunt neque modo . . . et fuit villa amerciata pro evasione ad 100 solidos, et collecta fuit predicta pecunia per porciones et extentas terrarum, et deberet solvisse dictus prior pro porcione 2 hidarum 10 solidos, nec voluit sicut prius usus fuit, et ideo veniunt in demanda super villam. It is not only the general probability that these customs of joint liability went back to the time when the hidage and the geld system were established that we have to plead in order to connect these feudal descriptions with ancient practices, but also the necessity of proceeding in this manner at a time when there was no staff of collectors appointed by central authority to watch over the incidents of taxation in regard to small people. All tribute was for this reason—not to speak of others—imposed and levied by repartition of lump sums from above. This did not preclude individual exactions and individual control as regards conspicuous and wealthy people. The lords of manors, and before them the thanes, were not merely included in their shires and hundreds, but made individually responsible. When the Danish exactions were at their height possession of land was actually made dependent on the payment of the geld. Cnut, ii. 49. *Thorpe*, "Dipl.," 452. Cf. "Crawford Charters," 76, and *Thorpe*, "Dipl.," 452.

74. Aethelred, iii. 3, 1. T., Lgg. Henrici, i. T. § 7. Cf. *Liber Eliensis* : per sacramentum vicecomitis scire et omnium baronum . . . et *tocius centuriatus*, presbiteri, prepositi, sex villanorum unius cujusque ville. *Thorpe*, "Dipl.," 383 (Edw. Conf., A.D. 1060 * Winebodesham cum hundredo et dimidio . . . et cum 64 socemannis ad hundredos pertinentibus. Even in later times the suit of all free tenants, or even of all freemen, to the hundred is sometimes required. For example, *Placita Quo Warranto*, 428 : omnes tenentes Abbatis de Burgho St. Petri . . . in villis de Scoter etc. . . . Solebant facere sectam ad wapentake domini Regis de Coringham. Ita quod quidam illorum solebant facere sectam ad wapentake illud de tribus septimanis in 3 septimanas. Et quidam eorum solebant venire ad presentaciones faciendas ad Coromam pertinentes. p. 780 : tres radmanni de Wycton alter natim faciunt sectas ad hundreda domini Regis de Hunnesford de tribus septimanis in tres septimanas pro omnibus predictis villis praeterquam de Erdinton. Et omnes liberi tenentes de Erdinton personaliter faciunt sectam ad predictum hundredum de tribus septimanis in tres septimanas. The last case gives a good instance of the passage from an all-round suit to representative suit. The usual course in feudal times was to call up all the freemen for the two law days of the great court leet.

75. " Rot. Hundr.," i. 240 (Ketelby et Saxtenby) ; Ibid.,

i. 362 (Abbas de Hachneby in Estbarkeworyt). Cf. *Pollock* and
Maitland, "History of English Law," i. 527. A curious consequence of this localisation of suits appears in the shape of tenements
called *hundredlands.* Plac. Q.W. 349 : homines qui tenent dimidium hundredylond. . . . Tenentes Henrici de Grey . . . qui
tenent duo hundredeslaunde, etc.

76. It has been seen that the principle of representation was
not confined in the feudal period to the tenantry in villainage.
On the other hand, it would be difficult to draw sharply the
distinction between the personal suitors of the hundred (the centuriatus) and the bodies of villagers represented by the reeve,
the priest and the four men. It seems likely that it was the
effect of the class distinctions enforced by the Normans that
led to a consequent development of contrasts such as that mentioned in the marginal note to the Phillips MS. of Bracton. *Pollock*
and *Maitland,* "History of English Law," i. 534. Cf. "Rot. Hundr.,"
i. 220 : Thomas Malmeris solebat venire ad communitatem hundredi de Ho ad audiendum precepta Domini Regis et auxiliandum
judicium dare de sanguine, vita et membris una cum hundredo
predicto. Examples of the methods of doing suit may be found
"Rot. Hundr.," i. 205, 215, 361 ; Placita Q.'Warr., 293, 346. In
Kent, where no villainage at common law was recognized, and the
whole tenantry was admitted to hold freely in gavelkind, the
system of representation by the borgeldor and four men was in
full vigour.

77. See, for example, the apportionment of service and military
aid by hides in the Domesday Survey of Berkshire.

78. Aethelstan, vi. ; Canute, ii. 20. A germ of the institution of
compulsory frankpledge (freeborgh) may be seen in the voluntary
association of the gegildan of Alfred's law, 27. Cf. "History of
English Law," i. 556. The intimate connexion between the territorial and the personal arrangements of the system of frankpledge
is especially worth notice. It is perhaps clearest in Kentish
cases. "Rot. Hundr.," i. 215 : villa de Nywendene quondam
fuit una burgha ad hundredum de S. et subtracta est per libertatem
archiepiscop. Ib., i. 220 : in hundredo de Hosunstres borghe.
Ib., i. 223 : Dimidia borgha de Westbrocton, scilicet tenentes Willelmi de Montecanisio subtrahuntur a secta dicti hundredi post
bellum de Lewes . . . Item dimidium quarterium unius borghe
in Hedyton subtrahitur ab eadem secta. Cf. P. Q. Warr. 350 . . .
borgha forinseca . . . iidem tenentes solebant . . . in omnibus
Scottis et Lottis sustinere tertiam partem.

79. "History of English Law," i. 551 ff.

CHAPTER V

1. A picture of an ancient English plough worked by four oxen is given in *Larking*, " Domesday of Kent," cf. *Peisker*, Zur Geschichte des Pfluges, " Zeitschrift für Social und Wirthschaftsgeschichte," v.

2. This point has been best elucidated by *Seebohm*, "Village Community."

3. The tenants holding land *in campis* are carefully distinguished from the *cottarii, cotsetle*, etc.

4. The early Anglo-Saxon laws are full of information as to the position of slaves. See, *Schmid*, " Glossar " to his " Gesetze der Angelsachsen," sub. v. theow, witetheow. A ceorl's "bireel" is mentioned Aethelbirht, 16. (Cf. *Jastrow*, "Die Strafrechtliche Stellung der Sklaven in angelsächsischem Recht," in *Gierke's*, " Untersuchungen zur Rechtsgeschichte.")

5. Agricultural services performed by socmen are very common in the early surveys. For example, *Round*, " Feudal England," 30.

6. The peasants on an estate are described as þeowbærde and burbærde (C.D. 1079). The conditions and frequency of manumission are well illustrated by the group of charters and entries in Churchbooks collected by *Thorpe*, " Diplomatarium," under the heading of " Manumissions."

7. On the percentage of slaves in the different counties at the time of Domesday, see *Seebohm*, " Village Community," map to 84.

8. They are equated with the twyhynd class in treating with the Danes.

9. *Seebohm* traces single succession in regard to tenements to this cause. " Tribal Custom," 512.

10. Most of the smaller free tenantry and socmen of the early surveys are holding virgates and bovates in the same way as villains, and even if we do not pay any attention to the free elements among the latter, it would be impossible to account for the development of single succession among socmen by the influence of their lords. See, for example, the entries in regard to socmen in the Black Book of Peterborough (Camden Society).

11. " History of English Law," ii., 268.

12. The best examples of the distribution of sub-shares in gavelkind sulungs are given in the still unpublished Black Book of St. Augustine, Cotton MS., Faustina, 1. Cf. " History of English Law," ii. 271. *Seebohm*, " Tribal Custom in Anglo-Saxon Law," 515. Gavelkind in Sussex. *Robinson*, " Gavelkind," 5th ed. (London, 1897), pp. 33, 37.

13. *Heusler*, " Institutionen," i. 230 ff.

14. The motives for holding family property together are clearly expressed in several Old English documents, especially in King Alfred's will (*Thorpe*, 484, ff.) and in Ketel Alder's will (*Thorpe*, 581).

15. For example. Dd., iii., 95 : Delvertana . . . Huic mansioni sunt addite 2 hidae terrae dimidio fertino minus quas tenuerunt 13 taini pariter die que Rex Edwardus vivus fuit et mortuus. The tenure in paragio is very frequent in Domesday.

16. Both the Domesday examples of " parage " and the passages of Glanville and Bracton as to socage imply that this Old English law of succession was largely shaped by local custom. This is one of the points which ought to remind us, that the evolution of the law was much more dependent on customary development and local variations in the Old English and early Norman epoch than our experience of the influence of Royal Courts in the age of Common Law would lead us to suppose.

17. " Domesday and Beyond," 331 ff.

18. *Konrad Maurer,* " Ueber angelsächsische Rechtsverhältnisse," in the " Kritische Ueberschau," 1853 ff."

CHAPTER VI

1. Æthelstan, ii. 2, 8.

2. The Old English statutes of guilds are conveniently collected in a section of *Thorpe's* " Diplomatarium."

3. The man-bót : Ine, 70, 76 ; " Lgg. Henr. I.," 69, etc.

4. Ine, 50.

5. Æthelstan, iii. 4 ; iv. 5 ; v. 1.

6. For example, Ine, 39.

7. Domesday contrasts the man who could go with his land where he pleased with those who could not do so. Sometimes the personal obligation is separated from the relation in regard to land (Dd. ii. 57 b ; 71 b.). On this subject see " Domesday and Beyond," 69 ff.

8. This is made especially clear by the Cambridgeshire Inquest, in which the entries are arranged according to townships and not according to manors. " Domesday and Beyond," 129 ff.

9. Æthelred, i. 1, § 10 ; vii. App. 3 ; Canute, ii. 31 ; Ine, 22.

10. *Toll* applies to the right of levying toll from objects bought and sold within the franchise. *Theam* means the perquisites of the lord in cases when warranty was pleaded. *Infangenetheof* and *Utfangenetheof* refers to proceedings against thieves. *Hamfare* means burglary ; *foresteal,* the crime of waylaying. On the variations of the franchise see " Domesday and Beyond," 266.

11. The attempt to assign to the holders of sake and soke merely the profits of jurisdiction without its substance does not lead to satisfactory results. It supposes too artificial a division between two sides of one and the same process, and is not supported by the evidence. The whole subject is treated in a masterly manner in "Domesday and Beyond," 259 ff, 282 ff.

12. Dd. ii. 130, b. : In Fernella jacet saca et soca T.R.E. de omnibus qui minus habent quam 30 acras. De illis qui habent 30 acras jacet soca et saca in hundredo. The thirty acres which are made the parting line between the suitors of the manor and those of the hundred would according to the average reckoning make up a virgate. Sometimes the distinction rests on the custom of using and not using the manorial fold ("Domesday and Beyond," 91). Of course, these facts testify already to the violent processes of simplification and encroachment which followed the Norman Conquest, and the terminology became definitely settled at that time, but there can be no doubt that the social contrasts of which we are speaking were to a great extent prepared by previous history.

13. The man under soke of Old English times comes to be the free tenant of Norman times. The books conveying sake and soke generally grant all dues and profits which may have accrued to the King from a certain district. For example, *Thorpe,* "Diplom.," 417 (Eadward the Confessor) : ic an eke fredomes þan haligen kinge Seynt Eadmunde. . . . And ic wille him þat so fele siðe so men gildeð here gilde to heregild oþer to schipgild, gilde se tunschipe so oþere men don to þe abbotes nede and þere muneke þe þer binnen schulen for hus seruen.—And ic an þan halegen Kinge þat lond at Mildenhale mid mete, and mid manne, and mid sokne, so it me on hande stod and þe half nigende hundredes sokne into Ðinghowe. And ic an hem al here tune sokne of hale here londe. Cf. *Thorpe,* 138.

14. Æthelred, iii. 3 ; Canute, i. 8, etc. The fullest treatment of the subject is to be found in *K. Maurer's* essay, "Kritische Ueberschau," ii 41 ff. Cf. "Domesday and Beyond," 286.

15. The *trinoda necessitas* is well known. For example, *Thorpe,* 384.

16. The five-hide unit is already conspicuous in the notices on the "thriving" to the rank of a thane. Cf. C.D. 116 (endorsed by *Pilheard,* 799, 802) : thirty hides have to send only 5 "vires" to the war (in expeditionem incessitatem. Dd., i. 56, d. (Berks) : Si rex mittebat alicubi exercitum de 5 hidis tantum unus miles ibat et ad ejus victum uel stipendium de unaquaque hida dabanturei 4 solidi ad 2 menses. Hos vero denarios regi non mittebant, sed militi dabantur. This reminds one very much of the Carolingian scheme, "de exercitu promovendo." Capitularia, ed. Boretius, i. 134.

17. The cases in which heriots are mentioned show what the technical requirements were in respect of men of great wealth and power. They are very instructive as to the outfit of warriors. *Thorpe,* " Diplom.," 499, 501, 505, 512. Archbishop Ælfric bequeaths to his lord, the King, his best ship and 60 helmets and 60 coats of mail. In Wulfric's will of 1002 we hear of " heriot land " (*Thorpe,* " Dipl.," 546). Cf. Dd. i. 56, b.

18. It was very common to make an arrangement as to the number of knights and soldiers required from certain estates or tenements. The monastery of Abingdon had arranged to send out twelve knights (vassalli). *Thorpe,* 64. The see of Worcester had also entered into an agreement as to its military obligations. " Victoria County History of Worcestershire," 256. The duties of the Lagmen of Stamford. " Rot. Hundr.," i. 352, 354. An example of a convention with a thane bound to perform military service is given by *Thorpe,* 451 : ea tamen conventione, ut pro ea ipse ad expeditionem terra marique (quae tunc crebro agebatur) monasterio serviret, pecuniaque placabili, sive caballo, ipsum priorem unoquoque anno recognosceret. Cf. " Domesday and Beyond," 156, 163, 295. As to the difference between these obligations and the later system of knight's fees, *Round,* " Feudal England," 261. On knights' fees, cf. " English Society in the Eleventh Century," pp. 41 ff.

19. Example from the Danelaw, Dd. i. 291 (Notts) : Wicheburne . . . duas bovatas de hac terra tenuerunt quinque taini. Unus eorum erat senior aliorium. Example from the West. Dd. i. 105 (Devon) : Brotone . . . Huic manerio sunt adjunctae tres terrae quas libere tenebant tres taini T.R.E., pro tribus maneriis . . . geldabant pro 3 virgatis terrae. Terra est 7 carucis.

20. Drengs are very conspicuous in the Boldon book. The notice about Lanfranc turning the drengs of the see of Canterbury into knights is well known. Radmen and "Radchenistres " are frequently mentioned in Domesday—for example, i. 38, 163, 172, 173, 187, etc. As to the lex equitandi of St Oswald's in the see of Worcester, "Domesday and Beyond," 303.

21. It is worth while to compare the facts of this evolution of a military class with similar developments on the Continent. See especialy *Brunner,* on the Reiterdienst, "Forschungen zur französischen und deutschen Rechtsgeschichte " (1894).

22. " Crawford Charters," 127 ; *Thorpe,* " Dipl.," 470 ; cf. 312 ; "Cart. Sax.," 1318 (iii. 653). Bishop Denewulf's grant—*Thorpe* 162 : its interpretation in " Domesday and Beyond," starts from the untenable supposition, that the ninety sown acres apply to the whole of the estate of hundred hides ; in this case there would not be much reason for gratification at the success of the colonising policy of the bishop. But as he says expressly that all the holdings were " gevered," that is defended themselves by paying the customary taxes, the express mention of farm-stock evidently applies to the home farm. *Earle.* " Land Charters," 235 ; *Seebohm,*

" Village Community," has explained in a suggestive manner the passage of the Rectitudines in regard to the stocking of the gebúr's farm.

23. " Domesday and Beyond," 67 ff.

24. The *veislur*, the feasting progresses of Norse kings and of their officers among the *böndir*, the free householders of the folk, are constantly mentioned and fully described in the Sagas, e.g., Olaf's Saga hins helga, 61, 111, etc. *K. Lehmann*, " Untersuchungen zur Rechtsgeschichte, " has given a survey of the subject.

25. E.g., *Earle*, " Land Ch.," 100 (A.D. 822 ; C.D. 216) : insuper etiam hanc predictam terram liberabo ab omni servitute secularium rerum, a pastu regis episcopi principum, seu prefectum exactorum, ducorum, canorum, nel equorum seu accipitrum, ab refectione et habitu illorum omnium qui dicuntur fæstingmen, etc. The " fæsting- men " have been taken as a designation of special officers entrusted with police duties (*Earle*, " Land Ch.," glossary, *sub voce* ; *Andrews*, " Old Engl. Manor," 96), but it is clear that the fæsting indicates the duty of quartering or, as it were, establishing (fæsting) men sent by the King. The sense is shown by the following instance, *Thorpe*, " Dipl.," 114 (A.D. 855) : Monasterium, quod nominatur Bloccanlech, liberabo . . . a pastu et ab refectione omnium accipitrum et fal- conum in terra Mercensium, et omnium venatorum regis vel prin- cipis, nisi ipsorum tantum qui in provincia Hwicciorum sunt ; simi- liter et a pastu et refectione illorum hominum quos Saxonice nomi- namus Wahlfæreld and heora fæsting, and ealra Angelcynnes manna and ælþeodigra rædefæstinge. Cf. *Thorpe*, 102 (A.D. 848) : ut sit liberatum et absolutum illud monasterium ab illis causis quas cum- feorme (feeding strangers) et eafor (?) vocitemus . . . nisi istis causis quas hic nominamus : præcones si trans mare venient ad regem venturi, vel nuntii de gente Occidentalium Saxonum, vel de gente Norþanhymbrorum, si venirent ad horam tertiam diei, debetur eis prandium ; si venirent supra nonam horam, tunc dabitur eis noctis pastum, et iterum de mane pergant in viam suam.

26. Boldon book (Dd. iii.), 566 : Villani debent facere singulis annis in operacione sua, si opus fuerit, unam domum, longitudine 40 pedum et latitudine 15 pedum.

27. The farms of one night, half a night and several nights are of common occurrence in Domesday. E.g., i. 75, 86, 162, b. ; i. 154, b. ; ii. 7, etc. As for the Saxon Charters, they mention constantly arrangements based on the provision of food and drink for one or several repasts. E.g., C. D. 143 ; *Thorpe*, 460, 496, 498, 509, etc.

28. *Barton* is very common as a name of manors. As an example of the passage from its appellative sense may be quoted " Rot. Hundr.," i. 205 : Magister Ricardus per potestatem officii sui occa- sionavit quendam Willelmum filium Johannis de Wenchepe ut faceret eum prepositum de Berthona de Westgate.

29. *Earle*, " Land Ch.," 302 (Eadward the Confessor): ic ánn þet S^{tus} Peter and þa gebroðra on Westmynstre habben to heora beolifan cotlif Stana, mid þam lande Stæninga haga wið innon lundone (corr. lande ?), and fif and þrittig hida sokne þærtó, mid ealca þam berwican. Cf " Historical Dictionary of English," *s.v.* berwick. Dd. i. 269, b. : In Neweton T.R.E. fuerunt 5 hidæ. Ex his una erat in dominio. Æcclesia ipsius manerii habebat I carucatam terrae, et Sanctus Osuualdus de ipsa villa duas carucatas terræ habebat quietas per omnia. Hujus manerii aliam terram 15 homines quos drenchs uocabant pro 15 maneriis tenebant, sed hujus Manerii beruuiche erant, et inter omnes 30 solidos reddebant. Cf. Dd. ii. 362.

30. " Cartulary of Burton," 21.

31. The small manors of Domesday, as e.g., Dd. ii. 311, b. (in eadem villa est unus liber homo de 40 acris et tenet pro manerio) may merely imply in some cases that the land in question was considered as standing by itself outside of any other estate organisation. Therefore the term manerium may alternate with the colourless *terra*.

32. Examples may be found almost on every page of Domesday.

33. " Crawford Ch.," 123 : *heafodbotl* in Purleigh. Sometimes a " haw " (haga) is mentioned in connexion with a central *ham*. *Earle*, 194 : Wulfric ealdorman grants " 7 cassatos "—and se haga an ham tune þe þærto gehyret. Cf. *ib.*, 246.

34. Dd. i. 285 : in Careltune habuerunt 6 taini quisque aulam. 285, b. (Normentone) 5 taini quisque habuerunt aulam suam et unam bovatum terræ et 5 partes unius bovatæ ad geldum. i. 283 : in dominio aulæ sunt 10 bovatæ de hac terra. Reliqua est socha.

35. Such cases are rare and occur mostly in the earlier period. Bede's narrative of the grant of Selsea mentions 87 hides of land and 250 slaves who cultivate them. As slaves are generally found on demesne land, the district must have consisted of small estates and single farms.

36. This would fit the cases in Domesday when there was a manor in a place but no hall. E.g., Dd. i. 286, b. (Fenton), 312 (Toritun), 312, b. (Bruntone).

37. This being the ordinary case, any page of Domesday will supply examples. On types of manors, cf. " English Society in the Eleventh Century," pp. 305 ff.

38. *Thorpe*, " Dipl.," 502 : of two brothers one gets the inland and the other the outland. The instance seems a parallel one to Dd. i. 26, b. (Bristelmistune) where of three aloarii one holds the hall, while the land of the two others is held by villains.

39. The direct opposition to *reeveland* is *thaneland*. One species comprises land which stands under the jurisdiction of the reeve and is occupied by peasant cultivators, the *villani* and *bordarii* of Domesday. The other applies to the demesneland held of a benefice and defended by the military service of the professional soldier. *Thorpe*, 569 : and Aylmer habbe þat land at Stoneham þe ic hym er to

hande let to reflandes.   Dd. i. 181 : (In Getune) Hugo tenuit ad firmam (unam hidam ad geldum).   Haec terra fuit tainland T.R.E. sed postea conversa est in reveland, et ideo dicunt legali Regis quod ipsa terra et census qui inde exit furtim aufertur Regi.—While *thaneland*, the hide in question was directly dependant on the King, whereas as reeveland it has been swallowed by the estate of a Norman lord, Humfrey the chamberlain.   The *heregeatland* of *Thorpe*, 546 (A.D. 1002), seems to be only another term for the demesneland of a thane, held by military tenure.   As to *geneatland, Seebohm*, " English Village Community," 116.

40. *Earle*, " Land Charters," 376 : inland as demesne in contrast with gesettland held by geneats and geburs.   In many cases *inland* is opposed to the *soke* of a manor, that is to land held by free tenants. E.g., Dd. i., 317, 336, 337, 338 b.

41. This is very clear in the cases of the Northamptonshire geld roll, of the geld rolls of South-Western-Counties of 1084, and of the Burton cartulary.   In this last document *wara* is nsed in the sense of a share in the taxed land.

42. *Round*, "Domesday Studies," I, 93 ff. who, however, does not take sufficiently into consideration the cases when *inland* and *demesne* coincide.

43. E. g. " Black book of St. Augustine," illi de halimoto qui tenent hinnlonde.

44. The Domesday Survey constantly mentions demesne farms taxed for the geld.   Cf. *Maitland*, " Domesday and Beyond," 457.

45. E. g. Dd. iii. 59: et pro i. hida quam tenent villani odonis fili gamelini non habuit rex geldum suum.

46. From this point of view the warland and the wara of early Norman Surveys would proceed directly from the *Cyninges utwaru* of Anglo-Saxon customary law, this last expression pointing not to the military service due from the demesne of a thane, but to the fiscal obligations of his subjects.   In corroboration of this view I should like to quote the following passages. *Earle*, " Land Charters," 235 (A.D. 1017–1023) : Ælfwerd, abbot of Abingdon, makes an agreement with Æðelmær as to leasing to him land at Norton for three lives, that is " 3 hida to inware and oðerhealf to utware, swa swa hit gebohte þa ða hit weste læg."   Dd. i. 165, b. (Bertune) : hoc manerium quietum fuit semper a geldo et ab omni regali servicio. Cf. Flintune : hoc manerium quietum est a geldo et ab omnis forensi servitio praeter ecclesiae   The forense servicium is evidently the "utwaru " comprising all claims of the government as to the estate, while the " inner " service is due to the Church which owns the estate.   In this sense the " inwaru " would naturally be wider than the utwaru, while inland would be applied to that portion of the land which was not subject to taxation and other requirements and might be contrasted with *warland* as the rateable land.

47 The treatise has been published by *Dr. Liebermann*, first

in the "Anglia," and lately in his edition of "Anglo-Saxon Laws."

48. This is the collective designation of the staff of overseers and stewards. It comes from *wic* = village.

49. Bede, iv. 13 : 250 "esnes" settled on 87 hides.

50. Peasants on the estate may be búrbærde or theowbærde. There are records of hereditary serfs on the Hatfield and the Spalding estates, and the people mentioned were not mere slaves but gebúrs.

51. E.g., *Thorpe*, "Dipl." 585 (A.D. 1049–1054) : concessimus autem Lefwino homini nostro virgatam terre, in qua mansum suum habet, in vita *sua* quietam.

52. *Thorpe*, 581 (A.D. 1050) : the testator sets, "alle mine men fre, and ilk habbe his toft, and his metecu, and his metecorn.

53. *Thorpe*, 147, 151, 517. The gafol in the first two cases is expressly stated to be agreed upon (ared, cf. gerad). In the third the tenant is said to pay rent (gafela), but there were some other duties incumbent on him (mid anre garan ?). There is a well known enactment of Ine directed against the raising of work service from tenements which were bound only to pay rent, and Canute had also to legislate against additional exactions of the landlords from people who paid in their "feorm," or rent in produce. (Canute, ii. 69, 1.)

54. Dd. i. 78 b. : Tavistock. The English equivalent of censores must have been *málmen*, or, possibly, *gavelmen*.

55. I think that we have to construe in this sense the words of the will of Wynflæd (*Thorpe*, 536, A.D. 995) : þenne an his þan hiwum þara gebura þe on þam gafollande sittað and þera þewra manna hio ann hyre syna datter Eadgyfe : The slaves are bequeathed to a niece, but the "boors" settled on land paying gafol (the warland) go to the abbey of Shaftesbury. The expression is identical with the term used in the treaty between Alfred and Guthrum. An indirect corroboration of the idea that the King's gafol may be meant may be drawn from the sweeping character of those classifications. Land held by gebúrs, or later villains could be aptly described as gafol-paying land from the point of view of governmental taxation including geld, but it would have been strange to speak of holdings performing all sorts of work as gafolland. When a tenant may be described as rentpaying he is taken special notice of as a malman, a gavelman, or a censor (censarius).

56. Ine, 70, 1, is the classical instance : Æt 10 hidum to fostre 10 fata hunies, 300 hlafa, 12 ambra Wilisch ealað, 30 hlutres, tu eald hriðru oþþe 10 weðeras, 10 gees, 20 henna, 10 cesas, amber fulna buteras, 5 leaxas, 20 pund wæga foðres and hundteontig æla. Ine, 44, § 1 ; 49, 3 ; 59, 1, supply other details as to rents in kind.

57. The principal parallels are supplied by the description of services in Tidenham (C.D. App. iii. 450) and in Stoke by Hythe-

burne (C.D.1077). It is impossible to use these descriptions as chronological landmarks and to speak, as Mr. Seebohm does, of manorial
customs of the time of Edwy, and of the time of Alfred (" English
Village Community," 157 ff.) As has been shown by *Professor Maitland* (" Domesday and Beyond," 334) both instances belong probably to later times and illustrate the practices of the eleventh
century, standing thus exactly on a level with the Rectitudines. It
is most probable that many of these customs go back to ancient
times, but how many and which, we cannot tell, and, especially,
there is no warrant for looking on these two cases as representing
the general condition of English landholding in the age of King Edwy
and in that of King Alfred.

58. The one " who holds the shire " of § iv. 6, need not be neces-
sarily a sheriff: the steward of a great lord could be meant also.
Cf. the " Gerefa," § 2.   *Liebermann* translates : wer das (Gutsvogtei)
Amt inne hat.

59. The *geneats* of Tidenham are also rentpaying tenants burdened
with riding and carrying services (ridan and averian, láde lædan,
etc.), which are not assessed in detail, exactly as in the case of
the Rectitudines. It is impossible to take the "wyrcan swa
on lande, swa of lande, hweðerswá him man byt " as a proof that
the geneat was completely at the mercy of his master. The only
possible meaning seems to me that the various errands and services
which might be required from him were not directly specified. (Cf.
the fela óðra þinga). The payment of gafol has to be supplied from
the term gafolland which gets to be opposed to inland in the classification of the holdings. The ceorls of Stoke by Hysseburne are
also mainly burdened with gafol and the services required from
them in the way of labour take the shape of gafol earth, that is of
ploughing and sowing some acres assigned to them in their own
time (on heara ægenre hwile). There is a mention of week-work
but it has not assumed a definite shape and seems to apply to occasional jobs and errands. (And ælce wucan wircen ðæt him mæn háte
bútan þrim, etc.)

60. *Round*, " Feudal England," 31.

61. The opposition between *geneat* and *gebúr* is quite clear in the
Rectitudines, separated as they are by the intermediate group of
cottagers and the different character of their respective duties.
Seebohm thinks otherwise, " Village Community," 130, and *Andrews*, " Old English Manor," is inclined to follow him.

62. *Seebohm* makes the plausible suggestion that the three remaining acres of the winter field were let off the first year because they
represented the gafol-earth ploughing which could not be required
from new settlers (" Village Community," 141). An interesting
parallel may be drawn from the practice of Glastonbury Abbey.

63. I take the end of § 5 to apply to all kinds of gebúrs, and not
only to those who have to provide honey.

64. The geburs of the Rectitudines and those of Tidenham pay some gafol, but these payments are of a quite subordinate order. In both cases the " operae," the week-work are evidently the most important part of the services.

65. The gafol-earth, ben-earth and græs-earth ploughings are characteristic of a stage in husbandry which lies, as it were, between the tributary arrangement which could dispense with a home farm and the manorial arrangement which was based on the concentration of dependent labour on the home farm. The peasant who had to plough gafolearth had also to sow it with his own seed and, in fact, as the examples of the Rectitudines and of the Glastonbury Inquisition of 1189 show, the gafolearth was simply a portion of his own holding, three acre strips out of thirty, which he cultivated in the interest of the lord. It would lie intermixed with the strips of other peasants and there would not be any separate home farm to speak of, if the whole of the arable in the domain should be distributed on this system. The next and more important step would be to enclose a separate home farm and to require the peasants to come with their ploughs so many times a week to do work on this separate farm. This stage is the most common one in feudal times, and it seems to have been reached on many of the Old English manors, if we are to take more or less literally the statements of Domesday in regard to the demesne land of manors at the time of Edward the Confessor.

Third Book

THE FEUDAL PERIOD

CHAPTER I

THE PRINCIPLES OF THE DOMESDAY SURVEY

WE have now reached the point when the Manor became the prevailing social institution and all the main facts of local organisation were made more or less dependent **The subdivi-** on its structure. We may speak with some **sions of the** **feudal age** right of a manorial system characteristic of the feudal age, though it will still be necessary to bear in mind that no system is in reality perfectly harmonious and well-balanced, that every historical system is pregnant with contradictory principles and various possibilities.

The advent of the manorial epoch is roughly marked by the Norman Conquest. This great event, or rather, series of events, gave the final touch to the formation of a military aristocracy, and called forth a more or less systematic settlement. In the course of the general description which I shall endeavour to present, it will be impossible to attend to minor features of historical development, but even a general description must reckon with the fact that the period with which we are dealing falls into two principal subdivisions, namely, the time of the establishment of feudal rule, and the time of its legal elaboration. The establishment of feudal society was achieved under the first Norman kings, William the Bastard, William Rufus and Henry I, and the interest of this epoch consists in the struggle between the principles introduced by the Conquerors, and earlier traditions; the final success of Henry II may be considered as its approximate close. With the legal reforms of Henry II, the second half of the period begins, and its achievements are chiefly embodied in the growth of central jurisdiction and the formation of

Common Law, which correspond roughly to the reigns of John, Henry III, and Edward I.

The very documents characteristic of these two subdivisions of the feudal period are to some extent different and crave a different treatment. The initiation of feudal rules is reflected chiefly in the great Inquest of Domesday, with its various satellites, while the legal elaboration of feudality is abundantly represented by the plea rolls and court rolls on the one hand, and by the fundamental treatises on Common Law on the other the material of chartularies and extents runs through both epochs, and provides the connecting links for our general description.

At the very outset we have to face a question in which the characteristic traits of the period, as well as the peculiarities of its subdivisions, are appropriately **Some Domes-** illustrated. Among the aspects from which **day problems** the Domesday inquest surveyed society, one of the most important is the attempt to consider all social relations of the time from the point of view of tenure, to reduce them to varieties of conditional land-holding. The inquest had primarily in view to collect material for the imposition and repartition of the geld,[1] but it was something else besides. Though the necessary facts were ascertained by communal testimony on the ancient lines of the associations of shire, hundreds and townships,[2] they were recast into a new mould of manorial hierarchy. Now this recasting of the evidence has not only added a difficulty to the labours of modern searchers of Domesday; it was, as it seems to me, more than a matter of order and form, and we still can see what pains the commissioners took in rearranging the entries of the Cambridge townships so as to bring out more conveniently what the fiefs of William of Warenne or of Hardouin de Escalers were. Evidently, besides the collection of the geld, one of the purposes of the inquest was to provide the king's officers with exact clues as to the personal nexus of the different tenements. This nexus was of capital importance in apportioning political and administrative responsibility and enforcing dues, and it was worth while to go through some additional operations in order to establish it in a firm and handy manner. *Two* questions naturally arise in connexion with these operations of the Domesday commissioners. In order to classify the material on the principle of tenure, it was necessary to assume that every person mentioned in Domesday was attached to some land in one way or another, and that every plot of land to which the man in question was attached, was a tenement, held as a grant from another person, eventually from the king. It was necessary, in fact, to acknowledge the feudal maxim—" *nulle terre sans seigneur* "—and we may well ask how it came that such a maxim had got to be universally acknowledged in England ? The second question applies to those who held under the chief tenants mentioned by Domesday. If the king was following a set policy in bringing all land into a certain relation to himself by tenurial nexus, did not his vassals act in a similar manner in regard to those who stood below them ? What shape did this subjection of undertenants assume ?

Let us turn to the first question, to begin with. All land in England is described in Domesday as belonging either **Tenurial** immediately to the king, or to his vassals of **nexus** different degree, or to churches which held it by direct grant from kings and from persons whose grants have been confirmed by kings, or to burgesses whose tenure though peculiar, still appears as a tenure, a form of conditional ownership. In this way, the rule " *nulle terre sans seigneur*," seems to fit the case completely, and in regard to every particular tenement the questions, by what service it is held and from whom, necessarily arise. But does this all-pervading rule come from the period preceding the Conquest, or from the Conquest itself ? In other words, is the feudal conception of land-holding to be carried into Old English society, and, if so, to what period of Old English social history did it apply ? Or is the feudal conception a generalisation of Norman lawyers, and, in this case, to what extent had it been prepared by older processes, and to what extent was it a change in comparison with former times ?

At first glance, the feudal rule seems to be fairly grounded in Edward the Confessor's time. The Domesday inquisitions generally try to establish the precedents for tenure in the conditions of the day when King Edward was alive and dead. But a closer examination will show at once, that even the state of things on the very eve of the Conquest was materially different from what took place after it. There were great estates before the Conquest, there were landowners who had land in many shires, there were obligations to send armed men at the king's bidding from particular estates and places, commendation and service both of persons and of plots of land were exceedingly common, But all these facts and relations had not been reduced to the comparatively simple network of feudal tenure and service on " the day when King Edward was alive and dead." On the contrary, they were intermixed in a most confusing manner. One man could be another man's personal follower, and hold his land from a third, and be dependent on a fourth in point of jurisdiction.[3] The numerous sokemen who could go with their lands wherever they pleased were not tenants of any particular lord in a feudal sense.[4] Indeed, many of the Saxon landowners still held their land by the witness of the shire, and not by any express or implied feoffment. And even those who had books claimed a privilege made out for them in regard to the ownership of land, and not to a conditional tenancy instituted by the grant.

The notion of service was not necessarily bound up with the notion of land-holding in the feudal sense, namely, in the sense of a certain quantity of service corresponding to a certain grant. Landownership was burdened with services, and might be exempted from them, as land may be taxed or exempted from taxes in any political body. But the element of mutual obligation inherent in the nexus of feudal tenure was not in any way a general condition affecting land-ownership. And although it was of common occurrence that kings granted land and people settled on the land, these grants proceeded rather from the notion of a sovereignty over the whole territory and population of the realm than from the idea of a *dominium eminens*, a supposed right

of ownership to all land in the realm from which all other
private rights in land had to be derived.

If we take all these traits into account, we shall be able to
estimate the import of the change brought about by the
introduction of the doctrine " *nulle terre sans seigneur.*" [6] It
involves the reconsideration and resettlement of all ties
and relations connected with the land, from the point of
view of tenure and service, and though Domesday laid stress
on tenure to begin with, the admeasurement and exaction
of service was sure to follow. In regard to military service,
this admeasurement culminated in the division of the land
into the knight's fees tabulated in the Red Book of the Exchequer and brought into system under Henry II.[7] And in a
less conspicuous way, the same was the case in regard to
sergeancies, to ecclesiastical fiefs, to socage tenements, etc.
The struggle in regard to the services and customary duties
of ecclesiastical establishment has been rendered especially
famous by the collisions between men of the stamp of Anselm
and Thomas Becket with Rufus, Henry I, and Henry II.
We may remember that Rufus strove to be every man's
heir, that is that he asserted his right as feudal over-
lord to enter into every man's tenement at his death, or,
rather, to translate the rhetoric of aggrieved chroniclers
into the prose of feudal custom, that he enforced his right
of resumption of tenement in regard to his tenants, and
perhaps in regard to people who thought they were not
his tenants at all. And the Domesday description, let us
repeat, shows that all these claims were advanced on the
morrow of Conquest and went with the Conquest settlement.

This being so, the recasting of the inquest from the mould
of communal testimony to that of feudal tenure turns out
to be a process threatening wholesale social changes. It
was not merely a matter of schedule, or even of a generalisation of services. Conditions which did not quite fit in
with the standard set in motion by the Norman commissioners had to be cut right in accordance with this standard.
And a number of people who could go with their land where
they pleased disappear accordingly, a number of others

who owned to confusing forms of dependency on personal
lords and lords of soke, were forced under the one or the
other of the convenient headings supplied by feudal terminology.[8] A few *allodiarii* were suffered to linger even in King
William's days,[9] but this characteristic "survival" only
pointed to a previous epoch when conditions which Norman
lawyers would have called allodial were anything but rare.
And, of course, these specimens of the engulfing tendencies
of feudal organisation which we are able to bring forth
from the records of the inquests, though they have the
priceless merit of being documentary evidence, make us think
of the much more numerous facts of violence and encroachment which have not been described in such an incontestable
manner.   And what is perhaps more important than all
single facts of oppression was the radical change in the basis
of social relations : people had now to look, not so much to
their time-honoured associations in township, hundred and
shire, as to their relations of personal and territorial
dependence.

And now we come to the second of those questions from
which we started : the inquest gives names and definite consideration to the affairs of the king's tenants
Changes in the lower classes in chief and of the most favoured and considerable among the others.   The rest were
entered in numbers and under general headings.   What
was their treatment likely to be, if in regard to the persons
expressly named such a change of conditions was taking
place ?

It is obvious that a similar process of generalisation on
the basis of conditional subjection was going on in all classes
of society, and that it was carried on even in a more
sweeping and reckless manner in regard to the small
than in regard to the great.   Its effects may still be
traced in two directions : the notions of territorial
dependence upon a lord and of service as a characteristic
of tenure are coming to the front ; the seat of the
great man, the manor, gets to be the centre of local society,
and economic as well as legal relations are referred to it as
much as possible.   The first of these points is especially

noticeable in the treatment of status by the thirteenth century law-books and plea rolls. The position of a person is determined by his services. We need not speak at length as to the state of a knight or a clerk, but let us notice a fact to which we shall have to revert again later on, namely, that the personal rank of a free man and of a villain is assigned to them on the strength of their services : the services of the villain are deemed base in their essence and uncertain in quantity, the services of the free—devoid of any debasing tinge, and certain as to quantity. It may have been exceedingly difficult to decide in the concrete what extent and kind of agricultural work rendered labour services base, and what was compatible with the dignity of a free man, but this had to be decided somehow ; the stuff of which society was made up had to be cut somewhere, and a sharp cut severed conditions which were nearly or quite identical, and assigned them henceforward to totally different classes. Our point now is to show that this particular mode of classifying society was chosen by the rulers and lawyers of the Conquest, and that it led gradually to a complete rearrangement of society. Traits which did exist before the advent of King William, but were not considered of fundamental importance, became the chief characteristic of status ; differences which were made much of in King Edward's time were disregarded now as of second-rate importance. It was damaging for a man of free birth to perform rural services for his holding, and it might, in many cases, lead him into servitude ; it was unsafe to be a person entirely taken up with rural work and might be construed as a sign of rustic condition implying rural services and a state of villainage. Distinctions might be drawn in such cases, but they were slender and not to be much relied upon, if the interests of strong men went against them. On the other hand, a clean pedigree of free descent and customary participation in the gatherings of the free in shire and hundred were not of much avail, if incidents of base tenure could be made out against one. As I have said, the prominence of the test of services is very noticeable in the full records of the thirteenth century, but it is obvious that the great recasting of social classification on their basis dates from the Conquest and is primarily expressed in Domesday. Indeed, what is the object of the new departure in nomenclature which is expressed in the Domesday classification of persons ? The Norman commissioners make an attempt to put the people engaged in rural occupations, as villains, bordarii and cotters, on one side, and the people entirely or mainly free from these occupations on the other : there is hardly any other possible basis of classification to be found [10] but this very rough one. The thanes and ceorls, the twelfehyndmen and twyhyndmen of old do not serve the purpose for an exhaustive arrangement of society. The test of wergeld had been rendered worthless by the disruption of kindreds, the intrusion of privileged Scandinavians with their fancy weres, the confusion between small freemen, *coloni*, and freedmen of different kinds. And the very names adopted by the Normans were significant—they were names drawn from modes of rural settlement, from the connexion with the township (townman-villain), from the separate small holding, the Norman *borda*, and from the cottage, all names pointing to village life and easily generalised under the common designations of rustics, villains in general. To what extent this feature of rural life was considered as decisive at the time of the survey, may be gathered, amongst other things, from the fact that the Kentish peasantry was included in the rank of villainage, although there were features in its life which gave it a peculiar place among the population of England, and ultimately helped it to attain a more favourable social position. Still, they were villains, bordarii and cottagers in the sense of being peasant shareholders of villages and settlers holding small plots of land and separate homesteads. It may be justly observed that, at this stage of its development, terminology speaks directly of occupations and not yet of services. This is literally true, and leaves some margin for future variations, such as that which occurred in the very case of Kentish men. But, on the whole, the villains, bordarii and cottagers of Domesday are taken as people who not only themselves, live by rural work on their tenements but who support other people by their work : they are entered as members of manorial groups, and thereby subjected to such services as were appropriate to their mode of life.   And this possibly explains why, by the side of the general classification fitting most cases, special entries as to freemen and socmen appear. Most of these were evidently also peasants, but they had succeeded in making it clear to the compilers of the survey that their services were not mainly base agricultural work. If the survey had been taken in a more consistent manner, these entries of small freemen might have been more numerous ; but, dispersed as they are, they bear witness to the fact that, already at the time of Domesday, the tests of occupation and services were applied to settle questions of terminology and status.

Another feature by which the Domesday Survey, when construed in connection with later facts, reflects a great **Spread of manors** change in the structure of society, is the spread of the manor as the organising unit of property and population.   The elements of the manor were, as we have seen, all elaborated in the course of former periods. At the close of the Old English epoch we already find a great number of estates whose owners held the surroundings population in economic subjection and were endowed with a certain amount of jurisdiction over it.   But this social formation was by no means uniformly constituted or generally prevalent all over England.   The great estates, more common in the west than in the east, were everywhere intermixed with smaller properties, and intertwined in their working with the free associations of the townships and the hundreds.   Indeed, even from the manorialising description of the state of England A.D. 1086 given by Domesday, we can gather that the manors were as yet ungainly combinations, usually straggling over the fields of many scattered townships, creations of haphazard possession as well as of economic union.[11]   And the reminiscences as to the time of King Edward disclose even a greater variety of forms, ranging from mere commendation of free villagers to different protectors, to the settlement of *coloni* and slaves by the lord on the soil of his estate.   When we compare these shades of subjection to the well rounded, compact manors, of the Hundred Rolls, we are struck by the progress made by unification and subjection. But it is quite possible to realise in a similar manner the great advance made by this very process in its earlier stage. We can well form an estimate of the engulfing and organising tendency of the rising manor, e.g., by an attentive study of the Inquisition of Cambridgeshire compared with Domesday : it is very noticeable how small estates, and entire batches of free sokemen disappear within the limits of some manor, and how the personal dependence of free settlers on divers protectors gets replaced by the attraction of free tenants by local manorial centres.[12]

Indeed, in the light of these observations, we may go a step further and enquire whether in many cases the same thing was meant by the expression manor T.R.E. and T.R.W. We are constantly told that where there is a manor at the time of the Conqueror there was one at the time of the Confessor ; or else that there were two and perhaps more. But are we sure that the Norman commissioners and the juries led by Norman questioners were exact in these equations of Old English and Norman arrangements ? Was not, in this retrospective survey, the condition of the Old English estate often only supposed or made up to be the equivalent of the Norman manor ? The wish of Norman organisers to see manors everywhere may well have been productive of real results in the formation of manors, and incidentally may have caused a good deal of perplexity to modern investigators, who try to construe Domesday expressions in too rigid a sense. It has been maintained with considerable ingenuity that the manor was meant at that time to be the place where the tax-collector applied to get the geld,[13] but closer examination has shown that such a reading cannot be upheld. To begin with, the tax-collector had primarily in view the hundred and the vill and not the manor ; the geld had a history of ancient assessment behind it which ran through the channels of the old local associations, and the Normans were not in a hurry to tamper with institutions which for a long time had done good work in enforcing fiscal dues.[14] Then again we find that manor freely interchanges with such vague expressions as *terra*, a piece of land.[15]   And what is even more important and conclusive to my mind, there is the evident connection of the term with two sets of facts which run through very long periods of English history, both before and after Domesday. On the one hand, we find the hall, the grange (comp. barton) and the berwick as constitutive elements and adjuncts of the manor, and this shows that the essence of the manor consisted in its economic organisation—it was an estate to begin with, whatever other meanings and applications the term may have had.   On the other hand, we find the manor definitely used as a unit of local government on the basis of an estate— such is the feudal meaning of the term.[16]   There is no suffi- cient reason to seek for an entirely special departure in the case of Domesday terminology which tends to make estates units of local government.   The solution of diffi- culties seems thus to lie in the idea that the conquerors not only found manors on English soil and described them as such in Domesday, but created manors where they were not as yet constituted, and described as manors complexes of property which were in the slightest degree similar to them. An estate with a hall, however small, a district with a grange or a counting-house, a tract of land in a single person's possession, were termed manors and became virtually the centres of attraction of tenure and services if they were not so before.[17]   The aim of the conquerors was, from this point of view, not merely to record the data for the exaction of the geld, or even to collect the material for new impositions and a verification of the old, but to organise the country and to obtain a hold on its resources.   And their most powerful lever of organisation was the notion of tenure and service, as the notion of responsible local associations had been the organising lever of old English society.   Not that the new notion entirely superseded the old : it rather tra- versed and modified it, but it is as material to grasp the motive of the new order of things, as to remember that this new order could not be set in motion without taking into account many things which had belonged to the former one.

The division of England into manors at the time of Domes-

day is a fact of the greatest significance and importance :
it meant that the new government wanted to supplement
the old scheme of local administration by a network of
feudal bodies which would act as agencies for military,
fiscal, judicial and police purposes. Of course, their
policy in this respect was also dictated by the fact, that
England had been conquered not by a popular host, but by
an army of knights whose claims had to be satisfied in the
first place. Anyhow, without losing their hold on the
ancient divisions, the Normans took advantage of the existing links of patronage and landownership to work out and
to spread a new feudal scheme. The very fact that the
Domesday manors are not all in a state of perfect readiness,
that they are, in truth, in all stages of rudimentary development, speaks volumes for the conscious stress laid on their
organization. As much as governmental measures could
help in such a process, the policy of the Norman kings did
help. The official stamp of the manor was often set in a
hurry on formations which were anything but ready to
receive it, but this only shows how intent the Norman rulers
were to introduce this stamp and to give it currency all
over the country.[18] It is hardly needful to repeat that the
manor itself was not a newfangled expedient, that it was
growing and ripening on Saxon soil, but it is only the wholesale settlement on feudal lines which gave it the completeness and the predominance which characterise it in the age
of Bracton.

The best commentary on Domesday, from this point of
view, is afforded by the history of the next generations after
the great inquest. This history is full of
Changes in the details as to the systematic simplification and
Constitution
of manors elaboration of the hurried manorial scheme
into a comprehensive and national order.
Some of the Domesday manors disappear—the tests of
actual life kill off a quantity of hybrid beings which
had no other real claim to act as centres of tenurial
rights and of local government than the *fiat* of the
Domesday commissioners. Some others, without losing
their independent existence, lapse into a state of subin-

feudation in regard to more powerful neighbours. In the opposite direction, some of the big manorial concerns get parcelled up and breed lesser manors by subinfeudation. In some extraordinary cases, a greater being than the manor itself—an "honour"—may arise.[19] The most common occurrence of all is that one of the manorial bodies attracts and swallows up tenements, plots of land, and even other manors which come into contact with it. All these eventualities may be exemplified by numberless cases from all parts of England.[20] Something of the same kind had been going on for ages in Saxon England itself, but we have not the same means of observing the facts, and, in a sense, the occurrences of the Norman epoch were more decisive, in so far namely as they brought things to a head on the definite lines of a conscious system and a recognized theory. One especially characteristic form of transition from Old English conditions to the feudal arrangement may be noticed in the case of so-called sokes. The soke is an Old English institution, and does not fit well into the scheme of feudal dependency. It was not originally a congregation of tenants around an economic and political centre, as the manor ought to be. It is only a congregation of small landowners around a large landowner who obtains certain political rights over them ; it is the outcome of protection, and not of tenure. The feeling of a distinct difference between manor and soke was so strong, and the traditions in this respect so much alive, that the manorialisation of England left some sokes standing by the side of the manors. The tendency was, of course, to assimilate them gradually. In some instances, a soke was added to a manor without a very definite distinction between its members and the free tenants of the manor. But some other cases remained to late times in which the incomplete organisation of the soke was preserved. Such, for example, was the soke of Rothley in Leicestershire.[21]

I may venture to point out that these instances are remnants of an order of things when soke and sokemen were more common, even though I should incur the reproach of searching after survivals —an unpopular business now-a-days.

A very remarkable side of this process is the relation of the results obtained by it to the ancient social organisation. We

Manor and Township

need not dwell on the cross influences between the manor on one side, the county and its subdivisions on the other. But most perplexing problems arise from the fact that there existed townships with economic and political features in the very places in which the manor appeared with its economic and political organisation, and that these townships were not rendered useless by the new organisation. We have already had occasion to point out that the townships were not destroyed or superseded by the manors : they went on with their functions, but of course they had to come to some arrangement with the newcomers. The natural tendency was to subordinate the townships to the manors in such a way that a township, or even several, were swallowed up in their entirety by the higher unit. When this was the case, and such a result was commonly achieved after a good deal of wrangling and encroachment, it was comparatively easy to work the combination. The vill or township attended to its police duties, made its presentments, appeared by its representatives in hundred, shire and circuit, and transacted economic business under the protection and the guidance of the manor, while this latter drew its suitors and dues, managed its conveyancing, organised its judicial affairs, by the help of the vill.

In fact, such a combination was the normal one, not only in the sense of most cases finding their solution in such a manner, but also in the sense that this solution was the most convenient one. It brought local unity with it, it provided the manor with a simple and compact economic basis, while the organisation of the vill was perfected by the institution of a court which could try offences of many kinds and by a strong showing of authority in the action of the lord.[22] It is to those normal instances that we are mainly looking when we speak of the fully grown manor and its elements, and it is those instances which are mainly illustrated by court rolls. But extents and cartularies show that such instances were, by no means, the only possible

outcome of the process of manorialization. There was no
sufficient material force to bring over to this simple form
all the badly constituted straggling manors of Domesday.
In numerous cases, the vill remained a body by itself and
several manors, as many as three or four, perhaps, had to
share their influence over it.

How were such cases to be met ? To begin with, the
advent of the manorial arrangement produced of necessity
the result that the several manors quartered on the
single vill, or composed of scattered portions of vills, came
to hold their separate courts, and this meant that the local
business of the vill had henceforth to be largely transacted
in different institutions. No wonder that, in process of
time, this led to a disruption of originally solid vills into
several minor vills with distinct names and courts. Many
of the villages with distinctive affixes to their principal
names must have originated in this way. Such was the
origin of the Bampton Poges and the Bampton Regis, of
King's Langley and Abbot's Langley,[23] etc. Sometimes
the breaking up of the old township led to an actual separa-
tion of the village, to the migration of one part of the population and the rising of new clusters of dwellings. Sometimes the adjoining manors went on using the commons
or some part of them together, and in such cases joint meetings of the tenants or even of the courts had to be arranged
to regulate the uses and inflict penalties for transgressions.[24]

One expedient which may have been in use was the recourse to a court on a higher rung of the ladder of infeudation,
if the manors in question happened to have common lords.
But as this was not always the case, informal meetings for
the formulation of agreements must have been often resorted
to, and then the enforcing of the customs had to be left eventually to decisions of the public courts. A good many
processes arising from intercommoning have come down to
us, and part of them evidently goes back to conflicts of
rights between different manors within the boundaries of
one and the same vill, while others are attributable to undivided uses of waste tracts not included in the boundaries
of any particular vill.

In any case, the tradition of the ancient unity of the vill
was kept up in a marked manner by administrative requirements.   In regard to frank pledge, the catch-
Administra- ing   and   watching   of   felons,   the   responsi-
tive existence
of the Vill bility   for   murder   committed   in   the   fields,
the   repartition   of   taxes,   presentments   of
neighbours, sworn inquests and the like, the vills continued
to transact business which formerly had fallen to the duty
of townships, and, in all these respects, if the vill was not
incorporated as a whole in a manor and ruled as a whole by
its court, there must have been meetings to elect representatives and arrange for the discharge of duties.   The automatism and reality which are appealed to sometimes do
not go far enough to meet possible contingencies.   I fail
to see how a distribution of duties between the manors
taking up parts of a vill could have taken place without
some definite agreement to start the custom, and more
meetings and agreements to modify it in the course of time
and events.   Nor is it easy to understand how men were
to be taxed, watch could be kept, and presentments made
without   some   kind   of   organisation   for   entrusting   very
important duties to suitable people.[25] All these villar arrangements, when they are intermanorial, remain in the shade
because there is no permanent institution to take care of
their records, while public and manorial institutions remain
indifferent to such transactions.

CHAPTER II

OWNERSHIP AND HUSBANDRY

As we pass to a closer examination of the manor in its component parts and in its working, we may remind the reader that the manorial organisation presents

Aspects of manorial arrangement three intimately connected aspects—the proprietary, the social and the political one. The manor is an estate surrounded by tenures; it is a combination of ruling and dependent, working and military classes ; it is a unit of local government. It is from these three points of view that we have to consider the subject.

The proprietary and economic aspect of manorial organisation is ruled by the main consideration that it is directed towards two distinct aims : it represents and formulates the interests of the villagers, and it acts as the machinery for the collection of duties and enforcement of services on behalf of the lord. In this way it is a standing combination between the township and the home farm or domain, and it would be wrong to lose sight either of one or of the other element of this combination. The manor does not exist for the exclusive use of the lord any more than it exists for the exclusive benefit of the tenantry ; it has to reckon with both.

In dealing with the village community which formed the basis of the whole, we need not revert to the description of its shareholding and open-field practices, as these matters go back to Old English arrangements, and have been examined at length in the preceding chapter. But we must dwell on those features which have undergone a change in consequence of the development of the manorial system. All the main traits in the life of the community have been more or less affected by this development.

To begin with, the legal theory of landownership under-goes a complete transformation. Instead of treating the **Landowner-** rights of the several dwellers and cultivators **ship** of the locality as originally independent and combining through mutual agreement, or as derived from an original communal ownership, the legal theory of the feudal state treats them as derived from a private and exclusive ownership of the lord.

The lord's ownership itself may be considered as a depen-dent tenure, and traced ultimately to a grant of the king, as eminent owner of the whole land in the country. But if we turn aside from this hierarchical conception, and remain within the precincts of the manor, we have to recognise the lord as the exclusive owner and to derive all rights and customs from his private ownership.

The freeholders of the manor are his tenants, and their possession of land, though guaranteed in every way, resolves itself into a hereditary feoffment.[1] As for the unfree tenants, they have no rights in the eye of the law but to follow customs by the sufferance of the lord, their posses-sion, as far as it exists within the manor, is included in the proprietary rights of the lord.[2] Such is the feudal theory clearly formulated by Norman courts and Norman law writers, and, of course, a theory of so absolute a charac-ter is productive of many and marked consequences. There follows from it, that in case of neglect on the part of the tenants in the fulfilment of their duties towards the lord the tenement may be ultimately confiscated.[3] This holds good even in regard to free tenants, though, of course, in this case, confiscation may be resorted to only as a kind of *ultima ratio*, after all other means and penalties calcu-lated to bring the tenants to reason have been exhausted. Fines, amercements, distraints, come first, but the possi-bility of confiscation is clearly contemplated, and some-times it is actually put into practice.[4] Inasmuch as both lord and tenant are freemen, their contentions will generally

take the way to the king's court : there are writs to suit the
needs of both, e.g. the writs *quare cessavit* for the benefit
of the lord, the writs *quare exigit, de ingressu* for the benefit
of the tenant, the writs of novel disseisin and of common
of pasture for both. But there is a manorial process besides which may be resorted to if the parties do not want
to take recourse to the king's court,[5] and though, as a matter
of fact, most of the suits between lord and freeholders went
to the royal courts, this was merely a question of choosing
the better procedure, of obtaining and enforcing conclusive decisions.

Other and common consequences of the same notion were
the right of the lord to claim escheated tenements, to take
into his hands the wardship of his tenants under age, to
draw profits in cases of the marriage of heiresses, and to
exact relief as a consequence of the investiture of heirs, all
well-known and very realistic incidents of feudal tenure,
derived from the idea that the *dominium eminens* of the
freeholders' tenement belonged to the lord.[6]

As to villains, all these traits are much more accentuated,
as they have no legal standing against the lord. The court
Customary rolls tell us currently of confiscations as a
tenure penalty for offences, of escheats in the lord's
hand in default of heirs, of stringent forms of heriot relief,
wardship and marriage, of which more will have to be said
when we come to questions of personal status.[7] A characteristic form, suggested by the quality of the lord as the
true and only owner, is to be found in the ceremony of
surrender and admittance by which every transfer of land
from the hands of one villain to those of another, in cases of
donation, exchange and sale, had to be accompanied. No
tenant in villainage had power directly to transmit his precarious possession to another person by his own will, from
his own hands and by pure agreement between two parties.
He could merely give up his tenement, or a part of it, to
the lord with the understanding that the lord should grant
its possession to the person intended. In most cases, the
proceeding was fictitious in so much as both acts of the transaction had been arranged beforehand. But the form was,

nevertheless, full of meaning : it served to reassert in a most emphatic manner the exclusive ownership of the lord. Not the least remarkable trait about this process is its development out of ancient symbolic customs which had nothing to do with villainage and the lord's proprietary right : the feudal practice has a precedent in Teutonic usages by which the passage of property out of the ordinary course of succession was guaranteed and sanctioned. A donation or a sale deprived the ordinary heirs of a person, the kinsmen who had a potential right over the land, of their claims and expectations. No wonder that complicated formalities were needed to establish the facts of the case beyond dispute, and to prepare a standing ground in case of a trial. The means to attain this end was to put a middle-man between donor and donee, or between seller and buyer : the surrender of rights on the side of the first was made particularly clear, and a third party provided to stand as witness and warrant of the transaction. But there can be no doubt that the surrender to the lord had yet another meaning than the part played by the " salman,[8] the middle-man of ancient custom." The lord was not legally bound to pass over the land he had taken into his hand, and the recurrence of his particular seisin was obligatory and not a matter of choice on the part of the donor or seller. Nevertheless, it is to be noticed that even in its new meaning of resumption of property by the lord, the surrender and admittance proceeding was originally in use, not merely in the case of villains, but also in that of free tenants. After all, the tenure of these latter was juridically a feoffment, though not historically created in all cases by real grants. As a feoffment, it stood on a common ground with villain tenure, though it was protected in a different way.[9]

In yet another direction, the doctrine of the lord's ownership of the soil led to practical results of first-rate importance. **Ownership of the waste** As the lord was supposed to be the original owner of the whole territory occupied by the manor, and all other claims had to be established by special leave or by customary repetition, portions of the territory which were not occupied by anybody in particular were taken to belong primarily to the lord.[10] Now, we have seen what part the waste played in the economy of rural life. It was largely used as common pasture, common wood, common turbary, and it afforded a reserve fund on which the rural population could fall back for purposes of colonisation and enlargement of existing resources.

The notion of the lord's private right ran counter to all notions of communal property which were bound up with ancient usages as to the waste. Still, as these contradictory tendencies had to be reconciled in practice, in one way or the other, the compromise took the shape of allowing the customary rights of usage of commoners to go on [11] when there was no express call to disturb them, but to insist upon the legal doctrine of the lord's private right as to the waste and to put it into practice by taxing common usages [12] and by asserting exclusive privileges in regard to enclosures and to the reclaiming from the waste for cultivation.

Customary payments of pannage for swine and cattle grazing on the waste, customs of so-called grass-earth labour, fines for cutting down trees, and especially hunting and fishing privileges are among the earliest manifestations of manorial lordship over tracts of waste land, and, of course, they get more and more elaborate as cultivation and social progress increase. We have already had occasion to speak of the right of approving. It is only necessary to add now, that by getting a firm hold on this branch of rural economy, the lords ensured to themselves a most advantageous position as regards eventual apportionments of claims. It was evident that the very extensive tracts of waste land still abounding in England had to be utilised sooner or later, and henceforth the lord's will and policy began to play a conspicuous part in this utilisation. The people chiefly interested in maintaining old ideas and customs in regard to the waste, the villains, forming the majority of rural populations, had no legal voice in the matter. They were reduced to the condition of matter-of-fact usagers, and the express claim of the townships to rights of common was construed to

mean the right of manorial lords, though from a historical
point of view nothing could be more inadequate than such
a construction.   And so the usages went on by sufferance
as long as there was some fear of getting into unpleasant complications by too rough a handling of the
lord's private right, and as long as there were no strong
inducements to oust the commoners for the purpose of
enclosing grazing grounds for sheep-farming on an extensive
scale, or of starting new farms, or of increasing the private
enterprises of the demesne.   Freeholders were the only
people in regard to whom something more than a respect
for traditions and self-imposed restraint were needed.   And,
indeed, they asserted their claims in the courts as often as
the villains asserted theirs by agrarian riots.   The outcome
of the struggle were the Statutes of Merton and of Westminster ii., in which it was at least recognised that the
land in the special occupation of the tenant was not identical
with the land measured out to him in the fields, but included
a flexible quantity of appendant usage in undivided territory.   Still, by help of these enactments and decisions, the
lord carried off all the residue which remained after an
estimation of the special needs of existing tenements as to
pasture, wood, etc., which was saying a good deal.   In a
way, the burden of proof was shifted :   the tenants had
to show what their needs were, and the lord got hold of what
was not expressly appropriated.

As the balance of claims was maintained in regard to the
use of commons chiefly by considerations of matter of fact
Submission to interest and tradition, even so, and perhaps
customs in a greater degree, the open-field system of
cultivation went on by the influence of custom, although
it hampered alike lord and tenants in the exercise of their
discretion and private enterprise.   It is characteristic
of the power of deeply rooted ideas and habits, that,
in a very great number of cases, the lord's dominical land
was often entangled among the intermixed strips, and
that the lords commonly submitted to the incidents and
practices as expressed in the by-laws and customary rules
of the village courts.[13]   But it is not impossible to draw the

demesne land out of the customary network, and we find more and more often that *culturae separales*, plots cultivated in severalty, make their appearance by the side of the open-field[14] shots, furlongs and commons.

This development of private cultivation is not yet strong enough, however, to endanger the whole fabric of the open-field system ; the latter remains predominant in the fields, and testifies by its vitality and strength to the customary hold of communalistic practices on the main arrangements of village life.

One side of the village community was greatly strengthened by the growth of the manor, namely, the arrangement **Consolidations of holdings** of the holdings. Although the shares were formed and their functions already developed in the Old English system, without regard for the difference between free and unfree tenements, and although, as we have seen, there were strong economic inducements for the free holdings to keep their unity as far as possible, there were still considerable forces which acted in the direction of dispersing the holdings of free owners and of disturbing their regularity. Occasional divisions among heirs, alienations by sale and donation,concentration of many tenements in one hand, could not be altogether prevented while the owners considered themselves to be perfectly free in regard to their property. The introduction of the manor brought a new element of cohesion into play. The holding had to be kept united, not only because it was the best means of preserving economic efficiency and sometimes, in the case of smaller plots, the only means of keeping up the necessary stock and the share of the holding in the field, but because it was in the interest of the lord that the value of his tenancies should not be diminished or endangered by pulverising processes of division.[15] The whole weight of his interest tended thus in the direction of regularity and equality. Regularity, because it was more convenient to collect the dues from holdings of one type, or, at least, of a few co-ordinated types, than from plots formed at random. Equality —because he had to look to the general condition of his subjects more than to the private interests of particular families, and naturally felt inclined to exert his influence in a levelling direction. A good landlord was like a good gardener, who has to ply the axe and the pruning-knife in order to rear a plantation of strong, even trees which must neither stifle each other by pressing in too great numbers one against the other, nor be left a prey to a few exceptionally powerful specimens. Manorial instructions make it the duty of the steward to see to a proper and equable distribution of holdings, to provide with land people who stood in need of it, and not to allow the concentration of tenements in the same hands.[16] Altogether, the holding, whether free or villain, became, as a rule, indivisible. Rules of succession and possession were strengthened which favoured the tenement, as it were, at the expense of the population born on it, and gave an entirely different standing to brothers according to their relation to the tenement. In this way the interest of the owner contributed powerfully towards the introduction and maintenance of standard tenements. And, of course, this tendency was not less conspicuous in the case of peasant holdings than in the case of higher forms of possession.

Primogeniture and Borough English, that is, the succession of the youngest son, appear as common expedients **Borough English** for securing the unity of peasant holdings. Borough English deserves a few more words and attention, because the peculiarities of this remarkable tenure are hardly sufficiently realised, although it has been studied so often.[17] The passage of the holding to the youngest son has been often explained as the outcome of the fact that the youngest remains longest in his father's house, while the elder brothers have generally opportunities of going out into the world, at a time when the father is still alive and able to take care of his land. Sometimes the reason of the custom is sought in the consideration that the succession of the youngest put a longer stretch between generations, and was, in so far, advantageous to the tenants, as it exposed them more seldom to the heavy dues of relief and heriot. But there seems to be a good deal more behind this custom. To begin with, the evident favour it shows to the

interests of the tenant makes it probable that it arose on
free soil as one of those customary checks on division, of
which we have been speaking in the third chapter, and not
as a distinct outcome of manorial villainage, though it probably spread under the latter influence. We come to the
same conclusion when we draw the deeper consequences of
a rule which supposed that elder brothers found provision
outside their father's household and in his lifetime. This
savours more of the mobility of early conditions with their
opportunities for emigration, warfare, colonisation, new
settlements, and of greater importance of moveable property
as represented by cattle and sheep, than of a time studiously
bent on immobilising cultivation and land-ownership as much
as possible. The Borough English rule is more fit for enterprise than for customary tradition. A last feature which
strikes us in analysing its practical meaning, is the fact that
it was surely not meant for large families or family communities : the element of hierarchy and authority is completely absent from it. The holding will go to the youngest
son when the elder brothers and their offspring are removed from it, and the youngest in the family is certainly
not the fittest person to represent and to rule anything but
his own household. This shows that the Borough English
rule came up among people living in small households. It
was a fit rule for the holder of a bovate and possibly of a
virgate, but hardly for anybody else. In this way, some
of the most common forms of manorial custom as to inheritance point to a state of society characterised by a break-up
of the larger groups into the smallest possible agrarian units,
but also to a free population gathered in them.

The customary rules of inheritance in the county of
Kent and in some few other places swerve widely, as
we have had occasion to mention, from the common
Gavelkind road which leads towards the unification of
holdings. It is well known that gavelkind
implied a succession on equal footing of all brothers, or, to
put it more properly, of all members of the same generation
and household. The unity of the holding was not given up :
it was maintained in the form of communities between co-

heirs, and by the allotment of ideal shares which were shifted according to the outfall of successive divisions of rights between these co-heirs.   These facts are very striking and interesting.   One thing which we see clearly is that they stand in a closer relation to the customs of tribal divisions than to feudal practices.   They are, in so far, more Saxon than Norman and more suitable for freeholders than for tenants in villainage.   All these observations are well in keeping with the systematic opposition between the custom of Kent and that of adjoining counties, as Kent was deemed free from the taint of villainage.

This being so, we might suggest that the motive for this perplexing abnormity of custom arose out of two currents of facts which may be perceived in the history of Kent. Gavelkind, succession in partible socage, was insisted upon, and worked out as a kind of badge of freedom when the time came for the growth of villainage and for the conscious striving of Kentish men against it.   But this explanation, which lays stress on the strenuous keeping up of Saxon tradition in this particular corner of England, would be insufficient by itself, as it is clear that the leaning towards gavelkind must have made itself felt even before the Norman Conquest and the complete victory of feudalism.   After all, gavelkind, in its well-known *later* forms, could hardly be described as the usual condition of tenure even in Saxon times.

It was peculiar in so far as it did not admit of the working of the customary checks on subdivision which were in use in Saxon England : we find such a number of recognised claims, such minute subdivisions of rights, such a complicated network of ideal shares, and so many allusions to real divisions among co-heirs, that we entirely lose sight of the ploughteam and of its well-known component parts which form the framework of the usual system of holdings.   We hear, indeed, of the sulung and of the yoke, but, at least in later times, they are much too big for their names, including two hundred acres, and fifty acres, respectively,[18] that is, agrarian measures which even the fervid imagination of a Walter of Henley would not dare to provide with real existence in the fields. And, on the other hand, we find crowds of people registered within sulungs and yokes, and some of those, indeed, most of those are endowed with very few acres, a couple of acres, single acres, half acres, and the like. In a word we have glaring instances of the pulverisation of big holdings which have lost their agrarian significance and which are entirely out of proportion to the customary plough-team and its divisions. All this shows that we are on peculiar soil, not only from the legal, but also from the economic point of view. We find on the lands of St. Augustine and Christ Church, Canterbury, not compact agrarian tenements joining in open-field cultivation according to ancient practices, but an individualistic society which seeks its living and gains behind a loose screen of ancient holdings, by a more intensive individualistic cultivation of the soil, sometimes on exceedingly small plots. It thrives, nevertheless, partly by the help of many pursuits which were anything but agrarian and which were opened to it by the privileged position of the county on the high-road from France to England, and partly by work on hire on the estates of local magnates and in the interest of merchants engaged in the lucrative trade of London and of the Cinque Ports. From this point of view, one may almost feel tempted to liken the conditions of Kent to those of Normandy and Italy, more than to those of Surrey and Essex. It lay on the most important trade route, and had, at a very early time, assumed a mobilised, commercial, pecuniary aspect, if I may be allowed to use the term. Indeed, it is worth while to remember that this early time of the close of the Saxon and the beginning of the Norman periods was in truth the time of the most concentrated importance and well-being for Kent. It was exceptionally situated in regard to gavelkind and denial of villainage, because it was exceptionally ahead of the rest of the country in point of commercial development and emancipation from manorial husbandry. This solution of the problem seems to be appropriate in yet another sense : it provides the best clue to the otherwise incomprehensible fact that the landowners of Kent, its lords and knights, did not, in any way, contest or

hamper the declaration of " the rights of man " embodied
in the well-known statement of Kentish custom, although
Domesday might have given them seemingly a very passable
standing-ground for opposing it. It was evidently not in
their interest to oppose this early emancipation, and their
reasonableness and fairness may be best accounted for by
the fact that they gained too much from the privileged
mobility and commercial pursuits of their subjects, to be
very anxious to reduce them to the strict rule of villainage.
And, as this commercial turn was taken in Saxon times, no
wonder that the individualistic customs of Kent are permeated with Saxon reminiscences and engrafted on a stock
of Old English traditions. In short, Kent seems to have
proceeded from the tribal system and the independent
village system directly towards commercial husbandry,
without going through the intermediate stage of manorial
husbandry which was common to the rest of England.[19]

One of the most potent factors productive of communalism
is the joint liability of members of a village in regard to
duties primarily imposed on every single one
Joint liability of them. We have seen that the imposition
of taxes and services by the government always took the
shape of wholesale requirements which were to be met by
the natural associations of the country, so that deficiencies
in the bringing up of the necessary fractions in one quarter
might be made up by extra exertions in other quarters.
The county would have to make up deficiencies in the
hundreds, the hundreds to guarantee the completeness of a
whole drawn from the contributions of its townships, and
the township to vouch jointly for the proper performance of
duties by its shareholders. This did not exclude a repartition of the burden between the parts in each case, and such
a repartition was effected, as we have seen, by assigning
to every component part or member a constituent share in
the whole. And a considerable decrease in the strength
of individual shareholders might produce, and often did
produce, a change in estimates, in repartition and in wholesale requirements. But the subsidiary liability of communities stood behind the scheme and helped to work it.

This communal liability may, indeed, be at the root of the
usual description of all organised local subdivisions as commons or communities.[20] However this may be, it is clear
that a similar policy was followed by the lords in regard
to the manorial dues and services.[21] The shortcomings of
individual tenants brought, indeed, penalties and fines
on their heads,[22] and the manorial administration did not
only look to the coming in of the entire bulk of rents and
services, but went into all details and addressed its requirements to every single tax-payer and rated household. But
at the same time, there is the idea that the township or the
community of manorial tenants ought to make up as much
as possible for deficiencies of its single members, and it is
curious to notice that these two divergent tendencies are at
work at the same time. A plot vacated by its holder may
be put on the responsibility of the whole township or may
be taken into the lord's hands, and this last takes place not
only when it seems advantageous to increase the cultivation of the demesne, but also when the township is so weak
and overburdened, or the disappearance of settlers becomes
so frequent, that it is impossible to proceed on the principle
of joint liability. The labour services of the tenantry,
again, are often imposed in a lump, so that the repartition
between tenants remains their private affair while the lord
demands the performance as a whole. So many acres have
to be ploughed by the customers of the township, no matter
which of them has to plough and how much.[23] The position
of the reeve and other elective officers of the manor is also
connected with the principle of joint liability. They represent the community of tenants and are therefore elected by
them, although their office gets to be mostly concerned
with the collection of rents and the organisation of services
for the lord. The centre of gravity of these offices is
moved, as it were, in the direction of manorial authority.
And the tenants who elect these officers are responsible for
their good conduct, and bound to make good any losses
that may be incurred by the lord through the mismanage-
ment or dishonesty of the reeve or other elective officers.[24]
One question arises in this respect which does not admit of

a general and conclusive solution, namely, the question as
to the extent of the liability of free tenants. Reeveship
becomes a mark of villainage on account of the part it has
to play in the manorial administration, only villains are
bound to serve as reeves and, indeed, to serve as reeve would
create the prejudice that the person who has taken upon
himself such duties, is of villain condition. And, still, the
reeve has to represent the township as a whole, and to insist
on the lord's interests even in regard to freeholders. Besides, the village as a whole is called upon to stand pledge
for his good behaviour and to take part in his election.
These are contradictions towards the solution of which we
have no trustworthy clue. It is by no means unlikely that
customs varied in these respects in different places.

A most conspicuous instance of communal liability and
communal action was afforded by the cases when a town-
The farm of ship farmed the proceeds of manorial authority,
the vill pledging itself to pay a certain sum on condition of getting the amount of the dues fixed and of
taking over the internal administration of them. Such
cases were by no means uncommon, and were exceedingly important from the point of view of the peasants. To
form some estimate of their importance, we may notice the
fact that they are managed on the same lines as the surrender
of administration by the lord of a city, a walled or market
town. The first step towards self-government and civil
liberty in these municipal cases was the establishment of a
firma burgi ; the farming of the borough's dues.[25] As the
lord was mainly interested in the fiscal proceeds of his rights
and did not much care personally for the mere exercise of
power, as it was easy to perceive that an amelioration in
rights and modes of government was one of the surest ways
to an increase in wealth and paying power, the rising municipalities did not find it very difficult to buy self-government
by bidding high for the farm of the town's dues. And
there can be no doubt that something of the same kind
went on among the rural population. Apart from the
fact that, as we have assumed all along, urban townships present originally only a higher form of the same

organisation as rural townships,[26] it would be really incredible that the inhabitants of manorial villages should strive so eagerly and sacrifice so much to get the farm of their manor, merely to obtain leave to collect their own dues.[27] Certainly, by getting rid of the bailiff, they freed themselves from many extortionate practices and pretexts for oppression, but this was not all. The farm was a round sum which was paid irrespectively of the actual amount the different incidents of manorial life would come to. It was a speculation on the part of the township, as well as of a private bailiff, to promise such a payment and to effect it, as in reality the proceeds of reliefs, heriots, fines, sales might turn out to be more or less. But, whereas for the bailiff there was a direct inducement to run the fines and amercements up as high as possible, in order to pocket the difference between their aggregate amount and the corresponding part of the farm, in the case of the township the tendency would be the other way, namely, towards a moderation of exactions which would have to come out of the purse of the farmers themselves. On the other hand, there was an inducement to make as much as possible out of the economic advantages of the farmed demesne and out of the labour services attached to it; there would be, in fact, an increase of economic energy hardly to be matched by the compulsory work organised by the bailiff. It would be impossible to trace the material changes brought about by the farming of manors by the townships in detail; but so much may be said, that even if radical change did not take place at once, farming arrangements, when they became frequent and constant, might well bring about considerable modifications in the character of duties and services, the abolition of vexatious and unprofitable services and a more flexible economic management. We have to notice especially that the farming by a township implied a thorough application of the principle of joint liability and a corresponding development of the idea of communal property and self-government.[28] The farm did not abolish the working of the demesne, of customary services and of manorial courts, but it took away the personal interest of the lord

in the details of this machinery. He got his income in a
lump, and would not have listened to complaints about a
bad harvest, a scarcity of labourers or remissness of payments in court. But if the township had to come up anyhow to meet all the stipulated requirements, it had also to
act as a close and active association in carrying on the
economic and jurisdictional affairs of the manor it had taken
over as a farmer. We do not know in what way the requirements of such a rural union were met and how the eventual
proceeds were employed, but it is not likely that the farming
operations of townships should have been undertaken and
carried out so often and with such apparent success, if
the township did not start from the very beginning from a
powerful communal organisation.

It may be said, in a sense, that the communal government of a self-farming township was only the most complete and active expression of a union which
existed all along under the cover of manorial
authority. And though the theory of cor-
porate rights and corporate personality is certainly insufficiently developed in those times, and it would be impossible to draw clear distinctions between the attributions
of the corporate body and of its members, the limits of
property of the community and of individuals, the aims
of the whole and of its component parts, the germs of co-
operative union undoubtedly exist in these municipal and
rural institutions as well as the terms,[29] and we may be
inclined to look with less scepticism on their modes of expressing themselves if we take into account that a similar indis-
tinctness is spread over the working of many individual
claims, for example, of the notions as to eminent and
useful demesne, as to land-ownership and tenant-right, as
to customary arrangements and legal arrangements.

If we now cast a glance at the organisation of the township as a whole we shall not wonder that it was considered
and termed a community. The name appears constantly
in the Norman documents which concern themselves with
rural affairs, and there are many details which show that the
name was not given at random, but corresponded to a very

The manorial vill as a community

definite position. The records employ it mainly on two
occasions : when a township is called up to perform some
duty, for example, to do help at harvest, make presentments,
to attend some court, to watch prisoners, etc., and when it
was amerced for the non-performance of such duties or
for some transgression.[30] The point to be noticed, a point
which becomes very conspicuous in the second case, is that
a very clear distinction is made between transgressions of
single members of townships and offences which were laid
to the charge of the township as a whole. Free-fights,
cases of battery, were, of course, of every day occurrence,
but it could happen that a whole township was fined for
maltreating royal or manorial officers, and the juridical distinction points generally to cases of popular resistance to
governmental exactions or oppression.[31] People are constantly fined for encroaching on highways, on the king's
woods and pastures, on the course of rivers, etc., but apart
from those cases stand others when whole townships are
made responsible for the encroachments,[32] and knowing
what we do about the arrangements as to intercommoning
and the use of waste land, we shall not hesitate to explain
those instances as mostly originating in some confusion or
misuse of communal rights or to uncertainties of delimitation.
On the other hand, it frequently happens that a community is
said to be injured in its rights by the action of some individual or of another community, and here again we see that
the community is taken as a holder of definite proprietary
rights and is capable of vindicating them,[33] though in feudal
jurisprudence the process will mostly take the course of an
action carried on by some of the members on their individual
responsibilities, the winning or losing of one or some establishing a prejudice in regard to all the rest.

Indeed there can be no doubt that the community of the
township was in a sense a juridical person, that is a compact
group, capable of holding property in distinction to its
members, of acquiring and alienating it and of taking
measures for ensuring the attainment of common aims and
the protection of common interests.[34] The usual object of
such property claims was that portion of the land which was

not hereditarily occupied by individuals—the waste, the meadows, such plots as remained for some reason exempted from individual possession. The communal right in these occasions may be obscured and complicated in the later law of rural districts by the intervention of the manorial element, but it is very clear in the case of urban communities, which are constantly found to hold land, to distribute it for temporary use, to sell and to buy, and possess jurisdictional and market rights which could not exist without a common chest and a fiscal administration of some kind.[35]

This leads us to the question which has been much discussed by German, and, of late, by English jurists, as to the theoretical essence of the village community. Have we to apply to it the strict Roman idea of the corporation as a juridical personality, excluding other personalities from its domain and proceeding from the complete unification of interests and rights of all its members for certain purposes ? Or the conception of joint-stock enterprise with limited ends and determined liabilities of members leaving them for the rest entirely independent in their actions and proprietary rights ? Or that of a joint ownership which, while leading to common action and common assertions of right by agreement of the participants, has no legal existence apart from these agreements and may be dissolved in case of disagreement ?[36] Or the rather indefinite Germanistic conception of a community mixed up with individual rights, and presenting an organic combination of both principles ?[37]

It is quite clear that the case under discussion does not fit the strict Roman conception of a corporation or juridical person ; the rights of individual shareholders are not entirely merged into it nor clearly kept apart from it : even in the use of commons, individual interests are constantly asserted ; in the arrangement of economic affairs it would be difficult to distinguish exhaustively between the rights of the whole and the rights of single members as to the arable and to the other constituent elements of the holding. The later legal process starts from the assumption of individual rights, though it leads to the filling up of this individualistic form with contents drawn from communalistic customs. Altogether the materials for building up the corporation are largely composed of disparate elements and lack the unity of will which is necessary to the idea from a Roman point of view.

The joint-stock theory is also insufficient in many respects. The shareholders are there and their joining together is directed towards certain aims, namely to the management of a complex system of open-field farming. But the aims are so general that they resolve themselves into a common management of life under certain economic and juridical conditions. The shares play a great part, in this life, though not so much for the creation of a joint will as for the apportionment of profits and duties. The possibility for the shareholders of outgrowing the common shell and of living a life of separate interests outside of it is not to be denied and has to be taken into account, but there is no clear limit of liabilities and everything depends much more on actual forces than on juridical distinctions.

Already in analysing the joint-stock conception we come to one feature of the arrangement which does not fit at all into the idea of joint ownership (Miteigenthum, Gesammte Hand). The fabric of the village community, or, to speak more generally and correctly, of the township community, is substantially organic. It grows, and is not based on agreement, people cannot accede to it or recede from it without being admitted, by some natural process, birth, marriage, adoption, to the union of the holdings, and, theoretically, it is the holdings in their unconscious and unwilling combination which form the group and define its aims. External forces—the action of the king, the intrusion of foreign conquerors, the misdeeds of a magnate may cut through this customary combination and modify it ; it may grow and send out offshoots, but all these facts will not be the results of any artificial agreement binding only those who have entered it under certain conditions : the reclaiming of new fields, the extension of the original unit and its shrinking through colonisation are events which proceed from the organic whole or from outward pressure and not from passing agreements of certain joint owners.

The fourth conception is wanting in precision and legal neatness ; [38] instead of defining contrasts, it blends them. But for this very reason it may be serviceable from a historical point of view. It undoubtedly corresponds to the state of mind of people who are less accustomed to speculate on legal abstractions, than to solve practical problems by the help of compromises providing against exaggerations of principle and extreme views. As a matter of fact, people had to till the land very much in common because their agriculture was very much mixed up with pastoral pursuits, because they settled close together for purposes of co-operation in defence and economic matters, because they built up their early land system on the principle of a commensurate allotment of households worthy of folkright.[39] At the same time they did not look up to their community as to a kind of socialistic providence watching over all the eventualities of birth and of death, of chance and miscarriage, cropping the allotments according to the supposed requirements of the seasons : not equality and redivision, but shareholding and customary tradition were the results, and these fundamental conceptions opened gaps through which individualistic development was free to shoot forth in a rank growth. People were bound up in scot and in lot with their township in more than one sense, but they were nevertheless allowed to thrive in their own way, and there was not much in the communal arrangements to prevent these latter from decay, if they could not hold their own in life's struggle. To such a state of things a rather indistinct theory of communal shareholding developing on organic lines seems best to apply in spite of its inherent contradictions.

The arrangement of services and rents plays a very prominent part in the economy of manorial life. One might fancy the whole existence of the lord and his household provided for by the services of the tenants, although there was almost always a nucleus of independent husbandry in the centre of the system. Still, we might describe the work performed by the tenants from the

Services

point of view of the lord's household, as contrived to satisfy all requirements. For the cultivation of the arable, the peasant holdings will send their ploughs three or more days in the week, with a full complement of beasts and labourers, to work from sunrise till noon. As the soil gets properly tilled according to the usages of the different seasons, the peasants will send their harrows to break up the sods and prepare the ground for the seed. This part of the arable, cultivated at fixed rates by help of the week-work, will probably be sown by the lord's servants and with his own corn. But another part, the gafol-earth, will be taken over as so many acres to be tilled, harrowed and sown by the tenantry. When the ground lies fallow, it will be ploughed up in time to prepare for the crop season, and the tenant's cattle and sheep will be sent to the lord's fields and will have to use his fold. When the harvest season comes, the entire population of the village will have to turn out to help the lord's labourers and the week-workmen in making hay and cutting corn. A sense of the extra value of such work is expressed by the fact that it is termed " precariae," which means that it is not supposed to be due, but has to be asked for. And if this boon-work has to be repeated several times, the labourers get food and even ale from the manorial economy to keep them in good humour.

The hay and corn harvest will be removed by the villagers in their carts, and they will come to the manorial barn to thresh the lord's corn. As for the grinding of it to flour, it will be performed in the demesne mill, but all the tenants will have to use this mill for grinding their own corn, a very important source of profit to the lord. There are also cases when the baking of bread gets to be a monopoly, and the brewing of ale and beer is generally subject to supervision and taxes.

Pastoral pursuits are also arranged and taxed at the lord's convenience ; though, of course, the exploitation of the tenants will mainly take the shape of dues in kind, of which more anon. Still, service may be required as day-works, for example for shearing and washing sheep, and fines will be exacted in the frequent cases of trespass and impounding of cattle.

A miscellaneous array of services is connected with build-ing and keeping up of dwellings and works of common utility. The labour of the villagers will be used not only for the construction of castles and fastnesses, the construction and repair of manor houses and barns, but also for the erection of complete summer dwellings for the hunting season, for the keeping in repair of bridges and roads. The erection of hedges, the management of drainage in fen districts, the work of keeping up ditches, canals and dikes were all con-sidered as manorial duties, included in the week-work and enforced by manorial officers.

Another subdivision of labour-services was formed by carriage duties of all kinds. Of the removal of the harvest we have spoken already. Every considerable manor was provided with an entire system of riding and driving services. Riding bailiffs, servants, and sometimes socmen, had to carry summonses, orders and messages, and sometimes to inspect workmen. The produce of the farming operations of the manor had to be sent to markets and to central courts, and all the obligations attending these carriages and " aver-ages " (*averum, affre*—horse used for carrying) were settled with the greatest attention to details.

A last class of services was formed by the duty of acting as an official or servant of the lord, as reeve, messor or ploughman, for example, and of representing the township in the royal courts and inquests, in the county and in the hundred.

All these services could be imposed both on villain and on free tenants ; although the burden laid on the first, was of course, greater, and especially the heavy week-work incumbent on them, while the representation of the manor in the county and hundred entitled to a higher considera-tion, and even to personal or tenurial freedom.[40]

As to rents, there were still numerous cases when produce was sent in kind ; loaves of bread, ale, cheese, honey, salt,

Rents

fish, eels, etc., according to the special occupa-tions of the district. Products of industry were also presented to the lord, when such industries existed within the manor. We often find mention of rents paid

in linen, cloth, iron implements.   Of the combination of
provender rents with farms of rights we have already had
occasion to speak.   As to duties involving the present-
ation of animals they had often the character of taking a
certain percentage from the whole stock of the tenant.   A
nag or a calf had to be given from a certain number of
similar animals, ostensibly for leave to use the pasture.
In the case of small rents, a symbolical meaning may be
sometimes traced.   Chickens were given, for instance, as
an acknowledgment of bondage, eggs represented the number of acres a tenant held in the fields,[41] etc.

Money rents occurred frequently, and it is to be noticed
that they were of two different kinds.   Some were payments originally imposed on the tenants, so-called *gafol*,
others were paid in commutation of services or provender
dues, and were called *mal* (*mol*) or *mail*.[42]   The rent-paying
tenant was naturally considered to be freer than his compeer
burdened wth services, as he was not subjected to personal
interference and discipline in the performance of his duties,
and there was a constant tendency on the part of the
peasantry to obtain the commutation of payments and
services.[43]   This tendency, which played a very conspicuous
part in the gradual emancipation of the peasantry, was
however, checked during the feudal period by the scarcity
of money.   Every fact facilitating intercourse and money-
dealings tended indirectly to further commutation.   In many
of the manorial extents, especially of the fourteenth century,
it is usual to make customary estimations of the equivalent
of provender dues and services if commuted into money.
These mentions do not imply a conclusive transition to
payments in money, but the eventual exaction of the dues
in one or the other manner.   They are characteristic, of
the binding force of customary rules even in such cases as
these, when one would expect a good deal of bargaining
and oppression.

It remains to be noticed that the fiscal requirements of
the government were imposed directly on the working
classes, and were not left to be gathered by the lords.   The
hidage and geld had to be paid by the hide and, as we have

already seen in the preceding chapter, the geld units, according to which they were distributed, fell largely on the land of the villains. Taxes on chattels had also to be paid by the villain landholders themselves, so that distinct property in moveables was evidently assumed in all these cases.[44]

If we look to the demesne land of the manor, we shall find at its centre the hall, with barns, stores, mills, stables, folds and, possibly, rabbit-warrens and dove-cotes, in connection with it. In many cases, the **The demesne** arable of the demesne lay intermixed with the strips of the tenants, a fact which by itself bears testimony to the gradual rise of manorial organisation from the open-field community. There was of course a natural tendency of the demesne to obtain a position of severalty and to enclose itself. If, nevertheless, a great part of the demesne land of the manor remains lying in open fields, it is clear that it was entangled in the champion farming by tradition, and subjected to its regulations because it stood originally not above the village community but inside it.

Enclosed plots of arable and private meadows, pastures and woods are also often to be found, and they occur more and more frequently as time goes on. We catch glimpses of the process of enclosure, and of the changes brought about by more intense and perfect husbandry. New sequences of crops are introduced, the soil of some portions of the demesne gets to be manured and cultivated more carefully and, to protect these ameliorations, hedges have to be set up, " intakes " are formed ; and these intakes represent the most advanced technical progress of those times.[45]

Considerable portions of the demesne were leased in separate plots to servants and farmers. As to the first, they often got their remuneration in this form **Forlands** instead of getting wages, and we find ploughmen holding some five acres of land for this reason. But besides these, farmers, settlers and squatters were accommodated in this way with small plots, so-called *forlands*.[46] A forland was out of the ordinary course of cultiva-

tion of the open-field community, and was managed in
severalty by the tenant who got a lease for term of years
or for life.   Thus we come again across a current of
individualistic management derived from the demesne
and constantly on the increase during the period under
observation.   The reclaiming of the waste, under the leadership and by the license of the manorial administration,
mostly took this course.   The protection of the lord was
sufficiently strong to safeguard such enterprises, and colonisation now takes mostly an individualistic turn, while
it was communalistic during the preceding period : evidently, there was more demand now for individual energy
and capital than for co-operation, mutual defence and
responsibility.   We come across some remarkable facts
in this direction : the Earl of Warenne, for example, was
empowered by Edward I to enclose in the waste so much
land as was necessary to give him a revenue of £200.   If
the rent is estimated at about 4d. an acre—a very usual
estimation in those times—this would mean that the earl
got license to enclose and colonise about twelve thousand
acres in the most favoured part of England.[47]

On the whole, however, the characteristic feature of
manorial husbandry consists in the working together of the
domain and of the community of the tenants.   In the
normal case, there is no distinction between this community
and the township of old, which is still recognised as the
administrative subdivision of the hundred.   The system
was reasonably balanced when the soil and the work of the
tenants was divided in such a way as to afford sufficient
means of existence for the demesne of the lord and for the
households of the tenants.   When this was the case, the
peasants generally succeeded in laying by some capital
which they used for gradually buying out their dues, while
the lord strove to enlarge the separate husbandry of his
portion, and to attract settlers for rack-rents.   Both tendencies were directed towards aims which by their development
endangered the existence of the manorial arrangement and
prepared a new departure in economic and social organisation.

CHAPTER III

SOCIAL CLASSES

LET us now turn to the social stratification of this period—
to the division of feudal society into classes, and to the
relations between these classes. We notice

Slaves   three principal orders of men on the soil of a
mediaeval manor : villains, freeholders and manorial servants.

We have already had occasion to speak of the various
elements of which the class of villains is composed. One
part of it proceeded from downright slavery, from the stock
of theows or esnes of Old English times ; but it is significant
that only a comparatively small number of *servi* is mentioned in the Domesday Survey,[1] and that the class, as
distinct from that of the villains, disappears in the records
of the thirteenth century. These facts are very important,
and have to be looked into with some attention. The
manumissions of the Saxon period are frequent, and we
find hundreds of slaves emancipated by their owners for
payments in money, especially in wills. Still, it is certainly
not philanthropy or the influence of Christianity that have
reduced slavery to the modest dimensions it holds in Domesday. Christianity introduced some humanitarian elements
into the treatment of the slave, recognised in him a being
with a soul of his own, and, by the voice of councils and
preachers, proclaimed some regard for the wretched existence of men who had no protection in law, though they
bore the likeness of God. But the Christian Church was
very chary in its social propaganda : it did not contest the
institution of slavery, and preached meek obedience to the
serfs ; it took good care to make as profitable and well-

ordered a use of its own serfs as was possible, and we know, even from our own experience, how easy it is for men to compromise with their conscience when their interest speaks loudly for the utility of compromise, and how the sanctification of religion may be appealed to in the case of most shocking violence and despotism. Therefore the fact that so many ecclesiastic and secular owners renounced the complete property of their slaves, and that slavery, though most clearly expressed in the enactments of Old English laws, became obsolete in the feudal period is best explained by social and economic, and not by religious or humanitarian considerations. Indeed, in one sense, the practices of serfdom did not cease, but went on and even spread in their application, as villains generally came to be considered and designated as serfs or natives, and subjected to many of the most characteristic taints of slavery. Villains could be bought and sold, villains were manumitted to personal freedom, villains had to " buy their blood " when they married their daughters and even their sons. In this sense, bondage became more general, and infected classes and persons which had originally been free from it.² But these are results of confusion and of a mixture of classes, and the other side of the picture is afforded by the fact that the slave or serf as a distinct being of lowest order disappears. Faint attempts may be traced in law books, law decisions and extents to keep up a standard of basest villainage and to characterise it by especially base services, such as scavengers' work, but these instances are rare and do not result in constituting a distinct class. And, as we shall presently see, in the general law of villainage there were many features derived from the status of freemen as well as from slavery––it was, in fact, a complex condition. The servi of Domesday, of the cartulary of Burton and of a few other very early extents, are, in this way, the last representatives of slavery in Old English laws. The personal character of their condition is illustrated, among other things, by the mention of *ancillae* in the Domesday Survey alongside of *servi*.³ They are not connected with any holdings, but are reckoned up after the description of the demesne,

so that personal bondmen, living in the **domanial**
court and working as labourers under the direct command of the manorial stewards, are evidently meant.[4]
There is no reason for identifying them with the *bovarii*
mentioned in some instances as dwellers on the demesne.[5] The bovarii may be serfs or may be of villain
stock, but the allusions to women slaves ought to teach
us that the expressions were not equivalent. There
could be other servants of unfree blood on the demesne,
besides the drivers of plough-teams. The servi are mentioned so casually and there are so few of them in some
cases that it is not impossible that the entries of this class,
which was not attached to holdings, may have been incomplete. Still, an inference must be drawn from the fact that
there are comparatively many serfs in the manors of western
counties, fewer in the midlands, and hardly any in the east.[6]
In conjunction with the gradual disappearance of the class,
this fact goes to prove that, as we have already said, the
dissolution of serfdom was produced by economic causes.
All through the regions occupied by Teutonic tribes there
was a habit of treating the serfs as dependent peasants,
or villains according to feudal terminology, while there was
no proper place for them in the household of the owner.
As a rule, the profits drawn from serfs were provender rents,
produce in kind, and as for the *ministeria*, the duties of the
household, they were performed, not by slaves, but by the
weaker members of the family, the old and younger people,
the women. Of course, it is not by the psychological peculiarities of the Teutons that such arrangements have to be
accounted for, but as in the similar case of the Celts, by the
cumbersome character of domestic slavery and by the appro-
priateness of a colonate burdened with rents in kind to early
stages of society. Matters changed to some extent when
the Teuton conquerors entered into the inheritance and
seized upon the loot of the provinces. But social intercourse soon returned to slow customary processes, and the
leaning towards an imperfect and easy-going but easily
administered system of colonate made itself felt at once.
Instead of constantly watching slaves and spending care

and strength in organising their unwilling labour, the upper classes of mediaeval society levied dues and services from villains who were attached to the soil and held in order by the interest they had in their own households. This was the secret of the whole labour arrangement of the manor, and of the conspicuous decrease in the number of serfs and in the amount of serfdom, if one may be allowed to use the expression.

In connection with the disappearance of personal slavery, we find a great change in the effects and character of manu-

Manumission mission. The class of freedmen is always very important where slavery is prevalent, because freedmen form an intermediate link between slaves bereft of all rights and personality, and complete freemen. Thus the *libertini* of the classical world played a great part in the administration of property, both in land and in money. They were left in a certain degree under the authority of their former masters, and helped them so much in their business dealings that the money-market was almost chiefly in their hands. In a similar manner, the early law of the barbarian tribes recognised a kind of half-free position of emancipated slaves, making entire freedom a rare exception and allowing freedmen to obtain a position of equality with tribesmen of pure blood only in the course of several genera-tions. Now, although the practice of manumission cer-tainly continues during the feudal age, its effects are much more restricted, and the freedmen as a class disappear entirely. It is possible that a remnant of them may be found in the *coliberti*,[7] who are found rather frequently in France and in a few instances in England, apparently in adap-tation of French customs and terminology. To judge by the prefix in their name, they were men who had been liberated by a collective act and, possibly, held together in some way either by their settlement or by their common manumission.[8] They were certainly accounted half free. But, whatever we make of this condition, it is a very exceptional one, at least in England, and there is no need to dwell long on it. As for manumissions of single persons, they occurred frequently, but did not make much change in the condition of those who were liberated by them. They did not lead to the formation of a special class. of men, but to the admitted status of men personally free,

Free men holding in villainage
though holding in villainage.[9] This certainly made a difference as to the possibility for the tenants of leaving the holding and as to the position of their offspring : theoretically, such men would be free to go where they pleased, and may in many cases have swelled the ranks of artisans and of the commercial people in the towns. But, on the one hand, it was not so easy even for them to cut themselves adrift from their households and native associations, and, on the other hand, even downright *nativi*, that is serfs, might often run away from their masters and begin life afresh. One might say that the customary life of the manor was rigid, and held in fetters even those who were nominally free, but that, on the contrary, even serfs did not find it difficult to leap out of their fetters, if they were not afraid of the risk of leaving their customary occupations and surroundings. Thus there was no very great difference between freemen holding in villainage and downright villains within the manors, nor between emigrants from both classes, when out of the manor. In any case, the traces of freedmen disappear as well as the traces of serfs, and in feudal records we never come across the numerous instances in which they are mentioned in former epochs—we do not hear either of their various employments in ordinary circumstances or the points of law which arose out of trials as to their condition. The enfranchisement from villain services and disabilities of villain tenure, is, of course, a material affair, but it is entirely different from personal manumission, and has nothing to do with the formation of a class of freedmen.[10] The contingent of manumitted serfs remained within the state of villainage, by tenure if not by personal subjection.

A third element of villainage was provided by ancient freemen who had sunk into a practical dependence on manorial lords. The steps of this process were different, as we have had occasion to notice. A ceorl might be obliged to become the boor, the

Subjection of freemen

colonus of a landowner, because he had no land of his own
and got a tenement from the owner of the manor. Or else
he might be constrained to surrender his land because he had
no capital to manage it with, and was reduced to take stock
from a neighbouring lord who was able to provide him with
it. The ceorls settled on gafol-land are best explained on
these suppositions. But then again, there were people who
tilled their own land and went on with their cultivation,
but had to seek protection and to commend themselves to
powerful lords, and that protection might easily become
a heavy burden : beginning, perhaps, with commendation
to whomsoever one pleased, and then getting to be constant
subjection of one who could not go with his land where he
pleased, and ending by a registration among villains at the
time of the Domesday Inquest. Even a subordination to
soke might, through oppression, be turned into villain ge,
and the Domesday commissioners have brought many such
cases to our notice, leaving, of course, many more in the
dark. Altogether, the Conquest, with its violent and wholesale expropriation, must have been the great crisis in the
life of small people, as the Normans were surely not
more careful of tradition or more fair in their dealings with
their subordinates than the King was with themselves.
Already, the comparison drawn by the inquest between the
state of the smaller tenantry, T.R.E. and T.R.W. shows a
great change for the worse, and we must remember that even
the description of the supposed state of affairs T.R.E. is to a
great extent a fiction, coloured by Norman terminology.

Interesting indications as to the history of the peasant
class are supplied by the terms which are used to designate
Norman term- its subdivisions. Most of the expressions
inology. employed are Norman-French and Norman-
Bordarii Latin, and the question naturally arises : did
they fit in exactly with the English expressions in use before
the Conquest, or were they an independent growth of the
Norman time to which the older expressions had to conform
as they best could. There can be no doubt that the latter
was the case. If we leave the cottagers and the sokemen

aside to begin with, as terms which have an English sense, we find that the most important of the terms used, *villani, bordarii, liberi homines*, are distinctly Norman and do not find any entirely corresponding equivalents in Old English usage.

This is especially clear of *bordarii*. The term is a wide generalisation, it covers not much less than one-half of the labouring population of the rural districts described in Domesday,[11] and it turns out to be a special term brought in by Domesday and hardly ever used either before or after, either in the Old English or in the feudal age. There can be no doubt that it aims at describing the smaller holdings which, without being mere cottages, do not amount to full shares in the fields.[12] In this sense, it comes from the Norman *bordarius* and *borda* (a croft). Later on, we find a great number of such small holdings, but they are ranged either as villain tenements or as free plots, so that there is no unity of condition between their holders who, on the contrary, belong to different social groups. The attempt to class them in one subdivision must be explained, partly by the influence of Norman-French conceptions and partly by the wish to obtain in the Survey not so much a record of legal as one of economic condition. It was material for fiscal purposes to know in a rough way how many normal holdings connected with plough-teams there were in a particular locality, and how many small tenements cut off from the arrangement into plough-teams, and, for this purpose, the distinction between *villanus* and *bordarius* was material, while it did not correspond to any definite legal distinctions. If we ask ourselves how the bordarii were called in Old English speech, and what Old English groups they represent, we shall have to suppose that they must have been either ceorls, boors, or possibly cotters. The fact that there were *cottsetle's* and *cottarii* by the side of them is evidently the outcome of some local distinctions within the limits of the group of small tenants, which do not affect the general classification. It is remarkable that there are comparatively few cotters in Domesday, while there is a great number of them in later records, so that a good many cottagers must have been entered as bordarii by the Domesday Inquest.[13]

Similar observations will occur to us, when we come to consider the Domesday class termed *villani*.[14] It does not

Villani correspond to the villain class of later feudal records. Not only does Domesday make no distinction between villains born and freemen holding in villainage, so that the villani class would, in any case, have to be taken as the aggregate of all tenants in villainage and not of villains by birth, but it is certainly meant to mark off a large group of tenants whose holdings are of a certain size and quality, namely, villagers who hold shares in the township according to fixed relations to plough-teams. They are considered as members of the township. *par excellence*, and termed *villani* for this reason. Later on the term was extended to all people in a certain legal condition of serfdom, thus including more and less than the Domesday group : more, because the greater part of the *bordarii* and *cottarii* came to be villains in a legal sense, less, because the rough and ready designation of villagers must have embraced a good many people who were members of the plough-team associations of the township without being unfree at the time of the Survey. To judge by the Kentish case, a number of people who were not even technically tenants in villainage were comprised by this terminological distinction [15] ; a dangerous precedent in the case of free peasants. When the term had come to imply serfdom, most of these were not as fortunate as the Kentish men, and did not recover either their free status or the free quality of their holdings. The same sweeping and ambiguous treatment of the *villain* class in Domesday is shown by the consideration of Old English terms which were represented by it. No single term applies. "Túnman," which would be an exact equivalent, occurs now and then, but is so exceptional that there can be no question of taking *villanus* as its translation.[16] Though the Domesday survey is very categorical in its affirmations that there were so many villains in such and such a manor, *temp. Regis Edwardi*, we can be perfectly sure that in the reign of Edward the

Confessor the people in the manors were either "ceorls" or "gebúrs," as no such thing as a villain existed in later Saxon terminology. The Latin versions of Old English laws, although belonging to the early Norman period, are not without significance in this respect : of course they often employ the term *villanus*, but they make it correspond both to "ceorl" and to "gebúr," and even to "g' neat,"[17] which, properly speaking, stands for the "follower," the *ministerialis*. As to "ceorl" and "gebúr," although these terms had become more or less vague in their application, there is nothing to show ᴜnat they had assumed the hard and fast legal sense which the later *villanus* carried with it. If "ceorl" had to be rendered by *villanus*, the common basis which made such a translation possible was evidently in the sense of both terms indicating *villagers*, members of the township ; and as for the common basis with "gebúr," it lay in the affinity of *villanus* with *colonus* which is the exact equivalent of "gebúr." My contention is, therefore, that the terminology of Domesday does not give any clue to legal distinctions between classes of persons, but rather applied to the size and character of the tenements, whereas both the Old English and the feudal classification start from legal and personal distinctions. The indiscriminate use which has been made of the one term common to Domesday and to the later classification, namely *villanus*, has been the origin of much confusion ; such a use may have begun very early, but in a historical account of social evolution we must be careful to distinguish between three sets of terms : the "ceorls" and "gebúrs" of Saxon times which included both free and unfree peasants, both owners and tenants ; the *villani* and *bordarii* of Domesday, who were the tenants of holdings of diverse standing in the township, irrespectively of legal condition ; and the "villains" of feudal records, who formed a distinct legal order of men.

What are the "sokemen" and the *liberi homines* of Domesday, and in what relation do they stand to the other **Domesday soke-**classes ? Here again we come upon distinc-
men tions which have no proper equivalents in

the period preceding the Great Survey and the Norman
legislation, although Domesday seems to imply by its
constant references to the numbers of " sokemen " and
liberi homines in King Edward's time that they were commonly recognised as such by the later Saxon classification
of men. The form " sokemen " seems at any rate to be
Old English in its derivation, while *liber homo* is a Latin
translation or a Latin generalisation of some other terms.
Beginning with " sokeman," we may notice that besides
Domesday it occurs in Latin versions of Old English
law, for instance, in the laws of Edward the Confessor
where a distinct fine is mentioned as appertaining to the
villain and the sokeman, the fine of 12 shillings for breach of
their home peace.[18] These instances show to my mind that
the distinction between villain and sokeman is a later
Norman one, and that originally both groups belonged to
the same class of " twyhyndmen " or " ceorls." Why
should otherwise the fine be identical ? It is applied to
two subdivisions which appear differentiated only in Norman
documents. There was no call for a differentiation of fines
in the time of Edward the Confessor, because both the
ancestors of later villains and those of later sokemen were
as yet merged in the one class of twyhynd ceorls.

Why did the Survey and Norman jurisprudence start
this very important division, and affirm that some
classification of the same kind existed in fact if not in
name in the time of Edward the Confessor ? Evidently
because there was a great difference of economic position
between different people belonging to the " twyhynd "
class, some being more implicated in services and subjection
in regard to the neighbouring lords and some less, though
even these last were to a certain extent under authority and
patronage. The departure taken by Domesday is to distinguish between members of the village who are taken to
be under manorial authority, and members of the soke who
are assumed to be merely under jurisdictional supremacy.
Some attempts in this direction may have begun already
in later Saxon times, but the terminological distinctions of
which we are speaking were not clear and ready even at

the time of the survey. We find the greatest number of
sokemen in the counties of the Danelagh and the adjoining
eastern shires, which seem in some degree to have followed
the example of Danish districts :[19] this may serve as a conclusive proof that the class of small freeholders with a very
independent status was exceptionally numerous in this part
of England, though we shall never know exactly how many
were submerged by the flood of the Conquest. But it
would hardly be safe to assume that the total absence of
sokemen in the enumerations of the western counties testifies
to a complete manorial subjection of ceorls in those parts
already in the time of Edward the Confessor. The retrospective character of these generalisations does not entitle
us to put too definite a meaning on their statements in
regard to Old English customs and conditions. The same
upper crust of the twyhynd class which was catalogued
separately under the heading of sokemen in the east may
have been included in the general order of *villani* in the west.
The fact would still be significant, but it would hardly do
to construe it too sharply and to assume an entirely different
course of development in both halves of the kingdom.[20]

What are the *liberi homines* with which the eastern
shires are studded ? Here again we are not entitled to
Liberi homines fasten upon any single term as an Old
in Domesday English equivalent of the Latin name. There
are some remarkable indications as to the direction taken
by Norman terminology in this case. The Latin versions
of later Saxon documents translate " thane " by *liber
homo*.[21] If we apply this observation to Domesday, we
come to the conclusion that twelve hyndmen were entered
as *liberi homines* in the Survey : the only difficulty would
seem to lie in the fact, that a number of the *liberi homines*
in Domesday are exceedingly small people.[22] But then we
have to take notice that, for once, thanes also are not
always big men, and that some of them perform very humble
services indeed, and own tiny plots of land.[23] It has also to
be remembered that in consequence of the treaties with the
Danse the quality of twelve-hyndmen was bestowed on all
the warriors of the Danish hosts : they were all reputed

" höldar " and " twelfhyndmen." Even this however will not
account for all the *liberi homines* of East Anglian counties,
and in their case two inferences would be probable : either
their social distinctions were affected by the example of
their Danish neighbours in respect of wergeld as well as of
patronage, or else that the rendering of Saxon terms by
liberi homines was more loose in this case, possibly including
not only those who are called " drengs " or " geneats " in
other counties, but rent-paying tenants in general, free
from servile work. This is a distinction towards which
many of the Latin records lead and it is by no means
impossible that it may have been applied locally by
some of the Domesday juries and sets of commissioners.[24]
On the other hand we should not like to argue too closely
from the scarcity of *liberi homines* and *liberi tenentes* in
the west, that all kindred groups of rent-paying tenants
and of personally free followers were absent there. The
safer inference would be, that the upper stratum
of tenantry did not obtain the same recognition of its
better position at the hands of western commissioners and
jurymen. The contrasts presented by different counties in
regard to the classes of their population ought not to be
disregarded, certainly, but these contrasts were not so sharp
or so devoid of intermediate shades as they look, when we
subject them to statistical abstracts, and take for granted
that all terms and designations were read and employed
in the same way all over England. This is assuming too
much from a Survey which had to overcome an immense
number of local difficulties, and had no clear body of legal
distinctions and no settled legal theory, either Saxon or
Norman, to start from.

The picture is different, when we get to the time of
regular jurisprudence, the time of Magna Charta, of
Villainage in the King's writs, of Bracton and Common
Common Law Law. We are then on firm ground and can
guide ourselves by the logical deductions of royal lawyers ;
we may even try to draw conclusions in their stead when
their direct testimony forsakes us. Nevertheless, the body of

doctrine they present to us is not free from contradictions
and inconsistencies : and no wonder, as they have contrived to throw into one mould three or four conditions of
men which meet our eye even in Domesday, not to speak
of former times ; namely, the slave, the servile labourer,
the *colonus* and the free ceorl under manorial sway. There
are no more " theows," no more *coloni* or " gebúrs," no
more *bordarii*, no more " ceorls " :—there are only villains
in contrast with free tenants, and these villains have
inherited traits from their various ancestors. We find,
to begin with, that they are free in regard to everybody
but their lords.[25] They are responsible for their acts, and
the criminal law does not concern itself with any of the
puzzling problems which arose in ancient society from the
misdemeanors of slaves ;[26] in " Crown " trials the expressions
freeman and villain may as well be omitted, they are
almost matters of courtesy ; a new departure appears only
when benefice of clergy is pleaded. Even in a civil suit
a villain may stand upon his right against any one but his
lord, and all the assizes will proceed in regard to him unless
the specific exception,—" the plaintiff is my villain, and I
need not answer him,"—is put forward by the defendant.
Still third persons may stumble against the peculiarities
of villainage, because, though they cannot avail themselves
of them, these peculiarities may be brought forward as a
screen by the villain himself : as a defendant he may say
that he is not capable of answering in his own person being
a villain, and transfer the action to his lord.[27] This is the
result of a second conception which is very different from
the one that a villain is free against everybody but his lord,
of the conception, namely, that a villain does not own
anything himself, but only possesses as much as his lord
suffers him to use and enjoy.[28]

In this way we are led to a second aspect of villainage
as a condition of serfdom devoid of any proper civil rights.
Civil disabilities The lord is the real owner of everything which
a villain has, and if the lord chooses to take
his own, the villain has no means of preventing it. The
courts will not listen to any claim or complaint of a villain

against his lord, and will dismiss the plaintiff without
entering into the material questions raised by his action.
on the formal ground of an " exception of villainage." [29]
There are still traces of a different view in feudal jurisprudence, there still exist records of early decisions which
recognise and protect at least some rights of free men
holding in villainage, but these decisions are inspired by
earlier principles which are losing their force : [30] they do not
prevail against the main current of jurisprudence which
knows no more of free ceorls and of contractual relations
between the rural settler and the landlord, but proceeds
from the assumption that villains are all alike and have
no actionable rights against the lord.

Consequences of a third conception are also visible. Villains
by condition belong to the lord in their bodies and persons.
Personal He may do with them what he pleases provided
villainage he does not kill or maim them.[31] They have no
leave to go away from him, even should they renounce their
holding or be without holding. He may use them as
labourers and servants ; he may sell them the right of
leaving the manor and staying abroad ; [32] they will have to
buy their own blood when they marry their daughters.
It is true that all these traits are characteristic of personal
villainage, and should not hang about those who are personally free though holding in villainage. But it is very difficult
to keep up such distinctions, and though they are clearly
recognised in law, we see from the Hundred Rolls that the
tendency of social evolution was to make all villains alike ;
—hundred after hundred appears in which all villains pay
merchet and are subjected to servile customs, and thus
one of the clues to a distinction between the two classes
disappears.[33]

Such are the complex foundations of the law of villainage.
We have lost sight of the distinct groups whch went to
the making of the class, and of the peculiar Domesday
estimates of the tenements. What we have before us is
a kind of serfdom in which theoretical disabilities are miti-
gated by custom and practical considerations.

The rightless condition of the villain in regard to the lord

is the juridical basis of the whole construction. It would
be wrong to define it as praedial servitude or ascription
to the glebe.   There is nothing in law to bind a villain to
particular plot of ground : he may be transferred to-morrow
to another plot, he may be sold out of the manor or bought
and settled in the manor ; he may be deprived of one part
of his tenement or of the whole of it, he may be " com-
mandeered " to work on the manorial farm.[34]   Even if we
take into account the customary connexion of villains with
their holdings, it must be remembered that it did not go
further than to bind the chief of a servile household to a
tenement ; all other members of his household were liable
even by custom to be transferred to other places, and thus
" origin " or " nativity " would not go further than to
establish a sort of connexion between them and a particular
manor where they had been hatched ; [35] a connexion convenient for the purpose of proving their villain status, but
not legally binding in any way.   As a matter of fact, the
staff of personal attendants and manorial servants was
recruited by the lord from among his villains : they belonged to him as persons, and were not merely attached
to land which belonged to him.   This last could only be
said of free men possessed of villain tenements, but even
in regard to those the idea of praedial servitude may be
misleading.   Their condition can be described as praedial
servitude in so far as their duties were imposed in respect of the holdings, but there was no legal tie between
them and their holdings, though there certainly was an
economic one : it may have been convenient for them to
till their land even at the cost of villain services, but they
could throw over their tenure if they pleased, and their
children were not bound legally to their birthplace ; on
the other hand, their tenements were held by servile customs and under servile disabilities quite as much as those
of downright villains.   Altogether, the attempts which
have been sometimes made to establish an exact equation between villainage and the colonate of the later
Roman empire are hardly to the point. They do not
take notice of the fundamental fact that the colonate

was a compulsory institution binding both sides, binding
the tiller as well as the landowner, and guaranteed in its
conditions by the State.

In the case of mediaeval villains, as we have seen, personal
subjection was expressed by exactions of various kinds
Personal which had no foundation in the use of the
exactions tenement. Such was merchet, the fine on
the marriage of the daughter, which in some localities was
extended to sons. This extension was only defensible
on the ground that the lord might levy a tax on all chief
occurrences in the life of his serfs, but the ordinary merchet
had a somewhat different colouring. It probably originated
in ancient times from a participation by the lord in payments made to the kindred for their woman, a participation
which ultimately became a monopoly. Besides, the merchet
got a special extension when the married woman went out
of the manor, the lord losing his rights over her and her
offspring : in such cases merchet was a kind of redemption
of eventual and actual rights, and was accordingly increased.
The same would be the case when a villain was made a
clerk and thereby emancipated. Some customs curiously
couple a fine paid on selling a calf or a nag with the merchet
for marrying a daughter ; and the motive may be the
same—a transfer of property out of the range of the lord's
power. Another characteristic outcome of villain tenure
was the payment of heriot on the death of the tenant.[36]
This exaction was quite distinct from the fine paid by the
heir on entering the tenement, the so-called relief. Heriot
arose from the assumption that the tenement had been
provided with stock by the lord, and that in fact all the
chattels belonging to a villain were his lord's, and liable
to be resumed at pleasure. In mitigation of such a practice
of resumption the heriot came in, implying the surrender
of the best horse or ox. In feudal times the heriot was a
servile custom, as we have said, but it was not servile by
history or by nature : it had grown out of a resumption
of loaned goods which might have taken place in any tenement however free. We know of the " Heregeatu " of
Saxon earls and bishops consisting of warhorses and

armour ; and this once more reminds us that the law of
tenure had common roots in the case of noble and of base
tenements : there was the element of precarious grant in
both.

Both as an object of property, and as a subject of power
the villain could be taxed at the lord's will.[37]   There was
nothing to prevent the owner of the manor from imposing
a tax on the villain population of his estate, and the amount
of the tax would be dictated by his own discretion.   And,
lastly, the duty of serving as a reeve at the lord's command
was also deemed a mark of villainage, because such an
office took up much time, placed the holder of it in direct
intercourse with the steward and exposed him to all sorts
of unpleasant and unforeseen requirements.

But although in this way the formula of disability was
by no means a dead letter or a meaningless fiction, it would
Custom of the be preposterous to look to it as the one regu-
manor lating factor of rural life.   The very root of
villainage lay in the impossibility for owners and lords
to work their dependents at their will and pleasure.   Feudal
law could lay as much stress as possible on the idea that
everything a villain acquired is acquired for his lord, and
that there was nothing to prevent any exactions what-
soever on the part of a lord : villains were in the ordinary
course of things peacefully possessed of their lands, moveables
and money, and the exactions of the lord assumed a fixed
customary character in amount and in kind.   Villains buy
and sell ; sometimes they buy their own emancipation
from their very lord with what is theoretically his money.[38]
They are taxed by the Government in their own chattels.
They transact all sorts of affairs both within the manor and
out of it ; and the laws regulating these transactions, even
when manorial and customary, are similar to the laws
practised in the King's courts.   Actions in the nature
of the assizes of novel disseisin and of mort d'ancestor,
of writs of entry and of common of pasture are sued by
villains in the manorial courts as frequently as by free
people in royal courts.[39] and these minute signs of legal
arrangement are significant proofs of the regularity

by which the relations of the villains were characterised. There is no question of the arbitrary rule of stewards or of the caprice of slaveowners. Whatever violence and oppression may have existed in single cases, the daily life of the peasantry followed a steady and orderly course. The villain has also another name which describes him in this respect : he is called a customer—*consuetudinarius*— and nothing is so important in this particular sphere of national life as the rule of custom. The medium between the privileged and seemingly autocratic position of the military class and the claims of the working class to a tolerable existence is found for a time in the reign of custom, which appropriates a good deal of the labourers' work for the benefit of their master, but still leaves a sufficient margin for their exertions in their own behalf. Villains are not admitted to prosecute in the king's courts, but their standing in the manorial courts is anything but an abject and rightless one : a body of customary law is evolved in all these local tribunals which keeps in close touch with the development of the common law, and paves the way towards the ultimate recognition of the binding character of customs. At no time was the tradition and authority of customary arrangements greater, nor directed towards so close a regulation of all the details of rural life and work, than in the epoch of the theoretical sway of the lord's will. No period has produced such records of customary possession and customary services at the period when the extents and custumals of manorial administration were compiled.

The ambiguous, or let us say the many-sided character of villainage is expressed not only in the contradictory **Tests of** aspects from which its law may be analysed, **villainage** but also in the evolution of the decisive tests by which the condition was established and recognized.[40] The question of the tests of villainage is discussed many a time in the trials as to status and tenure, and a characteristic confusion is noticeable in the opinions of judges, and in the verdicts of inquests as to this matter. Legal learning seemed to have taken hold of a convenient rule by putting forward the theory that villainage was the condition of a

peasant whose services were uncertain, who did not know
to-day what might be required of him to-morrow, who
could be ordered about at the pleasure of his lord. But this
definition was in truth a tautological one : it would amount
to saying that the status of a man was uncertain, if
shown to be uncertain. Or else it had a very slight practical value, because, whatever may have been the talk of
the lawyers and the exceptional meddling of stewards,
a villain nearly always knew exactly what he was to do
to-morrow and next week, and in fact in all the weeks of
the year ; and if there was some option as to the choice of
requirements, these requirements were still regulated by
very explicit and minute customary rules. In truth the test
of uncertainty was more the expression of the possible
result of the enquiry than of the clues from which it had
to start. As a clue, it would have fitted slavery and may
have been suggested by a theoretical opposition between
the uncertain work of a slave and the certain liabilities
of a free man, which remain a matter of agreement even
when base and unpleasant in their material aspect. Cases
could, of course, be decided on this test, if an express agreement could be proved, or, on the contrary, if it could be
shown expressly that people had been taxed at the mercy
of the lord or made to work at random.[41] But what was to
be done in the vast number of cases when the relations
between the parties were traditional and not formally
contractual ; and when, on the other hand, there was no
distinct swerving from customary arrangements ever repeat-
ing themselves in the same way ? The law got hold of two
other clues in such cases : it tried to ascertain whether the
people in question had been subjected to the incidents of
personal villainage, to merchet, the payment of toll on the
sale of animals, serving as reeve, etc. This would establish
a presumption that the stock of the men concerned in the
trial was villain by blood. But the very fact that such
a presumption had an important bearing on the question
of status produced a very undesirable extension of these
incidents to people who were originally free from them :
what began by being a taint of particular persons came to

be a feature common to all the peasants dwelling in certain counties and hundreds. The other eventuality presented itself when there were no personal incidents to go by. Men might be free from paying merchet or paying fines on the sale of their nags, and still might be implicated in villainage by reason of their tenure. Then the characteristic test of services was applied : people were made out to be labourers subjected to base and servile work. What was deemed to be such work ? Setting aside work by agreement, villain service was deemed to be agricultural service, when base or complete. Work with the fork and flail, spreading manure, cleansing drains and removing refuse were deemed forms of particularly base work establishing a presumption of villainage. Week-work in agricultural service extending to a regular exploitation of a peasant's household by the lord, was also deemed a villain's service. Occasional customs of agricultural service, such as were quite common among the smaller freemen and socmen, were not sufficient to establish villainage. Still the inference seems to be that after the Conquest, in the time of Domesday and of the manorial settlement, a treatment of such questions fatal to the legal standing of a great mass of the peasantry came into force. Villainage was assumed, and its consequences in regard to legal disabilities and refusal of protection by the courts were drawn on the strength of the general idea that customary tenure burdened with agricultural services was *prima facie* villain tenure. Such a rule must have played havoc with many men who had been considered free and enjoyed legal protection in Old English times ; but it was quite in keeping with the main principles of feudal society, which placed so much stress on the character of services.

Roughly speaking, villains were peasants, as freemen were knights or rent-paying tenants. And, after all, the very distinction between villains born and freemen holding in villainage seems to point to the same train of thought. It was not so much personal qualifications or disqualifications which produced villainage : it did exist apart from the personal qualifications ; its root was the possession of land by base agricultural services. The villain was primarily a peasant, and as such surrendered by feudal conquest to the discretion of his lord and the protection of local custom.

We must not leave the subject of villainage without taking notice of the fate of small tenements during the feudal period. In law there was nothing to distinguish a **Small tenements** cottager and the holder of a croft or plot from a virgater, both were villains or freeholders as the case might be, and in the numerous trials as to status and tenure no distinction whatever is made in regard to the size of the tenement. Most cottagers were, in fact, villains or serfs. As to the *bordarii* of Domesday, we can recognise their successors both among the villains and among the free tenants of the Hundred Rolls : [42] a number of these small holders had succeeded in emancipating themselves. But the progress of emancipation seems to have been more rapid among this group of the peasantry than among the shareholders possessed of ploughteams ; nor is this fact an astonishing one, as the customary arrangement of the manor was chiefly built up on the basis of the regular plough holdings or freeholdings (*terra in campis*), while the small tenants stood in a loose relation to it, and there was no particular reason for holding them to villain services.

The remarkable history of the small tenants is well worth consideration in many respects, though it has been hardly appreciated rightly by modern scholars. The *bordarii* class, as I should like to call it in agreement with the Domesday inquest, had evidently a very important part to play in the economic life of the manor, although no distinct legal position was assigned to it. The crofters and holders of plots represented two requisites of first-rate magnitude : though their tenements if taken singly were scattered and insignificant ; they furnished the chief contingent of agricultural labourers and their situation in regard to the cultivation of their patches of land was an individualistic one. These observations follow from the insufficient size of their tenements and from their being cut off to a great extent from the advantages appendant to the plough-holdings. They could seemingly send their cattle to the common pasture

and they were entitled to use wood for building, repairs
and fuel, but 'they certainly had no part in the use of
meadows, and it is doubtful whether they could make use
of the fallow pasture in the fields which were partitioned
among their neighbours. However that may be, it is clear
that a patch of five acres was a poor provision for a household,
especially as its holder had no regular means of joining his
neighbours in the formation of a plough team. Nothing
was left for a *bordarius*, if he was not merely a member
of a shareholder's family endowed with an extra plot of
his own, but to cultivate his land as an orchard with spade
and hoe, to use it as a little dairy, a smithy, and to
look out for hire in the manor and out of it. In the
aggregate, a considerable item in the life of mediaeval rural
society was formed by these people : it appears that around
the regular settlement of the village shareholders a good
many scattered householders were clustered which sent
their hands out to work for hire, managed the accessory
industries of the village, and carried on cultivation by
individualistic processes less dependent on the agrarian
customs of the open field and less burdened with service
in regard to the manors. No wonder that this class is considerably ahead in point of economic development, though
not settled on such a solid basis as the regular plough-
holders.

Small free tenements are more frequent than free
virgates, and the services of *bordarii* or *cottarii*, starting from
mere Monday work, get commuted into money rents at a
very early period. At the same time, it must not be forgotten that the processes which went on among the small
tenants reacted from all sides on the plough peasants and
vice versa ; the overflow of population and energy from
the plough-holdings spent itself chiefly in the formation
of small plots, and the overflow of population and energy
from the small plots went to provide the plough-holdings
and the manorial farm with the hands of which they stood
in need. Thus, cross-currents were created which could not
be directly reflected in the instantaneous photographs of
extents and custumals, but which left conspicuous results

after them hardly to be explained on any other supposition.

Proceeding with our description of classes, we come across a social group whose intermediate position is characterised **Villain socage** by its very name, I mean the group of *villain socmen.* The law writers and the law courts of the thirteenth century were careful to note that there was one set of peasants which did not come under the general rule that villains are rightless as against their lords : such villains under legal protection, termed villain socmen, were to be found in manors which had belonged to the Crown at the time of the Conquest, but had subsequently passed into the hands of private lords. The conditions on which the privileges of Ancient Demesne depended have to be noted carefully : neither ancient royal manors still held by the kings, nor manors which had been in the hands of the kings for some time after the Conquest and then have passed to subjects, are Ancient Demesne.[43] This means that, on the one hand, the King did not want to bind himself by fetters from which his subjects were free, and that, on the other, the mere fact of having belonged, at any time, to the King, was not sufficient to constitute privileged Crown Demesne : there had to be a pre-conquestual element in it in any case. Before offering an explanation of this pheno-menon, let us notice that the exceptional protection bestowed upon the tenants in Ancient Demesne was of a peculiar kind. They were admitted to the public courts for the settlement of disputes with their lords, but they were not admitted to the benefit of actions granted to freeholders. They could not use against their lords, the Great Writ of Right, the Assize of Novel Decision, the Assize of Mort d'Ancestor, the writ *Quare exigit,* or the writ *De communitate pasturae,* but had to content themselves with a bill or plaint to the King and with the grant of a Little Writ of Right, or a writ of *Monstraverunt.*[44] These technicalities had a definite sense : they meant that the peasants who thought themselves aggrieved by their lord had no standing-ground against him in strict and common law, but had to implore one from the equity and the private interest of the King, their former master. Having obtained a favourable hearing of their complaint, they were allowed to use means which were at the disposal of the manorial jurisdiction of the King, and sued for redress in the very manorial court which had come to be held by their present lord, although with these important deviations from the purely manorial course, that the process could be taken up to the public courts and went on under their inspection, and that even in the manorial stage the lord appeared as a defendant in his own court. These two deviations formed the dividing line between a trial on the basis of villain socage and the examination of complaints against stewards and officers which could arise in the court of any royal manor, even if it was not Ancient Demesne in the sense of having been granted to a private lord.[45] The case being such, it seems at first glance that the peculiar and exceedingly valuable privilege of Ancient Demesne was merely the outcome of the special grace and interest taken by the King in his former subjects. But the second qualification, the fact that merely demesnes of Old English formation were admitted to it, shows that there was yet another idea underlying this institution. This idea is clearly expressed in the law books,[46] and fits into the complexity of facts which have come down to us from the social evolution of those centuries. It amounts to a recognition of the fact that it would be a hardship to deprive the tenants of manors which had been held by the Crown in the time before William the Conqueror, of the recourse to public tribunals in the settlement of disputes, and of the consequent legal guarantees as to tenures and services which they had enjoyed in Old English times : they ought to continue in the same state as their ancestors, and the courts have to see that their holdings are not wrested from them, nor their services increased. They are villains by nature of their rural services and manorial subjection, but they are socmen at the same time because their services are certain and safeguarded by law courts. In this way, the loss of legal protection which is so characteristic of villainage in general, is arrested in the case of these privileged villains as a consequence of conquest which ought not to apply to the ancient tenants of the King. The whole institution is interesting from several points of view : it professes to set before us the material conditions of rural life as they existed in the age of Edward the Confessor ; it is built up on the consideration that the refusal of the courts to interfere in disputes between lords and peasants is an innovation from after the Conquest, and it attaches clearly the quality of tenure by agricultural work to villainage.

There is even a curious train of reminiscences of the fact that if legal interference was to be practised in regard to relations between lord and peasant, it had to distinguish between different classes of the peasantry, and, while protecting the villain as a former ceorl, had not to meddle with the power of the master over slaves. Attempts to distinguish between these classes in manors of Ancient Demesne are made in the thirteenth and fourteenth centuries,[47] but they are lame and confused, and no wonder, as the ancient divisions had been mixed up in the mould of villainage.[48] Of course, the privileges of Ancient Demesne were so conspicuous and great that there are constant attempts on the part of the peasantry of all sorts of manors to obtain the rights of villain socage.

By the side of villain socage, stands free socage, and the reason for distinguishing it from ordinary free tenure **Free socage** seems to be historical. Free socmen, or socmen without any adjunct, are customary freeholders who have obtained their position and name by tradition cf free stock and possession without any expressed beginning by grant and feoffment,[49] and with the idea that they were free owners subjected to soke, to political lordship, and not tenants or settlers on a landowner's land. In this sense, those very persons who are termed villains in the Domesday of Kent are sometimes designated as socmen by later records.[50] In many cases they are burdened with some rural services, although their obligations in this respect appear accessory when compared with the work imposed on villains in the same localities. Anyhow, their work is certain because their tenure has been recognised and protection granted by the courts, and as to the motives of such a recognition, besides a vague tradition and a name, the consideration of the accessory character of their services may have played a great part. The line between them and the villains was drawn to some extent in an arbitrary manner, and it is only too likely that people of substantially the same condition were entered right and left of this line among the wolves and among the lambs. But such is the nature of all sharp social distinctions, and the more important the consequences are, the more relentlessly the decisive line has to be drawn at some fatal moment of history.

That the difference between a socman and a freeholder is not a material one may be gathered, among other circumstances, from the fact that the tenure of the socman, socage, was also the main tenure of the freeholder. It has only to be said that free tenure is wider than socage as it includes, besides, burgage tenure, the military fief, the tenure by sergeanty, and, in one sense, the tenure by frank almoign. All these are certain, therefore free, and protected by Magna Charta and the Common Law. But the other forms of free tenure have all a certain special adjunct which gives them their peculiar cast : they are complicated by military or ecclesiastical obligations.[51] As for burgage, it is only a variety of socage and distinguished from it by its connexion with a privileged town, a borough. Socage remains the typical free tenure, the holding in which the services are certain, whether they take the form of rent or of services in kind. In this sense, socage is primarily a holding by contract, by definite agreement.

Besides these cases of express contract and the tradition of socmen as free members of a soke or free owners under **Molmen** soke, it is interesting to notice the existence of a deeply rooted view, according to which free tenure is the holding by rent service. It is quite common to find in the surveys and extents that tenants paying rent are described as more free or even simply as free, in contrast with tenants who have to work.[52] From this point of view, molmen are freer than workmen, and this is no mere word-play, because the necessity of performing work placed the person burdened with it, in the condition of a subordinate to be ordered about by the stewards during so many days a week and perhaps half the year, if taken all round, while the obligation to pay a rent merely meant the paying in of the charge on specified days without any further personal complications. Besides, buying off services in money took partly the shape of getting rid of some of the more hateful and cumbersome duties, such as merchet, for instance, and thus appeared as a kind of emancipation by instalments.. These observations have a bearing on the historical evolution of peasant holdings, both in their passage from the Old English age to the feudal period, and in their transition from the feudal period to later times. At the Conquest, one of the tests for classifying tenures as free or unfree seems to have been their position in regard to rent and to work, and in the fourteenth century one of the most potent factors which brought about the dissolution of villainage was the commutation of services for money.

Another feature indirectly connected with the conception of villainage as the workman's tenure, is the fact that persons of villain condition who had to perform duties not included in the ordinary routine of rural work, but called forth by requirements of the government, are deemed free. Such was the case of peasants who had to represent the township in the hundred, in the county court and before the assizes.[53] This representation was usually a thing settled once for all, and bound up with the possession of distinct holdings. The hundreders who had to attend on all these occasions, were said to defend the township by their suit, and to hold their tenements by suit of court. They were deemed and called free, because they were liberated from the ordinary drudgery of their neighbours, and no doubt this customary freedom would establish a presumption for their being treated as free in case of dispute with the lord. And still, historically, these men came of the same stock with all the villains around them.

All these facts point in one direction, namely, to the conclusion that the distinctions between free and unfree, between socage and villainage, were largely a creation of the Conquest, and that the hard and fast lines drawn by

feudal jurisprudence between the people living under
manorial customs, and the people under the direct protection
of the King's courts have produced artificial simplification
and concentration of classes which had been developing in
very different grooves; although the basis is the broad
economic difference between people burdened by agricultural work and people free from it.

There remains to be considered one more group of the
population of the manors, namely, the officers and servants
Servants and of the lord. This administrative staff was of
Stewards great importance in the economic arrangement
of the manorial institutions, although it was not recognized as a separate order by common law. Stewards
and beadles were either free or villains in their personal status, either holding in villainage or holding freely,
or not holding at all, in their relations to land. The
class which is characterised by the name of *ministeriales* in
the German surveys and law documents does not legally
exist in England. And, nevertheless, it exists economically
and plays a very conspicuous part in the life of the whole.[54]
It was necessary to provide for the discipline, the control
of labourers, the holding and auditing of accounts, and
numerous servants drawn from different classes are engaged
in this work. The larger the manor, the more powerful
the lord and the more extensive his possessions, the more
complex and influential his administrative staff becomes.
We have already spoken of the divers branches of office into
which this staff was divided to meet the requirements of a
large estate. But we must now cast a glance at the personal
conditions in which it was placed in order to perform its
work, and at its relations to other groups of manorial
society. Occasional labourers were generally hired and
the price of their board and lodging was subtracted from
their wages. Permanent servants must have also received
some remuneration for their services, though their wages
seem to have been very small, while their board and clothing
were comparatively good, and were provided at the expense
of the lord. These servants were usually drawn from the
subject population of the manor and were enlisted to do

their work by command. Skilled artizans, hunters and
men-at-arms had to be often engaged from other places,
and were paid high wages or attracted by other boons. In
the case of the higher servants, officers and accountants,
a very common expedient was to provide them with plots
of land, and even with regular holdings, from which they
could draw profits in remuneration for their services. We find
ploughmen, stewards, porters, smiths among the tenants,
and their tenements are free, in so much as they are un-
encumbered by customary work.[55] Sometimes these relations give rise only to temporary leaves, but this may be
the beginning of actual free tenure, if the charge and the
tenement remain long in the same hand or even go by
hereditary succession ; a very common thing in those times.
The riding men of the Old English period go naturally over
into Norman times, but as the laws of military tenure and
of sergeanty get developed, the higher standing among
them are generally enlisted among the military class and
settle on definite conditions of knight's service, while the
smaller mostly live in the castles with their lords, and a
few are quartered in separate tenements on the land
of the manor. In great administrations, a complicated
feudality springs up, fees of the kitchen, of the cellar, of the
gate are formed, and it becomes no easy matter to hold
this presumptuous and grasping population in awe and
discipline. It was partly in the lord's own interest that the
power and influence of the administrative staff was matched
by liberties and customs of the subject population. The
enrolments and the surveys made on the strength of sworn
manorial inquests served not only as records of the various
duties exacted by the lord from his villains and free tenants,
but also as a check on the malversations and encroachments
of the stewards and officers. This side of manorial life
is better understood when examined in its relation
to political organisation, as a unit of local government.

**Communal or-
ganisation for
administrative
purposes**

The part it played in this respect comprises
both its functions as a representative of central
government in the locality, and the expression
of the private power exercised by it over the

subject population. To begin with, the manorial arrangement was, of course, taken into account and used by the king and the estates in order to enforce the common needs of governments. It played its part in military organisation, in the collection of taxes, in the administration of justice and in police.[56]

It is characteristic of all these functions of the manor that, with the exception of military service, that they are all organised on a collective or communal basis. In most cases it is not the manor itself which appears on the scene, but the township or vill underlying it. The local unity does not act through the personality of the lord of the manor, but through chosen or customary representatives of a community, a " commune " of its members. And when we come to look at the organisation of the manor for its own home purposes, to the framing of enactments, the settlement of disputes and the infliction of penalties, we find the same communal character carried out in all minutest details. There is no question of enforcing the rule of a local potentate, of an absolute ruler and owner ; there are not even exceptional attempts to manage the business of the manor on the principle of a single will pervading the whole and of secondary administrative powers derived from it. We hear often of confiscations by the lord, of injunctions made in his name, of coercive measures taken by his officers, of extortions and oppression by his servants, but we never hear of a single manor governed as an estate is governed nowadays by the single will and disposition of the owner. With a regularity which presents the exact counterpart of the consistent parcelling up of the country into manors, the chief traits of the customary self-government of the manorial community are repeated over and over again ; surely a brilliant expression of the fact that we have to deal, not with the varying arrangements of private owner- ship, and not with the arbitrary sway of local despots, but with local forms of organisation, which are worked out under the constant pressure and control of a central government, and on the firm ground of an immemorial tradition of communal action. Before proceeding to examine

single points I cannot help dwelling a little on this remarkable phenomenon, which though certainly not unknown
to modern investigators, has hardly been appreciated at
its full value.   When in the feudal ages we find the country
cut up into manors, the Domesday survey cataloguing place
after place as manors, and the records of the courts treating
all cases of ownership from the point of view of the free
tenement in a manor, we are struck by the strength of the
idea of personal ownership pervading such an arrangement,
and feel inclined to trace it back as far as possible, to assume
that private will and private interest are the deepest
foundations of social life in England, and that everything
else is only a modification and combination of private
wills and interests.   But it is worth while to reflect a little
on the astounding spectacle of the communal structure
of all these manorial cells which look so individualistic
from the outside.   Why did the landowner never try to
establish a system of thoroughly personal government ?
Why did the courts and representative institutions recur
over and over again to local bodies which were assumed
to be under the complete sway of the manorial lord ?   Local
custom seems to obtain in this respect a similar force of
uniform organisation to that which feudal jurisprudence
with its writs and decisions exercised in the royal courts,
only that the secret of its power and of its consequent action
is more difficult to unravel, as the processes by which
uniformity is obtained in this case take place in numberless
secluded corners of England where petty potentates are
declared to be owners and rulers.

In two important respects the manorial organisation
is certainly not beyond control : as a centre
Court leet
of franchises, jurisdiction and police it is
a part of political machinery and under the direct
influence of the central government and of its judges.
The Hundred Rolls and the *Placita quo warranto* testify
to Royal supervision over the political attributions of
manorial lords.[57]   And from this point of view it is
material that the government considers a communal
organisation and representative institutions as a constant
and necessary element of the manor, whose administrative

structure is moulded on that of the township and already clearly indicated by the practice of the hundred and county court. The court leet, the committee of five or six hundredors, and the twelve representatives of an urban vill proceed from political arrangements which were in full play in the later Saxon age, but were fitted into the manorial system during the feudal period. A manorial lord would have lost most lucrative franchises, if he was not able to show that he had sufficient elements for the constitution of a leet, for the judgment and punishment of certain offenders ; and, of course, no royal court or commission of enquiry would have deemed his personal interference sufficient in such respect. A court must be a court in earnest, and the first factor to make it such was a sufficient number of suitors.[58]

The second reason which imposed a customary constitution on every lord was the fact that he was not a mere **Court baron** owner of serfs, but that he had to deal with free tenants as well. It was his recognised right to hold a court for the settlement of their disputes amongst one another, and for the transaction of conveyancing business for them within the precincts of the manor. This was the foundation of his court baron. But though this was a privilege which accrued to him as a part of his lordship, it could be set in motion and realized only on the condition of the actual or virtual participation of the free suitors for whom the court was held. No free-holder would have submitted to personal commands and arbitrary decisions of a lord whose free tenants were his peers, and stood on an equal footing with him in the king's courts. The court baron was of necessity a collegiate court, as the court leet was of necessity a communal court ; the first for feudal reasons and the second for political reasons. And when this point is reached it will become evident that the theory of later lawyers, that some free tenants were necessary to constitute a manor is not without its reasonableness.[59] The presence of free tenants made the arrangement of customary self-government not only optional but compulsory. The lord had no hold on them but by the law of the free, and had to submit to conditions which guaranteed their freedom and a fair representation of their interests.

But the most significant item in this manorial arrangement is provided by the fact that it is not merely when the **Customary court** manor comes into direct contact with the state, or when it deals with the civil affairs of its free tenants that it forms courts and acts on collegiate and communal lines, but also and most often when it settles questions of internal economy and deals with the requirements and offences of villains. The customary court is quite as much a court in the communal sense as the court leet, and more than the court baron, which is more collegiate than communal. It is true that the lord, or his *alter ego*, the steward, is declared to be judge of this court, but he is never single judge, he acts always with a court composed of free and villain suitors ; customs are declared by these and not by him ; inquests and juries are empanelled from among them ; the agrarian business of the customary court is entirely of their making ; and altogether the communal life of the township, the *villata*, appears to be as energetic as the action of the Old English township had been.[60] And though there is such a wide distance in point of right between villains and free tenants, they appear together as suitors of the customary courts, and take part in the management of affairs as members of the same community. We may notice how the free tenants work out separate privileges in many respects ; they object to sitting on inquests, they act sometimes as judges when villains only are admitted to make presentments ; they claim separate juries to try their cases ; they are privileged in regard to the means of executing manorial judgments ; they refuse to act as permanent manorial officers, though their acting as exceptional overseers is often noted. Still both elements of the court are indissolubly knitted together,[61] and indeed the differentiation between free and villain suitors appears in some respects to be a later one ; at any rate, there is no common theory as to differences in their attributions, and such differences appear in various modes and degrees according to local custom, and sometimes do not appear

at all. Not less significant is the fact, that the various
manorial courts are later ramifications of the one *halimote*,
originally the only meeting for the arrangement of all sorts
of affairs.[62]   Later on the halimote is especially taken as the
customary court, and it is not unimportant that such should
be the case, as the halimote certainly includes villains, and
if it was the main court of the manor the customary constitution of the manor must be traced to the development
of ideas which include the villains.   On the face of the very
terminology of our evidence this traditional root of communal action is afforded by the township, the *villata*,
round which the manor clung as a shell.

Thus from several points of view we come always to the
same conclusions. The economic development of mediaeval
rural life is to be accounted for by the formation in Old
English society of a village community of shareholders
which cultivated the land on the open-field system, and
treated all other requisites of rural life as appendant to it.
The evolution of individualistic husbandry and of political
protection produced the growth of lordships which culminated
after the Conquest in the arrangement of the manor, a
complex institution partaking of the character of an estate
and of a unit of local government.   The influence of the
Conquest and of the subsequent formation of common
law was decisive in submitting society to a system of personal rights and relations ; but underneath this system
ancient principles of communal action and communal
responsibility were still fully alive.

BOOK III

NOTES TO CHAPTER I

1. "Domesday and Beyond," **3.** Cf. On Legal Principles in Domesday Book, "English Society in the Eleventh Century," pp. 219 ff.

2. *Round*, " Feudal England," 44 ; " Domesday and Beyond," 11.

3. Dd. ii. 57, b : Et hæc terra quam modo tenet G. fuit in abbatia de Berchingis . . . sed ille qui tenuit hanc terram fuit tantummodo homo antecessoris Goisfridi, et non potuit istam terram mittere in aliquo loco nisi in abbatia. Dd. ii. 250, b : huic manerio adjacent semper 4 homines de omni consuetudine, et alii 4 ad socham tantum. Dd. i. 249, b : Medietas istius hominis fuit antecessoris Bainguard commendationis tantum, et alia medietas S^{ti} Edmundi cum dimidia terra. Cf. " Domesday and Beyond," 68 ff.

4. Dd. i. 58. Pater Tori tenuit T.R.E. et potuit ire quo voluit, sed pro sua defensione se commisit Hermanns episcopo, et Tori Osmundo episcopo similiter. Cf. *Round*, " Feudal England," 28.

5. The earliest attempts to establish a direct relation between land tenure and service are connected with grants of *loanland* for term of years. C.D., 1287. Cf. " Domesday and Beyond," 305 ff.

6. *Freeman*, " Norman Conquest," iv. 25 ; v. 21.

7. *Round*, " Feudal England," 295 ff.

8. Dd. ii. 163 : In frainghes unus liber homo 20 acrarum terra et valet 16 den. De hoc habuit suus (Willelmi de Warenne) ante. cessor comendationem tantum, et Stigandus socam. ii., 124 : In ailuertuna 2 liberi homines T. R. E., unus et dimidius Alnoth, et dimidius Aluredi commendatus. Has tenuit Rogerus Comes quando se forisfecit, post Godricus in manu regis. Modo tenet Aitartus, homo Rogeri Bigot, medietatem unius, et 15 reclamat ad feudum episcopi Baiocensis. Dd. i. 36, b : In Copededorne hundredo tenet Seman unam virgatam terre, quam tenuit de rege Edwardo, sed ex quo venit Willelmus rex in Angliam seruiuit Osualdo reddendo ei 20 denarios. Hic se potuit vertere quo voluit T. R. E. Dd. i. 210 : In Estone tenet Willelmus de Caron dimidiam hidam et dimidiam virgatam de episcopo. . . . Hanc terram tenuit Aluuinus homo episcopi Lincolniensis, et quod voluit de ea facere potuit. Soca tamen semper episcopi fuit. Dd. i. 287, b : In brunestada unus liber homo 15 acrarum, et in Horseia unus liber homo 12 acrarum. Ex his non habuit Ailwinus suus (Rogeri Bigot) antecessor etiam commendationem t. r. E., et tamen eos reuocat ad suum feudum ex dono Regis, quia ille Ailwinus habuit commendationem ex eis t. r. W.

9. Dd., i. 63, b ; i. 1, etc.

11. *F. W. Maitland* has tried to establish a distinction between villains and socmen on the basis of taxation : the first are said to have been so poor that the Government had to apply to their lords in order to collect dues from them, while the latter were dealt with in person (" Dd. and Beyond," 141). This distinction rests, however, on the doubtful proposition, that the taxes of villains were collected by their lords, and cannot be upheld if we come to the conclusion that both in regard to assessment and to collection the townships were in direct communication with the sheriffs and the Exchequer.

11. " Domesday and Beyond," 396,

12. See e.g. the descriptions of Swafham and Dullingham, Inquis. Cantabrig. 12 ff. ; 17 f.

13. " Domesday and Beyond," 120.

14. Prof. *Tait,* " Engl. Hist. Rev.," 189, 7, 770 f.

15. *Round,* " Engl. Hist. Rev.," 1900, 293 f.

16. E.g., Dd. i. 272: In Neuuebold cum 6 Berewitis, Witintune, Brimintune, Tapetune, Cestrefeld, Buitorp, Echintune, etc. Cf. i. 230 : huic manerio pertinent subsequentia membra.

17. Istos homines posuit Ingilricus ad suam halam. The hall is the centre of the home farm. Cf. i. 12 ; Ipse abbas tenet Setlingas manerium sine halla, quod se defendit pro 6 solins. Terra est XI carucis. Nichil in dominio. Ibi 30 villani habent 10 carucas. Dd. i. 285, C : Habuerunt Elmer, Elmis, Osbern, Grim, Edric, Stenulf quisque aulam suam, et unusquisque unam bovatam terrae. i. 164 : In Lindene fecit comes Willelmus unum manerium de 4 terris, quas ab eorum dominis accepit. ; i. 208 : Dicunt . . . terram Aluuini Chit de Westone per se fuisse manerium et non pertinuisse ad Kembaltone, sed tamen eum fuisse hominem Haroldi comitis. The fact that a manor is commonly considered as an organisation of labour services is clearly apparent in cases when there was some notable irregularity in the arrangement of work. e.g., Dd. i. 182, C (Elmelie, Herefordshire) : Ibi 4 hidas geldabiles. Terra est 8 carucis. Alterius villae homines laborant in hac villa et reddunt 37 solidos et 8 denarios. ; i. 181 : In Niware sunt 2 hidae et dimidia quae in Bremesse hundredo conveniebant et operabantur. What can the manors mean but small estates in cases like the following : Dd. i. 269, 5 (in Blackeburne hundred). ad hoc manerium adjacebant 28 liberi homines, tenentes 5½ hidas et 40 carucatas pro 28 maneriis.

18. Examples—" Domesday and Beyond," 116 f.

19. *Maitland,* " Manorial Rolls " (Selden Soc., ii.), 49, as to the
honour of Broughton belonging to the Abbey of Ramsey. In
Domesday Broughton is entered as one of the ordinary manors of
the Abbey. Dd. i. 204.

20. Comp., e.g., the description of *Horseth,* Cambridgeshire in
the Rot. Hundr., ii. 420 ff ; with Inqu. Cantabr. 29 ff ; and Dd. i.
103, b; 198 ; 199, b.

21. Dd. i. 230. Cf. " Domesday and Beyond," 115.

22. In these cases the *villata* or township appears as the body of
tenants in the manor in contrast with the lord and his stewards.
Maitland, " Manorial Rolls," 36, 90, 98, etc.

23. " Domesday and Beyond," 367.

24. The Aston and Cotè case. " Villainage in Engl.," 392, 450.
Maitland " Law Quart. Rev.," ix. 216 ff.

25. " History of English Law," i. 599 ff.

NOTES TO CHAPTER II

1. *Bracton,* f. 432, C.   " History of Engl. Law," i. 212 ff.

2. *Britton,* ii. 13 : Villenage est tenement de demeynes de chescun
seignur, baille a tenir a sa volunté par vileins services al oes le
seignur.

3. " Hist. Engl. Law," i. 333.

4. " Ib.," i. 335.

5. Two conflicting currents may be traced in the law on this
subject : the feudal and the public one, if one may be allowed to
use the latter expression.   The writ *cessavit per biennium,* although
suggested in form by Canon law, proceeds in substance from the
feudal notion that a fief is a tenancy held under certain conditions
and liable to forfeiture if these conditions are not fulfilled.   On
the other hand the Royal Courts were apt in their exercise of early
Common Law to regard the holder of a free tenement as endowed
with a right independent of the feudal nexus, and to treat the
enforcement of feudal services as if they were personal obligations
guaranteed by a gage.

6. " Hist. Engl. Law," i. 288, 299, 332.

7. *Maitland,* " Manorial Rolls," 29, 39, 121, 122.

8. " Villainage in England," 371.

9. *Madox,* " Formulare Anglicanum," 54.

10. The distinct formulation of the view that the lord is the real
owner of the waste belongs to the later half of the feudal period.

11. The lords often recognised binding customs, even when they
seek to enforce their private rights : e.g., the formulae in use when
a trespass in the lord's private wood was brought to the notice of a
manorial court are indirectly characteristic of the force of custom
in regard to common of pasture and wood. *Maitland,* " Court
Baron " (Selden Soc., iv.), 43 : des arbres coupes en le boys les

seignur ; le forester ly aresona e demanda par ky counge il coupa
cel cheyne ; e il y respondit et dit que ben ly lust cele cheyne couper
ou autre merine illukes prendre ans i com de la commune que est
appurtenant a son franc tenement ; le forester ly respondit et
dit que ces fu le seueral boys le seignur. Ib. 41 : de bestes
pestes en Ie pre le seignur—e pur ceo a tort, que la ou il ad suffi-
saunts pasture en la commune de a taunt de bestes et de animalz
com il ad e com il appent de auer solom le fraunc tenement que
il tent de ly en meme la ville. In both cases the contention is
between a lord and his free tenant, but it starts from the contrast
between the rights of the lord in regard to land held in severalty
and his position as to commons where the customary apportionment
of usages holds good.

12. A Domesday example of pasnagium as a payment. Dd., i. 154b.

13. A conspicuous instance may be found in the account of a trial as to the open fields of Tilgerdesley," Villainage in England," 230.

14. *Maitland*, " Manorial Courts," 170 ; Ricardus juvenis custos porcorum, deputatus per totam villatam in misericordia, quia pascebat plures porcos quam habere debet in separali cum porcis domini.

15. Seebohm considers the consolidation of the holdings as a specific result of manorial organisation.

16. Cartulary of St. Peter of Gloucester (Rolls Series), iii. 213.

17. e.g. *Elton*, " Origins of the English People ; " *Pollock*, " Land Laws," 2 ed., 148.

18. See my paper in the " English Historical Review," April, 1904.

19. " Villainage in England," 205 ; Hist. Engl. Law," i. 166.

20. " Hist. Engl. Law," i. 520.

21. " Hist. Engl. Law," i. 614.

22. *Maitland*, " Manorial Courts," 167 : Ricardus le Fette in misericordia, quia accepit . . . garbas in autumpno per liberacionem prepositi. Plegium tocius ville. Cf. 168.

23. " Villainage in England," 279 ; Cf. Dd., i., 174, b : In Bricstelmestune sunt 10 hidae. Ibi ; 10 villani et 10 bordarii cum 6 carucis, et arant et seminant 6 acras de proprio semine.

24. *Maitland*, " Manorial Courts," 168 : dicunt eciam quod Johannes dictus Lord bonus est domino messarius ad custodiendum oves matrices, et tota villa manucepit pro eo, quod bene et fideliter et cum omnis diligencia eos custodiet et respondebit pro eo. Dicunt eciam quod Johannes filius Johannis atte Grene necessarius est ad custodiendum multones domini, et admissus est, et tota villa manucepit pro eo.

25. See on this subject Madox, Firma burgi, passim, " Hist. Engl. Law," i. 635.

26. Tait, in his remarkable review of Domesday and beyond, refers to the example of Calne, "Engl. Hist. Rev." 1897, p. 774. Cf. Dd., i. 298 : in geldo civitatis sunt 84 carucatae terrae, et unaquæque geldabat quantum una domus civitatis.

27. This is the meaning of the arrangement as understood by the "Hist. Engl. Law," i., 618. The struggle to obtain the farm may be illustrated by the proceedings which took place in Castor, Lincolnshire. Placita Quo Warranto, 411 : presentatum est quod cum convenisset inter homines qui sunt sokemanni domini Regis de soka de Castre ex una parte et quosdam P.M. (et alios) . . consokemannos de eodem soka ex altera, videlicet quod predictus Petrus et alii compromiserunt et se obligaverunt predictis hominibus quod tantum facerent erga dominum Regem, quod dominus Rex faceret eis cartam suam quod haberent predictam socam ad firmam, per quam prius ipsam tenuerunt habendum et tenendum ipsis et heredibus suis imperpetuum . . . impetrarunt cartam ad firmam per 20 annos. "Rot. Hundr.," i. 265 : Yongcastre, soka domini Regis : Dicunt, quod Yongcastre est dominicum manerium domini Regis, et est in manu sua, et valet per annum 50 libras, tenetur per liberos sokemannos. Liberi sokemanni solebant tenere dictum dominicum manerium in capite pro 38 libras 7 solidos et 10 denarios de blanca firma ad scakarium domini Regis per manum eorundem persolvenda, et modo reddunt pro eadem 50 libras per scriptum quod habuerunt de domino Rege Henrico ultimo, patre Regis nunc. "Rot. Hundr," i., 354 : villa de Graham tenetur per liberas sokemannos eodem modo quo dominus Johannes Rex Angliae eam tenuit. Manors held by villains in Surrey, T. R. E. and T. R. W., "Victoria County History," 290, 291 (Dd., i., 34, 36. b). Dd., i. 127. (Wellesdene) : hoc manerum tenent villani ad firmam canonicorum Cf. Dd. III, 5, 7, 67.

28. "Villainage in England," 360.

29. *Maitland*, "Manorial Courts," 172 : Ad istam curiam venit tota communitas villanorum de Bristwalton et de sua mera et spontanea voluntate sursum reddidit domino totum jus et clamium quod idem villani habere clamabant racione commune in bosco domini qui vocatur Hemele et landis circumjacentibus, ita quod nec ipsi villani nec aliqui tenementa sua in posterum tenentes aliquid juris vel clamei racione commune in bosco predicto et landis circumjacentibus exigere, vendicare vel habere poterint in perpetuum. Et pro hac sursum reddicione remisit eis dominus de sua gracia speciali communam quam habuit in campo qui vocatur Estfeld qui jacet in longitudinem ad viam que se extendit de la Rede Putte ad boscum domini qui vocatur Hamele. Remisit eciam eisdem communam quem habuit in bosco eorundem villanorum qui vocatur Trendale, ita quod de cetero idem dominus nulla animalia habeat depascencia in communia supradicta sine in bosco predicto. Concessit

eciam dominus quod villani quam cicius dominus tempore pannagii
intret boscum ad pannagiandum porcos suos in bosco suo de Hamele,
intrant et ipsi cum porcis suis usque ad diem S. Martini.   Prof.
Maitland remarks most appropriately : " the villains of Bright-
waltham, men who were reckoned as personally unfree, nevertheless
constituted a community which held land, which was capable of
receiving a grant of land, which could contract with the lord, which
could make exchange with the lord."   Cf. *Petit - Dutaillis* " Studies
and Notes Supplementary to Stubbs' Constitutional History,"
translated by *W. E. Rhodes*, Manchester, 1908, pp. 4 ff.

30. " Liber Niger de Burgo " (Society of Antiquaries), f. 191 : tota
communa tocius ville metit una die in principio Augusti, ita
scilicet quod quilibet hominum inveniet ea die unum hominem.
" Rot. Hundr.," i. 384 : Thomas ballivas Regis cepit de communitate
ville de Hollebeck pro eodem felone 20 soL   " Rot, Hundr.," i. 275,
308, 497, etc.   Cf. " History of English Law," i. 552.

31. F. ex. " Rot. Hundr.," i. 54 : ibivenit ballivus de Kenet . . .
et tota villata dictum Galfridum et Alanum verberaverunt,
vulneraverunt, etc.

32. " Rot. Hundr.," ii. 666.   Dicunt quod villata de Gomecestre
fecit quamdam purpresturam super regalem viam et appropriavit
sibi de regali via ad valenciam tercias partis unius rode.   Thomas
de Berkele inclusit in villa de Enescerie de regali via et de communa
pasturi ad valenciam unius rode.   Dicunt quod tota *villata* de
Eynesberia fodit in regali via et obstruxit regalem viam ad nocu-
mentum tocius patrie.   Pipe Roll of 12 Henry II, p. 49, quoted
in the " History of English Law," i. 553 ; the township of Maltsby
owes 4 marks for having ploughed up the King's highway.   The
authors of the " History of English Law " think that the fact of
the township being treated as an amerciable unit may have been
produced by the practice of fining townships for neglect of police
duties.   But in the end all these references would still lead to the
primary position that the township was a real unit and not the
product of casual police expedients.

33. *Massingberd*, " Court Rolls of Ingoldmells," 43.   The township presents that John Mareis has injured the King's way to the
detriment of the whole community.   A certain William de Boston
dug a certain pit throwing the land upon his own land, injuring the
common way, when he ought to have thrown it upon the common
way.   " Rot. Hundr.," i., 386 : Prior de H. inclusit quandam
placeam . . . et fecit quoddam conigearium quod solebat esse
commune tote villate.

34. " History of English Law," i. 622 : the community is not
incapable of suing, but it rarely sues, because it has nothing to sue
about.   The fact is true, but the explanation hardly adequate.
Each community had a variety of customary rights and
interests, but it took action to defend them, not so much in the
way of direct litigation before the Royal Courts as by manorial

procedure (presentments, distraints, execution, measures against fresh intrusions and encroachments), or by the action of some individuals belonging to it, or by that of its lord. These were the most convenient ways to follow in view of the individualistic tendencies of the Royal Courts and the customary methods of manorial courts.

35. Placita Quo Warranto, 708. Communitas Villae Salop summonita fuit ad respondendum quo warranto clamat tenere placita corone et habere returnum brevium domini Regis et wayf. in villa Salop. . . . dominus Henricus pater Regis nunc concessit Burgens ibus Salop quod ipsi habeant omnia placita et querelas . . . concessit predictis burgensibus predictam villam ad feodifirmam (pro 44 marcis).

36. *Meitzen,* "Wanderungen," etc.   *Heusler,* "Institutionen des deutschen Privatrechts," i. 266; "History of English Law," i. 619; *Maitland,* "Domesday and Beyond," 350.

37. *Gierke,* "Deutsches Genossenschaftsrecht," ii. 68 ff., 80 ff., 90.

38. *Maitland,* "Domesday and Beyond," 341.

39. The juridical and historical construction given to these matters in the "History of English Law," and in Prof. *Maitland's* "Domesday and Beyond," starts from the following assumptions : 1. The economic ties of open field cultivation had no great or direct importance for the development of village organisation.   2. This organisation was mainly produced by seignorial and governmental pressure.   3. As the Common Law of Royal Courts considers society mainly from the point of view of individual rights and relations the juridical value of communal ideas and institutions is very small. 4. The phenomena of co-operation disclosed by the evidence are easily accounted for on the principles of *reality* and *automatism,* i.e. of a constant and mechanical repartition of duties between holders of certain plots of land.   My statement of the details of township organisation proceeds on different lines, and I may be allowed to sum up its main features in the following manner.   1. The basis of the rights, duties and organisation of the township is to be found in the economic peculiarities of the open field system.   2. Seignorial and governmental pressure may have considerably modified and hardened the township organisation, but it has neither produced it nor can it account for many of its features.   3. The domain of manorial legal custom has as much to be reckoned with in the juridical appreciation of the village community as that of the Common Law of Royal Courts.   4. Reality and automatism may account for a great deal in the perpetuation of customs and practices, but they are entirely unfit to explain the rise and changes of these arrangements.   The element of conscious co-operation and organisation cannot be eliminated from the life of the township. (Cf. "History of English Law," i., 677; "Domesday and

Beyond," 142, 147, 149, 346, 350.) It is not without interest to compare the English evidence with similar continental cases. The comparison with the German Markgenossenschaft has been often made. As to France, see *Flach*, " Origines de l'ancienne France," 103, 131, 137, 155, 332.

40. " Villainage in England," 279 ff.

41. Ibid., 288.

42. Ibid., 291.

43. Ibid., 307.

44. Dd., iii., 7 : et pro 10 hidis de terra heraldi quam villani regis tenent non habet R. geldum. Cf. 19, 25, 67.

45. " Villainage in England," 226.

46. Ibid., 328, 332. Portions of the demesne conceded to small tenants were sometimes called *inlands* because the Old English for demesne had been *inland*.

47. " Abbreviatio Rotulorum Originalium," ii. ; 5 Edw. III, Kanciae, rot. 7, p. 50., quoted by Prof. *Petrushevsky* in his " History of Wat Tyler's Rebellion," ii. 181 (Russian).

NOTES TO CHAPTER III

1. " Domesday and Beyond," 28 ff. Some 25,000 are entered in Domesday. On Social Classes in Domesday Book, cf. " English Society in the Eleventh Century," pp. 403 ff.

2. " Hist. Engl. Law," i. 413.

3. Dd., i. 219b (Nortone) : In dominio sunt 7 hidae, et 3 servi, et 2 ancillae.

4. Dd., i. 89 : (Walintone) . . . de ea sunt in dominio 3 hidae, et ibi 4 carucae et 31 servus, et 53 villani et 61 bordarius cum 25 carucis. Dd., i., 61 (Hingepene) : in dominio sunt 4 carucae, et 10 villani et 15 bordarii cum 7 carucis. Ib. : 20 servi et molinum de 12 solidorum. Cf. i., 4, b ; 31b.

5. Dd., i. 183 (Leine) : ibi tres serui et unus liber bouarius. I. 183, b (Lenhole) : ibi unus servuus et tres bovarii liberi. Ibid. (Alfetune) : ibi 4 hidae geldabiles. In dominio sunt 4 carucae . . . Ibi 6 servi et 5 bovarii. The last example shows that there was no constant ratio between the number of bovarii and the number of ploughs. *Round*, in the " Victoria County History of Essex," i. 362.

6. See the table in *Seebohm's* " English Village Community." There are no *servi* in Yorkshire or in Lincolnshire, 9 per cent. in Kent, but 24 per cent. in Gloucestershire, 18 per cent. in Devon. The reckoning is not exact, being based on Ellis' abstracts, which are not quite trustworthy. Still the figures may stand for purposes of general comparison. " Victoria County History of Worcestershire," i. 276.

7. Dd., i., 38, b. (Brestone): . . . In dominio sunt 2 carucae, et 11 bordarii cum 4 carucis et dimidia. Ibi 4 coliberti et 3 molendina. . . . In eodem hundredo est Dene quae adjacet huic manerio.— De isto manerio (Brestone, and not Dene, as Ellis thought, " Introduction," i., 35) habetur in Wallope 5 villani et unus servus, et unum molinum de 30 denariis, et 2 carucae in dominio, et coliberti (et Bures), ut supra, reddunt consuetudinem aliorum. It is evident that the coliberti rendering the rest of the dues are the four mentioned in Brestone. They are connected with the demesne land, as the serfs in other instances, and the gloss—*buri*, geburs—describes them as agricultural labourers. According to Ellis's abstract, 858 coliberti and 62 boors are mentioned in " Domesday."

8. The emancipation of slaves by testament took mostly the shape of manumissions of whole groups, and it is perhaps to this practice that one may have to look for an explanation of the coliberti.

9. *Pollock*, Land-laws, App. 202.

10. " Villainage in England," 87. Personal manumission comes again to the fore in the fifteenth and sixteenth centuries, when it gets to be the means of drawing profits from people who had attained a tolerably good position in society. *Savine*, The last days of bondage, " Transactions of the R. Historical Society," 1903.

11. *Ellis*, " Introduction to Domesday," gives about 82,600 bordarii.

12. Sometimes the bordarii are connected with the demesne. Dd., i., 175, b. : In Euesham villa, ubi sedet abbatia, sunt et fuerunt semper 3 hidae liberae. Ibi sunt in dominio 3 carucae, et 27 bordarii servientes curiae, et habent 4 carucas. i., 173 : In Tedford habet Rogerus (*Bigot*) in dominio quietam ab omni consuetudine, cui adjacebant t. r. E. 2 carucatae terrae, et modo similiter ; semper 2 carucae in dominio, 20 bordarii, 2 servi, 1 molinum, 13 acrae prati. De supradictis bordariis habet Rex scotum de suo capite tantum. Cf. " Lgg., Willelmi," 17: cil ki ad aveir champestre 30 den. vallant dest duner le den. sein Piere. (Le seignur par 4d. que il donrad, si erunt quites ses bordiers e ses bovers, e ses serjanz). The survey of Middlesex, which assigns hides and fractions of hides to the divers tenants, gives indications as to the state of the bordarii as smaller tenants, e.g., Stibenhale—tenet Hugo de Cerneres subepiscopo 5 hidas et 1 virgatam terrae.—Ibi unus villanus de dimidia hida, et 6 villani de 3 virgatis, et 2 bordarii de dimidia virgata et 3 cotarii de 2 acris et dimidia. In eadem villa tenet uxor Brien—1 villanus de dimidia hide . . . et alter villanus de dimidia hida . . . et 15 bordarii de 10 acris. In eadem villa tenet Ranulfus flambard de episcopo 3 hidas et dimidiam. . . . Ibi in dominio 2 carucae et 3 carucae villanorum. Ibi 14 bordarii de 1½ hida (altogether). . . . In eadem villa tenet Engelbricus canonicus de episcopo 1 hidam et 1 vergatam. Terra est 1 carucae, et ibi est

in dominio. Ibi 1 villanus de 1 vergata et 3 bordarii quisque de 7 acris. Cf. Inquis. Cantabrig., pp. 24, 51, etc.

13. About 5,070 cotarii (or coteri) and 1,749 cotsets according to *Ellis*. Dd., i. 127b: In Tuleham 22 cotarii de dimidia hida (altogether) et 8 cotarii de suis hortis.

14. *Ellis*, "Introduction," 108,407 villani.

15. "Villainage in England," 205 ff.

16. In the famous enactment of Edgar (iv., 8, 13), as to the witnessing of sales of cattle, the tunesmen appear as members of the township in general, without any distinction as to personal status or size of holding.

17. *Liebermann*, "Gesetze der Angelsachsen, Leges Henrici, i., 70, 1: In Westsexa . . . twyhindi. id est villani, wera est 4 librae. Quadripartitus, Ine 18: Regis geneat (id est villanus [colonus fiscalinus]); 22, si tuus geneat, id est [colonus el] villanus; Rectitudines, 2: Villani (geneat) rectum est varium et multiplex.

18. Lgg. Edw. Conf. 12: Manbote de occisis erga dominos quorum homines interfecti erant. Manbote in Danelaga de villano et de sokemanno 12 oras, de liberis hominibus 3 marcas.

19. According to Seebohm's estimate there are 45% of socmen in Lincolnshire, 16% in Norfolk, 5 % in Suffolk, ½ % in Kent, none in the Western and South-Western counties. The uncertainty in the use of these terms is very apparent when we consider the sharp contrasts between neighbouring counties placed in substantially the same conditions. The general number of socmen in Domesday is about 23,000.

20. The relative position of villains and of socmen at an early period is best seen in the Black Book of Peterborough (Camden Society).

21. *Liebermann*, "Gesetze der Angelsachsen, Instituta Cnuti Canute," ii. 71, 3: Liberalis hominis qui habet consuetudines suas, quem Angli dicunt Kinges þegen debitum post mortem eius (heregeat) . . . 4 librae; § 2: Mediocris hominis, quem Angli dicunt læsse þegen illius heregeat est equus et arma, aut halsfang, quod est 10 solidi.

22. Dd., ii., passim, e.g. f. 230, b. (Bertuna), f. 272, 273; Dd., iii. 99 (Hesterige): In ista mansione tenuit quidam liber homo 9 agras terre et 2 agras nemoris, set non potuit de mansione separari.

23. E.g. some of the thanes in Yorkshire, Dd., i. 330b, or in Dorset, i. 84b. The classical example of thanes burdened with some work is the Lancashire one. Dd., i. 269b. The Domesday of Lincolnshire supplies a curious instance of *socmen thanes*, Dd., i. 337b (Grantham). Later Anglo-Saxon practice admits the possibility of some thanes being mere twyhyndmen. See Canute's

writ, *Thorpe*, " Dipl.," 308 : ealle mine þegnas twelfhynde and twihynde. Cf. *Round*, " Victoria History of Essex," 357.

24. There is a remarkable difference between Norfolk and Suffolk in this respect. The Suffolk Survey in Domesday mentions chiefly *liberi homines* and reckons them at more than a third of the whole number of tenants (35 per cent.), whereas in Norfolk we find rather less than a third (32 per cent.) equally divided between socmen and *liberi homines*. The entirely different treatment of these classes in two adjoining counties may have been suggested by a strong admixture of Norsemen in Norfolk, as the term *socmen* is chiefly applied in counties where the Danish invasion had left conspicuous traces. According to Ellis's computation there are in " Domesday," 10,097 liberi homines, and 1,287 homines who were also evidently considered free. As minor varieties of freemen the *censarii* and the riding servants must be mentioned. E.g. in the Glastonbury Inquisitions of 1189, " Villainage in England," 167 ff. Cf. Dd., i. 298b. (Sceltun, Yorkshire) : De hac terra tenuit Torber 2 carucatas cum halla et 6 bovatas. Nunc habet sub rege unus censorius, et sunt ibi duae carucae et 6 villani. i., 302, b. (Wiltone) : Haec tenuit Eld pro uno manerio. Nunc Thomas habet ibi 15 censores habentes 7 carucas. Dd., i. 174b (Poiwic) : Ibi fuerunt 8 radmans . . . habentes inter se 10 carucas et plures bordarios et servos cum 7 carucis. . . . Ipsi radmans secabant una die in anno in pratis domini et omne servitium . quod eis jubebatur faciebant. As to radmen or rodknights, see " Victoria County History of Worcestershire," 250, 251. Some of the tenants entered as socmen may have been riding servants. Liber ecclesiae de Burgo (soc. of Antiquaries) : socomannus facit servicium cum equo suo pro 1 virgata. Cf. also the drenghs in Lancashire. Dd., i., 269, b. (Walintune). Ellis reckons 369 radmen in Domesday and 369 radchenistri.

25. " Villainage in England," 64 ; " Hist. Engl. Law," i. 404.

26. *Jastrow*, " Die Strafrechtliche Stellung der Sklaven."

27. " Villainage in England," 68, 69.

28. Ibid. 159 ; " Hist. Engl. Law," i. 404.

29. " Notebook of Bracton," pl. 1237 : Dominus Rex non vult se de eis intromittere. " Villainage in England," 46.

30. " Villainage in England," 75 ff.

31. " Notebook of Bracton," pl. 1041. *Maitland*, " Select Pleas of the Crown " (Selden Society), pl. 3.

32. " Villainage in England," 157.

33. Ibid., 155 ; " Hist. Engl. Law," i. 356.

34. " Gloucester Cartulary " (Rolls Series), iv. 213, 214.

35. " Villainage in England," 48 ff.

36. Ibid., 159.

37. Ibid., 163.

38. Ibid., 86, 87.

39. *Maitland*, "Court Baron" (Selden Soc. iv.), iii. technical formulas of procedure in use in the King's Court employed in Manorial Courts. Prof. *Petrushevsky*, "Wat Tyler's Rebellion" (Russian), has given much attention to this feature of manorial life.

40. A more detailed discussion of this subject may be found in my paper on Agricultural Services, in the "Economic Review," 1901.

41. It has been shown already that the formula "to do what he is bid" does not necessarily imply an uncertain condition of servitude. It is commonly used to express the fact of being at the lord's disposal as to the quality of the work in the case of tenants of high and free standing. E.g. Dd., i., 174, b.: Willelmus f. Corbuz tenet Dormestun. Waland tenuit T.R.E., Ibi 5 hidae et in dominio 2 carucae, et 2 villani cum 14 bordariis cum 3 carucis. Predictus Waland secabat prata domini et omne servitium quod jubebatur faciebat. (Cf. ib. Poiwic). i., 219, Rex tenet Lufenham et Scaletorp. . . . Ibi sunt 12 sochemanni et 16 bordarii cum presbytero habentes 12 carucas.—Homines operantur opera regis quae prepositus jusserit.

42. Comp., e.g., the description of Horningeseye, Rot. Hundr., ii., 42, with Inqu. Eliensis, p. 103 (Hamilton).

43. It was convenient and usual to inquire whether a manor had been in the hands of the King at the time of the Conquest by a reference to Domesday. Such a reference did not create a title, but only gave the means of ascertaining it. There could be cases like that of King's Ripton, when the condition of Ancient Demesne may have been established by other methods ("Hist. Engl. Law," i., 382). But in one way or the other the claims to a privileged position rested entirely on the status of the tenantry before the Conquest.

44. "Villainage in England," 94 ff.

45. Ibid., 108 ff.

46. *Bracton*, f. 7.

47. "Villainage in England," 114 ff. The Stoneleigh Register is especially instructive in the distinctions it draws between the different classes of the tenantry in Ancient Demesne manors. I take this occasion to protest against the attempt to set aside the evidence of this survey on the ground of its being a late fourteenth century document. (*Seebohm*, in his review of "Villainage in England," "Engl.sh Historical Review," 1893). Though compiled in the second half of the fourteenth century the Stoneleigh Register is based on original records going back to Henry II's time. Its information agrees well with other evidence on the subject and presents some features of ancient demesne in a very clear light. As far as I am able to judge about records of that kind, the survey in question

seems to me to be one of the most valuable documents bearing on the condition of mediæval peasantry, and it is only to be wished that it should be published.

48. The passage of " Villainage in England " (p. 118), in which I ventured to criticize the motives of the decision of Hengham Ch. J. and others in the case of Tavistock, has called forth the indignation of Prof. Ashley and of Mr. Leadam. My reviewers have not taken the trouble to show, however, why we have to reject the ruling of all other judges in similar cases in order to maintain the authority of Hengham. If it had been necessary to show in every case of Ancient Demesne that socmen had been mentioned in the Domesday descriptions of the manors, nine-tenths of the Ancient Demesne trials would have gone against the tenants claiming the privilege. I am content to accept the reproof for unnecessary severity preferred against me by the " Hist. Engl. Law," i., 382, as it is admitted by this authority that the reason challenged by me is bad.

49. " Villainage in England," 198.

50. " Rot. Hundr.," i., 201, 202. " Notebook of Bracton," pl. 1334.

51. Socage is termed by the " History of English Law " the residuary tenure—quite appropriately, if by residue is meant not an adjunct, but the basis from which other more complicated conditions proceed.

52. " Villainage in England," 186, 187.

53. Ib., 191.

54. Ib., 319.

55. " Villainage in England," 323.

56. " Hist. Engl. Law," i. 600.

57. " Placita Quo Warranto," 12 : Idem comes (Humfridus de Bohun) cognoscit quod venire faciat decennarios suos extra comitatum Bedeford usque in comitatum Hertford ad presentandum presentaciones que in turno vicecomitis et in visu franci plegii presentari debent, quod non est juri consonum. Cf. 5, 7, etc.

58. " Rot. Hundr.," i., 205 : Mattæus de Kingeslond ballivus Regis noluit tenere hundredum ad deliberandum quendam prisonem nisi haberet dimidiam marcam, et sic evasit a prisona, pro qua evasione prior ecclesiac Xpi Cantuariae cepit de borgha de la Leye 100 solidos, et pertinet hujusmodi ad dominum Regem. " Placita Quo Warranto," 8 : Abbatus de Waltham. . . . dicit quod revera multociens fuerunt latrones judicati in curia sua de Alrichesheye et suspensi ad furcas vicinorum, quas accommodaverunt, et post ultimum iter evenit quod quidam Thomas latro captus fuit cum manuopere . . . et in curia sua judicatus, et pretextu charte Regis in qua continetur quod habeat Infangenetheof, primo tunc levavit furcas sicut eiene licuit.

59. In the well known Domesday case of socmen borrowed by Count Roger from Picot the sheriff to hold pleas (propter placita aua tenenda), *sua* may stand for *ejus*, or for *eorum*, but whether it be the first or the latter, the existence of a court in private hands has to be surmised, and to this private court men who were otherwise entitled to go to the public courts had to do suit.

60. " Villainage in England," 368 ff.

61. *Massingberd*, " Court Rolls of Ingoldmells," Introduction.

62. *Maitland*, " Manorial Courts," 163, 164. *Savine*, " The English Village in the Age of the Tudors," 1904 (Russian), thinks that the customary court is of late creation, probably coming up at a time when the manorial arrangement was going to pieces, and there arose the necessity of settling the affairs of single customary tenants in places where there were no free tenants. We need not express any judgment on this theory, but the main point is clear : whether the court baron or the customary court be eliminated, there remains only one manorial court, besides the leet— *the* court which deals with the affairs of both classes of tenants.

INDEX

Abbreviations : C.—Celtic ; O.E.—Old English ; R.—Roman ;
R.E.—Roman Empire ; Dd.—Domesday Survey.

The numbers in small type refer to the notes.

Acreware, 153, 253
administrative staff of manor, 359–360
aettleiding, 241–242
agnatic principle in Celtic society, 7–9, 10–11, 12–13
in Teutonic tribes, 135–137
agri arcifinii, 54
agri per extremitatem mensura comprehensi, 57
agri compascui in the R.E., 65
aillts, 24, 29
allotment of holdings, 176–178
alltuds, 29–30
árborenn, 90
argluyd, 33–34
artisans in R. Britain, 45
assarts, 170–173, 260–261
assessment in the R.E., 57–61 ; in the O.E. and feudal period, 158–161
automatism, 185–187, 306, 372–373
averagia, 328

Barton, 224, 282
berewick, 224, 283
bócland, 142–144, 244-248, 209
ból, 266
boldgetæl, 250
boneddig, 35
boon works (precariae), 327
bordarii, 337–338, 374, 352–353
borgaldor, 191, 271, 277
borgh, 138
Borough English, 314–315
bovarii, 334, 373
bovate, 201, 208
bunda, 240
buri, 374
by-laws, Scandinavian, 265 ; English, 185–189, 268–271

Caeth, 24–25
cartron, 17
carucate, 153–158, 252–255
casatus, 243
cattle breeding, 180–181
Celtic elements in R. Britain, 39–42, 101–102
censores, 376
census, 57–58
centuriation, 54–55, 87
ceorl, Kentish, 123-124 ; West Saxon and Mercian, 124–125, 130, 133 ; O.E., 202, 278
chieftainship in C. society, 31–34
clann 7–8
classes of C. society, 35
clients, C., 30–31
coaration, 19
coliberti, 335, 374
colonate in the Eastern provinces of the R.E., 81–82, 111–112, 113
colonate in R. Africa, 79–81, 109-110
colonate, general character of, 76–79, 82–83
colonisation in the feudal period, 331
comitatus, C., 34
common appendant, 168
common of estover, 259–260
common of turbary, 169
commons, 166–170, 260
communalistic origin of property in land, 18, 92
commutation, 329, 331, 353
Conquest, Anglo-Saxon, 117–120, 237
Conquest, Norman, 291–292
cotsetle, 201, 278, 233, 338–339, 375
court baron, 363–364, 379

court, customary, 364–365, 379
court leet, 362–363, 378
cumal, 35
currency, O.E., 125, 237
custom, manorial, 310–312, 368–369, 348–349, 361–362
custom in the O.E. period, communal, 171–173
cwide, 143, 248

Da, 34
dadenhudd, 22–23, 94
daer ceile, 30
Danegeld, 227
demesne, ancient, 354–356, 337–378
demesne in manor, 312–313, 369, 330–331
drengs, 220, 281, 376
dwellings, tribal, 15

Earl, O.E., 124
ἐμφύτευσις, 25, 108
ἐπιβολή, 60, 75
erfeland, 248
esne, 229, 285
estates in O.E. period, 221–223, 281–282, 227–234
etheling, 124

Feasting duties, 223, 282
finè 7, 89
fællesjord, 263
folcland, 142–143, 244–245, 247
food rents, C., 28–29, 98–99
  O.E., 224, 282
forlands, 330–331
forspreca, 243
frankpledge, 250, 198, 277
fredus, O.E., 123, 237
freemen, economic condition of Welsh, 25–28
fundi in the R.E., 61–65, 105, 86, 104 ; in R. Britain, 87, 114
fyrd, 127, 198, 217–218

Gafol, 232–233, 286
gafolearth, 225, 283, 233, 237, 286–287, 327
gafolgelder, 127–128, 238, 240.
galanas, 10, 12
Ganerbschaften, 206
gavelkind, Irish, 20 ; O.E. and Kentish, 141–142, 205–207, 278–279 ; 315–318
gebur, 129–130, 133, 233–234
gedalland, 174

geneat, 238, 220, 232–233, 286
geneatland, 225
gerefa, 191–192, 272
gesithcundman, 125–126, 237–238, 128, 239, 217–218
gesettland, 225, 284
gilds, O.E., 146, 250, 212–213
gore, 262
greave, 190, 271
gribsjord, 263

Haga, 182, 267
halimot, 365
hauldr, 131, 132
headland, 262
heafod bótl, 224–225, 283
herdsmen, 190, 271
herdwick, 224
heriot, 347–348
heywards, communal, 190
hide as family holding, 141–142, 162–163
hide, field, 161–164, 257–258
hide, geld, 151–158, 252–255
hiwisc, 141–142, 250
hlaford, 126, 213
holdings, alienation of, 208–209
holdings, single succession to, 207–208
holdings, unity of, 204–205, 278, 313–315
hundred courts, O.E., 193–194
hundreders, 358
hundredlands, 277
hundreds, O.E., 144–145, 249–250
hunting rights, 167, 259
husbandry, general character of C., 16–19

Immigration into America, Bryttonic, 40–42, 100–101
inheritance of land, 12, 90–91
inland, 225–227, 283–284, 373
intakes, 330
intermixture of strips, 175–179, 312–313
invasions, Anglo-Saxon, 117–120, 237, 145
invasions, Danish, 121–122, 131, 146, 251
inware, 284

Jurisdiction, O.E., private, 214–216
jurors of the hundred court, O.E., 193–194
jurors of the vill, 193–194, 272–273

Kin and descent, 23, 95

Labourers, free, 229–230, 285
læts, O.E., 124
landrica, 193, 216
latifundia, 69
Latin words in Bryttonic, 44, 102
leysing, 132, 203
liberi homines in Dd., 299, 366–367, 342–343, 375–376
loanland, O.E., 209–210

Maeg-burg, 138
maegth, 138–141, 242–273
maer, 28, 29
maer tref, 28, 38
maintenance, right of, 22–23, 94
manor in Dd., general character of, 299–302, 367
manor, definition of feudal, 307
manors, O.E., 224–225, 282–283, 228–229, 231–234, 285–286
manumission of O.E. slaves, 203, 278, 332–333
manumission of villains, 335–336, 374
manure in medieval agriculture, 181–182
marriages, 11, 90
massa, 64, 69
meadows, 173–174, 261
merchet, 347
methods of investigation in the pre-English period, 3–7 ; in the R. period, 43 ; in the O.E. period, 185, 189, 194
molmen, 329, 357–358

Open field pasture, 179–182
open field system in R.E., 66–67 106, 84–85
open fields in medieval village 175–179, 263–267, 312–313
ornum, 263
otting, 264, 266
ownership seignorial, 308–312

Pagi in the R.E. C., 48–49, 103
paragium, 206–207, 279
pasture, communal, 169–170
patronage in the R.E., 70–73 ; in the O.E. period, 126–128, 129–130, 212–213
pencenedl, 31–32
penteulu, 22, 95

pit villages, 39
plou, 52, 104
plough, R. and C., 44–45, 102–103 O.E., 201, 278
priodarii, 96, 97
progenies, 13, 89

Radchenistres and radmen, 220, 281, 376
re-allotment of holdings, 178–179, 263–267
rebdragen jord, 263
Reebning, 179, 263–267
reeve, O.E., 191–193, 271–272, 228–229
reeve of the feudal period, 319–320, 369
reeveland, 225, 283–284
rents in kind, O.E., 231, 285, 328–329
rents, O.E., money, 230
rents, feudal, money, 329
Romanisation of Britain, 37–38, 83–87, 221
Romanisation of continental Celts, 46–48, 103
Romanisation of the provinces, 45–46
rotation of crops, 182–183
run rig system, 175
rural life in the R.E., 47–48

Saer ceile, 30
sake and soke, 214–216, 279–280
saltus, 70, 106–108
scot and lot, 196, 275
sept, 8
serfs in C. society, 25–29
servi casati in R.E., 76–77
servi in Dd., 332–335
services of Celtic freemen and serfs, 28–29, 95
services of peasants in the R.E., 80, 110–111
services of tenants in the feudal manor, 326–328
setene, 239
settlements, C., 16, 91 ; in R. Britain, 85 ; in Anglo-Saxon Britain, 140–142, 147–148, 184–185
share holding, 150–151
shifting possession of arable, 174–175, 261–262
sixhyndman, 125–126, 237–238
slaves, C., 27–28 ; O.E., 202–204,

283, 229, 332–334 ; of the feudal period, 332–335
small proprietors in R.E., 67–68, 106
socage, free, 356–357, 378
socmen of the feudal age, 356–357
soke, 215–216, 280, 303
sokemen, O.E., 215–216, 280 ; in Dd., 294, 299, 366–367, 341–342, 375
solskifte or solrebning, 265–266
subseciva, 65
sulung, 155, 254, 262
surveying in R.E., 54–55
systems of agriculture, R.E., 65–67 ; O.E., 180, 182

Taeog, 15, 25–29, 97
tenures in Dd., 293–299
tenures, free, 308–309, 368
tenures, villain, 309–310
tenures in provinces of R.E., 52–54, 55–57
terra carucis in Dd., 254–255, 156
terra reipublicae iuris, 244
terra testamentalis, 209
terra unius familiae, 141, 243
territorial subdivisions of C. tribes, 26, 97–98
Teutonic elements in O.E. history, 120–121
thane, Scotch, 33 ; O.E., 127, 128, 218–220, 280–281, 232 ; in Dd., 342, 375–376
thaneland, 283–284
township and taxation, O.E., 194–196, 273–274
township and police, 198, 277
township and the law courts, 197–198, 270–277
township moot, O.E., 194–196, 273–274
trev, 15
trevgyvriv, 19–20, 92–94
treweloghe, 20–22, 93–94
tribal hidage, 250
tributarius, 243
tún, 146–149, 251, 150–151, 252
tunc pund, 29
tunesman, 133–134, 241, 339, 375
twelvehyndman, 125, 237–238
twyhyndman, 133, 241
tyddyn, 15

Uchelwr, 15
utwaru, 239, 284

Veislur, 282
vici, 49–52, 104, 82, 113
vill as a community, 322–324
vill, legal constructions of, 324–326, 372–373
vill, farm of the, 320–322
vill in its relation to the manor, 304–306
vill, solidarity of the feudal, 318–322, 362–365
village community, causes of formation, 84–85
village community, general character of, 165–166, 258
village courts and meetings, 187–189, 268–271
villains in Dd., 297–299, 367, 336–337, 339–340, 375
villains, personal status of, 333, 344–348
villainage, freemen holding in, 336, 345, 346
villainage, legal theory of, 343–352, 377
villas in R. Britain, 38–39, 69, 106
virgate, 201, 208

Wapentake, 144, 249
warland, 225–227, 284, 230, 285
waste, approvement of, 170–173, 260–261, 310–312, 368–369, 331
wealh, 126
week-work, O.E., 233–234, 286–287 ; feudal, 327–328
wele (=gwely), 13, 20–22
weorthig, 183–184
wergelds, Kentish, 123, 236–237 ; West Saxon and Mercian, 125–128, 237–238
wicneras, 228, 285
wite theow, 202, 229
women in C. society, 9–10, 90
women's title to land in C. society, 12, 90–91 ; in O.E. society, 143–144, 248–249
woods, 168–169
woodwards, 190